Magic City Nights

MAGIC CITY

NIGHTS

*Birmingham's
Rock 'n' Roll Years*

ANDRE MILLARD

Wesleyan University Press • Middletown, Connecticut

Wesleyan University Press
Middletown CT 06459
www.wesleyan.edu/wespress

Manufactured in the United States of America
Designed by April Leidig
Typeset in Garamond by Copperline Book Services

For pictures and more stories and to add your comments,
go to our Facebook page: https://www.facebook.com/MagicCityNights
/?skip_nax_wizard=true. For pictures and profiles of musicians and to listen
to some of the music, go to http://www.birminghamrecord.com/brc/.

Library of Congress Cataloging-in-Publication Data
Names: Millard, A. J.
Title: Magic city nights: Birmingham's rock 'n' roll years / Andre Millard.
Description: Middletown, Connecticut: Wesleyan University Press, [2017] |
Series: Music/interview | Includes bibliographical references and index.
Identifiers: LCCN 2016035697 | ISBN 9780819576972 (cloth: alk. paper) |
ISBN 9780819576989 (pbk.: alk. paper) | ISBN 9780819576996 (ebook)
Subjects: LCSH: Rock music — Alabama — Birmingham — History and criticism.
Classification: LCC ML3534.3 .M586 2017 | DDC 781.6609761/781 — dc23
LC record available at https://lccn.loc.gov/2016035697

5 4 3 2 1

For
Ben Saxon, Johnny Powell,
Topper Price, and Matt Kimbrell,
who kept the faith

◆

Contents

Magic City Nights

For Max

with Best Wishes

Andy Milland

May 2017

Introduction

This book is the product of an oral history project begun by Aaron Beam at the beginning of the 1990s. As a music lover and club owner, Beam had made friends with the bands that played his venues, and he became interested in Birmingham's rock 'n' roll history as he listened to their stories. Southern musicians are essentially storytellers, and to tell a good story well is to perform. These recollections can cover the rise to fame of a group of musicians, the rags-to-riches stories that are at the heart of rock 'n' roll mythology, and the corresponding, but no less dramatic, fall from grace. There are creation stories about bands, the writing of a great song, and the early years of a local musician who went on to become famous. Many of these rise-and-fall stories have a moral: the dangers of hubris, the pitfalls of sudden wealth, and the consequences of forgetting one's friends. Every working musician can be relied on to recount at least one notable adventure of the road, or in a performance in the kind of place one only sees in the movies. The stories often begin: "I remember one night we were playing..." and then, acknowledging a comrade, "He tells it better than I do." Longtime session man Roger Clark, looking back on forty years in the business, said: "I got a lot of stories. Some of 'em I can't tell you about... I'd have to leave home... I can tell you a lot of stories, and some of them I wasn't there."

Giving interviews to journalists or historians could be taken as merely another performance. I have heard the same stories wonderfully recounted by authors like Peter Guralnick and Robert Gordon in their books duplicated more or less word by word by the same storytellers, at different times and different places. I have also heard the same story told by several different respondents in which the leading role had been appropriated by whoever was telling the story. No matter; these are good stories, and Aaron Beam heard so many of them that he thought it was a shame that no one had ever collected them and written them down. What Beam envisaged was a history of the leading rock bands that played in Birmingham in the 1970s and 1980s based on the recollections of the musicians.

This oral history project was initiated at a significant time in the city's music scene. The growing popularity of indie, postpunk rock had broken down the barriers of geographic location and business infrastructure that had hindered Alabama musicians' breakout into the national scene in previous decades. It had also inspired a wave of indie bands, attracting the attention of talent agents and record companies. So at this point in Birmingham's musical history, optimism was widespread about the possibility of a breakthrough — a national hit on a major label — that would propel a local band into the center of America's popular music scene and reflect well on their city's cultural reputation. Several Birmingham bands had just snagged the all-important record contract with a major record company, and several seemed on the cusp of doing so, and this drove local pride and gave hope that a local band would make it big, thus validating both the city and its music, as it had done recently to other cities in the New South, such as Austin and Athens. Aaron Beam and his many friends in the Birmingham music scene agreed that this was the right time to uncover the history of Birmingham's leading rock bands, make it part of the permanent record of popular music in the South, and give credit where credit was due. It was, in Beam's words, giving "proper recognition" to a music scene and local musicians.

The first step of this project was to identify these bands. The people who compiled the list of musicians to be interviewed based those decisions on how inspired or impressed they had been by each band's performances. The oral histories were not intended to provide a complete and unbiased narrative of rock music in Birmingham, nor were they intended as a hagiography of those successful musicians who had left Birmingham for greener pastures; it was more a compendium of everyone's favorite local bands. Aaron Beam said, "The focus of the book is more about the music scene in Birmingham and the people, and I personally want to have a lot about the people who are still here." The history gathered was essentially a narrative about who formed these bands, and their performances, recordings, and personnel changes. In this way the project was to be as much taxonomy as history: following the convoluted paths of musicians joining and leaving bands turned out to be a major endeavor, one that took up most of the time of interpreting the transcriptions of the interviews. Interviewing musicians began as a means to identify what bands they had played in and then use this data to build up a picture of where the major bands came from and how they evolved over time. The final product was intended to be a guide, organized by bands and containing their individual histories and vital information. This sort of approach had been pioneered by record collectors who had built up their own histories of their favorite bands based on the recordings they made. There were also books like C. S. Fuqua's informative *Alabama Musicians: Musical Heritage from the Heart of Dixie*, which comprises short biographies of musicians listed alphabetically.[1] Aaron Beam's project aimed at covering bands from more than one genre within rock 'n' roll (the record collectors histories had been largely confined to 1960s garage bands) and building up a flow chart that chronicled the birth, death, and resurrection of the important bands. At the very beginning of this ambitious project we agreed that it would be impossible to interview everybody, and as the pile of interviews grew larger and larger, we discovered that, as Aaron said, "the universe of what we don't know is getting smaller."

Aaron Beam agreed with many of his colleagues and customers that the city of Birmingham had not received its due as a center of southern music. They were all convinced that Birmingham was undervalued as a cultural center in the New South and that there was a need to set the record straight and put Birmingham up there on the pantheon of southern music, perhaps not as high as Memphis, New Orleans, and Nashville, but definitely up there with cities like Atlanta and Chattanooga. Beam's associates in the music business (who tended to be mobile as well as entrepreneurial) believed that Birmingham had not only produced great musicians but also had a local music scene as good as anything in the New South. Birmingham's bar bands had cultivated a loyal audience who were convinced that the music they heard every weekend was as authentic and virtuosic southern rock 'n' roll as one could hear anywhere. There was a consensus that Birmingham's music scene was on the rise and that it deserved some sort of written record. A better understanding of the musical history of the city would also be useful in the continual comparison of Birmingham with other cities of the New South, a process that covered culture as well as politics, the economy, traffic, food, and lifestyles.

The sense of being overlooked and undervalued fit in perfectly with the overall mind-set of a city with an inferiority complex. Birmingham was only one of the new cities in the New South, but it was known as the "Magic City" because of its rapid growth, and expectations that it would be the greatest city of the New South were always unreasonably high. Its inhabitants were always mindful of the competition to become the leading economic and cultural center of this self-conscious and well-publicized urban movement to modernize the South. Music is only one part of the social makeup of an urban community, but it punches well above its weight in assessing the quality of life and in determining a cultural identity. The lack of a musical identity to compare with some of Birmingham's neighbors in the New South, or even an acknowledgment that there was a local music scene, struck longtime residents as another injustice — the final straw after fifty years of bad press and unwarranted criticism. Memphis claims rock 'n' roll, New Orleans sells itself as the birthplace of jazz, Nashville means country music, and even Vicksburg can claim to be the "key" to Mississippi music. But Birmingham has nothing to claim despite the impressive list of great musicians who had once called the town home. The 1990s was a decade of rapid economic growth and raised expectations in Birmingham. The town's self-esteem was buoyed by the outstanding performance of its new service, health, and communication industries. Its elevation in the media to the status of an attractive, livable city and a "best-kept secret" was the source of immense pride to its inhabitants used to finding themselves at the bottom of every list. Aaron Beam was one of the founders of HealthSouth, one of the fastest-growing and most profitable businesses in the nation, and his outlook reflected a new confidence in the future of a city that had previously failed to live up to every one of its New South promises. Birmingham was moving forward on a wave of local pride and record earnings reports, and expecting even greater things as the millennium approached. A history of rock music in Birmingham would be a timely reminder that the city could provide entertainment that was not as bad as everybody thought, and that this was something to be proud of in a community reasserting itself into the cultural life of the South.

The entrepreneurs who founded the city had great ambitions for culture as well as the production of iron. They wanted to give the new city the veneer of high culture, and chose to import "classical" symphonic music as the means to accomplish this goal. The people who started this oral history project also chose the classics to demonstrate the cultural accomplishments of their community, but in this case it was classic rock, southern rock, and all its offshoots into country rock, folk rock, art rock, and so on. I think it was Duke Ellington who said that there were only two sorts of music: the good music and all the other music. The definition of "good," however, is highly subjective. By the 1980s the term "classic rock" was considered pejorative in some quarters, but positive in others. The young musicians of the New Wave had criticized the aesthetic and pretensions of 1970s rock 'n' roll much more effectively than any parent or minister had done in the 1950s. In turn professional musicians with a decade or two of experience on the road laughed at the amateurism and pretensions of the New Wave. The direction the oral history took depended on who was asked, and this in turn reflected the musical knowledge and tastes of the people arranging the interviews. Even a small city like Birmingham produces too many musicians to include everyone in an oral history, so there was never any intention, or commitment, to provide an inclusive and complete history, although this was the standard often expected of it.

"Birmingham: Greatest City in Alabama / You can go across this entire land, but there ain't no place like Birmingham."

When I joined the project in the mid-1990s, it had stalled in its efforts to create a taxonomy of popular rock bands because there was far too much information to be easily digested and too many discrepancies in the information gathered in the interviews. The context of the project was always the baby-boomers' understanding of what popular music was and what it stood for — the 1960s idea that music meant much more than entertainment and that loyalty to one band was a virtue for both musicians and their audience. In the 1960s you stayed with a band for life, but thirty years later one chopped and changed between different bands, and there were so many highly mobile musicians, and so many bands, that it was virtually impossible to keep track of them. There were so many different versions of who was in the band, what instrument they played, when they played, who they replaced, and even how to spell their names. I fear that the last issue will never be satisfactorily solved because it is difficult to read people's handwriting, even when it is in capital letters. I want to apologize in advance to everyone whose names we misspelled and whose true role in the band was overlooked. I want to thank my friends in the Birmingham Record Collectors club, especially Johnny Powell and Charlie Bailey, for all the help they gave me in uncovering the history of sixties bands and locating the surviving musicians. The flow chart of the formation and progress of rock bands that the pioneers of this project had envisaged grew so large and complex that it had to be discarded.

A native of Louisiana, Beam knew little of Birmingham's troubled past as America's most segregated city and brought with him no local pride or loyalties. He was interested in southern music and not the New South. What he learned about Birmingham's history came from the stories about the good/bad old days he heard from members of bands, and most of all, from the music they played, which was largely unapologetic about the city's racial politics. Like my friend Aaron, I am an outsider in Alabama and an alien onlooker with no personal investment in interpreting its history. As a professional historian I came to this project well aware of the city's racial past and the global impact of the fight against segregation. What I saw in the growing number of interviews of musicians was a means to examine the history of the city through its music. Birmingham is a creation of the New South and a splendid example of a New South city, not only in its first incarnation, but also in its postsegregation experience. Birmingham was coming under the influence of urbanization (even gentrification), increased Latino immigration, reverse immigration from African American communities in the North, a new demographic that included a more educated workforce, and the challenging of the politics and social norms, which were often as much Old South as New South. A musical history of the city of Birmingham might be able to supplement and even inform the many political and social interpretations of its history. What I envisaged as the final product of this project was a scholarly book based on these interviews that would provide a narrative of the city's musical culture. As this covered over a hundred years, it would have to be an overview rather than a detailed account, but it could act as a foundation for further investigation.

I therefore successfully lobbied to broaden the outlook of the project to include more musicians, more sorts of music and more of the history of the city. The project was enlarged to cover a much longer time period (as far back as anyone living in Birmingham in the 1990s could remember), a much broader definition of what counted as rock 'n' roll, and as many other musical genres as could be practically investigated. I knew that Birmingham had a widely acclaimed jazz heritage, and when I thought about the city's music, it was Erskine Hawkins's "Tuxedo Junction" rather than Randy Newman's "Birmingham" or Lynyrd Skynyrd's "Sweet Home Alabama" that immediately came to mind. I was also aware that many of Birmingham's jazz greats were coming to the end of their lives and thus there was no time to waste in getting their stories down on paper. In the first few years of my management of the project, Birmingham lost the Lowe brothers, Sammy and J. L., who had played a significant role in creating Birmingham's jazz heritage and were active in keeping it alive.

As someone whose musical education began in London in the 1960s, I came to Birmingham with a grounding in the history of the blues (more than a lot of native Alabamians, both black and white) and a belief in the blues myth of racial purity and expression. My generation was profoundly touched by the blues and probably bought into the myths of the blues more than any other group of affluent Europeans. What better place to learn about it than a major urban center in the Deep South with a historically large African American population? Before coming to the city, I had never heard or read about a blues player from Birmingham, but it seemed to me that a city usually ignored in the history of the blues ought to have some "real" blues music in its past. My own journey of exploration in this project was to go fearlessly and naively into the uncharted waters of African American culture and get to the heart of what I believed was the southernness in southern music.

The first problem was that there were hardly any blues players from the golden age of the 1920s and 1940s still alive in Alabama and ready to talk. Much of the blues history I heard had been passed down from enthusiastic, middle-class whites who recounted the stories told to them years before by bluesmen, or friends of bluesmen. The history I was hearing was secondhand, and probably fashioned to suit white sensibilities and molded by the blues myth. The Alabama native Johnny Shines had been a friend of the legendary Robert Johnson and was full of interesting stories about the great man and their life on the road. I pounced on these stories, but I could not help wondering, as I heard them told and retold, how much they represented the reality of bluesmen versus their mythical life as enshrined in their songs. During the 1990s a blues joint in an industrial suburb of Birmingham called Gip's Place emerged into public consciousness (Henry Gipson opened his place back in 1952, he says), and quickly lost its best-kept-secret status to become extremely popular. Gip's Place soon made the national media, the AAA's *Alabama Journey* magazine, and the Travel Channel. This was the so-called authentic blues in my own backyard. The music came to me not on vinyl or MP3 but in video clips sent to me via cell phones by my friends and students. It sounded very good, but it made me wonder if the music I heard was an authentic voice of the African American past in Alabama or an entertainment directed to a white audience of college kids, tourists, and hipsters that had to conform to their expectations, and the widely held stereotypes of the blues and its players. Gip's Place now has its own Facebook page and sells a line of merchandise. Was Gip's the real thing, or was it another commodification of a music already heavily commodified in television commercials and in franchised blues clubs like the House of Blues?

Birmingham had its own black business and entertainment district during segregation, places deemed sites of authentic black cultural production, just like Memphis, Atlanta, New Orleans, and Chattanooga. In her engaging history of Bessie Smith, the "Blues Empress" of black Chattanooga, Michelle Scott describes how the process of rural to urban migration (Bessie Smith's family came from Alabama), industrialization, and the creation of a black working class provided the context for the rise of a blues culture and the creation of African American entertainment stars. Chattanooga worked just like Birmingham in supporting a segregated entertainment in a clearly delineated district that offered street performers, tent shows, music halls, bars, and rent parties in private residences in addition to retail and hospitality businesses. Along with historians Robin Kelley and Tera Hunter, Scott argues that black recreational spaces served as alternative sites of networking, economic enhancement, and protest. They allowed African Americans to enjoy themselves, be themselves, and "share their true feelings about economic hardships, relationships, and racism in a social space away from the gaze of an oppressive white population."[2] Music was an important part of what Lawrence Levine called the "necessary space" that had existed between the slaves and their owners in the antebellum South. He described how the "sacred world of the black slave" — their religion, folklore beliefs, and music — prevented legal slavery from becoming spiritual slavery. When this "necessary space" shifted to urban centers like Chattanooga or Birmingham and came under the same economic forces as the rest of the country, blues culture moved beyond self-definition and personal liberation to economic opportunity. It was, in Grace Elizabeth Hale's words, "a dangerous dialectic," one in which "slaves constructed masks of simplemindedness and sycophancy, loyalty and laziness to play to their owners' fantasies while securing very material benefits."[3] The white-run entertainment business provided these material benefits as it mediated the space between the races, which depended on serving both black and white customers. That is why the first accounts of African American music in Birmingham come from white observers.

The blues figures large in the identity of black southerners. In her study of race, class, and regional identity in the postsegregated South, Zandria Robinson points to the centrality of this musical culture in defining what black is ("and what black ain't") in the South. She describes African Americans' collective search for ancestral American history in which the South "stands in for a cognitively and geographically distant African homeland. Blues, soul, and gospel are the soundtrack." Blackness, she argues, can be found in these "originary soundscapes."[4] In many ways this assessment of the power of blues music to create identity and encapsulate history is not much different from white blues enthusiasts who buy the commercial products of blues culture. Bessie Smith became the Empress of the Blues through the popularity of her recordings in white America, and by the 1920s the blues

covered a very wide range of music. The bandleader Paul Whiteman competed with Bessie Smith as representing blues royalty, but his palm-court
hotel music is as embarrassingly white as Bessie Smith's music is excitingly
black. There was no firm correlation at this time between racialized music
and racialized bodies. Karl Hagstrom Miller describes a music industry
at the turn of the century in which black and white performers "regularly
employed racialized sounds," but by the end of the 1920s listeners expected
musicians to *embody* them, allowing African Americans to challenge the
minstrelsy conventions that supported blackface.[5]

The story of Bessie Smith shows that the rise of the blues as a popular
music provided opportunities for entrepreneurship, especially when it was
co-opted by the white music business and popularized for broader con-
sumption outside the segregated districts of the New South. Several students of Birmingham's great music teacher, Fess Whatley, played in Smith's
band and got a chance to tour the country and make some good money.
Bessie Smith played a large part in taking the blues out of its birthplace in
the backstreets and byways of the black South into the mainstream entertainment of the industrialized West. She certainly benefited from it — her
stage shows articulated the wealth and luxuries that fame brought her just
like the current stars of hip-hop flaunt their wealth in their music and performances. I am certainly not arguing that these economic transactions
between whites and blacks were fair and reasonable, but even the most
criminal exploitation of blues musicians provided some small inducement
to continue playing the system. Robert Toll, in his groundbreaking study
of minstrelsy, stressed the mobility and opportunities of advancement to
be found in blackface. However meager the returns of playing for the white
man, they were preferable to the other outlets for employment and entrepreneurship. When Bessie Smith was making a career in regional vaudeville and appearing in the blacks-only theaters in Bessemer and Birmingham, she went back to working as a laundress in Birmingham during the
times she was not on the music hall circuit.[6]

From the meager number of interviews with elderly African American
musicians in Birmingham, and from a study of the literature and discogra-
phies, a pattern of entrepreneurship and opportunity emerged in Birmingham in which African American music during segregation was essentially a

commercial endeavor played by professional musicians. In this conclusion I am on exactly the same page as Karl Hagstrom Miller. In his book *Segregating Sound*, he shows how southern music was compartmentalized first by the record companies and music business according to race, and then these divisions were reinforced by academics and listeners. This "logic of segregation" has become commonly accepted, but as he convincingly argues, this compartmentalization failed to reflect the music actually being played. Karl Hagstrom Miller starts his book with a quote about Robert Johnson from his traveling companion Johnny Shines: "He did anything he heard over the radio. *Anything* that he heard . . . It didn't make him no difference what it was. If he liked it he did it." Miller argues that the blues and country music sold as products of "modern primitives" in fact emerged from long engagement with pop and commercial music. He discovered that "the very idea of southern musical distinctiveness" came not from southern musicians playing in the South, but from the touring shows of vaudeville and minstrelsy and from southern migrants who moved to the North and Northeast.[7]

If we define blues music as a commercial endeavor that drew on a wide variety of sources and was successfully engaged with the music business, then its links to authenticity and black identity come into question. That it provided entrepreneurial opportunities for African Americans colors the content and tone of the memories of Birmingham's black musicians. The first blues players who hustled from street corners in downtown Birmingham were content to play whatever their audience wanted. Birmingham's first jazz musicians, schooled by the legendary Fess Whatley, played "society jobs" as often as they jammed for friends and neighbors — the former gigs were preferred because they paid better. Seeing their music as a profession, as their job, meant that African American musicians in all genres of the blues — from street corners to concert halls — had a particular take on segregation that did not dwell on its evils but rather on the opportunities it provided. It wasn't that they ignored the racial injustices and violence going on around them; rather, they did not think it was worth it to stop carrying out their profession to confront these evils — they just kept on playing. As J. L. Lowe concluded about decades of performing big band jazz in the segregated South: "We did what we were supposed to do: we played." Mat-

ters of blackness and whiteness took a back seat to considerations of green
dollars; helping to define black identity and providing a record of racial
injustice were all very well for subsequent generations of commentators and
academics, but it did not pay the rent at a time when making a buck as a
black man in Birmingham was very hard work.

Comparing the two sets of interviews — one from southern rockers and
one from big band jazz musicians — provided some surprising similarities.
Both groups of musicians put a high value on virtuosity and expressed a
pride in their professionalism. Both provided plenty of stories about the
decadence of the road; the only difference was that it was harder to extract
all the interesting details from elderly African Americans. Both were convinced that Birmingham and its musicians had been undervalued in the
history of American popular culture, and they wanted to see more credit
being given to their city and its music.

The coming of rock 'n' roll clearly provided more entrepreneurial opportunities for black musicians, despite claims that they were shortchanged
when the music was stolen from them by the white entertainment industry,
which indeed it was. But the black roots of rock music were appropriated
just like the country ones, and there was no color bar to being cheated. In
his excellent book on the music scene in Memphis, Robert Gordon sees
rock 'n' roll as the result of a collision of two musical cultures rather than a
happy comingling of enlightened musicians, club owners, and record producers. Reading this book and enjoying the stories expertly recounted by
Gordon reminded me of the same sort of stories told in our interviews with
Birmingham's musicians. Birmingham and Memphis are considered to be
similar cities of the New South, and the same goes for their rock 'n' roll
experiences. They usually begin with first tentative explorations of black
music by budding white musicians, starting with the radio and ending with
the personal interactions by which all musicians learn their trade. Gordon
assigns the telling quote "Everybody learned it from the yardman" to white
guitarist Jim Dickinson, but I have heard the same thing from no end of
Alabama rock guitarists. Dickinson's band went through all the experiences of every garage band in Birmingham, from visits to pawnshops to get
instruments, then to learning songs from records, to the triumphs at high
school hops. Musicians in both cities had to navigate the same enormous

changes in the music business caused by the Beatles. Businessmen in both cities exploited the British Invasion to sell stuff and to claim to be hip. But most important, the emergence of rock 'n' roll in both cities was inspired by, and drawn to, African American music. As Dickinson remembered: "My band played the blues, and we played it like white boys, because that's what we were." Perhaps this is what leads Gordon to conclude that "whites were unable to exactly mimic black music, and their failure created another hybrid . . . Rock and roll was white rednecks trying to play black music. Their country music background hampered them and they couldn't do it. That's why we don't call what they made rhythm and blues." Rather than condemn racism as immoral and unproductive, Gordon sees it as responsible for rock 'n' roll. Dickinson points to the venality, racism, and exploitative nature of white businessmen not as an aberration that undermined the new music but as an integral part of its creation. A gentle coming together of musical cultures could never have produced the edginess and energy of early rock 'n' roll: "The racial collision, it has to be there."[8]

White boys playing black music imperfectly was hardly new, nor were the profits of exploiting black music and dance going to white-owned businesses. This process did not begin with the Rolling Stones or with the Original Dixieland Jass Band; it started way back in the nineteenth century with the universal popularity of the minstrel show, which emerged in the northern states in the antebellum era. Minstrelsy traded on images of black difference and inferiority, but according to Karl Hagstrom Miller, it was the primary medium through which nineteenth-century Americans came to understand musical authenticity, "not rooted in history of heritage but in consensus — minstrelsy taught that authenticity was performative . . . imitating black performance remained a constituent component of white identity."[9] This theme has been picked up by historians David Roediger and Grace Elizabeth Hale. In *Making Whiteness* Hale asserts, "Blackface became essential to the creation of a more self-consciously white identity as well."[10] In this way whites imitating blacks was a tradition that began well before the blues. This was the heritage carried forward to the era of rock 'n' roll. Criticizing white rock musicians for copying black music and thus undermining the racial and aesthetic purity of the music ignores this great American tradition.

In the mediated spaces of the blues music business, blacks were also given the opportunity of mimicking whites. As minstrelsy became the popular music of the industrialized West in the late nineteenth century, African American performers were allowed onto the bandwagon and were able to get their share of the revenue streaming in from the minstrel shows. Some of the largest and most profitable minstrel shows that entertained thousands of whites in Birmingham were African American productions. In putting on the same blackface as the white performers, blacks got to see African American identity through white eyes. As Hale points out, these professional musicians had "in effect to play whites." The creation of these "miscegenated styles paradoxically subverted white spectators' expectations and declared black musical freedom to match white methods and survey the full measure of musical sources."[11] In this way, blacks imitating whites imitating blacks became another American tradition carried forward by rock 'n' roll.

To my mind, the story of minstrelsy effectively challenges the concept of distinct racial musical traditions, as well as historians' commitment to narratives of difference. It also provides us with a different take on the birth of rock 'n' roll and the amount of white guilt to be assigned to the co-opters and exploiters of black culture. The white teenagers who played in garage bands in Birmingham acknowledged their debt to black musicians and freely admitted, like Jim Dickinson, that they played the blues like white boys. But they made it their music too, despite coming from the wrong side of history and the color bar. There has been a friendly takeover of blues music in the twentieth century. The blues is the foundation music of white players in Birmingham and has been for many years. It is white boys' music played exclusively for white audiences. Teenagers learning how to play electric guitar naturally lean toward blues rhythms and progressions because it's easy, and it actually sounds better if you don't have clear amplification and intonation. Martin Stokes has written about the musical construction of self and place: "Music is part of modern life and our understanding of it, articulating our knowledge of other things, and ourselves in relation to them." Yet he argues that "people will use music to locate themselves in idiosyncratic ways," and this surely covers white teenage Alabamians who think of the blues as their own.[12]

"At the Dark End of the Street"

For all the similarities between the musical experiences of Birmingham and Memphis, two very important differences stood out: the relative successes and failures of recording studios and the differing attitudes toward race. Both of these differences can be used to explain why Memphis is regarded as a music city and Birmingham isn't. If only Sam Phillips had moved to Birmingham rather than Memphis! If only those famous studios in Muscle Shoals had been established in Birmingham rather than out in the sticks! Alas, this did not happen, so Birmingham remained a backwater in American popular music. The creation of a successful recording business is founded not, as popularly believed, on great local music, but on commercial considerations such as infrastructure, geographic location, and marketing networks. There was every reason to believe that Atlanta would have become *the* recording center of the South rather than Memphis or Nashville. In the 1920s it was the recording center of the South — there were no studios in Memphis or Nashville at this time — but it lost this lead in the 1940s, never to regain it, and the musical development and reputation of *the* city of the New South suffered accordingly.[13]

The story of the rise of Muscle Shoals' recording studios has been told and retold, but I am not going to apologize for including it in this book because it plays such an important part as a comparison with Birmingham. Many of the players who made Muscle Shoals famous came from Birmingham or would have willingly moved there if there were equal opportunities. The rise of Muscle Shoals as a recording center reveals the importance of racial integration in rock music and explains why Birmingham never made it into the urban version of the Rock and Roll Hall of Fame. Only a few miles up the road, Muscle Shoals provides the perfect comparison with Birmingham and proves that racial tolerance plays a vital part in a dynamic music scene. If there is one scholarly conclusion to be taken from these interviews it is that Birmingham's racial tension suffocated its musical aspirations in the rock 'n' roll era.

White Alabamians who loved black music and respected black musicians felt privileged in a segregated society because their musical tastes allowed them to mark the difference between them and their schoolmates and parents who condemned black music as "trash" and "animalistic." The garage bands who played blues and R&B could say later that their music placed them apart from the rest of white Alabama, and this is true, but an interracial musical culture does not necessarily create interracial harmony or equality; it might *suggest* interracial harmony, but it does not actively *produce* it. As my colleague Odessa Woolfolk pointed out, if you didn't march you couldn't claim to be part of, or even a friend of, the movement for civil rights. The young white men who played black music lived the same divided lives as their schoolmates and parents, keeping the races separated and making a distinction between the African Americans who brought them up and served them, and those who were demonstrating for civil rights downtown. In remembering the dark days of 1963 there does appear to be a collective myopia in white Birmingham; the dramatic events unfurling in downtown Birmingham managed to attract the attention of people all over the world, but the news failed to go "over the mountain" to the more affluent suburbs of Birmingham.

Music marked out white identity in Birmingham just as it did for black self-awareness, but it also gave white blues and R&B fans the means to take sides without getting involved in violent confrontation. Many of our white respondents admitted that their love of black music had to be kept secret in the 1950s and 1960s. Modern communications technology provided the means for whites to cross the color bar in secret, and even those brave or enthusiastic enough to make surreptitious trips across town on Saturday night could return to their privileged place in a segregated society on Sunday morning—the most segregated time of the week, according to Dr. Martin Luther King. It is pretty easy to condemn their passivity with the benefit of hindsight and the safety of the twenty-first century, but I can't blame anyone for not wanting to get beaten up or lose their business license. Those who challenge the credibility of their interracial yearnings have a point, but the young men who played the white-boy blues and idolized the black musicians who had popularized it sincerely thought that they were the good guys in the struggle for desegregation. I couldn't include a lot of white guilt in this narrative because it was hard to find any in the music lovers we interviewed. Unfortunately, the racial politics of Birmingham's history leads to white voices being valued less and in some cases completely discredited. Yet white voices are still a part of the story and should carry the same weight as the heroes of desegregation in recounting the musical history of Birmingham.

Looking back over the transcripts of the interviews, I found out that within the community of interviewers and interviewees in this project I was known as "the Professor," and my modus operandi was to focus the interviews around the topic of race. I admit that I am a history professor, and as with most, or all, history professors, what interests me most about the history of Birmingham is race. Not only did I orientate the oral histories toward African American music, bringing in the first interviews of black musicians, I also interrogated everyone else on the matter of race, often to the annoyance of those being pressed to talk about an issue that they considered had been dead and buried for many decades. Yet in my well-intentioned but naive efforts to make this a scholarly history of music in Birmingham that incorporated both the black and white experience lay the seeds of my defeat and the impossibility of ever producing a one-volume history of music in Birmingham that encompassed the experiences of two musical cultures. There was never going to be enough race in this project to satisfy academe.

The first problem was getting access to black musicians and gaining their consent to give interviews. This oral history project was originated, managed, and executed by whites. One of the main changes I made when I came to this project was to increase the number of people who went out and did the interviews. The first group of interviewers was largely adults — musicians or other members of the music business who were long-term residents of Birmingham. Under the direction of the hard-working Jon Van Wesel (who did the majority of the interviews), investigators Keith Harrelson, Gigi Boykin, Jay Dismukes, Brian Haynes, and Nancy Belcher went out and did the interviews. I exploited my position as professor at the University of Alabama at Birmingham (UAB) to bring in students to this project, which created a younger group of interviewers, who were music lovers rather than musicians and who had much broader and more eclectic tastes in music: Courtney Burks, Alison Oden, Tonya Wise, Brandy Lepik, Rob Heinrich, John Gilchrist, and Caitlin Moore. My experiences directing the American Studies program at UAB, a public school with a large percentage (around 25 percent) of African American students, taught me that they know almost nothing about blues culture and care little for the history of black music, slavery, and civil rights. As budding doctors, lawyers, and engineers, they find little to attract them in this part of black heritage. While it was easy to convince my white students to take part in this oral history project, it proved almost impossible to recruit young African Americans. Although we in Birmingham live in an integrated city and enjoy life in an interracial society, the black and white communities are still largely self-segregated, and there remains some discomfort about white people coming in with clipboards and lots of questions. It was possible to reach out to the older generation of black musicians to tell their story, but finding out about modern African American music proved to be much more difficult. Hip-hop in the 1990s was a closed society in Birmingham. Because of the opposition of city government and the impossibly high insurance premiums, there were few hip-hop concerts, and the performances that did take place tended to be private and underground. Again there were significant incursions across racial lines, which muddied the waters of authenticity because hip-hop culture remains amazingly popular within the white suburbs, but one can hardly imagine the howls of protest that would have followed a history of hip-hop in Birmingham drawn largely from whites.

The other problem was that musicians look back on the segregated past with different viewpoints than other people, especially white liberal academics. It was easy enough to get African Americans to talk about the horrors of segregation. Here is a typical quote from Bruce Martin: "It was bad back then . . . people shouting at you as you walked down the street, throw a tin can full of pee at you . . . Lots of black women had to work, worked for whites, and get abused, you know. Go home and tell their man, nothing he could do about it. That's where all those high yellahs come from! It was the Dirty South, not the Deep South, the Dirty South." Bruce is a taxi driver and was in a good position to understand the reality of segregation. But a black musician sees segregation in starkly different terms than those in other occupations, and it turned out that the last place one was going to find outrage and disgust about segregation in Birmingham was in music venues and clubs, or in the recollections of musicians of both races who had made a good living during that period. How much the rules of racial deference in public continued in this era of good feelings toward African American musicians is hard to evaluate, as no side is eager to stress the power dynamic of these business relationships. Yet it is uncontestable that both sides were profiting from these relationships, which had always allowed African American musicians to work in places where many other blacks and whites were not allowed, and to get much higher returns for the work they did.

In fact, one could argue that many of the viewpoints expressed in these interviews go completely against the prevailing views of academic historians and what one would expect from downtrodden African Americans in what used to be America's most segregated city. The first time I heard an elderly African American speak wistfully about the good old days of segregation and how much better life was back in the 1960s I was shocked, but I soon got used to it and understood that musicians interpret history differently than professors or politicians. If we see their music as a commercial endeavor rather than staking out black identity and articulating black resistance, this begins to make sense. The same economic forces that powered African American music into the mainstream of popular culture were never going to dwell on the injustices or the immorality of segregation. By choosing to record the experiences and viewpoints of musicians, rather than garbage collectors, taxi drivers or policemen, the final product was never going to meet the expectations of the academic community who were the peer reviewers of the scholarly narrative I hoped to publish. The binary racial politics of Birmingham were never going to be reflected in the mediated and mobile space that musical culture occupies in between the races. Leaning on a group of respondents who were pretty much politically incorrect to start with was enough to condemn their recollections as debased and unimportant within the contested cultural history of the Deep South.

The boundaries of racial politics are not permanently fixed in time, and racial signifiers also shift over time. Mike Butler has studied southern rockers in the postsegregation decades and found that the Confederate symbols these musicians proudly displayed no longer represented traditional southern racial ideologies, in which the flag was associated with the Ku Klux Klan and other racist organizations, but the changing racial identities for white males in the South. Although this new construct of male southerners was not accepted by all males in the South, those involved in southern rock rejected the racist imagery of the flag in favor of a pride in regional imagery, while at the same time "openly and frequently paying homage to the blues musicians who influenced their own creative musical style." In the 1960s and 1970s this was a rebellious posture that counteracted the accepted image of these musicians as "frightened racists."[14] While southern rock still carries with it the burden of southern racism, it has to be accepted that music has healing, redemptive properties, and this is especially true for a popular music that was the product of some elements of racial integration. As Mark Kemp wrote, "Southern rock offered an emotional process by which my generation could leave behind the burdens of guilt and disgrace, and go home again."[15]

"We've got Newark, we've got Gary / Somebody told me we got L.A. And we're working on Atlanta."

Birmingham, Alabama, is what George Clinton would call a "Chocolate City." In the postsegregation era it has a majority African American population, a local government run largely by African Americans, and a large and affluent black middle class. In her book about black identity in the postsegregated South, Zandria Robinson defines two distinct urban Souths: the historic urban South, which has experienced increased African American population growth but maintains many of the old black/white binary populations and power arrangements, and a new urban South, characterized by an increasing racial and ethnic diversity. She then enhances her definition of the new urban South to encompass the idea of a "Soul City," in which cities like Birmingham "carry on the musical and political legacy of the civil rights movement even as they attempt to reconcile the racial and socioeconomic realities of the post-soul era." Like Jackson, Mississippi; Greenville, South Carolina; and Raleigh and Greensboro, North Carolina, Birmingham has little of the Old South's Confederate heritage or the glitz and sophistication of the fashionable cities of the New South, like Atlanta.[16]

"Soul" is a perfect way to locate a time, a place and racial identity, and Robinson expertly joins the components of the music and its southern black experience. She explains how the music of soul artists like Aretha Franklin and Otis Redding "recast southerners as instrumental in the political and cultural struggles of African American communities."[17] But soul music as a signifier of black southernness is not without paradox. This blackest of post–rock 'n' roll African American music was also the most integrated of southern music up to that point. Ironically the first meaningful racial musical interaction in the postsegregation South ended up articulating black pride and power. If you had to condense soul music into one brand, it would have to be Stax Records in Memphis, and here we see white and black musicians working together — it is difficult to think of the Stax sound without thinking of Steve Cropper and Donald "Duck" Dunn, who came to the Stax rhythm section from the Mar-keys, the first integrated band to play in black circuit in the early 1960s. How come a soul classic like "The Dark End of the Street" was written by a two country boys from Vernon, Alabama, and LaGrange, Georgia? If I were to find a consensus in all the interviews of white music lovers active in Birmingham in the 1970s about the genre of music that appealed to them the most, it would have to be soul. Even though this was the heyday of southern rock in Birmingham, it was soul bands that reached the high points of that "ecstatic commonality" (in the words of Ellen Willis) which drew us all to the rock performance in the first place. Soul touched white music lovers in Birmingham in ways that would be unimaginable in a politically correct world. Birmingham's garage bands were probably unique in how quickly they incorporated horn sections into the lineup of three guitars and a drum set: and horns mean soul.

By pointing to the popularity of soul music in Birmingham I do not want to understate the amount of white anxiety in postsegregation Birmingham. I agree with Madhu Dubey that the move back to authenticity in the popular culture of the 1970s, and the amazing popularity of folk and roots music, was a response to the empowerment of African Americans in a new New South, a Nuevo South in which the old binary code of black and white that had served the South so well was upturned by a new and more complex formula.[18] Music plays the same role in defining both white and black culture in the South, acting as a performative and ideological glue that holds identity together. In her book on rock 'n' roll culture in Liverpool, Sara Cohen argues that music is a "shared code" that gives "a strong sense of allegiance and identity."[19] It also helps define a time and a place. Reaching for authenticity in music meant going back to a time when the races knew where they stood, and stayed in their place; and if there is one thing that defines southerners, it is that they know their place. But times have changed, and we now live in a Chocolate City that has overcome its tragic past and looks forward to a prosperous multiracial future.

Yet neither the New South nor the new New South has lived up to its expectations and realized the identity politics of its boosters. The history of the civil rights struggle in Birmingham remains a critical part of its identity and the justification of its rise as a Chocolate City. But as Diane McWhorter has pointed out, reconciliation has become an industry in Birmingham. The fifty-year anniversary of the historic events of 1963 was an orgy of self-congratulation and self-promotion, tempered only by the continuation of poverty of many of its citizens and the uncontested tradition of bad government. If you ask white people what it was like to live in Birmingham in the 1960s under the leadership of Bull Connor, they will tell you about the hopeless corruption and inefficiency of a comically inept government. If you ask anybody in Birmingham right now about city government, they will tell you more or less the same thing. While Dr. King's "dream" is much closer to becoming a reality in Alabama, it is still a work in progress. Hip-hop artists have taken up the role of documenting the lives of the poor and disenfranchised in today's "Dirty South." In her study of hip-hop in Memphis, Zandria Robinson profiles the artist Erykah Badu, who sings about a Dirty South of poverty, drug trafficking, and violence. Robinson calls this protest music "post-soul blues," which seems an appropriate term for the postsegregated South.[20]

The city of Birmingham continues to live in the past, unable to shed its historic stigma of racial hatred and to find an alternative to defining itself in terms of African American resistance. City government has enshrined its famous musicians as well as its civil rights leaders in its efforts to build a more acceptable and comforting past. Building monuments to musicians who grabbed the first chance to get out of Birmingham, and sometimes denied ever coming from the city, has more than a touch of irony. I don't disagree with those African American musicians who told me that the Motown sound was really Birmingham music (and musicians) transplanted to Detroit — but what does that say about the city they left behind?

"Sex & Drugs & Rock & Roll"

After it became evident that it would be impossible to produce a one-volume history of music in Birmingham that was politically correct and adequately covered all the music made in the city since its inception, the question remained what to do with the pile of interviews we had amassed — over a hundred by the end of the 1990s. There was so much good material about punk, postpunk, and all the many varieties of the New Wave that it seemed possible to assemble a history of rock music in Birmingham from the 1950s to the millennium that would cover all the different declensions of rock and show how it had developed or perhaps regressed — a sense of progression and change is central to the ideology of rock 'n' roll. This was still an ambitious goal, but it would provide an opportunity to address some beleaguered issues in rock music, such as gender and virtuosity, and also cover some of the transformative effects that new technology had on the music industry.

It came as quite a surprise to me that a city as conservative as Birmingham should have had such a lively punk scene, but on reflection, the very fact of its tradition of conservatism was only going to encourage rebellious youth. Although the city was far from supportive of the New Wave, it did allow it to exist, in much the same way that gay bars survived in the 1970s and 1980s. What punk represented was part of the fabric of rock 'n' roll — the challenge to keep it the music of rebellion. As Michael Azerrad noted, rock 'n' roll in the 1980s was seen as a force for change, not just a commodity.[21] Just like the folkies and worried white supremacists, rock 'n' roll enthusiasts' desire to return to simpler (but more subversive times) reflected discontent with the status quo.

Punk aimed to "break a few rules," in the words of Ian Dury, and of the many rules punk rockers broke, the gender rules were probably the most influential. The popular music business has been a male domain from the beginning, and it was female musicians like Bessie Smith who challenged male dominance and articulated a new sexuality in their work. Birmingham can claim one of the most outspoken female blues artists in Lucille Bogan, and it is unfortunate that her music and influence are not better recognized. While country music was traditionally open to females, its louder and more energetic cousin rockabilly was dominated by males and the popularity of this music in Birmingham marked the beginning of rock 'n' roll in Alabama. There were a few notable instances of female rockabilly stars coming from Birmingham, but regretfully I was never able to locate the survivors or find anyone who remembered their performances in enough detail to analyze it. As the music of white working-class southerners, rockabilly conformed to the tradition of keeping the women at home. I was told that "good girls" didn't go to rockabilly joints (which were sometimes joint business ventures with prostitution), so being a female rocker in the 1950s required some mental and physical toughness. The music they made certainly sounds as tough and as assertive as that of their male counterparts.

Susan Cahn has described in detail how rock 'n' roll highlighted the sexual tensions of the 1950s South. Much of the fuel for resisting integration and rock 'n' roll came from fears of how white girls would fall prey to sexually evocative, black-influenced music. Cahn paints a picture of the sexually charged spaces in high schools and dance floors and the "coming out of teenaged girls' sexuality, with rock music at the conspicuous center." Yet for all its sexuality and surface rebellion, rock music in the 1950s was dominated by males. Cahn recounts the career of Janis Martin, "the female Elvis," who openly expressed as much sexual longing as the male Elvis and paid the price for it. Female rockers had brief careers, short-changed by deejays and stifled by the disinterest of record companies. Cahn concludes that "a female performer singing about her own sexual desires, satisfactions, frustrations, and fantasies seems to have deviated too far from sexual norms. The men controlling the music industry preferred the dynamic of a sexy male singer eliciting giddy, hysterical reactions from girls."[22]

The rise of the counterculture in the late 1960s enshrined sentiments of sexual liberation, but the pursuit of hedonism was still ordered along the lines of gender. For all its claims of sexual equality, the 1960s were sexist. Ellen Willis has pointed out that the counterculture still treated women "as chicks — nubile decorations — or mothers or goddesses or bitches, rarely as human beings." Rebellion was still part of male assertiveness, and the liberation that came with new sexual freedoms served to excuse males from the traditional obligations of respecting and supporting women.[23] Women in 1960s rock 'n' roll were seen as groupies, backup singers, or the object of love songs, but not as players; their place was in the audience, not on the stage. Only a few musicians, like Janis Joplin, managed to break into this male club.

While the folk revival of the 1960s encouraged women to join in, to play guitars and write songs, the male domination of rock 'n' roll continued into the 1970s. Acoustic guitars were open to both sexes, but electric guitars — the mainstay of rock 'n' roll — were considered boys' toys. Electric guitars and amplifiers are complex technological systems that have always been a male preserve in America, and the great power of amplified guitars meant that only strong males could control them. The absence of women in rock prompted feminist writers such as Patricia Kennealy-Morrison to question the core values of this musical culture. In her wonderfully titled article "Rock around the Cock," she articulated her own fantasy of becoming a guitar hero — a heresy to the rock establishment and its audience.[24] But punk challenged both the concept of a guitar hero and the gender conventions of rock 'n' roll, opening up rock music to all races and both genders. Punk allowed women to get their foot in the door and participate: The music and the business have been much the better for it. Nowadays young female guitarists are courted not only by the popular music industry but also by the manufacturers of electric guitars.

The technology of rock music has changed drastically over the past three decades. When this project started, you still bought music in record stores, and very few bands thought of using a computer to record music or to reach out to their fans. Aaron Beam's oral history of music in Birmingham happily spanned the most significant changes in the popular music industry since Thomas Edison invented the phonograph. Here was a chance to evaluate these changes from the perspectives of the musicians rather than put it into a context of the history of technology. In fact, all the changes in rock music and the music industry in the twenty-first century seemed better illustrated by the experiences and opinions of musicians than by any scholarly interpretation. This realization returned the focus of this project back to the interviews themselves: no longer the basis for the narrative, but the narrative itself. And this is the book you have before you. A history of rock music in Birmingham told by some of the people who played it, listened to it, and tried to make a living from it. A history of rock music in Birmingham that explains how it changed lives and how it reflected individual identities and perceptions of the city itself. Although it has plenty of rags-to-riches episodes, it is not a story of success aimed to boost the reputation of the city and attract more investment and tourist dollars; rather, it follows the cycle of raised and lowered expectations. It relates the experiences of professional musicians rather than rock stars, and how their dreams and desires were translated in the harsh realities of the music industry. It is a story not about rock 'n' roll's triumph but of its evolution and survival.

CHAPTER ONE

Rock 'n' Roll Comes to Birmingham

Rock 'n' roll came to Birmingham in the form of recordings — shiny black lacquered 78 rpm promotional discs sent to radio stations by the record companies. Station WVOK went on the air in Birmingham in 1947. An AM station of 10,000 watts, it covered most of North and Central Alabama as well as good portions of Georgia and Tennessee. It was the work of the Bends and Brennan families, and Dan Brennan was there from the beginning: "When we signed on, a Capitol transcription library was our only source or primary source of entertainment. Big 16-inch discs, and they had some interesting programming, among others they had Duke Ellington, Gene Krupa, some others, Pee Wee Hunt. They had a number of singers and some country & western, Tex Ritter and some of those people, Nat King Cole and the King Cole Trio. They would have maybe four or five selections on each side, and it would be just an opportunity to play them. The other form of music was a 78 rpm record . . . The only company that gave us records in the beginning was RCA. We did get some help from them, but most of the others did not. We actually had to purchase records. When we first signed on, we played a form of pop music; the Capitol library was pop. We did have some country & western too, but it was primarily pop, then within the first couple of years we had switched over to country & western. Partly because of audience demand, and partly because some of the live bands we had on the air were country & western.

"We had dances and we had bands that would perform at the Bessemer City Auditorium. We just did that as a means of kind of spotlighting the groups that were playing on the air. We gave them an opportunity to make a few dollars and also to make the station look a little different. Not many stations in town had any live functions like that that they participated in. We played records while the bands took a break. I remember one of the dances at the Bessemer Auditorium. I remember the first record, first true rock 'n' roll record I played: 'Rock around the Clock' by Bill Haley. I remember people did not dance — they looked like they did not know what in the world they were hearing. I knew at the time [1955] it was still, it was very popular already in some parts of the country, but our audience we had on that dance floor did not know what it was. Our first exposure to rock 'n' roll was really rockabilly. It was kind of Jerry Lee Lewis, Carl Perkins, and some of those Sun recordings. As a matter of fact, we played a combination of country & western and rockabilly in the beginning and it was probably a transition to rock 'n' roll music."

Baker Knight was in a rockabilly band called the Nightmares in 1955, with Shuler Brown on bass, Nat Toderice and Glen Lane on saxophone, and Bill Weinstein on drums. They had, in his words, "a country rock sound" with steel guitar and piano. "We had started a band when Elvis came out and I had learned to play guitar well enough to get a band going." Knight said they were "the first rockabilly band in Birmingham . . . and the American Legion [venue] in Leeds [a community close to Birmingham] was the first time the Nightmares played." Later on they played "the Mountain Brook Lodge, which had mostly pop groups, and the people came rushing in to hear rock 'n' roll, people had never heard it before . . . People would come and stand around bandstand and stare up at us, whatever songs were popular, 'Blue Suede Shoes,' black music, I could sing that stuff . . . R&B [rhythm and blues] brought them together, Bo Diddley stuff, people loved it — it was something different."

The radio stations playing that "Bo Diddley stuff" in Birmingham were some of the few African American stations in the country. As the South was segregated, Birmingham's biggest radio stations — WAPI, WBRC, and WSGN — broadcast to a predominantly white audience. The first inroads into the segregated airwaves were short programs devoted to African American sacred music, featuring the gospel quartets whose sweet harmonies and soaring lead vocals appealed to both races. William Blevins, Nims Gay, and Sadie Mae Patterson all broadcast gospel shows on white radio in the early 1940s. The African American businessman A. G. Gaston sponsored Birmingham's Gospel Harmonettes on WSGN. On April 19, 1942, WJLD started broadcasting from Bessemer. It carried gospel shows, popular music, and news. In 1946 a white disc jockey called Bob Umbach began the *Atomic Boogie Hour*, playing rhythm and blues and imitating the patter of black deejays, just like Dewey Phillips in Memphis. It was the only station in Birmingham that broadcast black music. The *Atomic Boogie Hour* was so popular it often ran for hours every day, and it lasted until 1953.

In 1949 Shelley Stewart got a job with the newly opened WEDR, a white-owned station aimed at the black audience, and as "Shelley the Playboy" he brought the exciting sounds of R&B and rock 'n' roll to an awed audience of teenagers. Ed Reynolds, who managed WJLD, started WEDR radio in 1949 — another station aimed at the African American audience. By the 1960s WENN was the premier radio station in Birmingham programming African American music, with two of the city's most popular deejays: Shelley Stewart and "Tall Paul" White. Record collector Ben Saxon remembered: "You grew up listening to WJLD and WENN and Shelley the Playboy and Tall Paul." "Can I get a witness!" roared Shelley over the air after he played a hot song, and thousands of Birmingham teenagers agreed with him. As one of them said: "We was all listening to Shelley." Baker Knight: "B. B. King was just starting in and they were playing his records on the black radio station... This was 1952. I was over at the black radio station before white people knew that they had such things... We went over to the black radio station, and that was unheard-of in those days, and we'd listen to B. B. King records." The black stations had an illicit attraction: "You had to get closer to the music," remembered David Bryan, and this meant traveling to the black sections of town, ducking down in the car as you traversed the mainly African American Northside. If you could not get the signal, you were left out of it. Tony Wachter: "So it is strange how cut off we were. I felt extremely cut off. Even though WENN was broadcasting in my youth, if they were I didn't know what it was — we could not get it."

Listening to the radio at night was one of those shared rock 'n' roll pleasures. Ben Saxon: "I don't know how I first started listening. Transistor radios were just coming out. I had one that was in the shape of a rocket ship. It was only AM, of course. The nose was the pull-up antenna... I had a really strict father, who would make me go to bed at eight at night.

I would take the radio with the earphones and have a great time listening to the music until I went to sleep." On a clear night you might be able to pick up *Louisiana Hayride* coming from KWKH from Shreveport, or B. B. King playing records at WDIA in Memphis, the "mother station" of rhythm and blues.

As rock 'n' roll became more accepted, more radio stations began to program it. Loud, brash, Duke Rumore ("the loud mouth of the South") established himself as the leading rock 'n' roll disc jockey at WSGN — the major player in Birmingham's radio in the 1960s. Vocalist Henry Lovoy and Ben Saxon remembered him and "all that New Orleans soul and R&B that he used to play. It was kind of like an Alan Freed of the Birmingham area. He brought that new sound here to us." Bob Cahill: "You could listen to black radio, but I don't think other than in the morning when you were going to school, because for most teenagers the Rumore brothers probably had their ear in the afternoon. The reason was that they would play the latest, and if Duke said, 'Hey, I've got a new record from somebody,' everybody would listen and he would play it at 4 [p.m. — after school]." Davy Roddy was another popular rock deejay. Fred Dalke: "One of the biggest things in the '50s and '60s was that radio had personality, they had radio personalities, as compared to today — a lot of these deejays are clones. In those days every deejay that became big and popular had their own way of doing things, like Dave Roddy, and they called him 'Rockin' Roddy,' and he was on WSGN and he was like *the* deejay to listen to, he was cool, and all the kids listened to him on Friday nights."

Disc jockeys were well connected to their audience; they did their business in person, meeting the listening audience in the numerous promotional activities they arranged. Duke's brother Joe Rumore of WVOK — at 50,000 watts the most powerful station in the state — had one of the most recognized voices in Alabama. His daily presence on air made him a family friend for those who listened in: "I couldn't get through the day without Joe," said one of them.[1] Joe would deal with as many as 250 letters from his listeners every day. In 1954 the two brothers opened Rumore's Record Rack on 1802 Second Avenue, which gave them a retail outlet for the records they played on air. Deejays played a more personal role in music than they do now; they were there on the stage introducing the artists, making appearances at retail stores and record hops. Ben Saxon and Henry Lovoy agreed, "We had a radio family at one time in Birmingham. Back then you knew or felt like you knew Dave Roddy or Dan Brennan or Joe Rumore. They were your friends."

Popular Entertainment in the 1950s

Much of Birmingham's live music at this time was being played by dance bands — not the great swing bands of the 1940s, but smaller, more flexible groups. Harrison Cooper started playing saxophone at Ensley High School in the 1930s: "I organized a little Lombardo-type band. Guy Lombardo. Everyone liked him then. So we just got bitten by the bug and his music, and started copying his arrangements and we were just teenagers. We played Birmingham, but it was actually after high school. So we had this real professional-sounding band and we would broadcast on the local radio stations WBRC and WAPI and just go all over the country. The signal went out and we would get letters about going to different places to play . . . We played all around Birmingham at different clubs, the hotels, dances at the country clubs. It was a very danceable-type band. In 1935 we were playing at the Ritz Theatre and there was this girl and her husband who liked our band a lot and they were moving to South America . . . They liked our band so well that they told us when they left that they would try and book us down there. Sure enough, they did. We went down there in January of 1935 and stayed for six months in Buenos Aires. That was really the climax of that band. After we came back from South America we played around Birmingham for a while and I guess it just kind of wore off. We all just went in different directions." After graduating from school Harrison Cooper joined Herbie Kay's band in Chicago: "I played with that band until I was drafted in World War II. Then when I got into the army I organized a band there. I was fortunate to have a band all during the war. We had a big Glenn Miller–type band at that time. That was about 1941–45. That was about the swing time. There was Benny Goodman, Glenn Miller, and there were a lot of big bands at that time. So after the war was over I came back to Birmingham and stayed about six months, and then I decided to go back up to New York, and when I got there I got a job with Benny Goodman.

I was with Benny for about two years, and I came back to Birmingham to organize my own band here. That was about 1947. So I picked up where I left off years ago. We played all the places around Birmingham. The Pick-wick Club was very popular. They had a big dance hall in the back of the hotel. It was very popular, all the high school proms were held there and it was just a very busy place. We also played at downtown at the Municipal Auditorium, we played a lot of dances there. The Thomas Jefferson Hotel, the Tutwiler, they all had ballrooms. Country clubs like the Fairmont, Hillcrest, Birmingham, Mountain Brook, we played a lot of those places, a lot of those social dances. We were a busy bunch."

Tommy Charles had started training his voice for opera, "but I saw people around me who had less voice than I did making a lot more money and having a lot more fun singing ballads, pop . . . Don Cornell [vocalist of the Sammy Kaye band] was an influence, Sinatra was an influence, Perry Como, who is a guy you haven't heard of. Bing Crosby, of course." Charles was soon making a name for himself as a radio personality: "I made national radio with a band called Horace Height, which was a national touring band that was on CBS, and I made them in 1953 . . . Back then I sang everywhere . . . I played here at Mike's South Pacific, and also played at Carmichael's [nightclub] . . . And Carmichael was a real hip kind of guy, dressed in real fancy clothes, and he introduced me . . . and I came roaring out from the sidelines and the band's playing the introduction to my song and I grab the microphone off the stand, and I'm going to put on a show, then I knock my tooth out and it falls on the floor." The life of a musician in the 1950s was "with whiskey and people having a good time . . . But some of the things I could tell you, you couldn't put in a book. Because back then, performers just got women. I don't know why . . . and I don't mean it with anything illicit necessarily, just women like to meet performers. And the sexual revolution hadn't taken place yet, so it was not a big deal."

In the 1950s the record companies and radio stations served the adult audience. Dan Brennan: "We really wanted to get, for our clients, more of the adults than we did the young children. We reached them with rock 'n' roll too. I think as many adults liked Elvis as did the youngsters. I don't think our goal was ever to try and just reach teenagers or anything like that . . . So while the first listeners might have skewed toward the younger age groups, the final result was a family audience . . . So for commercial reasons it was more profitable to us to sell our sponsors' products to adults than it was to sell them to youngsters."

Birmingham had many dance bands and venues for them to play. Vocalist Cousin Cliff: "I want you to write down Harrison Cooper first . . . He is a pianist and is just wonderful . . . Dewitt Shaw, he had one of the best bands in Birmingham. He really played most of the dances around here, he and Harrison Cooper. They used to play the old Pickwick [Club] . . . Buddy Harris had a real nice dance band that was real sophisticated, but they were not real big though . . . Another person would be Tant, Buddy Wallace Tant . . . Eddie Stephens had a band also . . . He had a big band, about fifteen or twenty pieces. He used to play at the Cascade Plunge and the Cloud Room. Do you remember Cascade Plunge? They used to have those big dances out there called convocations of social clubs . . . Just a lot of big bands out there . . . Ted Brooks is another person, boy, he was really good . . . in fact, he played shows with me at the old Shades Mountain Country Club . . . Lou Mazzeret was a band director, and he used to play down at the Blue Note Club. That used to be downtown. Henry Kimbrell is another one. He used to play at all those society functions . . . Back when I was going to school, Woodlawn [High School] and all, we used to have sorority and fraternity parties. We used to have lead-outs, where all the boys bring out the girls through this pretty arch and all, and they have this big theme and usually have big bands."

The scores of bands that played the big hotels downtown, the dinner and dance clubs like the Pickwick and Blue Note, the country clubs and private supper clubs, all depended on providing music for dancing. Harrison Cooper: "Bill Nappi had a dance band that was pretty big. It was a dance band mainly. These were all mostly dance bands that were around here. There was Paul Smith. There were a lot of little old bands like that around Birmingham at that time. They were very popular. There were as many dance bands around at that time as there are rock bands that are around now. Everything is rock now; back then everything was dance."

Tommy Stewart, one of the great trumpet players of the swing era, hit the road early: "The snake oil and medicine shows used to come from Atlanta, and a lot of them left with musicians who could read [music]. Plenty of tent shows came through. Over by Parker High School, there was a big old field over there. These guys came through and sell you some Hadecol, snake medicine or something — some of that stuff was colored water. They had live bands and I played with some of them. I made some money when I was about sixteen traveling with a circus . . . Birmingham was a hotbed for music ever since I was a little boy. You had bands like the Fred Avery Band, John L. Bell, a piano player had a band, John Hands had a band in the 1940s. Fess [Whatley] had a heck of a band. When Sun Ra left [around 1946] his band was still playing here."

Birmingham's segregated African American community had its own entertainment. Clarinetist and saxophonist Frank Adams "saw Cab Calloway at the Masonic Temple. I remember seeing him perform on stage. It was a black-only concert. There was no integration at that time. I remember seeing Duke Ellington for the first time at the Masonic Temple . . . I used to wonder how luxurious it was to see someone at an auditorium. They had a balcony, where we would sit and look out. I was really impressed with Duke's band." Tommy Stewart: "The Madison Night Spot on Bessemer Highway was the place; it had a big hall to dance: $2.50 to see B. B. King or Bobby 'Blue' Bland, Ray Charles, Howlin' Wolf. There were a lot of clubs, five or six clubs along Auburn Avenue, some holes in the wall and some very good. Fess was playing at country clubs. Birmingham was real dirty, but there was a lot going on, the music scene was going strong and a sports scene was really something. Willy Mays — I saw him play at Rickwood Field. Birmingham had a lot of race problems. Fourth Avenue and Seventeenth Street was a black business district full of black businesses, a lot more thriving than you do now. I'd rather be in segregation any day because the music was better — you had four or five big bands, five or six combos making money, with guys working six days a week. On weekends you would go along Fourth Avenue, it was like a brand-new city in the middle of the city. It blew my mind when I first went down there . . . You could go down Fourth Avenue on Friday night and see the [tour] buses, they got stranded, or stopped to get a motel in the district or stayed in homes. It's tough now when you read about it [segregation], but then they did not pay any attention — they liked to play, they were making music, they worked regular and they were doing all kind of stuff." Frank Adams: "Live music was big. Tuxedo Junction was a park where they played. I can think of so many places where musicians played. I can think of so many, like the old Congo Club, which was out on Bessemer Highway. Monroe's Steakhouse was another one. A lot of people got names for clubs in Birmingham after places that had opened in New York. We had a Cotton Club here . . . There were sometimes musicians who would sit out on Fourth Avenue and play. It was comparable to the French Quarter . . . Fourth Avenue was thriving at that point. It was downtown, and it was all that we had. It was the heart of entertainment. You worked all week so you could come into town on the weekend. You spent your money on Fourth Avenue."

Things were changing for big band players in the postwar entertainment scene. Tommy Stewart: "Jazz musicians from the swing era, when work got slim at the end of the 1940s, a lot of them went into small bands. Louis Jordan was jump jive. His band was the Tympany Five, those smaller bands, he got it from Chick Webb. At this time the small bands were coming up, because there was less costs . . . Well, there were two factions of small bands: followers of Louis Jordan and [followers of] Charlie Parker. Jazz used to be dance music, popular music entertainment, then Louis Jordan went toward R&B, and jazz became intellectual listening music. R&B would still employ music from big bands. For example, the Clovers and Drifters — their first arrangers were old jazz musicians." Tommy got hired to play trumpet in R&B singer Jimmy Reed's band: "I had gone back to Gadsden [about sixty miles from Birmingham] and had formed a jazz band, three or four students, and we went with Jimmy Reed, we were just teenagers. We had sharp stage suits, you know, the Ivy League pants and big-brimmed hats. There I was playing in New York City at fifteen. Here comes my mama . . . That killed me right there! We played mostly black joints . . . Jimmy Reed had a big white following. I think the last club my mama pulled me out of was the Birmingham Country Club — she came over there and got me!" Frank Adams landed a spot in the great Duke Ellington band, which kept swing alive in the 1950s, albeit in a more modern form. Erskine Hawkins became an arranger and bandleader for James Brown, who was making a big impression with the African American audience for his soulful stage show. Sonny Blount (aka Sun Ra) worked with Wynonie Harris, a wild R&B singer who inspired Elvis Presley with not only his music but also his outrageous stage act. In 1948 Harris cut a record for the independent King label; "Good Rockin' Tonight" was a hit and a portent of some important changes to come in the business of popular music.

"Good Rocking Tonight"

Written by Roy Brown in 1947, this influential song started off as a jump jive number: swinging tempo, heavy on the beat, and with clearly enunciated lyrics. Brown's vocal style owed a lot to gospel and influenced singers like Bobby Bland and Jackie Wilson. Brown tried to sell his song to Wynonie Harris. He was not interested, but the song impressed the owner of the independent De Luxe Records, Jules Braun, to sign Brown and put the record out. Released in 1948 it reached number 13 on the *Billboard* R&B chart, and a year later Wynonie Harris's cover made it to number 1 on the chart. This attracted some attention from country artists looking for up-tempo songs. Bill Haley was one of them. His cover of Jackie Brentson's "Rocket 88" had done very well, and he followed this in 1953 with "Rock the Joint," a pioneer rockabilly record. The beat, structure, and lyrics of the song owed a lot to "Good Rockin' Tonight," but changes replaced the names of R&B dances to country dances, and there was a lot more echo effect in the recording and a penetrating guitar solo by Danny Cedrone, which he used again on "Rock around the Clock."

Country and Rockabilly

Bill Haley was not the only country artist trawling through the R&B charts looking for suitable material for audiences wanting faster tempos and more exciting rhythms. Sidney Louie "Hardrock" Gunter of Birmingham was also trying to cross over. Gunter was a singer who got some of his first gigs on radio — playing guitar behind the Delmore Brothers on the *Alabama Hayloft Jamboree* show. Gunter formed the Hoot Owl Ramblers in 1938 to broadcast on local radio — allegedly the band came from Hoot Owl Holler in Birmingham. In 1939 he joined Happy Wilson's Golden River Boys, who had a regular spot on WAPI radio, which helped them get booked into the Princess theater chain, which covered Alabama and

Georgia. Gunter acquired his nickname after a trunk lid fell on his head while unloading the group's gear and he continued unhurt. Much of his music harked back to the string bands and comedy routines of the previous generation of old-time players, but it was changing with the times. He told the story of country music's postwar transformation in a song he wrote called "I'll Give 'em Rhythm." This is a song of two halves: one with steel guitar breaks and lyrics about "purty love songs," country homes, and the "good ole radio." But he laments that there's something wrong — they don't like my songs, they want rhythm with a solid beat. The song takes off in a faster tempo with roaring saxophones and pounding drums as Hardrock proves he can deliver what he calls "rhythm and blues." Although it "hurts his soul to dig for gold," he does it anyway, along with hundreds of his contemporaries, black and white, who were looking for inspiration across the color bar. In 1951, he recorded a song with Roberta Lee, the raunchy "Sixty Minute Man," which was one of the first country records to cross over and appeal to R&B audiences.

Gunter was so popular on local radio that Manny Pearson, the owner of Bama Records, approached him with an offer to make some records. Bama was a small, independent local label with no offices and no recording studio, so Gunter went to the studios of WAPI to record "Birmingham Bounce," and "How Can I Believe You Love Me." The Golden River Boys (renamed the Pebbles for the session), were made up of Hardrock on guitar, Billy Tucker on fiddle, Ted Crabtree on steel guitar, Huel Murphy on piano, Jim O'Day on bass, and Bob Sanders on drums. "Birmingham Bounce" soon became a regional hit and Hardrock played for large crowds as he toured the Deep South. "Birmingham Bounce" is about having a good time in "a town we love called Birmingham." Gunter's song rocks along with a pounding boogie-woogie piano and drum beat, yet prominent fiddle and steel guitar breaks mark this disc as country. Gunter's music sounds like old-time radio with a folksy spoken introduction and down-home banter, but it also has enough rhythm and excitement to qualify for early rock 'n' roll, even though the trademark twangy electric guitar is absent. Country singer Red Foley recorded a version for the major Decca label that quickly climbed the national charts, finally making number 1 on the country charts for several months.

Bama followed the success of "Birmingham Bounce" with another single in 1950: "Gonna Dance All Night" / "Why Don't You Show Me That You Love Me." This record has a place in the history books as it claims one of the first mentions of the term "rock-'n'-roll," years before deejay Alan Freed popularized it. Gunter remembered later that he had often heard the term at dances, especially after a good up-tempo number. So he started to use it in his introductions —"here's one you can rock 'n' roll to"— in order, as he admitted, to be "in with the kids."[2] Bill Haley had done the same thing: he had picked up the phrase that formed the title of his song "Crazy Man, Crazy" from the teenagers in his audience. Country singers and their fellow professionals in R&B were incorporating the vernacular of their audiences in their songs and putting both "rock" and "roll" in the lyrics. On "Birmingham Bounce" Hardrock sang, "When the beat starts rockin,' no one's blue," and he added to this on "Gonna Dance All Night" with: "We're gonna rock 'n' roll while we dance all night." While solidly in the country genre — his next Bama release was "Dad Gave My Hog Away" / "Lonesome Blues"— Hardrock was playing rock 'n' roll and defining it as up-tempo songs that "the kids" can dance to.

Unfortunately for Gunter, his regional hits did not help his career as a recording artist, and he remained in radio and television. In 1953 he returned to Birmingham, where he was a deejay on radio station WJLD. The program director there was Jim Connally, who was related to Sam Phillips, owner of the small Sun label in Memphis. Phillips had expressed an interest in recording Hardrock in Memphis, but Gunter could not find the time to travel up there, so he remade "Gonna Dance All Night" at a Birmingham radio station. The tapes were sent to Memphis, and in May 1954 Phillips released it on the Sun label.

Elvis Presley was another country singer signed to Sun. Phillips always told the story that he was searching for a young white kid who could put over the rhythm and blues that was so popular with his black customers, and Presley turned out to be that person. "Birmingham Bounce" was Sun's #201 release and soon after came Sun #209, "That's Alright Mama," a reworking of bluesman Arthur Crudup's earlier record. Sun Records were trying to cover all their bases for Presley's first release, for on the flip side of this R&B cover was a country standard, "Blue Moon of Kentucky," done over in a much faster and louder rockabilly style. Elvis's second Sun release, "Good Rockin' Tonight" (Sun #210), was a cover of Wynonie Harris's hit. Birmingham musician Lenard Brown: "See, black people were doing that for so long before Elvis, it was unreal. They [Sun Records] just had the money to put behind it — he was not doing anything different."

Enter the King

Although the country radio stations steered well clear of "Good Rockin' Tonight," Sam Phillips and Elvis Presley knew that they were onto something. During 1954 Elvis continued to perform as "The Hillbilly Cat" (backing Bill Haley and the Comets on one occasion) and playing gigs in Alabama, including one-nighters in Sheffield and Montgomery, and some say a honky-tonk in Prattville. Elvis Presley was gaining exposure, especially after he secured gigs on *Louisiana Hayride*, a Saturday night country radio show that was broadcast all over the South. One day in November 1955 Ken Shackleford was eating lunch with RCA executive Ed Hines in Gulas's restaurant in downtown Birmingham. Shackleford was a new entry into the record business: "I got out of the navy and came to Birmingham and went to work in a bank. I won a contest to sell accounts, and I won and got a tape recorder — a reel-to-reel. Being a musician myself, and I met this guy, a saxophone player and he said, 'You need a mixer.' So I went out and got a Boken mixer. My friend said, 'We should go downtown and start a studio.' I had a friend downtown who had a blood bank, who gave me the upstairs for nothing. We go in and build a studio... We would tape a session and we would send our tapes to RCA [in Nashville] and then they would [custom] press them. We sent them the tape and they did the rest. We knew nothing about soundproofing and recording... The only thing [recording studio] they had at that time was Homer Milam [of Reed Records]. He's a good friend, but he didn't have the kind of equipment we did. At the time the best stuff on the market was an Ampex two-track reel to reel... Homer had a three-track, that's what he did all the Reed stuff on... In the meantime we were recording various people, a session for Marion Worth, who got a Columbia record contract, she was like Patty Page." While the two were eating, Ed Hines, "the RCA head honcho in Nashville," blurted out "We bought Elvis's contract from Sun Records for $35,000!" Shackleford was shocked: "What! My God, did somebody lose their mind?" This was an unheard amount for a little-known singer and the most that any record company had ever paid for an individual artist. An entrepreneur with a background in carnivals and a fake military title called Colonel Tom Parker had taken over managing Elvis from Sam Phillips, and he steered the young man away from Sun Records to RCA — one of the five or six major recording companies. RCA proclaimed their new signing as an up-and-coming star of country music and his first release on their label was a country song, "I Forgot to Remember to Forget" (recorded in Sun Studios in 1955). The B side of this disc was the sublime "Mystery Train," one of the great rock songs, and its relegation to the B side indicates where RCA thought the core audience for Elvis might be. Yet RCA alerted their dealers that Elvis's records should be catalogued as both pop and country.

Twenty-one-year old Elvis made the journey to Nashville at the beginning of 1956 and found himself in RCA's recording studio under the watchful gaze of Chet Atkins. This was a complex of studios, first-rate equipment, and some of the best guitar pickers in the nation — a big change from the tiny, primitive independent studios like Sun in Memphis or Shackleford's Heart Studios in Birmingham. When "Heartbreak Hotel" was released in January 1956, there was an anxious feeling in RCA's offices in Nashville and New York that someone had made a big mistake. A few weeks later no one was worrying anymore; "Heartbreak Hotel" was racing up the charts — not just the pop charts, but all the charts. It had reached number 1 in pop and country and number 5 in the rhythm and blues charts by March. Its sales were astounding. Even the black radio stations were playing it. The next time Shackleford and Hines met for lunch a few weeks after that November meeting, Hines said: "Ken, you are not going to believe this but we are shipping records out of Indianapolis in boxcars" — that is, in railroad boxcars instead of in trucks or U.S. Mail packages. The national network of record distributors operated by RCA was spreading the word of rock 'n' roll in the form of this single disc.

The Rock 'n' Roll Show

The first national tours of artists playing the new music came to Alabama in 1956, such as Bill Haley, the Drifters, Bo Diddley, and Big Joe Turner, whose "Shake, Rattle and Roll" had been the basis of many successful covers by white artists, including one by Bill Haley. These were the days when a concert was more than one headliner and an opening band, but as many as fifteen nationally known artists all performing on one bill. Music promoter Tony Ruffino: "There was eleven acts on one show and they all did one song. The radio would only play one or two songs. So therefore no one would ever have more than one or two hits." The next year Alan Freed's *Biggest Show of Stars* came to the Deep South with some of the emerging names in what he had labeled rock 'n' roll: Fats Domino, Paul Anka, Frankie Lymon, Chuck Berry, the Drifters, and the Crickets, led by a bespectacled teenager called Buddy Holly. Ben Saxon remembered that evening: "This was the big show of 1957." Saxon acquired some photographs and records given to the person who cleaned up the auditorium after the show: "He would help them unload their equipment . . . He got this kind of stuff from them. He got this one signed by Fats Domino. Here is Buddy Holly. This is 1957, two years before he died . . . Buddy Holly was it. I will be fifty-two years old tomorrow [1994]. If you took a survey of people that were three years older and younger than me, Buddy Holly would be their favorite artist. Not Elvis Presley. I'm talking about here in Birmingham . . . I was in Panama City, Florida, the first time I heard him. I was only a kid. I heard him on the jukebox. They had all the black artists, like Muddy Waters, on there. All of a sudden I heard this white voice and did not know what to think. I still liked it. I was adapted to the black sound."

While the traveling shows of stars were eagerly awaited, they were rare and wonderful events in the lives of Birmingham's teenagers, who wanted more than a once-a-year rock 'n' roll fix. So they looked to other entertainment venues. Although television in the 1950s is usually considered to be a force of cultural conformism which illustrated a classless, lily-white version of the American Dream in its family friendly programming, it did provide an important outlet for new music. Elvis Presley's controversial appearances on *The Ed Sullivan Show* might have outraged many viewers, but the size of the viewing audience (a quite amazing 82 percent share) made it clear to the entertainment business that rock 'n' roll was far too popular to be ignored. It is not too surprising that his movements on stage — all learned from black acts he saw on Beale Street in Memphis — were deemed too provocative for the family audience. Yet it was these gyrations that made rock 'n' roll so attractive to teenagers.

Elvis's controversial appearances on *The Ed Sullivan Show* became part of his legend, and the dramatic rise of "the King of Rock 'n' Roll" owed a lot to extensive exposure on television. Elvis's first recording sessions in RCA's Nashville and New York studios were fitted into a crowded schedule of live performances and TV appearances — the Dorsey Brothers', Milton Berle's, and Steve Allen's nationally viewed shows — and a screen test for Hollywood producer Hal Wallis. By the 1950s television sets were installed in millions of American homes and the exposure it gave to music was quickly making it as important as radio in marketing records. Birmingham's two television stations, WBRC and WAPI, were part of the NBC and CBS networks and carried the syndicated variety shows of Ed Sullivan and Steve Allen. The jubilation or horror that accompanied Elvis's performance on *The Ed Sullivan Show* was shared all over the country. That Birmingham was part of this audience, a nation seated in front of blue-tinted screens, was part of the New South's integration into a national popular culture.

Radio played all kinds of pop music, not just rock 'n' roll; television networks were wary of delinquent teenagers and their music; and the major record companies were still not fully convinced that rock 'n' roll was anything more than another passing fad. But Hollywood producers looked at the numbers and realized that the youth market might replace the adult audience lost to television. What propelled Bill Haley's "Rock around the Clock" into the hearts and minds of American youth was not just the playing of the record at dances like the one at the Bessemer City Auditorium or in jukeboxes all over Birmingham, but in a few minutes of a movie. *Blackboard Jungle* (1955) was a film about a rebellious group of students at an inner-city high school tormenting an exasperated teacher played by Glenn Ford. "Rock around the Clock" only played for a few seconds in the beginning and end credits (and as a short instrumental interlude in the film), but its impact was immediate and unprecedented. Those who watched the movie in the Alabama Theatre were struck not only by the power of the song, but also by the power of its amplification as it came over the mighty sound system of Birmingham's picture palace: it was the loudest music anyone had ever heard. Dave Bryan was there: "Oh, yeah, it was loud . . . It was at the Alabama Theatre, 1956, I saw it; oh, jeez, there were folks, after the first run of it, there was people coming out, around the Alabama Theatre, the word got out about it, there were people around the theater, waiting to get in. It was the start right there of rock 'n' roll. That's what took it right there in this town."

This slight exposure took a B side of a little-known country band and made it into an iconic recording in American popular music. Film and rock 'n' roll had a symbiotic relationship; the sound and look of the new music quickly appeared in films aimed at the youth market. With his record in the charts, Bill Haley appeared in two movies in 1956. These were cheap, exploitative vehicles quickly turned out by Columbia Pictures. There was no attempt to associate the new music with the threat of teenage delinquency, as was the case with *Blackboard Jungle*, which scared parents and theater owners alike, and Haley's *Don't Knock the Rock*, which tried its best to persuade audiences that these were good kids after all. Elvis made his first movie right after his first RCA recording sessions and television appearances. In 1956 he started a career in Hollywood that was to eventually eclipse his music. Presley's first film gave him no opportunity to expand his rock persona, but the next year *Jailhouse Rock* not only produced some exciting new music, but also served as a primer for rock 'n' roll stardom, reflecting the meteoric rise of a southern working-class bad boy in the entertainment industry. From the beginning rock 'n' roll was obsessed with its history, a self-conscious entertainment that dwelt on its origins and focused on its transformative powers. It shifted southern musicians' aspirations from working on local radio to appearing in films shown all over the country, from buying a new car to owning a fleet of Cadillacs.

Birmingham's film theaters quickly got into the act by using local bands to help promote rock 'n' roll films, and by turning their theaters into venues for amateur musicians. Budding rockers Jerry Woodard and Bobby Mizzell secured dates at the West End Theater performing there after movies such as *Go, Johnny, Go* and *Rock around the Clock* were presented. The manager of the theater said he booked them for a return appearance because "there was such a demand for the boys" by the audience. Some theaters dispensed with the traditional Saturday morning show of cowboy and adventure serials to replace it with "Teen Time" shows of rock 'n' roll films with live music. The talent show moved from its origins in radio to film theaters and television studios as the rock 'n' roll craze caught on.

Each movie brought more converts. Henry Lovoy experienced his initiation at the Alabama Theatre in 1957, where he saw Elvis's *Jailhouse Rock* in a house packed with teenagers. Henry had been drawn to music at a very early age: "My wife had my picture in the paper on Sunday because it was my birthday. The picture . . . was when I was five years old and singing with the Harrison Cooper Orchestra. It was at the Pickwick Club. They used to have a lot of dance receptions, wedding receptions, and other dances. My aunt's marriage was one of the last receptions there . . . It had two stages. It had a bandstand stage and a regular stage . . . They had Elvis movies that played at the Alabama Theatre . . . I remember going to the premier opening of the Elvis movie. At the end of the movie you could see this clump at the side of the stage. Bands didn't have much equipment in those days. The band was Sammy Salvo, who was singing his song '[Oh] Julie.' He had about three or four pieces with him. He was dressed up like the Elvis-type guy. He was dressed up in '50s attire with the white buck shoes and a white coat. His hair was [combed] back . . . I was sitting in the mezzanine and looking over to watch him. Girls were screaming in the movie. When the movie was over, girls were screaming at him. The girls were going wild. I thought, This is the life for me!"

CHAPTER TWO

Records and Rock 'n' Roll

The coming of rock 'n' roll to Birmingham produced a surge of activity in the newly established commercial recording business. After World War II many new entrants to the record industry were created to take advantage of postwar innovations in sound recording, in which tape recorders replaced the expensive, sensitive machines that cut recordings onto acetate discs. As Ken Shackleford found out, all you needed was a tape recorder, a mixer, and some microphones, and you could set up a recording studio in a shop front or office. The Sun record label was the work of a businessman from Alabama called Sam Phillips. Born and raised in Florence, one of the three communities in northeastern Alabama with strong industrial ties to Birmingham, Phillips moved to the nearest city to advance his career in broadcasting. After starting with WLAY radio in Muscle Shoals, he then moved to Decatur, Alabama, and then briefly to Nashville and finally to Memphis in 1944 to take a job at WREC radio. He set up the Memphis Recording Service in a storefront on 706 Union Avenue with the intention of recording "Negro artists . . . who just wanted to make a record and had no place to go."[1] He loved the music of his youth, the music he had heard on his father's farm and in black churches. He recorded B. B. King and Jackie Brentson's historic "Rocket 88." Sun was not big enough to market these recordings, so the masters were sold to larger companies such as Chess in Chicago (which released "Rocket 88") and RPM on the West Coast. Sun was building a reputation as being "the expert in recording Negro talent," but this wasn't profitable enough to support a storefront operation with two employees, so Phillips had to make a living recording anything from wedding speeches to bar mitzvahs. "We record anything — anywhere — anytime" was the motto. For $3.98 anyone could make a recording on a fragile acetate disc. In the summer of 1953 Presley walked in to 706 Union Avenue, and there occurred the most fateful meeting in the history of American popular music.

Birmingham in the 1950s was primarily an iron and coal town, but it had also become the technological center of the region, a communication and broadcasting hub. When Rick Hall decided to set up a recording studio in Florence, he had to come down to Birmingham to get some of the equipment. Soon after the war was over the first independent record companies and studios were established in Birmingham — the work of entrepreneurs who wanted to record local country and gospel acts for limited distribution in northern Alabama. They were small, shoestring operations linked to local musicians and locally financed. The Vulcan and Bama labels were the first two. Both used acetate disc recording equipment in radio stations to record masters, until wire and tape recorders became available in the late 1940s. Charlie Colvin established his first studio in Albertville, a small community in northern Alabama, near Huntsville: "Well, I had a studio in Albertville back in '49. We took the root direct to disc. Tape was just an invention at the time. Ampex made the first recorder, and I happened to go to Nashville one time. I had written a song, and there was a publisher up there who had run a check on it, and there was this Ampex tape machine and I thought, well, you know, it's just like wires [wire recorders]. In my studio in Albertville I was recording mostly the gospel groups around. Then I came to Birmingham to get into the business. I left for a while and went to school and then I came back here in '57. Ken Shackleford and all of them had started a studio called Heart and Soul Studio. It was above a blood bank on Third Avenue... Of course we had mostly black artists. We were right in the middle of Fourth Avenue [the black business district] there: so we had a lot of black artists in there."

Charlie Colvin thinks that the first studio in Birmingham was established by Ted Bilch, a guitar player and head of the musicians' union, probably in his home in Birmingham with Ampex or Presto equipment. Several others started recording in their homes and then progressed to building studios in rented properties. Homer Milam was the pioneer of commercial recording in Birmingham. After operating several small studios in the suburbs, he built his Birmingham studio in two rooms above a restaurant at 1917 First Avenue North in the early 1950s. Described by some musicians as a "dump," it was old, dusty, and nasty. There was an office and a room with a direct-to-disc recorder in it — a device that inscribed the sound on a flimsy Presto acetate disc. The rest of the equipment was equally primitive — an Ampex tape recorder and "one microphone, one of those all-the-way-round things." Yet Milam's Reed label produced some exciting recordings and played a big part in bringing rock 'n' roll to Birmingham.

Reed was not the only record company driving the spread of rock 'n' roll and rockabilly in Birmingham in the late 1950s. Charlie Colvin's label was releasing records produced at Heart Studios, while Squire Records was releasing rock and rockabilly numbers, including Slick Lawrence's "Little Mama." Although the rock 'n' roll records are the best-known, much of the recording activity of the small labels was directed at the large audience for sacred music in Alabama, where gospel quartets thrived. Arlington Records produced songs of the Birmingham favorite, the Harmony Four, and many other gospel groups. Some of these small labels were formed specifically to record gospel and several were directly linked to the singing groups. Vulcan Records was set up by Peter Doraine in 1955 to record local R&B groups. Charlie Colvin worked closely with Heart Records as a producer and writer, setting up sessions for his singers to make the demos he would hawk in Nashville: "Tony Borders was the first artist that I recorded. I took him to Nashville and recorded a song that he and I wrote . . . Then we had the first release on Smash Records [one of his labels], which was Mercury's [one of the larger independents set up in Chicago after the war and then established in Nashville] first 'Indian Blues.' I don't know if they printed up the labels for us . . . I did a lot of rhythm and blues, recording mostly black musicians. I also had a little white group that was really quite good. They were just kids in high school. God, I can't remember their names. They were a singing group. I put out a record on my label [Colvin Records] called 'Let's Dance.'"

Many of the records produced in Birmingham were of gospel or R&B groups, and this naturally influenced the sound of the music being made there. Charlie Colvin: "I wish I had some more names but the sound in Birmingham, it kind of went to the . . . I don't know what you call it, it was the first teenage sound, came right after the Big Bopper [J. P. Richardson], and Ritchie Valens and Buddy Holly. It was that kind of music, but it had more of a teenage feel to it. Birmingham did have its own sound, and most of it was black influence . . . You had a cross between Memphis and Nashville. That was what the Birmingham sound was back then . . . I used to go all through the black community and get musicians, and I got pretty good at it at one time. The most fun was looking for musicians and black players. I would go out there and say: 'Do you know so and so?' 'No. No, I don't know them, they don't live around here.' I would say, 'Well, I heard he did, and I have some money I need to give him.' 'Oh, you mean *that* so and so!' That was how I would have to find them. It was really fun back then . . . In Fairfield there was Freddy's Lounge over there and then the Blue Gardenia. Actually, there was more happening in the black community than there was in the white community . . . I was the only white guy in the place usually, because I was booking black talent, you know . . . There was one place that was the Choral, and it was country, and we used to always go down there. I could see all the guys from different bands. There was a lot of country, a lot of good country singers came from here, but I still think that you ought to do a little thing on the gospel that was going on here. It was big here! All-night singings and back then they were on the radio on Sunday mornings . . . R&B definitely had an influence on most everything that happened in Birmingham. They just had the feel! They called it 'soul,' the soul feeling, you know? Excitement! That's what it was. It was excitement!"

Ken Shackleford was joined by Gary Sizemore at Heart Studios: "Just out of college — this was before Elvis — I answered an advertisement in the paper for a salesman for RCA Records . . . I wasn't making any money, so I quit and went to work for Jake Friedman for Southland distributors . . . I was selling records: Rumore's Record Rack, Newberry's, Loveman's [department store] was the big album outlet, E. E. Forbes [piano and musical instruments] was big . . . It's 1956. 'Heartbreak Hotel' came out. I am selling records like crazy . . . People were making lots of commissions on Elvis. I was selling independent records, like Mercury's 'Little Darlin' [by the Diamonds], 'Searchin'' [by the Coasters], I promoted the B side — 'Young Blood.' We were selling them in batches of a hundred in Birmingham. I took it to all the deejays — Duke Rumore was the first to play it. And then it went national." Sizemore worked for several independent labels: "There was a lot of payola in those days. I am supposed to offer him [Buddy Dean, a Baltimore deejay] half the publishing, or half the record [sales], and I don't know what . . . I went through the same thing with all the deejays, I didn't know a thing. Time to get back to Birmingham. Then I met up with Ken — that was 1958 or 1959."

With Gary Sizemore traveling the country promoting Heart's records, Ed Boutwell and Glenn Lane joined the organization and learned how to be recording engineers on the job. Ken Shackleford: "I was a loan office [at a bank] and I was working every day. I was the absentee owner. Glenn Lane and Ed Boutwell did the engineering." Ed Boutwell started recording music in 1956: "I was working for Channel 13 TV and WAPI radio doing production and people would ask us to do a jingle. So we did not know what we were doing, but we did it. We had a lot of fun. I did a lot of jingle recording up there and just commercials . . . the only recording instruments were at the radio stations." Shackleford: "The studio was busy all day. We had a little tape duplicating thing. Loop tape thing, we were dubbing some of those and staying pretty busy doing sessions. Basically it was people coming in and asking to do some sessions." To get into Heart Studios you had to go through the blood bank, full of "riffraff" waiting to sell plasma, and walk upstairs. When you entered the studios you found yourself in a big room with worn carpeting, and glass dividers to isolate the sound as it was recorded. Gary Sizemore and Ken Shackleford would be lounging in the office with cigarettes and coffee, telling stories, while Ed Boutwell would be setting up the microphone and checking the levels on the mixer consol. They often used a single microphone, and only one or two tracks to record on. Re-recording was unknown. Henry Lovoy recalled, "You had to do everything in one take . . . We just did the whole thing. I don't know how many cuts we made, I remember that we had to unplug the air conditioner, because it would pick up on the microphones . . . I remember that the studio was dark and shabby looking. They had some baffles. I was literally squished behind a baffle, singing on this microphone . . . We were in and out of the studio in two hours. They gave me an acetate copy." They learned quickly; each recording session was a learning experience. Charlie

Colvin: "There were very few professionals here . . . I can go to Nashville, and I can cut four decent sides in three hours [the industry standard]. It would take me two days to cut four sides here."

Birmingham's Rock 'n' Roll Recordings

Strolling into these primitive recording studios came the young men who were the pioneers of rock 'n' roll in Birmingham: Baker Knight, Sammy Salvo, Dinky Harris, Bobby Mizzell, and Jerry Woodard. Thomas Baker Knight was the first of them. A few trial recordings (called demonstration records or "demos") made in Reed Studios brought him to the attention of Alan Bubis of the independent Kit label: "He came to see us play and he took us to Nashville to Owen Bradley's studio, and we cut five or six sides. It was all done awfully fast!" Making "Poor Little Heart" and the upbeat "Bop Boogie to the Blues" "was a good experience but nothing came of that. We came back to Birmingham and he came down again with a microphone that Bradley's studio had leant him and we went to another studio and recorded 'Bring My Cadillac Back.'" This was sold to Decca Records, and "it sold forty thousand copies in two weeks." This was the hit record that all rock musicians dreamed of: "It was my very first professional song and it didn't take long / before the record was playing on every jukebox in town," Baker Knight wrote later in a song. "We had a big page ad. In *Billboard*, but the stations stopped [playing] it because they said it was a commercial for Cadillac!" The next recording sessions were carried out in Decca's studios in New York City, and the Nightmares released three singles on Decca in 1957. This showed how fast the system could work when it smelled talent.

Sammy Anselmo had begun singing as a child: "I could do imitations. The whole family would have me do it at parties. They would say, 'All right, Sammy, go out there and sing.' Then I would do [Enrico] Caruso. They tried to teach me Italian. I couldn't understand it. I made up the words as I went along. My father was an opera singer. He used to have an Italian [radio] hour every Sunday in Birmingham. He would broadcast from the back of the hotel . . . When I was in the army [in the early 1950s], I used to go to the library and listen to opera." His brother George picked up the story: "Sammy went into the service in Fort Nix, New Jersey. New Jersey was a Yankee town where they were singing country & western. Country & western has a kind of soul sound. Maybe that is what it was with those service boys. I went to visit him while he was on active duty. He was singing at a local club with a boy [Horace Wheat] from Georgia. There had to be three to four hundred people in there. They were standing on a circular stage in the middle of the club singing country & western music. I didn't know that my brother could sing country & western because he had never sung it before." Sammy: "I would do Webb Pierce and Jimmy Reed stuff. I would do the harmony and Horace would sing the lead. The club invited us to come in on that Sunday. They wanted us to do a radio show . . . I got up and I had a smooth voice back then. About two hours later the whole parking lot was full. That was my first professional experience. It was professional, but not professional. We drank all that we wanted and had a good time. We didn't make any money."

When Sammy came back to Birmingham after his stint in the service, he took up singing professionally. His experience shows how important the radio deejays were in the music business: "We were introduced to Joe Rumore. He was a country & western disc jockey. I also met Dan Brennan. I was on Dan's show first. Horace and I got up and did some country stuff. The next thing you know, Joe told me that he needed a singer with Curly Fagan [Joe's right-hand man]. I said yeah, I'll be glad to. So I started singing with Curly. We got more involved with Joe after that." George: "Joe was a very powerful man in music. If he thought you were good, he gave you a push." Sammy: "Yeah, he sure did." George: "Joe was a personal friend of Sammy's. He was Sicilian also. Joe played a lot of country & western. He played Roy Acuff and Roy Orbison. He didn't get into that kind of rock stuff. Dan Brennan was playing all the rock stuff. When Sammy was doing country & western — that was just a step into rock 'n' roll. That was all back in 1956." Sammy: "It was rockabilly. 'Heartbreak Hotel' is more rockabilly than it is rock 'n' roll."

After playing some gigs and appearing on radio, the next step for any aspiring musician was to cut a record. Sammy: "We wanted to do 'One Little Baby' as a rockabilly song. That was the first one. We cut that in Joe Rumore's basement. He had a studio in his basement. There was recording equipment in Joe Rumore's basement as nice as RCA's studios." George: "Joe Rumore was nice enough to do it. I had hired a studio, out in Irondale [suburb of Birmingham]. This guy really screwed it up. His name was Homer Milam. He had a little old studio at the time — it is out on Highway 78 ... This is when I went back up to Nashville with a master tape. RCA would press for other people. I was going into my own distribution." George had decided to start his own record label. He had the support of Joe Rumore and the example of Sun Records: "I started thinking: what is there to a record company? Just looking at that piece of plastic, I knew it wasn't worth much. With some machinations behind me, I figured out how to start a company. Up to that time I had never heard anyone doing that ... I figured: Well, hell, I'll start my own company ... The name on the label was Mark V Records. I went from Birmingham to Dallas, Texas. I came back through Dallas and went through Little Rock, Memphis, then back to Birmingham. In between here and there I hit every radio station I could see. I used to hand out these small lighters. They looked like miniature Zippos. They said 'Sammy Salvo' on the side, with a musical note. They were really cheap. I got about five hundred made. They were really pretty ... In 1956 I was only twenty-one years old. I only needed about four hours of sleep and I was driving and talking all of the time. I was on the road for about two weeks. I was using whatever I could to get them to play it and pass it on to everybody. I never told them he was my brother. I was out there selling records and getting them hot. I really learned a lot then."

George Anselmo was doing such a good job of pushing Sammy's record that RCA began to take notice: "Steve Poncio [a record distributor in Houston] heard the record and made me order some more. I called RCA and they shipped ten thousand more. They assumed Sammy had a hit, since he was selling so many records. It was breaking in Jackson and Meridian, Mississippi, and Baton Rouge and New Orleans. I stayed in Houston for about a week. That darned thing just took off. Within three days it was number 8 on the Top Ten [local radio chart]. When I got back to Birmingham, Steve had called me. They wanted to buy my rights [to Sammy and his record] for ten thousand dollars. They wanted to give Sammy 5 percent and they wanted to give me 10 percent of the sales. They wanted to know where Sammy was. I told them that he had gone to Nashville, because Chet

Atkins wanted to sign him up. He signed for RCA that day. I caught him at the Biltmore. He said, 'Yeah, I signed.' I said, 'I'll be there in a minute.' I was driving up to Nashville. I was looking at the contract. It was so thick. I knew that there was no way of breaking it."

A recording contract with RCA! One of the biggest record companies in the world — the label that had made "Heartbreak Hotel" a global hit and Elvis Presley a star! Sammy Salvo was over the moon: "I was so excited to be signed on RCA. I got 3 ½ percent. It was the kind of deal they gave brand-new artists. That was of the retail sale price. They gave me a three-year deal." George: "I wasn't excited because I had the thing sold for $10,000. I knew that we would be getting more from the other day [working with Poncio and selling their own records]. I was very humble. I told Chet Atkins that he didn't need my brother, because of all the big names that he had. I told him I would like the contract back. He said he was sorry, but it had already been worked."

When he got to Nashville, Sammy was given four songs (enough for two double-sided 45 rpm singles) and spent a week rehearsing them before going into the studio. During a lunch break a deejay brought in a demo of a song called "Oh Julie." This song had been written by singer Ken Moffet and released by Ernie Young of Ernie's Record Shop on his Nasco label. A local group in Nashville called the Crescendos performed it. Chet liked the song and told Sammy to rehearse it: "We cut it. It only took us three takes. It was a really easy song. We did that, then we did the other three songs." On the B side of the RCA single, he recorded Wayne Handy's "Say Yeah," which had been released on the Renown label. "Oh Julie" is a ballad done in rock 'n' roll style, but many stations played "Say Yeah" because it was an up-tempo dance tune. The Crescendos' version of "Oh Julie" beat Sammy Salvo's record into the *Billboard* Top Five in December 1958. Sammy made it to number 23.

The outlook for Birmingham rock musicians in the late 1950s was promising. Baker Knight and Sammy Salvo had achieved the rock 'n' roll dream of a contract with a major record company. Jerry Woodard, a young singer who got his musical training in his father's Church of God ministry, was the next budding star to record in Birmingham. Jerry could sing both church music and country. His friend Jerry Grammer noted the similarities with

Elvis Presley, who could sing gospel songs with the best of them. Charlie Colvin had no doubt: "Jerry Woodard was wonderful, probably one of the most multitalented singers of the guys who came out of here. Jerry is dead now. He cut 'I'm Just a Housewife' for RCA, and he cut a lot of demos for me." Pianist Bobby Mizzell: "I met Jerry at WHTB in Talladega, Alabama. He had a radio program there, like I did. I just remember we both liked rockabilly and early rock 'n' roll boogie and all that stuff, so we got together because of that . . . We cut songs at WHTB . . . and the people there made little 45 demos for us . . . Jerry Woodard and I both left Talladega because of Country Boy Eddie, he had a show on WBRC-TV and WAPI-TV . . . This is how we first got recognition in Alabama, through the medium of television there." Country Boy Eddie: "I always wanted to be what I called a 'radio star.' I met Happy Hal Burns and he kindly helped me along . . . I was on in the morning from about five to seven, and at night from seven to ten. That was during the time when rock 'n' roll came along. Even though rock was hot, I still had the number 1 show in Birmingham . . . At that point I wanted to get on television . . . So I went to this fellow named 'Big Hearted' Eddie Right. He had a used car lot . . . so I got him to sponsor me on Saturday night on Channel 13 . . . From there I went to Channel 6 TV . . . That was in 1957, and I stayed on there from 5 a.m. until 7 a.m. through 1993 . . . I think it was the longest-running country music show with one host in America." Bobby: "When Jerry and me came to Birmingham, the first club we played was the Starlighter, then we played Pappy's Club and the Escape Lounge too." In 1957 Woodard recorded his first singles in Birmingham: "Six Long Weeks" / "Blue Broken Heart," backed by Jerry Reed on guitar and Charles Matthews on piano, followed by "Downbeat" / "Our Love and Romance." In 1958 he recorded "Who's Gonna Rock My Baby" for Reed Records, which became his best-known release. This song was the lament of a young rock 'n' roller conscripted into the army (and the fate of Elvis that year). "She's a Housewife, That's All" was a slower country song about the way many teenage love affairs ended up in tedious domesticity. These two tracks were good enough to be picked up by RCA, and Chet Atkins re-recorded them in 1959.

Jerry Woodard and Sammy Salvo's hot records propelled them into larger markets, and they were soon performing outside Alabama. Both were asked to appear on Dick Clark's *American Bandstand*, the most popular music show on television, with a huge audience of teenagers who watched it every afternoon after school. "Oh Julie" propelled Sammy Salvo's career, and he now lived the life of a teen idol: "There were a bunch of screaming girls. It was fantastic . . . The first car I ever bought with any money that I made was a 1950 pink Mercury. That was what I used to travel around in. After that I bought a T-Bird. It was special. I didn't ask the salesman how much it was, I just told him 'I want that car there.' There wasn't all that much money in the business at the time. The companies made a lot of money. They would spend all the artist's money before he even got a check. For instance, the check that I was supposed to get for 'Oh Julie' had been mostly spent when I got it. They spent all the money on promotion pictures and album covers." George: "The artists paid for their own sessions. The money came out of their advance. Back in the 1950s it cost you forty-two dollars a minute to record." Sammy: "I had a three-year contract. I had to live with it. I couldn't have quit. They wouldn't have let me record [with another company]. It would have been over with. They held me there for three years. It started wearing out for me. The tempo changed to something I didn't know. I just wasn't getting any hits. I wasn't doing the right tunes. I don't know. Maybe I was out of the groove . . . I was on my way down. I was singing at a place called the Southern Steakhouse. It was in Bessemer in 1961. There was a knockdown drag-out fight, and I ducked from many a beer bottle."

Bobby Mizzell and Jerry Woodard cut acetates in Birmingham studios and radio stations in 1958. The duo formed a band (Bobby on piano, Jerry on guitar) and also did session work in studios, backing vocalists Sammy Salvo and Len Wade (whom Bobby recorded on his record label singing a song he had written called "Found Someone"). Bobby and Jerry added other band members over time: Newman Cohely on guitar, Billy Self on drums, Tommy Willingham on drums, Lee Hood Carzle on bass, Johnny Carter on drums, and Sam Newfill on guitar. They backed the big-name singers when they played in Alabama: Buddy Knox, Jimmy Bowen, Mark Dinning, Brenda Lee, George Morgan, Roger Miller, and Tex Ritter. Their first record on Reed was Jerry's "Don't Make Me Lonely," and Mizzell had the instrumental "Atomic Fallout" as the flip side — an appropriate title

for a country in the grip of the Cold War. Mizzell played on Jerry Woodard's "Who's Gonna Rock My Baby" and on numerous other records cut in
downtown Birmingham. Two tracks he produced for Reed in 1959 caught
the attention of 20th Century Records and were released on their label.
"Heart and Soul," his best-known song, was issued in instrumental and
vocal versions. It had more than a hint of the boogie-woogie piano style
that was to make Jerry Lee Lewis famous. On the B side was "Same Thing,"
with vocals by Jerry's brother Lee Wayne Woodard.

Dinky Harris met Jerry Woodard at Birmingham International Race-
way, where he was racing his car, "TV6." Jerry needed work done on his car,
Jerry had his tool kit handy, and the two got to know one another while
working on the motor. Dinky had been playing music since high school,
where he had gotten together with a classmate who played bass and with
guitarist Carl Hanson. Dinky was the only member of the band with a
day job, so he bought a drum set and they started to play a few gigs. After
meeting Woodard, Dinky reorganized his band as the Spades, with Jerry
Woodard, Bobby Mizzell, Johnny Carter, and Frankie Benefield. In 1959
they recorded "She Left Me Crying," written by Jerry Woodard. It was
recorded at Homer Milam's Reed Studios and released on the Fad label,
a company formed by Woodard that Jerry, Dinky, and Bobby used as the
vehicle to market their music. "She Left Me Crying" was an outstanding
rockabilly number — a song described later as capturing "lightning in a
bottle." It became a Birmingham favorite. Duke Rumore had a call-in request show that most teenagers listened to, and "She Left Me Crying" became the number 1 song on the station's chart.

As rock 'n' roll became more and more popular, the output of Reed,
Heart, and Fad Records increased exponentially. Dinky Harris was record-
ing under many different names: Dinky Harris and the Nuggets ("Linda"),
Dinky Harris and the Draft Dodgers ("Who's Gonna Rock My Baby"),
Dinky Doo ("Think It Over, Baby"), and plain Dinky Harris ("I Need
You"). Bobby Mizzell formed his own Kim Record label (named after
movie star Kim Novak) and released rockers like "Rock and Bop Blues,"
"Birmingham Boogie," and "Knockout" (an outstanding piano instrumen-
tal still prized by collectors).

Producing a hit record was something like winning at the roulette table: so much of it was chance. Charlie Colvin had been producing Jerry Woodard's records on the Heart label, but in 1960 he released Woodard's "You Just Wait" on his Colvin label. The A side was written by Kenny Wallace, and the B side was penned by Woodard's bass player Henry Strzelecki, who noticed a guy with a big cowboy hat in a restaurant where he was bussing tables (it was Tex Ritter). Henry Strzelecki played in several local bands in Birmingham, including the Four Flickers and the Four Counts. "Long Tall Texan" had a laconic vocal and a certain charm, and its history reveals how the record business worked. Ken Shackleford: "The original song 'Long Tall Texan' was done at my studio. Jerry Woodard and Bob Cain had been there all night long. They phoned me early on Sunday morning, and he [probably Woodard] said: 'We got a hit record.' We leased the song to Johnny Vincent [who founded Ace Records in 1955 in Jackson, Mississippi], and then Murry Kellum covered it." Kellum's version on the MOC label (financed by his parents) was the national hit in 1963. Heart Studios was selling its output to whatever record company, big or small, which was interested: "We would record black artists and send the masters to people like [Berry] Gordy in Detroit, who was struggling just like us."

By 1959 rock 'n' roll was in full swing in Birmingham as its recording studios produced a stream of up-tempo dance music with a pounding beat and loud guitar accompaniment. Pat Riley and the Rockets cut "I Need You Baby" and "Little Bop a Little." Lawrence Shaul and the Aristocats covered Little Richard's ribald hit "Tutti Frutti" and another R&B standard, "Hey Little Mama." Paul Ballenger and the Flares produced several records, including one just called "Pig." Reed's output in 1959 shows the diversity of music in Birmingham: rock 'n' roll and rockabilly, country ballads, comedy numbers, and sacred songs. Gene Cole with Clyde's String Masters recorded "Coal Miner's Blues," and the Jubilaires quartet produced their version of the old blues and vaudeville standard "Birmingham Jail." Sacred music was recorded by several other quartets: the Rhythm Masters recorded "Rainbow of Love," the England Brothers covered "Jesus Save Me," and Wallace Odell and the Chordaires did "Walking Towards Heaven."

Country music dominated Reed's output in 1959, especially when it leaned toward pop. They made covers of hits like Hank Williams's "I Don't Like This Kind of Livin'," Mason Dixon's "Cold Cold Heart," and Newt James's version of Hank's big hit "Jambalaya." Country music fans enjoyed comedy numbers such as Ronnie Wilson's "You Love That Guitar More Than Me" (backed by Jerry Woodard) and Country Boy Eddie's "Hang in There Like a Rusty Fish Hook." Rock 'n' roll was man's music, with female voices only as backup, but Birmingham had a few women rockers such as Abby Lee, whose "Waitin'" is a classic of rockabilly. The sound is raw and powerful. She also recorded "I Want Your Lovin'" for Reed. Patsy Tidwell was another female rockabilly singer from Birmingham with two records on Reed: "I Dig You the Most" and "Sit and Rock and Roll Blues."

Reed and Fad Records were Birmingham's own versions of Sun Records: small operations run by entrepreneurs in the same mold as Sam Phillips and staffed with local talent. The pioneers of commercial recording in the New South formed a business and social fraternity; Ken Shackleford, Ed Boutwell, Charlie Colvin, and Gary Sizemore knew Phillips personally and did business with him over the years. They are full of engaging stories about this legend of rock 'n' roll, oblivious to the fact that it could easily have been one of them. Yet it was not to be, and for one simple reason: Sam Phillips and later Rick Hall found success and a measure of immortality by recording African American artists and by incorporating a lot of black music into the records they produced. All of these Alabama record producers shared an appreciation of African American music, but this was the segregated South, and nowhere was segregation stronger than in Birmingham, Alabama. As African American bass player Cleve Eaton pointed out, "They did not let blacks into the studio then." The idea that a hybrid form of country and R&B — an amalgam of white and black music — could be the music of teenage America, which seems so logical today, was frighteningly novel in the Deep South of the 1950s.

CHAPTER THREE

The Garage Bands

Rock 'n' roll had been pioneered by the front man — the handsome singer — and the first wave of Birmingham rockers followed this pattern: Baker Knight and the Knightmares, Sammy Salvo, Pat Riley and the Rockets, Jimmy Wilson and the Flames, and so on. Elvis had been their inspiration and guiding star — southern boy done good. Henry Lovoy was five years old in 1953: "That's when rock 'n' roll was getting started and so was I. I was singing and dancing at dancing school and in various hospitals and army bases surrounding the Birmingham area and other cities in the Southeast. I was dubbed as Little Elvis and my mother painted on my side burns and I gave Elvis a run for his money at the age of six." In the 1960s rock 'n' roll became the music of youth; and youth was in the ascendant as the mighty baby-boom demographic reached puberty and its discretionary income rose. Musician Doug Lee of Dogwood: "Our generation changed it so much, back then pop music, rock music whatever you want to call it, was played by kids for kids . . . Back then it was all kid music." The next wave of amateur rock 'n' roll musicians were younger and less experienced than the first, and they did away with the handsome front man and formed guitar groups.

A powerful new technology was driving these changes. A pounding boogie-woogie piano or raucous saxophone had been the siren calls of rock 'n' roll, but these were difficult instruments to master and quite expensive to buy. The electric guitar, on the other hand, was cheap and easy to play. As thousands of mass-produced Gibson Les Pauls and Fender Telecasters rolled off the assembly lines, more aspiring young musicians were tempted to buy into this technological revolution. Gradually the electric guitar became the voice of rock 'n' roll, replacing pianos and saxophones for the leads, and cumbersome standup basses with new electric Fender Precision basses. Musical instrument shops stocked the new instruments, and even retail outlets like Sears and Montgomery Ward started to sell them. The Chicago Pawn Shop downtown provided many of the instruments for start-up bands. Entry into the world of professional musicians had always been guarded by the high value put on virtuosity. Rock 'n' roll and cheap electric guitars changed all that. You could master the three or four chords that underlay rock music in a matter of months; energy and enthusiasm was more than a match for virtuosity in guitar bands. Guitarists like Buddy Holly provided the example for millions of young men: they copied his playing note by note as they craned over their portable record players or got closer to the television.

All over Birmingham in the waning years of the 1950s thousands of hours of grass cutting, errand running, and room cleaning were converted into the dollars that would finance a trip to Forbes Music or Nuncie's Instruments. "I had to mow a lot of lawns to get that guitar!" remembered Terry Powers of the Bluedads and the Alabama Power group. His rock 'n' roll upbringing took pretty much the same path as many other Birmingham musicians': "When I was a baby my mother put a radio in my room to help me sleep at night. So I started off listening to all that old rock 'n' roll . . . The first guitar I ever played was when my uncle moved to Clanton [Alabama]. He pulled it out and started to play all these hillbilly songs and I could not get over it. I was just infatuated; he was my hero. I started playing guitar when I was six. My first guitar idol was Chet Atkins and also Buddy Holly. Ahhh, the sound of Buddy Holly!" Electric guitars were easy to obtain; they were traded, mail-ordered, or picked up at pawn shops. Buying one was a high spot in many musicians' memories of the 1960s — nobody ever forgot that first electric guitar, how much they paid for it, and how it looked. Keith Harrelson still remembers the wondrous day when his brother Mark came home from Nuncie's with a brand-new Fender precision bass — the product of many months delivering papers. Keith was impressed with how the shiny new instrument looked with its pearly white pick guard and lustrous brown finish, sparkling like a jewel in a bed of crushed red velvet in its fitted case.

All over Birmingham, back rooms and garages were converted into practice areas as hundreds of excited young men embarked on the first steps of a journey that had no limits in their imagination. Being in a band got you some prestige in high school and was a great way to get some attention from the girls. Terry Powers: "When I went back to school after the Christmas vacation I was already singing and playing. I went down there and got on the auditorium at Lake View Elementary [School] and sang 'Cotton Fields Back Home' and that was the first time I ever played in front of anyone. Everybody just laughed and all the girls just screamed and they thought that was cool and all. So that was my first live performance . . . My first real electric guitar I got when I was fifteen. It was stolen and I got it for $150. It was a Mosrite made in California and it had a hollow body and the guy who sold it got it from David Crosby. So my first electric belonged to David Crosby . . . Then I started to play with some high school boys in their bands because I could play rhythm. I was then inspired to play lead from this guy in Homewood named Larry Benyon. He was unbelievable. He showed me how to do everything, and I practiced until my fingers were numb."

The ease of learning a few chords on an electric guitar created a more egalitarian standard for amateur musicians, and forming an instrumental band of guitars and drums gave a measure of anonymity to players who were not too confident in their solo skills. Bands were being formed in high schools wherever there were music-loving teenagers. Larry Parker started his musical career in high school in 1957: "I got to Woodlawn High School and took music instead of art. I had been taking art for all those years and had no talent. Music was something that I could get recognition in. That is what I was looking for. I put a vocal group together called the Veltones. Woodlawn had fraternities and sororities for social clubs. They were the Top Hatters, the Suitors, the Esquires, and the Tri Ws. The clubs would have lead-outs every year. They would always bring in the black groups. They would bring in the Coasters or the Drifters or Hank Ballard and the Midnighters. They were big groups. We would come up with the money. The guys would spend the better part of the year raising money. It was very elaborate, the lead-out. The guys were in tuxedos, the girls in evening gowns, and we had bands all night . . . When the school teacher in the eighth grade told me that I should consider music as my career, that summer I made a real effort to try it. I went down and auditioned for *Teen Time Talent Hunt*, which was by Jim Lucas at the Alabama Theatre. He was a deejay at WSGN radio. He had a great voice and had this show live every Saturday at the Alabama Theatre. I went down for the audition on an early Saturday morning. I did a lip-sync on the Four Coins' 'Shangri La' [a hit record in 1957]. Jim took me off the stage and we sat on the steps and he said, 'Larry, you have a good voice and you don't seem to have any fear on stage, but groups are what's happening. You should put a group together, instead of trying to do it solo.' This is in 1958. Jim told me to get a group together, and that is where the Veltones came together. We began performing as a regular on *Teen Time*... We put the group together and we didn't like the name. We only kept that name for about a month. We were a doo-wop band. It was a four-part harmony group. This was Top Ten at the time... Jim Lucas was very encouraging to me. We performed at the Alabama Theatre as the Swinging Teens... Then we were invited to do a television program on Channel 6 every week. They wanted us to come up and play there... About that time I decided that we needed a band. All I could handle was the group. I decided to put my own band together. I found a guy named Jack Pyle. He found the rest of the guys, including Bill Campbell, and they formed a band called the Nomads. They backed the Swinging Teens... The following summer I met a guy named Hal Painter. We found another guitar player and a drummer and we put together Larry and the Loafers. That was in 1960... My father was the one who named the group. One night he asked where I was going. I told him that I was going out to spend some time with the guys and go play. He said: 'When are you going to stop hanging around those loafers?' When I saw them, I told them that they were now the Loafers."

Forming a guitar band was something that you did at high school in the 1950s, like playing football or writing for the yearbook. In Birmingham the first wave of garage bands emerged from local high schools in the late 1950s: the Counts, the Premiers, the Epics, the Ramblers, the Ramrods, the Gents, Rooster and the Townsmen, Charles Smith and the Ram Chargers, the Nomads, and the Roulettes were the best known, but there were more. Larry Parker: "Bands started to pop up everywhere. Anybody that wasn't participating in my group started their own group in order not to feel slighted. Anyone could do it. There wasn't any competition; we even tried to help each other." Although they were not musically accomplished, the enthusiasm of the garage bands spread rock 'n' roll throughout teenage America. These amateur guitar bands were to transform the musical landscape of Birmingham in the 1960s and create a new paradigm for professional entertainment that would last for the rest of the twentieth century.

Dale Karrah gave Fairfield High School friend Howard Tennyson a bass guitar and said, "Here! Learn to play this!" Bringing in another friend, Bo Reynolds, led to the start of a band called the Satellites — named for the current headlines about the Russian satellite Sputnik. The band consisted of Dale, Howard, Bo, and a drummer named Skeet, who played a new set of drums made by Premier. Dale and Howard re-formed the band as the Premiers in 1956. Their name came from the brand of Skeet's drums — an indication of the importance of equipment in the mind-set of these youngsters. When Skeet left, the Premiers had to find a new drummer. Larry Graves bought his guitar from Sears after Chuck Berry's "Johnny B. Goode" inspired him and started a band called the Nomads. When Bo Reynolds asked him if he wanted to be in the Premiers, Larry brought his guitar for the audition, but ended up playing the drums. Pat Thornton had learned to play piano at Fairfield High and he also got an invitation to join the Premiers. The band practiced the garage below his house in Fairfield, and this explains where the term "garage band" originated: "We had a ball! There were only four or five bands when we started out, but everything was changing."

The life of a garage band revolved around rehearsing. Record producer Ed Boutwell remembers this conversation with a concerned parent: "I am just so worried — they are spending so much time doing that, and I am afraid that they are going to go out and work at these nightclubs and all, and get in trouble. I said, 'Pardon me, but where are they every afternoon?' 'In the garage out back playing that darned music.' I said, 'Yeah, every afternoon, seven days a week right?' 'Yes.' I said, 'Where do they go then, once or twice a week? — they will go work a gig, right?' 'They are there for two or three hours and then come home and they will get right back out in the garage and start rehearsing again.'"

The Premiers were acknowledged as the leading rock band in Birmingham. Ned Bibb: "They were powerful for one thing. Dale Karrah was a powerful lead player for the times. I would go to Duke's and just stand in front of him in awe. He played a Fender Duo Sonic. That was the kind I had to get, because that is what he played. My wife tells me that I started looking like him . . . They were all football players, and one time they came out on stage in their football sweats. They played really loud. They were older than us, so naturally they were all role models. They did mostly Bo Diddley songs — that was their big thing." Henry Lovoy: "Dale was before his time. He was like Jimi Hendrix before Jimi Hendrix. He was doing all this whacking off the guitar and that stuff. He also had experimented with feedback, which nobody did. He was just wild."

The Ramrods were formed by a bunch of students at Woodlawn High School in 1959: "We all went to Woodlawn together, the ones that started the band. We had Joe Lackey [vocals, guitar], myself [Larry Wooten, guitar], and we all went to Woodlawn. Jim McCulla [drums] that went to Banks [High School], Joe and I and Paul Newman here, and Harry Looney went to church together. That is really how we got started, and Joe bought a guitar and I sort of got interested in playing the guitar after watching a program at Woodlawn High School that featured a band that was already there. That is what motivated me to go out and buy a guitar. I couldn't sing very well but I could play the piano. So I went out and bought a Silvertone [an electric guitar sold by Sears], a double-pickup Silvertone and an amplifier. Joe and I would practice in his living room: rock 'n' roll songs. We were a rock 'n' roll band. We played songs like 'Suzie Q' by Dale Hawkins, Chuck Berry stuff, but it was mainly rock 'n' roll, and not much Elvis. Mainly Buddy Holly, Chuck Berry and folks like that, and some Little Richard rock 'n' roll stuff." High school garage bands were in a constant state of flux as trends in popular music changed: "Then we picked up some other folks. See Joe was in a choral group at Woodlawn, the Warblers, they sang barbershop harmony and they put on a minstrel show. It was a big group . . . So they started doing some doo-wop stuff. So we went from rock 'n' roll to doo-wop when doo-wop became popular. We had a couple of girls that went to Banks High School that did songs like 'In the Still of the Night.'" The Ramrods' name was inspired by a record by Duane Eddy, the king of the guitar instrumentalists, which had become very popular — "the stuff came back in that featured a lot of instrumentals like Freddie King, the Ventures, and groups like that." Guitar instrumentals were perfect for garage bands, requiring a minimum of musical expertise and doing away with the lead singer altogether — the group was now the thing. Duane Eddy's "Rebel-Rouser" in 1958 started the trend, and it continued with a guitar band from Seattle called the Ventures. Their big hit "Walk Don't Run" of 1960 encouraged numerous other guitar-based bands to emulate their twangy, echoing electrified sound.

Phillips High School produced the Epics. Rick Hester played lead guitar, Terry Ryan played guitar and bass, Ross Gagliano was on the drums, and Joe Ardivino was the vocalist. Rick was the lead guitarist for the band, and Joe was the lead vocalist. The Churchkeys started around 1962 with a group of students from Ramsey High School: Tommy Allison on drums, Mike Easter on bass, Rob Hackney on guitar, Bert McTyer on sax, and Tommy DeBuiys on piano. After Bert and Tommy left, Charles Feldman and Chuck Butterworth joined and the band was renamed the Bassmen. Again, their name came from their equipment, in this case the name of a Fender amplifier. Ramsey High School produced the Ramblers around 1961. This was formed around the guitar-playing talents of Tommy and Eddie Terrell, Van Veenschoten (on lead guitar), and Chip Sanders, with Johnny Robinson on drums. True to form, the Ramblers practiced in Robinson's garage. The Romans had members from Ramsey and Shades Valley Schools — this group was managed by Buddy Buie, who was to have some influence on southern rock 'n' roll. The Counts were formed around 1962 in Robert Alexander's basement. Robert and Ned Bibb played guitars and teamed up with Bobby Marlin on drums.

As with many other Birmingham teenagers, Ned Bibb's introduction to rock 'n' roll came from the movies: "My inspiration was Chuck Berry from when I was thirteen years old [in 1958]. I had gone downtown on the bus on a Saturday. I decided to go see a movie. I went in to see a rock 'n' roll movie that had Chuck Berry playing the guitar [probably *Go, Johnny Go!*]. This was the first time that I had seen how music was made. During that time there was no television that had rock 'n' roll . . . I decided that I wanted to play the guitar, but I didn't have any idea how to play one.

I didn't even know how to tune one. I think the insurance guy came by the house one day and tuned it for me. I would just play the record and learn the notes . . . The first live band I saw was the Road Runners . . . We were going to the movies and the band played after the movie was over . . . I just flipped out over their music. They played mostly Little Richard and Buddy Holly songs. I saw them play at the West End Theatre. They were a very big influence on me. I moved to West End in 1959. I met up with Rob and Bobby and them. I was in high school in West End and they all went to Ensley High. My cousin had a boyfriend named Jack Kelley, who turned out to be a musician was well. Robert [Alexander] invited me to come over to his basement one day to play. I was the only one who could play lead guitar. I was really shy the first day. They wanted me to play a song. I asked them if they knew anything from Buddy Holly. They didn't. They wanted to know what key it was in. I didn't know, I just told them to start on a certain fret. I started to play the lead part, and they had never seen anybody do that. They thought I was fantastic! Robert Alexander was the spark plug. He was the one who wanted to have a band. We got rid of Jack because he wanted to play country music and didn't like me playing the lead. We recruited Bobby Marlin on drums. We played a little show. Our first little gig was at Calico Corner. We played at the Southern Steak House on Bessemer Highway. We were not of drinking age, but that wasn't a problem. They were not nearly as strict back then. The fraternity parties were a lot of fun. At first we played for high school parties and sororities. A year later, as our band progressed, we played at Tuscaloosa [University of Alabama] and at Auburn [University]. It was a very important market. Those were the good paying gigs."

The Counts later added Jim Larusa, on bass. They started playing Chuck Berry and Bo Diddley songs and recruited young Henry Lovoy as vocalist: "As I grew older my interest in music grew even higher to higher expectations and I knew that entertaining would be my life . . . When I was fourteen I played football at Ensley High School. If we won, I would sing Bo Diddley on the football bus. One day a fellow player knew some guys who were putting a band together and needed a lead singer . . . My first job in a nightclub was when I was fourteen years old. I became a lead singer in a rock 'n' roll band. I could also play drums too when the drummer was not around. The first group was called the Counts, and my first break came when we played for Duke Rumore's record hop at Duke's in Ensley. That is when we got radio time, and that was important for local bands. I played in and out of clubs for about five years while going to high school."

Ned Bibb underlined the importance of gaining this powerful deejay's support. "In order to get those gigs you had to have exposure. That is why Duke was such an important stepping stone. He had the armory shows in the late 1950s... At first it was called Duke's in Dixieland and then just Duke's. They had sock hops there: you would take your shoes off and dance in your socks. High school kids went there. That was the big time: if you could play Duke's, the fraternities and sororities wanted you. Playing Duke's for the first time was so important... Duke had a big influence on what bands learned. He controlled what people listened to. If Duke didn't play it on the radio, nobody was interested in learning it. He had a show in the afternoon. It came on about 3 o'clock, when the kids were getting out of school. He played mostly black music and a lot of rhythm and blues. He played a lot of Jimmy Reed and Fats Domino. Birmingham was influenced a lot by New Orleans, Memphis, and other southern cities."

Most of these electric guitarists were self-taught, but there were music education programs at Birmingham's high schools that trained students in piano, saxophone, clarinet, and trumpet — instruments that could add a lot more to the standard lineup of lead, rhythm, and bass electric guitars along with drums. The Premiers, Bassmen, and Ramrods often used a piano rather than a guitar lead, and the Epics, Ramrods (after Ronnie Eades joined), and Bassmen employed a saxophone to supplement the lead guitar. The Torquays had a trumpet (Barry Bicknell) and a sax (Steve Salord) in addition to electric guitars and drums. The Epics were probably the first band to have a horn section, bringing in Jim Anderson on trumpet and Bob Sheehan on sax. Larry Wooten: "So doo-wop went out and then the Memphis sound came in with the horns. So we took on a saxophone player and then we took on two saxophone players. One of the saxophone players could play saxophone or trumpet. So we had that Memphis sound for a while, and then we got away from that because that went out and stuff came back in that featured a lot of instrumentals like Freddie King."

The Garage Band Scene

The primary venue for bands made up of high school students was naturally the high school, whose extensive social events usually had live music. Doug Lee: "You knew you had a band when you got a paying gig. Yeah, once you got paid, you had a band, a real band . . . I can remember football games when I was a starter, a pretty good athlete, and immediately going back to the locker room, changing clothes and putting on my rock 'n' roll duds and going to the gym and jumping on stage and my band was playing the dance after the football game!" The biggest draws were the lead-outs of the fraternities and sororities, and the shows staged at local armories. Each school had its home armory: high schoolers from West Birmingham went to the shows at Ensley Armory sponsored by Duke Rumore, those from East Birmingham went to Opporto Armory and Dave Roddy. Bunkie Anderson: "You go in, they drive the tanks out and they set the bands up, you would set up two little amps and you'd play, and it would take you fifteen minutes to break down and go home." Frank Ranelli of the Things: "When I was a teenager and all, every weekend I wanted to go and hear some live music. It was just like the thing to do! The big deal was to go somewhere on a weekend and dance and hear music. Or go to the drive-ins and hang out. We used to go to the Oporto Armory. WSGN used to do it, and they had live music every Saturday, and it got for a while where they were doing it Friday and Saturday. That was a great place to go. You go out there to dance and meet girls or whatever. That is what we did. Of course we would try and play some music too." The armory shows were squeaky-clean high school fun. Pat Thornton: "The kids picked up by parents at Duke's, they always had four or five police at hand, so the fights ended quickly, no one could bring in booze there." But someone else added: "You were drunk when you got there!"

Just like everything else in Birmingham, high school music was segregated by race, but it was also divided by school affiliation and geography. Birmingham's teenagers kept in groups with high school friends. Bob Cahill: "They sold Cokes there, there was a big dance floor, and you just sort of milled around, you probably saw people from all the schools in the city, you would end up seeing people and they would say 'I am from this school,' and you would say, Well, do you know so and so?" Garage bands usually drew musicians and audiences from the same school. Record producers Courtney Haden and Mark Harrelson think this had a significant effect on retarding the music scene in Birmingham: "One of the reasons Birmingham never really penetrated back in the '60s and maybe even today is that the kids were a lot more segmented by neighborhoods. You have kids in Birmingham: I was from Vestavia and Courtney is from Homewood. We had people who knew each other growing up, but it is still a city of neighborhoods. There were Vestavia bands and there were Homewood bands. In Tuscaloosa there were just bands."

One famous armory show is remembered by many in Birmingham; as Ben Saxon said with a sly smile, "Oh, it was huge, everyone was there . . . In fact, I hardly know anyone who lived in Birmingham in the 1960s who says they were not there . . . The armory only held about five hundred people. I believe that there could have been eight hundred people inside and outside the building." It was a Duke and Dixieland show at Ensley Armory. At the back of the room girls were standing on their boyfriends' shoulders, and Ned Bibb estimated that there could have been nine hundred kids at the show and that they were stacked three high by the end of the night. The climax of the show was provided by the Premiers — acclaimed by many as the best band of the time and a favorite of Duke Rumore. As a tape recorder captured it for a record and posterity, the band sang one of their own compositions, "Are You Alright." Ben Saxon: "It was a favorite because everyone always liked to say, 'Hell yeah!' They were all trying to be on the recording saying, 'Hell yeah' . . . It was kind of chaotic, there lots of fights . . . Duke kept saying 'You'll all be sure of saying, Well, yeah.'" Ned Bibb: "The only original music they did was 'Hell Yeah.' There was a national hit called 'Flamingo Express.' It was just saxophones. There were no words, but it was a real popular tune. I don't know who put the words 'Hell Yeah' to it. I don't know if Bo Reynolds did it or who did it. Somebody started to play those two chords back and forth and saying 'Are you alright? Hell yeah!' They repeated it over and over. It was such a big deal to go to a public place and shout at the top of your lungs 'Hell yeah!' This was a very rebellious thing for us. We weren't allowed to do that in this town. We were not taught like that . . . We had fabulous times. We were innocent.

Just to be able to say 'Hell yeah!' in public was mind-blowing. A girl once told me that the Premiers had so much control over those kids they could have marched them downtown if they had wanted to."

As rock 'n' roll became more popular with teenagers more venues opened up. Larry Wooten: "We played for high school parties, what they call lead-outs. High school sorority, fraternity lead-outs. We started to play for church outings, we played social clubs and outings. It was good when you played, but it wasn't real consistent... but we had fun! We played some [gigs] down on the Warrior River at a nightclub. We played a place out here, the Clover Club on Highway 31. It was pretty dilapidated when we played. I was a sacker at a local grocery store during the day, and I had to get off a little bit early to go play there one night, and I was already tired because I had worked a full shift, and they kept throwing so much in the kitty, I think we finally finished about three or four in the morning... We did radio... WVOK was a big station out here on the western end of Birmingham. We played there several times. These were live. Then we did some taped stuff for one of the local television channels, talent shows. We would tape on Thursday and they'd show them on like Saturday. We did fraternity parties. We did a fraternity party at Birmingham Southern [College]. I remember that. It was a good party! The theme of it, it was a commode party!"

Once the band was established and the first gigs completed, the players started to think about making a recording. The rise of the garage bands provided much more business for recording studios because the ambition of every band was to make their own record: "We wanted to make a record" was the mantra of numerous musicians as they recalled their days in a garage band. As incomes rose in the 1960s and rock 'n' roll took hold on the mass audience, the record companies found a larger market for rock records. The recording studio now became a center for amateur musicians. Mac Rudd and Sydney White were in the Strangers. "Sydney had talked his way into Boutwell Studio at one time, and I believe told him a lie about who he had played with. Of course Ed knew it was a lie, but he humored him and liked him and after that Sydney and I sort of, we just hung out! We were kids that would hang out at Ed's studio, this was in the old church... Had the whole congregation area set up as the recording area... Ed had built a plaster of Paris reverb chamber in a sort of a closet, and he had a microphone stuck in there, and it worked very well! I do remember one time in the old church, going and looking back behind where the choir was, and it was the first time that I had seen Jesus depicted as black . . . Shortly after that Sydney and I, we did a lot of session work over there. We played with the Rev. Parker on a lot of gospel albums, black gospel albums. We came in, and the reverend and the organist. We would ask them, What key do we play in, how does this song go? He would just say 'Fall in and go for yourself!' and he would start pumping away at that organ, and we just sort of fell in and he made albums that were put out. I felt the Spirit! I felt the Spirit because a lot of times we would do this recording on a Sunday afternoon in the summertime, the choirs were of course about fifty or sixty people crowded in there. I don't believe we had air-conditioning, and it got really hot and the Spirit moved us. There were some ladies in the choirs that had outstanding voices, but they had some, either fainting spells from that, or the Spirit was moving them! It was exciting to play, I had grown up hearing that."

The rise of rock 'n' roll fostered a spirit of entrepreneurship as musicians began to form their own record companies. Inspired by the legend of Elvis and encouraged by larger crowds at their concerts, musicians like Larry Parker and managers like George Anselmo went into the record business themselves. After a producing a master recording at one of Birmingham's studios, the budding producer could farm out the pressing of the disc to independent operations, like Rite Records in Cincinnati, or to the custom pressing departments of the major record companies — George Anselmo's Mark V Records were pressed by RCA in Tennessee. Many rock 'n' rollers remember the exciting trip to the bus station in downtown Birmingham to pick up boxes of their records (cash-on-delivery). Some of them had business plans for these discs, like Sammy Anselmo or Larry Parker; others had no more ambition than to show them off to friends and hand them to girls.

Birmingham garage bands recorded on a mass of small, homegrown labels: Jo-Jo, Vibrato, Vesta, Lemon, Gold Master, Modern Enterprises, Malone, Vaughn-LTD, Malcolm Z, Dirge, Chyme, Knight, Holly, Ara, and Tinker. The Tikis recorded for Finley Duncan, who ran a local juke-box operation and formed the Minaret label for them. Duncan had great plans for the Tikis and took the band to Nashville and Muscle Shoals to record in their prestigious studios. The Tikis went on to release records on the Dial, United Artists, and Atco labels. In 1963, the Ramrods went into the Baldwin Recording Studio in Woodlawn, Birmingham, and recorded two original songs. Larry Wooten: "We made a record that Joe wrote one side . . . and side A was 'Fire Power' by Paul Newman . . . It was on the Bright label, I don't remember his first name, his last name was Bright, he saw us up in Blount County paying for a benefit or something and he liked our music and said that he would like to record us and put us on a record . . . So we went to either Florence or Sheffield to record 'Night Ride,' which was released on Rick Hall's 'R and H' label."

The Ramblers produced a record called "100 Miles Away" on the Brooke label. The song was written by an acquaintance of the band called Brooke Temple, who wrote the song about a girl he dated in Montgomery (a hundred miles from Birmingham) and asked the Ramblers to record it. His mother paid for the recording session and the disc pressing, so they used his name for the label. In 1967 they made their second record on their own Tommy Tucker label. As Johnny Robinson remembered: "The total for the packing slip was $123.10 for 510 records. That made them 24 cents each. The studio time was $300, as I remember. That made the total cost 83 cents each. Of course, we did not make the records to make money — we gave most of them away to try and book more jobs."[1]

CHAPTER FOUR

On the Road

D rummer Bunkie Anderson remembered: "In like the early '60s you played either of two places. You played the honky-tonks or the armories," either squeaky-clean armories or raunchy roadhouses. Rock 'n' roll had grown up in Birmingham in adult venues like Pappy's, which was out on Highway 78 West, stayed open very late, and always had good music. Pappy's was owned by Jim and Margaret Wallace, who were known for their penchant for breaking up bands to get the right combination of musicians to play in their club. Many of the big names in Birmingham rock music played Pappy's and remember it with affection. Jerry Woodard even recorded a song about it, called, appropriately, "I Got Loaded at Pappy's." Jerry Grammer remembered it being pretty decadent; there was a strip of motel rooms along the parking lot to cater for out-of-town bands and ladies of the night. Being a house band involved a lot of work, and it could get dangerous. Pappy's attracted some tough characters, and even the formidable Bobby Ray, the chief bouncer, once got his ear bitten off.

There were also the bars and restaurants along Bessemer Highway. Ned Bibb recalled that these places were roadhouses rather than restaurants because they had stopped serving food years before and were "sleazy joints, serving only live bands and vulgarity. We didn't get to play too many clubs because we were so young. We played the Southern Steakhouse because they were so lax about age. We played this crummy joint out on the highway once on New Year's Eve. We played at a club on Bessemer Super Highway called the Colonial Inn . . . They'd have girl fights and ask you if you have a gun when you come in. If you don't have one, they give you one.

Ha ha!" Mac Rudd: "There were roadhouses out on the Bessemer Super-highway, the Twilight Club, the Bessemer Sportsman Steak House ... in downtown Birmingham across from the Greyhound bus station we played at a club called the Shamrock." Bunkie Anderson: "Back then they had the redneck kind of roadhouse bars up between here and Jasper. Jasper was a dry country and they had, I mean, rough, rough bars over there. There was only one rule back then: don't stop playing. If you stop playing, everybody will know there's a fight, and everybody will start fighting." Johnny Carter played with Jerry and Bobby Mizzell: "You had to be drunk or crazy to play there ... Warrior River rednecks were the worst — they would pull a knife on you if you danced with their girl."

As rock 'n' roll became the music of youth rather than drunken adults, new venues opened up for teenage musicians. Skating rinks provided safer and steadier work for guitar bands. Roller skating was an important teenage fad in the 1950s: there were rinks all over town, and it wasn't too difficult to turn them into venues for live music. The Roebuck Skating Rink was booked by Richard Dingler, who later started the powerful Southeastern Attractions booking agency. Huffman Skating Rink was an especially good place to play, as it was reputed to be the spot to pick up girls. Rudy Johnson: "That was a hot spot." Wayne Perkins: "That was a very hot spot!" There were also several bowling alleys that hired bands to play at weekends. The swimming clubs or playgrounds were an essential part of summer entertainment in the Deep South at a time when few public places were air-conditioned. These venues brought in live music to supplement their attractions of swimming and boating. The Cascade Plunge on Tuscaloosa Highway had local bands every weekend, such as one where the Counts performed on Saturday and the Cajuns on Sunday. Entrance was only a dollar, and the entertainment was described as "Rock 'n' roll Band." The Cloud Room in Eastwood had a bandstand and dance floor close to the outdoor swimming pool. There was also Holiday Beach, which had a pavilion for dancing in addition to the swimming pool. Henry Lovoy was a teenager at high school when he first moonlighted as a vocalist for the Counts. One of the band's first major engagements was at the Holiday Beach resort. Henry fondly remembers the pay: five dollars and a hamburger!

As rock 'n' roll became established in American popular culture, it infiltrated the adult bastions of dinner and dance clubs, such as the Pickwick Club or the Hollywood Country Club, as well as the ballrooms of the nice hotels that had once monopolized entertainment in Birmingham. Mac Rudd: "Sydney White and myself formed a group called T. H. E. Trolley. We got a job playing at the Redmont Hotel. It was a scene! This was the Red Room Lounge, and you never could tell who was going to come in. You never could tell when somebody with a gun was going to walk through the door." Birmingham in the 1960s listened to sedate music in hotel lounges, supper clubs, and "rooms" named after their décor — the Cork Room in the Parliament House (featuring Denise Lumiere on piano) — or their fare — the Sirloin Room in Michael's restaurant. When these venues put in a guitar band, it was as much a concession to the prevailing fashion in music as it was a novelty for their customers, for, as Tommy Charles remembered with some regret, "You didn't sing rock, you didn't get booked."

Steve Lowry joined his first band around 1964: "The Echoes were a roving band. We played teen dances all over town: Misty Waters, the Cascade Plunge, and the Redmont Hotel were all weekenders. We did record hops. Neil Miller had us play for him at the National Guard Armory Shows. We used to play a lot for him out in Calera." His second band was called the Tynsions, "named because at fifteen years old we were told that women go to bed with the 'tensions.' We were the house band at a club called the Starlight Lounge. It is now a parking lot across the street from the Federal Building downtown, next to the Patio Lounge, which was the first go-go bar in Birmingham." There were plenty of problems for a group of underage teenagers breaking into the world of professional entertainment, including the lack of a Musicians Union card: "They never came around here and checked. We had a manager that got us in, and I think that he cut a deal with the local union, because we were underage . . . The story behind the Starlight Lounge is that a number of entertainers that played at Boutwell Auditorium would go for a nightcap after they had played their show. I became the bass player and the singer of the band in just one night. The whole thing. We were playing Wilson Pickett's 'Land of a Thousand Dances,' when someone gets up out of the audience [he was snookered] and said: 'Son, you don't play that right.' I was going 'Excuse me?' because I have a natural ear and I thought that I was a big stud playing it right. It turns out that guy is Tommy Cogbill, who was the original bass player for Wilson Pickett — he was one of the greatest bass players in the history of bass players . . . We were just kids, and this was where we got our musical education."

Charles Smith and the Ram Chargers were jubilant to get a chance to play at the Southern Steakhouse on Bessemer Highway, a rowdy bar where you might have to deal with obnoxious drunks and dodge bottles from fights on weekend nights. They played from 8 p.m. to 2:30 a.m. Monday through Saturday, and each member made seven dollars a night. Fred Dalke started off in a band called the Coachmen and also played drums for the Ram Chargers: "Oh yeah, we played all the major clubs in Birmingham . . . some of the big clubs we played in were the Starlight Club, the Patio Club right next door, and that was where all the teenagers, people in their early twenties, would go . . . I take it back, you had to be at least twenty-one to get in. We were teenagers, but we got to go in because we played in the band . . . When I first played, see, I didn't have my driver's license. I played first at fifteen. My mom was real supportive, so she had to drive me."

With the minimum wage hovering around $1.50 an hour, the rewards of playing rock music were impressively high for teenagers. A big armory show could bring in $250 for the band if the place was packed. The three members of the Ramblers split $9 among them for their first gig, but with a bit more experience and a self-produced record ("Stop That Twisting") out there, they were soon pulling in from $75 to $100 a night. Steve Lowry: "When I got in the Tynsions, that was five nights a week from 8 p.m. to 2:30 a.m., and I would get up at 6:30 a.m. and go to school. I did that for two years and it almost killed me. I made decent money, which was $250–$265 a week and all that we could drink. We drank a lot, like fish." With a popular record out in Birmingham, called "Goin' Wild," and enjoying lots of airplay on local radio, the Ram Chargers were on the way up: "Let's see, I think the first night I played I got thirty bucks, that was a lot of money for a sixteen-year-old, that's tax-free. I couldn't believe I was getting paid for something I loved to do." For fifteen-year-old Bunkie Anderson, the experience of playing in a band was priceless: "I loved it. I remember when they put six dollars in my hand and I said: You mean you paid me? There was the end of my life as I knew it. I went from being a church boy and a good student — my life was over. They gave me money. I would have done it for no money."

As Fred Dalke points out, there were more than monetary rewards for playing in a rock band: "I think the moment I'll never forget was when I was playing in a club on the West End called Misty Waters. It was a teen-age nightclub, and they didn't have any alcohol, or there wasn't supposed to be any alcohol in there. And the local station, WSGN, was promoting us and playing the record, and when we got there that night it was a packed theater, you know just hundreds and hundreds of kids and they were just all going wild and having a great time. That was a special night. They made us feel like we were superstars or something."

The Fraternities

The most sought-after gigs for Birmingham's garage bands were the college sororities and fraternities. Auburn and Alabama were large public universities with a well-funded social life, and they became one of the most lucrative audiences for rock music in the state. The number of garage bands in Birmingham would have been much smaller if there had not been such a large market for rock 'n' roll just an hour away. As band members got older and obtained the keys to a car, they were able to play these gigs. (In those days access to an automobile and the ability to drive were considered equal to musical ability when you were trying to get into a band.) These were valuable gigs. They could pay one hundred dollars a night for three or four forty-five-minute sets. Some bands played for the fun of it and for drinks, many drinks, sometimes all the beer they could drink: "The next time they hired us they said they'd rather just pay us a flat fee of four hundred dollars a night because they lost money on the beer payment deal."[1] Despite the contracts that stipulated the duration of the gig, college boys wanted to party late into the night, and this suited the musicians — young and eager and full of the relentless energy that was rock 'n' roll: "We would play until the last man was standing," said one. The fraternities of the University of

Alabama had a well-deserved reputation for being, in the words of Johnny Sandlin, "animal houses . . . I will probably get shot for saying this . . . Fraternity parties down there during the period convinced me that I did not want to go there. That was the '6os, you know, it was pretty crazy! Gosh, I had one too many beers spilled on my guitar."

Tuscaloosa was Party Central in Alabama in the 1960s. The toga, jungle, and football parties were legendary, and the potent mix of testosterone, alcohol, and excitement placed a premium on loud music with a beat that you could dance to. It was quite a "culture shock" for a band that had only played the armories to work in the alcohol-fueled atmosphere of the fraternities, remembered Tommy Terrell and Johnny Robinson of the Ramblers. Entertaining "a bunch of drunks" took a lot more energy and a larger repertoire. In addition to rock songs, there was also a place for a few slower, more romantic numbers so that the young men could get closer to their dates. Rhythm and blues was the ideal soundtrack for a keg party, and in the fraternities it was R&B or nothing: "We had to play black music," recalled Rick Hall of the Fairlanes, or be thrown out.[2] When Bunkie Anderson's band went to Tuscaloosa, "we wanted to play Beatles and Kinks and Yardbirds, but all they wanted to hear was black music: Temptations, Four Tops, J. J. Jackson's 'But It's Alright.'" Henry Lovoy: "Everyone had to do the Beatles thing, because it was so popular. You had to go with the times . . . When we did the English stuff, we still had our soul sets. When we played the fraternity houses at Auburn and Alabama, we played the Beatles stuff with our soul stuff. They still wanted that doggone southern blues music. We were doing stuff like 'Sweet Soul Music' by Arthur Conley. At one fraternity house I must have had to play that song twelve times in a row, because that's all they wanted to hear."

Ironically, while Governor George Wallace famously stood at the door of the University of Alabama to deny African American students access; the frat houses had been employing some of the leading names in African American music for years. It was an Alabama tradition. The soul star Rufus Thomas said: "I must have played every fraternity house there was in the South . . . I'd rather play those audiences than any other."[3] Bob Cahill enjoyed many R&B acts while in college: "Arthur Alexander. I can remember him playing the song 'Anna' in Auburn, and this was about 1966, and if he played it once everybody wanted him to play it again. I think he played it about five times, to the point where the other members in the band were saying No! No! . . . I remember seeing Little Anthony and the Imperials in a packed house. We saw Dionne Warwick." The embarrassment of rhythm and blues riches in Tuscaloosa had a powerful influence on young musicians in the area, for even if they were not enrolled in the university, there were still plenty of places you could hear outstanding African American performers play once they had earned their money at the fraternities. Future stars of southern rock Paul Hornsby, Chuck Leavell, and Eddie Hinton all started their lifelong infatuation with R&B while growing up in Tuscaloosa.

For lovers of rhythm and blues, the great public universities of Alabama offered wonderful opportunities to hear some good music. You could get an invitation to a fraternity party and spend the evening listening to Arthur Alexander or Wilson Pickett, or if you were *really* lucky you could find yourself playing behind Otis Redding at an Auburn fraternity party. When one of Redding's backing band found himself unable to play, aspiring guitarist Bob Cahill got the chance of a lifetime: "This was in the fall of that year [1962], when Otis Redding was unheard-of. The band was sent from Georgia to perform at a fraternity party, and they sent the wrong band and the guitar player got pretty drunk there on the fraternity's booze, and by the time the party started, he could not play. The guy that I had gone down to see and his brother were there, and he told his brother that I could play, and this singer and I figured out what songs we could play and we played for the rest of the night." Redding had just cut his first record for Stax in Memphis, and a few months later Duke Rumore played "These Arms of Mine" on the radio. "Five or six months later this friend of mine called and said, 'You have got to listen to Duke Rumore, he's playing a song by this guy!' So I said that that sure did sound like him. I don't even think that we knew his name, but he had a real good voice. So when he came to Birmingham we went to see him, but when we saw him he did not remember us and I can understand that. It was, however, the same guy, and it was Otis Redding."

Panama City Blues

Being underage, not having a license or a vehicle, working part-time jobs and homework restricted many teen bands to playing only around town at weekends, often relying on friends or parents to take them to their engagements. But those lucky to be in the nether zone between high school and college or full-time work grabbed at the opportunity to take their music outside Birmingham and onto the road, especially if that road led to the sun, sand, and girls on the Gulf Coast. Driving down to the beach became an important part of the garage bands' experience as their members matured both as musicians and drivers. Touring was an adventure, part of the newness and excitement that characterized many memories of the 1960s, in which a generation of amateur musicians tasted the life once reserved for fearless bluesmen and hard-drinkin' country acts. Terry Powers: "I used to play with Hot Light, and that was with Eddie Chandler, Wayne McNight, and myself. We were just a guitar trio and we did pretty well. Jerry Beetlesom and I played in my first band together when we were eighteen called Crystal Magic. We had the life of Riley on the road. It was fantastic."

Financed by loans from parents and boosted by high expectations, Birmingham's garage bands took to the road on worn-out tires and vintage automobiles. Many of the stories about touring in the 1960s have at their center vehicles made in the early 1950s or 1940s. The love affair between these young men and their vehicles led to songs and bands named after them: the former about the kind of beat-up cars they drove, the latter about the kind of prestige vehicles they yearned for. Rock songs about cars depict them as things of beauty and power, listing their attributes and making them the heroes of narratives of speed and conquest. For teenage musicians the automobile represented the American Dream at its most immediate and potent, and they crammed into old Dodges and Chevies for long-distance journeys that took them to the Gulf Coast. They pulled U-Haul trailers loaded with gear. They brought their instruments and band outfits but very little money: Larry and the Loafers fell out in Panama City with only $2.65 between the five of them, and the Ramblers pawned some of their PA system for $5 worth of gas to get home. Driving long distances at night on narrow country roads was scary enough to persuade some of them to retire from touring. All shared the same trials and tribulations. Country musician Bill Morrison: "The good, the bad, and the ugly of traveling in passenger cars pulling those darned trailers, with the drummer's stinky feet resting on your lap while you tried to get a little sleep" during the long rides, guitars between your legs in the cramped interiors, and the inevitable breakdowns. Engines blew up, transmissions failed, tires burst, and trailers became disengaged and took their own way home. None of these hurdles seem to discourage the bands. This was an adventure. It made memories that lasted through adulthood and were fondly recalled in middle age.

The garage bands went on the road with varied goals. Some of them were playing to pick up a few hundred dollars to help get through school. Some played to pay their bar bills. Others had their sights set a little higher and dreamed of a recording session in Muscle Shoals or Nashville. Playing in a band could make an important contribution to a high school student's budget; a wad of bills for a few hours of fun seemed like a big deal at the time. Bandleaders were in constant negotiation with venue owners for increases in pay or beer. The meeting of band and venue owner usually went as follows, as related by Dale Aston of the Torquays: "A tubby middle-aged man greeted us and gave us the standard band greeting: no drinking on stage — no girls in the room — no smoking on stage — don't play too loud, etc., etc." But all the rules were there to be broken and the party that started on the bandstand often ended up in the sensuous confines of a motel room. Playing rock 'n' roll in Alabama was not without its peculiar dangers, especially where booze and girls were involved. And booze and girls were usually involved. Vodka and underage girls ruined one trip that the Distortions took to Demopolis. The gig at the party went well — "Man, we had a ball!" — and the band's celebration in the motel after the party went even better until the police arrived. Disaster! The story ended with the band spending the night in jail for underage drinking. The next morning the judge, who had earlier been at the party, fined the band all the money they had made at the gig.[4]

The thrills of the road went hand in hand with the maturation of the garage bands as musicians. Playing for money, and learning how to entertain a crowd, pushed amateurs to a level of professionalism. There was always that moment of epiphany when you realized that the band was really

playing together and you had finally made it. It might come at the end of a
set when the crowd cheered or when a promoter asked you what you were
doing for the rest of the summer. Some bands enjoyed a special moment of
triumph. Dale Aston remembers when the Torquays played Panama City:
"Our first night to perform at the Old Dutch was fun. We had a chance to
meet our fellow performers, Mark Dinning [known for his songs on *Teen
Time* in Birmingham] and the exotic dancer, White Storm. We began an
upbeat instrumental and brought her onstage to raucous applause from
around seventy-five well-lit people ready for the show. Remember, she was
only a few feet in front of us on the stage as she danced about . . . All of a
sudden White Fury turned her back to the audience, faced the band, and
tore her top off, revealing two bounding breasts with tasseled pasties at the
end. The drummer lost a stick, and the band lost it for a moment before
recovering. I don't think the audience even noticed the sour chord. After
the first night the strip act became routine for us and we hardly noticed
when the clothes came off. I guess we had finally become true professional
musicians."

The college fraternity circuit was easily the best place for a garage band
to play, but it only operated during the school year, during football season
in the fall and coming to a climax with graduation in the spring. The long,
dreary months of summer tended to drag on with little musical entertainment and employment opportunities for amateur musicians. Driving down
to Panama City, Florida, for the summer vacation became popular in the
1950s as this sleepy seaside town developed into a major tourist destination
for folks from Alabama and Georgia. By 1960 it was welcoming a million
visitors a year, and the "Miracle Strip" became an icon of southern culture
that also supported a lot of live music. It became a summertime tradition
to go down Panama City Beach. The route which went along the two-lane
highways to Florida became an indelible part of the memories of summer
for many in Birmingham. In the 1940s and 1950s the annual trip to Panama City was a family affair, with several generations crammed into an
automobile heading for a wooden cottage a few steps from the beach.

J. D. Weeks's love affair with Panama City began in 1949. "I knew the
routine. Take Highway 31 out of Birmingham, turn right on Highway 331
in Montgomery and go as far as you could, which was Highway 98 in Flor-

ida, and turn left." Some years later he would hitchhike with some of his fraternity brothers: "We were picked up about 2 a.m. by an already full car that included Dinky Harris another Viking fraternity brother. We did finally arrive and got right out near the Hang Out. After a lot of searching we found a lady that would let us sleep on the floor of her living room. Her cottages were all full and she felt sorry for us." Bad Betty: "Boy, back in the 1950s Panama City Beach was the New York of all high school kids. On Fridays we would load up and take off, heading to the beach. All the guys were wound up and would stay wound up the whole time they were there. Running along the beach, trying to make out with the girls, drinking a beer, going to the Hang Out and just having a blast. The sororities were all there trying to outdo each other. Dixie Debs were always around and flirting with everyone's guys ... The music was great, laughing and talking and meeting new folks. Sitting on the beach listening to the music."[5]

Music and dancing were central to the Panama City vacation. You listened to it on the radio as you drove down. Sarah Bradford Wear: "Seems we kept it on Duke Rumore until we got close to Montgomery, then the dial on the radio would get a workout ... looking for our finger-snapping, hand-clapping, and singalong favorites until we could get our luggage to the motel door." The Newspaper Boy: "We listened to WSGN for as long as we could, switching to WVOK and its 50,000 watts until it signed off at sunset ... We went through all of the small towns and tried hard to find a radio station playing good music. South of Montgomery we picked up a Tennessee station with a black deejay playing 'So Tough' by the Original Casuals." And when you got there, rock music was everywhere: from live bands at the Old Hickory restaurant and the Old Dutch Tavern, and from numerous jukeboxes at the popular Hang Out or at Aultman's or at Little Birmingham, a liquor store and gift shop: "The music was great, laughing and talking and meeting new folks. Sitting on the beach and listening to the music." But most important, the music was there to dance to, and the place to dance or just be seen was the Hang Out, a large, open pavilion right on the beach, with music blasting from several jukeboxes. Here you did the Bop or just watched from behind the wooden railing that enclosed the concrete dance floor. Don Campbell: "The Hang Out was *the* place to see and be seen on the beach, usually all night and all of the day. Some didn't have to get out of bed; they slept on the beach. The dancing started early at the Hang Out, with the jukebox playing the newest 45s continuously [six plays for twenty-five cents]. The music had to be loud to drown out the scratching of the sand between the dancer's shoes and the dance floor . . . The guys would spot who the best dancers were and who looked best in a bathing suit or a pair of white short-shorts with a golden tan. Many of the girls danced with a set of large curlers in their hair so they would look good that night." The Newspaper Boy: "The records on the Hang Out jukeboxes included songs we would always associate with PC [Panama City] and the Hang Out: 'Hully Gully' by the Olympics, 'You're So Fine' by the Falcons were great 1959 dance songs, and 'Searchin'/Youngblood' by the Coasters, 'Honky Tonk' by Bill Doggett, 'The Stroll' by the Diamonds, and 'That'll Be the Day" by Buddy Holly and the Crickets. We didn't spend much time on the beach because the music from the Hang Out drew us to it. The Hang Out was a concrete-floored open-air pavilion with a high gabled roof and a wooden railing around it with four jukeboxes." Henry Lovoy: "I was ten years old when I learned to Panama City bop, which was *the* dance. If you knew how to bop you could dance with the older women [sixteen and older] . . . I went to the Hang Out every night and bopped to the great rock 'n' roll music . . . At the Hang Out, at eleven o'clock, the big cop [Tom] would lock up the jukebox. Then we would go to a little place to dance called Aultman's, but then for only an hour, since it was late by then." Sarah Bradford Wear: "Of course we'd have to comb our hair again for the umpteenth time, freshen our drugstore lipstick and . . . carry our shoes to the concrete dance floor at the Hang Out that was still open and going strong. I was a good dancer too, one of the best . . . at least I thought. I'll bet everybody thought the same thing about their own smooth moving. I'd rather bop than eat, and I did, lots of times . . . We seemed to draw approval from the crowds gathered around us just about every time I'd get on the dance floor. That made it official: I *had* to perform my own 'stuff' . . . I guess I could say that Panama City is not where I was born, but it's where I started living."[6]

Teenagers maintained their Birmingham high school affiliations on Panama City Beach. Walter Norris went down with a group from Ensley High School: "We did run into some luck that first night there. We met a group of girls from Shades Valley High School who paid for a full week in a cottage . . . but to a person they were so sunburned that they were going home after four days . . . I made friends with a girl who was with a group from Woodlawn High School . . . soon her friends had met the other boys in our group and we were all just having a ball enjoying the beach . . . The girls from Woodlawn outnumbered us guys eight to four, so we were in teenagers' heaven!"

For Birmingham's garage bands, playing at Panama City was the closest thing to heaven. It was that potent combination of the music, the sand, the beer (ninety-nine cents for a six-pack of Old Milwaukee), and the girls ("we had a one-track mind . . . girls, girls, girls"). There was also money to be made, and also valuable publicity for the band. John Wyker of the Rubber Band: "Back in those days, and probably even today, the best place for a band to be seen was at a club at the beach. Every summer, kids would come to Panama City where they would be exposed to bands that they usually fell in love with. This would lead to wintertime gigs all over the South. I did my best sellin' jobs to my fellow band members, painting a picture of all the fun we'd have and all the girls we'd get, but mainly all the money we could make that next winter by bookin' parties and lead-outs for top dollar."[7]

In the 1950s most of the music in Panama City was provided by a juke-box, but as the garage band movement took over high school entertainment, the beach clubs and bars began to adopt live music and hire guitar bands. Some bands like the Swinging Medallions, the Rubber Band, and King David and the Slaves established their reputations at Panama City Beach. "Back then [1960] the Old Dutch was a jumping place. Always crowded with a large supply of pretty girls. We got in line to get inside. I happened to know the guard at the door, as I remembered him from the summer before. He was an ex-marine, well built, and his face looked like it had caught fire and someone tried to put it out with a track shoe . . . Back in those days no one checked your age. If the door bouncer thought you were old enough, you got in. If not, he told you to hit the road . . . The place was jammed . . . A band was playing and the noise was unbelievable. We could hardly hear our own voice . . . We were in hog heaven" ("KB" from Samson, Alabama).

Pop music that glorified the summer fun of beaches, sun, and golden-skinned girls enjoyed great popularity in the mid-'60s with the rise of surf instrumentals (played by guitar-slinging surfers like Dick Dale) and beach-themed ballads recorded by the universally popular Beach Boys. At least one celebrated Birmingham band drew on the surf and beach theme: the Tikis. Len Wade (piano and vocals), Billy Self (drums), Clyde Masters (bass), and Hayes Hopper (saxophone) played in the band that backed Bobby Mizzell and had years of experience playing the venues along the Gulf Coast. They also played gigs on their own along the Florida Panhandle as far west as Mobile. When they decided to form their own group in 1962, they picked a name that would fit their beach band reputation. "The Tikis" conjured up images of palm-tree lined beaches, Pacific breezes, luaus, and exotic cocktails. With the addition of Phillip Scott on trumpet, the Tikis could boast one of the best horn sections of the bands that played the beaches of Florida and Alabama.

Panama City was such a big deal for Birmingham's teenagers that one garage band produced a song about it. "Panama City Blues" by Larry Parker became the hottest record of 1960 in Birmingham. The production of this recording shows how radio interacted with amateur musicians in the 1950s and 1960s. It started at station WIXI AM-1480 in Irondale, where Larry Parker worked part-time and had the keys to the station. Working in radio attracted many high schoolers who had picked up an understanding of broadcasting in their classes and were interested in the electronics of their guitars and amplifiers. Musicians congregated at radio stations — to listen to the latest music, hang out with their fellow players, and maybe do a bit of business with the deejay. Larry's band the Loafers — Hal Painter, Delmar Smith, and one other — practiced at WIXI and even recorded a few songs on the station's transcription equipment to see how they sounded. Although the center of production for rock 'n' roll records was the independent recording studio, radio stations with transcription machines came a close second. These machines recorded and replayed programming to lessen the burden of providing live music or paying the record companies to play their records. They could also be used to produce trial recordings and demos, which were the currency of the popular music industry. The demo on a thin acetate record was the calling card and promotional tool handed to agents, promoters, record company A&R (Artist and Repertoire) men, and radio deejays, who all kept a record player close at hand to play these fragile acetate discs. The trial recording made at a radio station was much the same as one made in a recording studio, but with one critical difference — the person operating the machine had a keener sense of the commercial appeal of the recording, as he usually spent most of his day playing records to teenagers and gauging their response. Recording your music at a radio station was therefore a good way to find out how you sounded and get some input from a professional in the music business.

Larry picks up the story of recording his most famous song: "So let's get back to the studio at WIXI in Irondale. We borrowed two guitars, some amps, and a part of a set of drums. In short order I wrote 'Panama City Blues' and we recorded it on that late summer night as the A side . . . Everyone always assumed that 'Panama City Blues' was recorded live in Panama City, especially since the song opened with the sound of the water rushing onto the beach. That sound was created in the studio at WIXI, utilizing the running water in the shower and manipulating the sound volume. 'Panama City Blues' was the A side, and the B side was 'Till the End' . . . We recorded using an Ampex 601 reel-to-reel mono tape recorder." Larry played it for the deejays at the station, and they gave it some airplay. Ron Bowing of WYDE heard it, liked it, and played it: "The phones lit up and they were lit up all afternoon." Larry Parker's mind was racing — he could cut a proper master and have "an actual record." The next version of "Panama City Blues" was recorded at Reed Studios. "Reed was always a nasty place. It was old rooms in a building. One was the studio and one would be the office . . . There was only one recording [take]. We only had one chance to make it right . . . I am not sure where they were pressed, but I think it was Nashville . . . We got them three or four weeks later . . . I picked them up at the Greyhound bus station. I drove out to [WIXI] and we played it on the air. The kids loved it . . . I was in a real quandary about how I was going to get the record played and what I could do that was legal. The first thing I did was to quit my job at the radio station [WIXI, where he broadcast as "Jack Jackson"]." Duke Rumore was presented with some records: one was played on the air, and the rest were taken to Rumore's Record Rack and sold. "Duke was my hero. He did not realize that I was Jack Jackson on

the radio station. He found out about it and broke my record on the air . . .
Dave Roddy appeared at WYDE radio, and he played my record. He and
Duke had a falling-out. It was either/or. Duke and I were on the outs . . .
The next night Dave Roddy played my song on the air for an hour." Competition between deejays was ruthless. Ben Saxon: "If you had your record
on WSGN, you couldn't have it on WVOK. If you had it on WVOK, you
couldn't play it on WSGN. They hated each other. It was war."

As "Panama City Blues" took off, Larry and Duke Rumore reached a
conciliation. "Duke took me under his wing . . . It took some real schmooz-
ing and cost me several hundred records to get him to play my record again."
Rumore was not a man to miss a business opportunity, and he went on to
play the record all the time. He also got his brother Joe to play it on WVOK.
"Panama City Blues" was now heard on radio and jukeboxes, and it seemed
like everyone in Birmingham was listening to it. Larry and the Loafers' hit
song enjoyed a resurgence of sales every summer when Birmingham's teenagers started to dream of the beach and dancing at the Hang Out. In 1961
Larry and the Loafers — now Parker, Charlie Giambrone, Dale Serrano,
Wayne Gross, and Johnny Nations — produced another version of "Panama City Blues," this one recorded at Heart recording studios. "There was
a 4-track studio up there. This was major high-tech back then. There were
four microphones and four different tracks. It was wonderful. I took the
group up there and was abused by all of the producers and engineers and
whatever titles they gave themselves back then. I paid for that recording
time out of my own pocket. It cost me $125 for everything. It was a lot of
money for high school kids. We would get $20 or $30 for performing. Kids
in those days got around $2 for cutting the lawn."

"Panama City Blues" opened many doors for Larry and the Loafers.
They were invited to join the "Shower of Stars," an ambitious concert sponsored by WVOK, where they shared the stage with the best of Birmingham's
rock scene, such as Jerry Woodard and Bobby Mizzell, and with all-time
greats like Jerry Lee Lewis. The asking price for their shows increased dramatically, whether it was a private party in Birmingham or a large fraternity job in Tuscaloosa. "Panama City Blues" brought Larry and the Loafers
to Panama City, where they were booked to play Saturday and Sunday jam
sessions at the Old Dutch Inn. Larry always took several copies of "Pan-

ama City Blues" with him so he could replace those 45 rpm vinyl singles in the town's jukeboxes, which were constantly wearing out with all the play they got.

Kids just out of high school were easily impressed by the money to be made on the college and beach circuits in the Southeast, and all the fun that could be had, but it was hard work. For musicians looking to become professionals, touring was much more demanding than they ever imagined. Even an athlete like Sammy Salvo could lose twenty pounds on the road and come home exhausted. Larry Parker found that touring was wearing him down; he was losing weight and tiring out. As garage band players became semiprofessional musicians and spent more time touring, they came into contact with realities of the entertainment business: the broken promises, the ripoffs, the constant struggle with club owners and record producers, the alcohol and drugs. Youthful dedication to the music collided with seamier side of rock 'n' roll. Larry Parker watched the decline of several of his contemporaries: "We didn't like what we were seeing. Drugs were starting to show up in the music business. That didn't appeal to us . . . I didn't want to be a washed-up rock 'n' roll singer . . . I had seen Jerry Woodard slipping off the edge with his alcohol. He was drunk all the time. I did not want to be part of that." There was an even bigger threat to Birmingham's teenage rock bands: adulthood and its responsibilities. "I met a woman named Ginger that night. I asked her to go out with me for New Year's Eve . . . I asked her to go steady that night, within a year we decided to get married. I was twenty years old. I had my run as a rock 'n' roll singer and was looking for something a little more stable than what I was running into."

Nothing much came of the rock 'n' roll hopefuls from Birmingham, Alabama, and nobody was able to emulate the rags-to-riches story of Elvis Presley. Jerry Woodard and Sammy Salvo came back from the road and played bars and clubs in Birmingham and along the Gulf Coast. Baker Knight headed out for California with a few bucks in his pocket and made a career for himself writing songs. His beautiful "Lonesome Town" is about the pain of separation from home and family. Looking back, though, local musicians are far from downbeat about missing their chance for rock 'n' roll stardom. What they remember is the joy of playing and all the fun they had. Tommy Charles: "It's funny because the changes in music, from that era to today, even though it was rock back then, is dramatic. It was more fun back then. I think so and I'm pretty young and hip, but this music today is just too hard rock. Yeah, back then it was fun music and people smiled. They don't anymore, they're mad when they perform, back then it was just a beat, it was just rock . . . It was feel-good. I look at what they are doing today and I say, those guys are missing it, because they don't have any fun and the audience doesn't seem to be enjoying it . . . It is such a dramatic change in what has happened to music and to performers and to the audience. And that's too bad." Fred Dalke: "Because, quite honestly, rock 'n' roll was a lot more fun in the '50s and '60s. It was *fun*. It was innocent, and it was just a local group playing 'Louie Louie' and you didn't have to have a hundred thousand dollars' worth of equipment. And nowadays I feel sorry for the kids. It's just totally changed. I think a lot of the kids really don't know what they are missing. These groups now, they are all clones manufactured out of these record companies. See, one of the biggest major things that made the '50s and '60s what it was, as far as the music, was the local records. There was a lot of local groups and that was how they got started. Nowadays they don't have local records anymore."

CHAPTER FIVE

Race and Music in Birmingham

B irmingham, Alabama, will not be remembered as one of the leading cities of rock 'n' roll — like Memphis or New Orleans — but it was a hotbed of opposition to it. Anti–rock-'n'-roll rhetoric in Birmingham played an important part in the demonization of the music and its insertion into the discourse of race relations in Alabama. During the 1950s many adult Americans were alarmed at the undermining of the set of values and traditions they called the American Way of Life. With World War II won, anxieties over new threats, such as communism and juvenile delinquency, grew among the uneasy victors. Psychologists, politicians, and the mass media were quick to point to every crack in the edifice of family, sobriety, and the American Way of Life. Rock 'n' roll channeled all these anxieties into one easily labeled threat.

Birmingham was already in the midst of its massive resistance to desegregation when rock 'n' roll arrived in Alabama. Despite all the efforts of the record industry, the radio networks and the Hollywood film studios to reassure parents that the new music would not undermine the morality of youth, it was hard to deny its essential African American core. Likewise, it was difficult to completely censor all the songs about youthful drinking, promiscuity, and driving too fast at a time when national attention was on the moral decline of American teenagers. The more popular rock 'n' roll became, the greater the fears of its growing influence on a young and impressionable audience. Birmingham's parents viewed rock 'n' roll through the 1950s prism of Cold War paranoia, juvenile delinquency, and sensational journalism. One wrote, "We consider the situation to be as serious as an invasion of the enemy in war time, if we cannot stop the wicked men who are poisoning our children's minds."[1] Ed Boutwell remembered the

opposition to rock 'n' roll as racial: "It was all 'nigger music' to them, and
that would just turn us inside out when we heard that. It would make us
sick! I remember Elvis's first records were cursed by the elder whites."

Rock 'n' roll became the face of the many changes that threatened the old
way of life in the South. Fears about the breakdown of morality, the disrup-
tion of time-honored bonds in society, and the end of good manners and respect for elders coalesced in the opposition to rock 'n' roll. In Birmingham
it was perceived as urban music, with all its overtones of modernity. Folk
musician Joe White: "Birmingham was pretty much one generation away
from people coming from the country to get a job in the big town. Most
people's parents listened to country-type music, and most people's parents
enjoyed the music, and most people's parents didn't like rock 'n' roll music.
Just like the words from the Barbara Mandrell song: country wasn't cool at
the time. Rural was something that you didn't want to be associated with:
'No, I don't listen to that! I am from the city, I listen to rock 'n' roll." The
teenagers who watched *Blackboard Jungle* were energized by Bill Haley's
music, but so were parents, educators, newspaper reporters, and politicians:
a U.S. Senate Subcommittee on Juvenile Delinquency held hearings on the
impact of degenerate films on youth violence, *Time* magazine expressed
the belief that it gave support to communist critics of the American Way
of Life, and communities all across the country moved to ban it. As "Rock
around the Clock" sped up the *Billboard* charts and disturbances followed
showings of the film in North America and Europe, one psychiatrist di-
agnosed teenage enthusiasm for rock 'n' roll as a "communicable disease"
caused by "cannibalistic and tribalistic music." Saving the youth of America
was especially important to the Ku Klux Klan: "Don't let your children
buy or listen to these Negro records. The screaming, idiotic words and
savage music are undermining the morals of our white American youth."[2]
Popular entertainment became as important a battlefield in the war for
civil rights as public transport and lunch counters.

This was not the first time that an African American music was perceived as a threat to society; like blues, jazz, and voodoo before it, rock 'n'
roll was believed to have insidious powers over its disciples. Unlike the minstrel shows, another entertainment that mimicked black culture, rock 'n'
roll could not be placed into a pantomime that demeaned its creators. Had

the good old boys in the Ku Klux Klan looked a little closer at their own favorite songs — that old-time country music — they would have seen similar
worrying African American influences. Practically every one of their heroes, from Uncle Dave Macon to Hank Williams, acknowledged the debt
they owed to African Americans, especially in their formative years. Hank
had learned about music from a black street performer in Montgomery,
and he was far from being the only one who got his early musical education
from African Americans. The father of commercial country music, Jimmie Rodgers, worked with African Americans on the railroads and learned
their songs. "The Singing Brakeman" was as comfortable with the country
blues as any of the traveling bluesmen, who sometimes accompanied him
to gigs across the South, but when he came to Birmingham in the 1920s he
performed for a segregated audience.

The history of music in Alabama shows a constant interaction between
black and white players. African sounds and musical ideas began to influence southern culture from the moment that the slaves landed on American shores. During Reconstruction ex-slaves impressed their ex-masters
with their prowess on the fiddle, and soon went on to teach the next generation of white musicians how to play it. Many of the standards of old-time
music, like "Turkey in the Straw," were common to musicians of both races.
Folk songs like these were meant to be changed by the singer, who often
added new verses, and this particular standard was also called "Zip Coon"
when it was interpreted in black-faced minstrel style. In the Deep South
musicians had been exchanging ideas and instruments since the eighteenth
century. Stars of the fiddlers' conventions like Gid Tanner had numerous
African American songs and playing styles in their repertoire.[3] That great
American folk song "Home on the Range" appeared to reflect the western
frontier — the home of cowboys and little houses on the prairie — yet John
Lomax learned the song from an African American cook in San Antonio
who had heard it on a Texas cattle trail while working on a chuckwagon.

The record companies denied this racial interaction by inventing labels
that segregated the music. The first blues and jazz recorded were marketed
as "race" records for the African American market, and this was followed
by categories such as R&B, rap, and urban contemporary. When "rhythm
and blues" crossed the color line and entered the mass market, it became

"rock 'n' roll," even though the music remained much the same. Like "race music," the label "old-time music" was created by the record companies as they began to categorize their products in order to market them to specific audiences. Ethnomusicologists like Cecil Sharp had argued that the music of Appalachia was the purest expression of that mythical England so beloved by southerners, but that was just wishful thinking; old-time musicians were as flexible and impressionable as any other group of professional entertainers, and they would copy and imitate anything that caught their ear. As Rose Maddox, a star of Alabama country music, said: "I had got my songs and stuff in rhythm and blues, you know from the colored people's music. But I turned them around and did 'em my way so I thought I was doin' country music."[4]

The great exchange of musical ideas that led to rock 'n' roll was part of a long tradition of interracial sharing and copying that was accelerated in the twentieth century by color-blind recording and radio broadcasts. While segregation ordinances made it illegal for musicians of both races to play together on stage, the wider distribution of country and R&B records after the war made it easier for them to listen to each other's records and copy the bits that appealed to them. African American artists like Ike Turner, Bobby Bland, and Chuck Berry loved country music and incorporated some of what they heard into their own compositions.[5] After decades of musical intermingling, it was sometimes hard to distinguish the race of the voice coming from the radio. Many listeners in the 1920s had to be told that Uncle Dave Macon was not a black performer, a process that was repeated with Elvis Presley in the 1950s. Nims Gay was one of the pioneers of gospel on Birmingham radio in the 1940s: "I started with WJLD in 1942. That was the first . . . WJLD was the first station that blacks really began to work on . . . After I went to WDJC . . . this lady says to me 'They tell me you used to sing hillybilly.' I said I did . . . 'You are my sunshine, my only sunshine, you make me happy when skies are gray.' She said, 'Now you know you can't sing no hillbilly . . . They said that they wanted you at this white station because you sound . . . they didn't know whether you was . . . When you come on, I didn't know whether you were black or white . . . My uncle told me you used to be behind the curtain singin' hillbilly.' It was true!"

Ned Bibb remembered, "When Chuck Berry came out with 'Maybelline,' nobody knew that he was black. A bunch of country people loved the song: he didn't sound black on that song."

"Everybody learned it from the yard man."

The segregated South attempted to keep the races apart in education, transportation, public amenities, hotels, restaurants, and housing. Signs that read "Colored Only" or "White Only" marked the dividing line. Segregation was also present in all types of entertainment; many theaters, bars, and music halls catered solely to one race because of policy or their location. In a city where riding in a taxicab or playing checkers with a member of another race was a crime, there was every incentive to avoid interaction. George Anselmo pointed out, "In the early 1950s it was embarrassing to be in a car with a black man. Everybody looked at you funny."

Music became the vehicle for the cultural integration that was prohibited by law in Birmingham. Sacred music in the South was the product of interaction of the races, and while there were very few physical interactions in the city's numerous churches, the music they enjoyed was often the same. Everyone loved those old, "traditional" songs, whose long pedigree masked the interaction of black and white musical culture. Sheet music of gospel songs along with Methodist hymns was likely to be found in the homes of respectable white southerners. Ed Boutwell's mother was a soloist in the Highland Methodist church in Five Points, "but she would go to all the churches in the area and sing solos on Sundays and Saturdays. She would go to the synagogues and sing solos, and then run out and go to another church and sing another solo . . . Everybody in town had a maid, a black maid, and our maid was a church singer. She had the most wonderful voice, and she would tune in this radio show every afternoon between 3:30 and 4:00: Willie McKinstrie and his quartet, a black quartet that would sing spirituals. I would just run in there and just sit with her and sing along with her, with these spirituals, because they were just like the songs that Mother sang in church, and I love that stuff!" The Presley family were dedicated Christians, and much of Elvis's musical education was in church.

At the East Trigg Baptist Church, the pastor, Reverend Harper Brewer, remembered that Elvis was not the only white face in the congregation who came to listen to the stirring music. Gospel had such power and raw feeling that it attracted many white musicians. Mark and Keith Harrelson made a point of tuning in to African American religious music on the car radio while their parents were in their own church. Like other white musicians who came of age in the 1960s, they "grew up hearing gospel music." The musician and club owner Tom Baddley: "There was a black church at the golf course, and I would sometimes go with my father and he would let me go across the street while he played golf, and I would sit on the steps of that church and listen to the gospel music and I absolutely loved it."

Despite the best efforts of the segregationists, it was difficult to keep the musical cultures of working-class southerners apart. African American vocabulary, food, and culture were part of the lives of the white working classes. Music often provided the bridge between the two societies. Sam Phillips grew up on a large farm where he heard the farmhands sing while they worked. Carl Perkins claimed to have learned guitar playing from a black sharecropper who worked cotton fields adjacent to his family's plot. James Miller has pointed to the tradition in the South of "musical missionaries" like "Uncle" John Westerbrook, who inspired the music of Perkins, and "Uncle" Silas Payne, who converted Phillips.[6] As a child in rural Alabama, Gordon Evans hung out at his father's sawmill and went on to work next to the African American laborers. "I grew up with those people, worked with them, respected them, loved their music."

Some groups of working-class whites had closer connections with African Americans than others. This was especially the case for the Italian Americans who provided retail and commercial services in Birmingham's black communities. The Italian immigrants to the New South, especially the swarthy and often illiterate newcomers from southern Italy, were not considered the equals of native-born whites. In Birmingham the patterns of segregation discriminated between groups of whites along ethnic lines. For example, in the company town of Thomas, just west of the city center, the housing went from white to black, with a separate intermediate section for the Italian immigrants — the browns. Italians often ran the small neighborhood stores — precursor to convenience stores — in the working-class sections of town. Henry Lovoy: "I got influenced by black artists mainly because my daddy had a black grocery store. My daddy did not play anything but WJLD, which was a black radio station. He played all that stuff running through the store. I just kind of liked that music. The black folks would come into the store and eat lunch because he had a hot plate. They fixed egg sandwiches and bologna sandwiches. The plant workers from across the street would come and eat lunch . . . I really got turned on to the Delta blues artists like Slim Harpo, Lightnin' Slim, Little Walter, Ray Charles, and I can go on and on forever. They were a great influence on me wanting to be a musician." When asked about how music was breaking the race barrier in Birmingham, he responded: "Exactly! It always has. When I got started there were a lot of black musicians that we looked up to around here. Truthfully we were trying to imitate their sounds . . . and to me I just loved their sound so much that I wanted to sound more like them because I thought they had better feeling. Everybody says 'soul,' but it is just feeling they have . . . That is where I learned all that from. I was more of a black artist."

George and Sammy Salvo Anselmo were raised in Birmingham's Italian community. Of course they heard Italian music at home, on special programs for Italian speakers on the radio, and at weddings and parties, but several of their relatives had businesses in the black section of town, and it was there that the Anselmo Brothers heard gospel and blues from the radio and jukeboxes. George: "Black music was our thing: Muddy Waters, B. B. King. You got them on the radio on black stations. Back in those days, white stations would not play black music. Back in our day, they did not put black records on jukeboxes in white places. My uncle had a black café. It was called the Blue Moon Café. It was in Pratt City. I used to take all my white buddies out there. It was still segregated. The whites sat on one side and the blacks on another. The jukebox just sat in the middle." As they grew up and started doing those odd jobs that keep teenagers solvent, they found themselves working with African Americans and enjoying the rhythm and blues of Muddy Waters and Big Mama Thornton. Sammy: "When we worked in the store, there were several black employees. We all worked together and we all listened to the black station. It was good hard music. It made us feel like working."

Tom Baddley grew up in Tennessee and had played military bases: "I encountered interracial couples and stuff very early, so I, it seemed that and it struck me odd in Alabama, it was very segregated . . . I don't even recall Afro-Americans in the white clubs we played or in members of fraternities or sororities we played for . . . My father was very liberal for his day. He ran a service station, and I worked in that station when I was real young with the black men washing cars . . . So I got exposed to interracial mixing very early and I just loved R&B. I just loved it!" Many entertainers like Tom who played across the South found Birmingham to be the most segregated city: "Birmingham in my experience coming from Tennessee was much more segregated than from where I was from, or any place I have ever been, including Mississippi in a bizarre way. There was more hostility here."

Despite segregation, it was a tradition in the South for young white men to go to African American clubs and beer joints to enjoy the music and illicit booze — to cross the tracks and experience the wild side. Elvis Presley and Sam Phillips frequented the clubs on Beale Street in Memphis, where the music and carousing went on all night. In Birmingham, several young men who were later to make their mark in the music business remembered the first tentative trip to some of the city's famous black venues: the Blue Gardenia, the Madison Night Spot, and the Grand Terrace Ballroom. This was hardly co-option of culture, but rather a controlled form of reverse exploitation; the visitors got a chance to subsidize underpaid musicians, and the club owners got to cash in on all the excitement. Purchasing records or visiting black radio stations to listen to what they were playing on the outside speakers were the first tentative steps in each individual's journey from segregation to integration. The next step was to experience the performance in person if one had the courage to do so. Ed Boutwell: "I remember going to an all-black club and people were just looking at me, like, 'What are you doing here?'" Charlie Colvin routinely trawled the black clubs looking for talent to record, and admitted that he was "the only white guy in there." (The African American singer and producer Lenard Brown thought that Colvin had "large cojones" to do that.) Henry Lovoy and his bandmates in the Road Runners were escorted by their friend Joe Burnes of Poonanny to clubs like the Famous Flame in Fairfield and the Blue Gardenia, when "the racial thing was going on hot and heavy at that time. And this was in Birmingham . . . This was in early 1963 and 1964, right in the middle of the civil rights movement that gave Birmingham a black eye . . . I never did even think about things like that — the black and white issue — I knew that was there because I was raised in the South, but I loved my music and I loved the music they were putting out . . . They made us feel welcome in those black clubs back then." Frank Ranelli is a little skeptical of this racial intermingling in the world of music: "The Madison Night Spot, James Brown, Little Richard, they all played there, but you did not dare go down there and try and get in. It was like you invaded their territory. I used to hear guys tell me, 'Oh, I went down there and I heard James Brown' or something like that, but I don't really believe that they ever got in. It was kind of like, 'This is ours, you don't mess with it.'"

Yet the lure of great music was tempting more and more white teenagers to cross the lines of color that defined the New South. Music crossed racial boundaries with ease. Ned Bibb and his bandmates loved Freddie King's "Hide Away," and when they heard he was staying at the Gaston Hotel while playing a club date on Fourth Avenue, they decided to go and see him: "He was very gracious and we had a wonderful little visit." Ned asked him to play "Hide Away," but King said his guitar was at the club, so Ned loaned him his guitar and the great man played for these awestruck teenagers. After the worst of the racial tension in the mid-1960s was over, more budding musicians went to Fourth Avenue or Bessemer Super Highway to listen to the music, but this movement was for whites only; if any black teenager crossed the color line, he or she would be risking injury or death. In the late 1960s rock 'n' roll drew white teenagers into Birmingham's black neighborhoods. Herb Trottman: "When I was a kid in high school we used to go out on the Bessemer Super Highway to the Madison Night Spot, which was where Bo Diddley and Chuck Berry and all would come and we would listen to them outside . . . So there is a real vibrant thing, the industry was so intense, especially the mining and the mill work, and you will find this from the gospel people too, that a capella singing was an outgrowth of that."

There was a long tradition in the South of "sitting in" informally with other bands, which permitted some isolated moments of integration. This began with jazz musicians. Frank Adams had a long-standing gig for his combo at the Woodlawn Club, off Highway 78, playing for "the elite . . . This was into the 1940s. In the early 1950s we started to integrate at the Woodland Club. The white musicians would come out there about 12 at night. We would go until early in the morning . . . That is how we started to gradually integrate things together through openness." Henry Lovoy and his bandmates made the most of Joe "Poonanny" Burnes's friendship: "If you could get into a black club and of course Poonanny would make sure that we would be wanting to sit in, and we would sit in. And if we got them off, then we knew we were doing something good, because they have the feeling and we did get them off!"

Acceptance by an African American audience was the highest compliment that could be paid to an emerging rock 'n' roller. Kevin Derryberry of Telluride: "I was surrounded by African Americans because I was in Selma. That made up most of the population. I was in bands all through school, and in one band there were a lot of black members. So we did the junior high talent show in eighth grade and walked away with the trophy. It was cool. The school was mostly black, and we got on stage and broke into 'Proud Mary' and everybody just went nuts! It was another one of those moments in my life where I knew at that point that was what I wanted to do . . . We were close to Pritchard, Alabama, and there was this place that always had these blues people, artists, and we would always go there. We were always the only white people in there. It did not matter . . . You would be a little nervous but once the music started . . . we were all there because of the music."

But it wasn't always so easy for a garage band to connect with a black audience. When Tom Baddley was asked if he was ever uncomfortable visiting black clubs, he responded with this story about one night in the 1960s when the Companion Band played a black club: "I did! I mean, I am not stupid . . . The most uncomfortable thing that I ever remember was at the 409 Club . . . The first time we played, and we came out just as white as we could be, and we looked out and it was all black and dead silence. Ed Self [the vocalist], who is a good guy but he was extremely white . . . he called a song that was just . . . something like the Gentrys or something! I looked at those people, and it was not well. I said to Eddy, 'I am calling the songs from here on out,' and I forget the next song we did, but it was a black number and I cranked the bass up and looked at the drummer, who was Jimmy King, and I said, 'You better move with me,' and we finally broke through, and people got up dancing and it turned out to be a great night!"

Not every musician in Birmingham admired black culture and knowingly adopted it; some of the leading advocates of segregation were to be found among the ranks of country players. Rockabilly star Dinky Harris: "I loved the blues and the music of those blues masters like John Lee Hooker and Muddy Waters, but if the people I was hanging out with knew I was listening to black music they would have burned a cross on my lawn!" The high school kids who played in Birmingham's garage bands were well aware that they music they loved was not acceptable to their elders. Larry Wooten of the Ramrods said that teenagers were naturally rebellious and "wanted to form their own opinions about things. So we were closet rhythm and blues and blues listeners." Fortunately for them, you could listen to black music in Birmingham on the radio without risk of Klan retribution if you were careful. Larry: "We'd listen to WJLD, and they wouldn't turn their radio up real loud when you could hear Shelley the Playboy talking, but when the song came on they would turn it up . . . if they were in their car, but that's a shame it had to be that way, but you would really be ridiculed by other whites."

As rock 'n' roll took off in Birmingham in the early 1960s, the white radio stations played more Motown (the sound of "young America"), R&B, and soul, while black deejays like Shelley Stewart played Bobby Darin and Elvis as popular music became a little more integrated. Dan Brennan figures that Birmingham radio by the mid-1960s was playing black and white music in equal amounts, and Shelley Stewart agreed: "Rock and roll changed the dollars by removing black radio's power [of monopoly of R&B]." It soon became difficult to hear where R&B ended and rock 'n' roll began as the categories invented by the record companies lost their meaning. Shelley: "Now what the hell is rock 'n' roll? We have had rock forever. I have played what he [Alan Freed] called rock 'n' roll back with Ma Rainey. I mean, come on! With Bessie Smith. So don't tell me that he invented rock 'n' roll, when black people were doing it prior to that . . . the first damn thing about it. And I told Alan Freed, I said, 'I resent rock 'n' roll — you named it rock 'n' roll! You did that shit!'" While white-owned record companies got the credit for introducing rock 'n' roll, Shelley pointed out that black-owned record companies sometimes broke white acts, "you had your Abners, and your Jimmys [Ewart Abner and James Bracken of Vee-Jay Records], who actually brought the fertile Beatle records [which had been rejected by the Beatles' U.S. record company, Capitol] to this country on Vee-Jay Records."

Faced with strict segregation laws, Birmingham's theaters adopted the strategy of having two shows for each performer: one for whites and one for blacks. Some integrated shows went on without incident, such as the January 1956 tour of Bill Haley and R&B performers Big Joe Turner and LaVern Baker, but when Haley returned in May with the Flamingos, Platters, and Frankie Lymon and the Teenagers, he faced picketing and threats. If a visiting rock 'n' roll tour had only a few whites on a predominantly black bill, the white performers were often dropped from the show and told to stay in their hotel. This is what happened when Buddy Holly and the Crickets came to town, to the anguish and heartbreak of their fans, like young Ben Saxon: "This is 1957, two years before he died. What we lost out on, as fans here, we did not get to see Buddy Holly in Birmingham. We did not get to see Paul Anka. We did not get to see the Everly Brothers. The reason is because they did not let blacks and whites play on the same stage." People who listened to Holly and the Crickets sometimes thought they were African Americans, and while the band was famously welcomed in Harlem's Apollo Theatre, the opposition to racial mixing on stage eventually forced them to leave the tour.

The department stores, restaurants, and public places along Seventeenth and Eighteenth Streets — the border between black and white downtown Birmingham — were becoming the frontlines in the rising tempo of racial confrontation. One powerful weapon of the black community was the boycott: an exercise of consumer power that put pressure on white businesses. Birmingham had a relatively affluent African American community, which included thousands of industrial workers who spent their wages in downtown stores and other retail outlets. Although the Montgomery Bus Boycott is rightly emphasized in the struggle for civil rights, it was only one of several boycotts that occurred in the late 1950s and early 1960s in Alabama. The fight for integration in Birmingham began with a wide-scale boycott of white businesses in 1962 that was promoted by students from the historically black colleges in the area. If political and cultural barriers to integration were too strong to move, then economic pressure might be able to persuade white Alabamians to change their minds. One flyer used in a boycott summed up the strategy succinctly; it was titled "If You Need My Business..."

Behind the infamous confrontations of civil rights protesters and Birmingham police in the streets of the city center, the economic intercourse of blacks and whites continued, especially in the business of popular music. It was business as usual at Heart Records and the other recording studios that relied heavily on the gospel trade. Ed Boutwell: "Carlton Reese had a choir called the Carlton Reese Singers, and he put together that choir with three or four other choirs, and came to my studio in English Village in 1962. But English Village is in Mountain Brook, Alabama, and it was an enclave of white people, very rich people. The color barrier was profoundly maintained there for all these years, and my studio was on the line of Mountain Brook and Birmingham. All of a sudden busloads of black choirs show up and park in my parking lot behind the studio and pour out into the studio, and in come ten Mountain Brook police ready to save me! No joke! I just got tickled. I thought it was as funny as hell. I said, 'Well, I would appreciate it if you just guard us, because we are going to cut an album with these choirs.' Some of them grumbled, but most of them laughed about it." Racial harmony was an essential part of the music business in Birmingham: "I had all these wonderful musician friends, black and white, and we worked together all the time... In the studio, oh yes, if they needed a good hot guitar picker and they happened to be white, they would not keep him of their session and vice versa. It produced an atmosphere for me that made me feel very wholesome about it."

Black customers were also vital to the music retailers like the Forbes piano store at 1914 Fourth Avenue, adjacent to the black business district. This was a large store, with several floors of retail space and demonstration rooms. Here black and white mingled while choosing records, browsing through sheet music, or admiring a piano. French Forbes: "Business still went on. You had your good years and your not-so-good years... Everyone was making a living at it... We had plenty of black customers. We always had a large black clientele. We never had any problems with that.

We always had a number of black people working for us. They were fine people. I think the news media blew things out of proportion. But of course we were in our own little world and might not have been in tune with everything. I've gone out to black churches on Sunday nights when they would have meetings [during the civil rights struggle]. We would demonstrate organs and pianos for them. I've never had a problem in a black church. They always treated me respectfully and I returned the same respect." Newberry Records was another place downtown where the races came together — buying the 45 rpm vinyl singles, gazing at the posters of pop stars or just listening to records in the special booths where you could hear a song before you bought it. The economic interaction between black and white in Birmingham isn't usually part of the city's history, but while the confrontations in Kelly Ingram Park attracted the world's attention, a business that depended on the cooperation of the two races had to go on. Ken Shackleford: "I was right in the black area. A lot of the racial problems were hyped. They did have some problems, but it was nowhere near what the media put out. Our studio was a block from Kelly Ingram Park." Gary Sizemore: "There was a service station there on the corner, and there was this old black guy called Davis that run it, and he had his wife and daughter who hated white people — you could feel the hatred. Instilled that hatred in their daughter Angela." Ken Shackleford: "We had a deal with him, for a parking lot for Heart [Studio], and would go there once a month and she'd be there, home from school, and you could tell she hated me 'cause I was white but I always killed her with kindness. The old man was as nice as he could be."

The rise of rock 'n' roll in Birmingham had given some African Americans the opportunity to make money. Birmingham's preeminent back deejays — Shelley the Playboy and Tall Paul White — started in white-owned stations for very little pay. Shelley: "I started doing radio in 1949. They didn't pay me money really. They paid my transportation bus fare, which was seven cents . . . I was not paid until two years later after I came out of high school. I was hired full-time because I was doing a teen show . . . and my salary was $17.50 a week. I worked from 6 to 8 mornings, 12 till noon, and from 3 till 6." As Shelley the Playboy, celebrity deejay, he was able to earn much more money: "I had a very strong white listening audience.

Bull Connor would say, 'Don't let your children listen to that jungle music of Shelley the Playboy. Don't do that!' But I had a white fan club in the early 1950s!" He opened his own record store and played lucrative gigs for all-white audiences in record parties. These were violently opposed by segregationist groups, which were determined to stop Shelley from dancing with white girls: "No, I was not popular with the White Citizens' Council. I was not popular with the Ku Klux Klan. The KKK cut the radio tower while broadcasting over there at WEDR. They wrote 'KKK' on my windows in blood there. In 1960 they tried to kill me. I was appearing for a white audience over there at Don's Teen Town out in Bessemer. They tried to kill me."

Rock 'n' roll's conquest of American popular culture provided some opportunities for its originators to cash in and escape the discriminatory wage structure that was the foundation of segregation in the South. Joe Burnes played drums in high school and was asked to join a band: "So I went with him that night and man, they loved us, and they gave me all the hamburgers and french fries and Co'-Colas that I wanted — free! That right there, man! They started pushin' them off when I didn't even want one, I was like seventeen or eighteen. Then on top of that when I got home that night he gave me six bucks. Six dollars! Check this out! I'd been caddying eighteen holes for three dollars in the sun carrying two bags. Three and four dollars and he give me six bucks for all that fun! I went into the house that night, so help me God, I told my momma I was gonna be a drummer . . . and I knew then that that was what I was gonna do for the rest of my life. Here it is thirty-seven years [later] and I am still doing this. I don't wanna do nothing else!" Lenard Brown pointed out the amazingly high financial rewards in the entertainment business: "In high school for us at that time lunch cost twenty-five cents, and I was making fifty dollars a week singing for two nights a week . . . I was able to buy all my friends lunch."

The rise of rock 'n' roll pumped a lot more cash into the nightclub business, and some black musicians were able benefit from that. Joe Burnes of Poonanny: "I started playing here in Birmingham in 1957. It was so bad until we basically started playing white clubs . . . The blues is something that used to be real big in this part of the woods . . . It is mostly white folk that don't understand nothing but traditional blues . . . Poonanny is a success story, and what makes us a success story is that I did it the hard way.

I never recorded up until '93 and I started my band in '62 and I can think of some billion-dollar companies that went under from '62 up until '92, and Poonanny is still around and able to make it, and it's maybe 60 percent because of white audiences. Black people would like to think that it is the black thing that kept us going, but it was not. It was the white thing that kept us going! Now check this out: My record company representative, I was with him last week, he tells me that I am old rock 'n' roll. Rock 'n' roll is something that I record, and that is on a blues label, and it is blues, but it is a special kind of blues."

Although the memories might have been tempered by time and a much more relaxed atmosphere to race in post-1960s Birmingham, black musicians usually do not linger on the violence and oppression of segregation. Lenard Brown: "Because I was so into music and a lot of things . . . I did not have a bad life as a youngster. I don't remember a lot of it. I remember racism and all that was existent at the time, but at the time I ran into very little of it . . . We were doing so many things." Lenard played in a vocal group called the Controllers from the tenth grade onward: "The hottest place was called Jenkins' Blue Gardenia, yeah, and that was a hot spot, you know . . . There was every nook and cranny in Birmingham we played. So once we figured we got downtown, we could play any little place in town. We thought, 'Oh, we are downtown now. We have arrived downtown now!' We were playing at the hotels, and it was a gradual thing but at the time we had never performed there before." Asked if playing for white audiences in downtown Birmingham revealed Alabama's racism as the worst in the country, Lenard replied, "I disagree with that! Because I think that anybody who is honest enough to tell you . . . Well, you know, I like being with white people, I like being with my own . . . I believe that Alabamians are honest in their racism. If they are going to say, 'Yeah, I am a racist'— point blank, 'By God, I am a racist'— right off, there is no hiding. I think the worst kind are those who lie and cover up."

Foxxy Fatts made a living playing the white clubs, college gigs, and what he called the "society jobs," the country clubs and private parties in affluent suburbs like Mountain Brook: "You could go into the clubs and play for them, you just couldn't sit out, and if you wanted to sit down and have a drink or sit and eat, you had to go into the kitchen . . . It was real strange back then . . . Because I don't think I would have the nerve and the patience to do some of that again like sitting in the kitchen. I still don't, but I really wanted to play. That is my art. That is my craft, my life of work, and I love it!" He summed up the attitude of many young African American players in the music business of the 1960s: "I have no problem with color. My favorite color is green."

CHAPTER SIX

Music in the Struggle for Civil Rights

The civil rights struggle dominated the story of Birmingham in the 1960s and did more to determine the image of this city than anything else. Birmingham became famous during this epic confrontation, and the images generated are so powerful that they still resonate today. The pace of civil rights agitation moved parallel with the rise of rock 'n' roll, whose loud entry into American popular culture was made all the more worrying because of its association with dangerous R&B performers and low-class white guitar pickers. Much of the threat was in the timing. At the very moment when Elvis Presley was hitting the Top Ten, Rosa Parks and Dr. Martin Luther King Jr. were gaining attention as the leaders of the Montgomery Bus Boycott. The seminal recordings of rock 'n' roll were released at the same time that the nation first heard about sit-ins, boycotts, and the rising tide of juvenile crime. It seemed to many beleaguered Alabamians that the stability of their families, and the racial integrity of the New South, was being compromised by a conspiracy of civil rights advocates, communists, sexual deviants, and wild rock 'n' rollers. Both the supporters and opponents of civil rights acknowledged that popular music was playing a part in bringing the races together and that rock 'n' roll was a force for integration. The influence of popular music was taken seriously by the Ku Klux Klan and the White Citizens' Councils. While gradual economic integration might be under the segregationists' radar, the high profile of the entertainment industry made rock 'n' roll a highly visible battleground in the cultural warfare of the 1960s.

The leader of the White Citizens' Council in North Alabama was Asa "Ace" Carter, a fervent segregationist and a member of the KKK who had enjoyed a stint of radio broadcasting and was now leading the fight against integration. He was particularly incensed when white women, "frantic, screaming" women, mobbed black performers to get autographs. The Alabama White Citizens' Council argued: "The obscenity and vulgarity of the rock 'n' roll music is obviously the means by which the white man and his children can be driven to the level of the nigger." They picketed shows with signs that read "Jungle Music Promotes Integration," "Be-bop Promotes Communism," "NAACP Says Integration, Rock & Roll, Rock & Roll," and "Churches Must Speak Out against the Anti-Christ Forces."[1] Rock 'n' roll was feared as a force of modernity that offered transcendence from the restrictions of Jim Crow into a new world order of teenagers in which the hierarchy of racism was overturned. State senator Walter Givhan: "The reason we are here and the reason we've fought these battles is your little boy and little girl. That's what we are fighting for. We're going to keep these little white boys and these little white girls pure."[2] The first Elvis Presley records had been roundly criticized for being coarse and degenerate, and his televised performances had also offended many parents. Some of them were sure that these legendary Sun recordings were the work of communists. People in the white working and middle classes who criticized "the sensuous negro music" were not alone; Dr. King thought that rock music was degrading.

Within the rhetoric of rock 'n' roll was a new concept of race relations in which the music radiated healing properties and created an imaginary world where all people could get along, as Craig Werner has argued.[3] Brian Ward has catalogued the violence that sometime accompanied concerts of rock and R&B acts, but concludes that these interracial meetings "were the sort of joyous celebrations in which many . . . detected the roots of greater racial amity."[4] Rock musicians and fans in Birmingham considered black musicians "our heroes" and regarded their own love for music as color-blind. Bandleader and club owner Bob Cain said, "We really have a kind of bond. We know each other." The African American player Joe Burnes explained, "We was all like brothers in the same lodge," and there was clearly much love and respect between musicians of both races during the 1960s. Cleve Eaton claimed: "Music started integration. Jazz in particular, but music is what did it." Musician Rick Ranelli: "I was just reading the other day about what happened to Nat King Cole, how he was thrown off the stage. That stuff happened, but as far as musicians playing with colored musicians, and the integration of the whole matter, musicians have [been] and always will be cool about that. They want to know how well you play that horn; they don't care what color you are."

Birmingham embarked on its historic role as flashpoint for racial strife in 1956 when one of Alabama's most successful entertainers returned home. Nat King Cole was a star with a string of hit records to his credit. Born Nathaniel Adams Coles in Montgomery in 1917, he learned to sing on street corners and eked out a living until he moved to Chicago. Cole established a reputation as a jazz pianist with the King Cole Trio in the 1940s and later rose to a level that was well beyond the ambitions of most black performers — his own television show on NBC. He headlined the "Record Star Parade" of 1956, a major concert tour booked into Birmingham's Municipal Auditorium on April 10, 1956, just a few months after the January release of 'Heartbreak Hotel.' Female vocalist June Christy joined him on the bill, along with the Four Freshman singing group and the Ted Heath Orchestra — a swing band from England. There were two shows: "Whites at 7:00 p.m. and coloreds at 9:30 p.m." Birmingham's segregation ordinances prohibited "mixing of whites and negroes at public gatherings," and even kept ticket sales separated: "White tickets now on sale at E. E. Forbes [piano store] 403 N. Twentieth Street: colored tickets on sale, Temple pharmacy." Members of the white supremacist group the White Citizens' Council attended the show that night with the intention of breaking it up. Cole was getting too popular with American audiences. Asa Carter claimed that it was only "a short step . . . from the sly, nightclub technique vulgarity of Cole to the openly animalistic obscenity of the horde of Negro rock 'n' rollers."[5] He could be seen cozying up to white women on television, and the publicity photographs of the event showed Cole and Christy standing close together. That had to be stopped.

Cole had only completed the first two songs in his set when four men jumped onto the stage, quickly followed by several policemen. Many accounts of this incident describe a brutal beating and a distraught and traumatized Cole, but John Collins, a guitarist for the Ted Heath band, saw little violence: "On stage it's hard to see anyone coming from the audience because of the lights. I thought it was a joke at first, because they had Nat by the leg. Cops were rushing from the wings of the auditorium to apprehend Cole's attackers." It was probably the audience members who were the most traumatized — thirty-five hundred of them sat in stunned silence, many of them struggling to comprehend what was going on: "I'd never seen hate like that in anyone's eyes before," said one. The *Birmingham News* reported, "After the disturbance, Cole was brought back to the stage by cries from the audience. The Alabama born entertainer was applauded for nearly ten minutes when he returned. He told the audience, 'I just came here to entertain you. That was what I thought you wanted. I was born in Alabama.' There were yells for him to sing again, but he said his back was hurt. Then he walked off the stage amid more applause."[6] He did, however, perform for the black audience later on that night. He canceled performances in two other southern cities (Greenville and Charlotte) and never performed in Alabama again.

Charges were made and fines levied, but this did little to dispel the sense of shame in the white community, especially as the attack made the national news. Bob Cahill: "Well, it got national precedence and I would imagine that 95 or 100 percent of the people there were shocked and just did not know what to do." Diane McWhorter describes the growing discomfort of "big mules" of Birmingham's economic and political elite as the city's hateful reputation spread. They were no strangers to racism, but as McWhorter artfully points out, "the crude shirt-sleeved version of the bigotry" embarrassed them. They feared its effect on their social standing and businesses. U.S. Steel dominated the economic life of Birmingham and had made as much profit from segregation as anyone, but when an executive argued that Bull Connor and George Wallace were giving Alabama a reputation for "reaction, rebellion and riots, of bigotry, bias and backwardness," it was clear that this was bad for business.[7]

The recording industry also carried out its own policies of segregation, and paid much lower fees to African Americans. Those bluesmen who had gone up north to record in the 1930s and 1940s had to use the freight elevator to enter the studio, and so did local gospel singers when they broadcast from Birmingham. Nims Gay: "See, when the Gospel Harmonettes started here in Birmingham, they used to go to the station to do [a broadcast] when they done their first recording. They had to rework the elevator at the *Birmingham News* [who owned the building]. So you had to get on the elevator and up — the freight elevator." One reason Sam Phillips set up Sun Studios was that it was "the only recording studio that I know of in the South at that time" that was open to African American males. "Black singers have never been given the opportunity to record," he remembered, and this reality was evident to Birmingham's black jazz and R&B players as they struggled to get into recording studios.[8] Despite police chief Bull Connor's threats directed at recording studios that employed black talent, Birmingham's record producers continued to work with African American musicians and businessmen.

But outside the usually friendly confines of recording studio and practice room, things were very tense in Birmingham, "the Johannesburg of the South." The blues player Johnny Shines told Davey Williams that he hated to go through Birmingham from the moment he alighted at the bus station: "That place was so rough, especially for a black man, and it made the worst part of Chicago seem like a park." Buddy Causey found himself in the same dangerous situation when his vehicle was stopped on the way to a gig and he had to explain what he was doing with black men in the vehicle. When Spooner Oldham and Arthur Alexander drove down from Muscle Shoals to play a gig in Birmingham, they found a hostile reception: "Arthur was scared to fucking death. He would not get out of the car." Donnie Fritts was with them that day, and his conclusion speaks volumes: "Birmingham was dangerous back then, and I mean dangerous, son."[9] It was especially dangerous for black Americans testing the bounds of segregation. Nims Gay: "In fact, my dad, he came here from Cleveland, Ohio . . . It's funny to me cause he came to visit and the streetcar ran down Tallapoosa Street over there in East Birmingham where I was, and I got on the bus, me and another lady, and sit down, sit down right at the front, you know, and we weren't allowed to sit in front. My daddy got the next bus out of Birmingham. He told my sister and my brother, 'Everybody gone crazy down there.'"

Freedom Songs: "The Soul of the Movement"

The threat of rock 'n' roll imagined by the White Citizens' Councils never materialized, and its effect on the struggle for civil rights was negligible. For all its subversive posturing, rock songs very rarely made a political statement. The Bobby Fuller Four were singing, "I fought the law, and the law won," but this required guitars, amplifiers, and some work in the recording studio to be heard. A powerful force of activist music came from another quarter, one that Carter and his friends in the Klan had never imagined might pose a threat. It was not a cultural invasion of troublesome northerners, nor an illegal import brought by those "outside agitators," but a homegrown tradition close at hand. The music of activism, later called "freedom music," came from deep southern roots. Its main strand was sacred music, the music of the black sanctified churches; another was the songs of union organizers and strikers, and another was the ballads and commentaries of folk music. Freedom music came together in the heat of the civil rights struggle and was created outside the commercial framework of popular music that had embraced rock 'n' roll.

Gospel songs joined with the music of mountain men, cowboys, chain gangs, bluesmen, union organizers, and gandy singers in the construction of an American folk music that was recorded by ethnomusicologists John and Alan Lomax in the 1930s. Their recordings often crossed over into popular culture and made stars of performers like Huddie Ledbetter and Woody Guthrie, who went on to inspire a generation of young folk musicians in the 1960s. Folk music also had more practical uses as creators of identity and tools of solidarity. During the Great Depression songs were employed in the rhetoric of protest, such as "The Scottsboro Boys Must Not Die" and the iconic "This Land Is Your Land," written by Woody Guthrie, whose guitar bore the inscription "This machine kills fascists." African American work songs and sacred music were included in anthologies published by unions and the communist party. Lawrence Gellert included them in his *Negro Songs of Protest*.[10] Freedom songs as popularized by performers like Paul Robeson reached far beyond their southern home and kept a canon of resistance music alive — to be discovered by the baby-boom generation as it came of age in the 1960s.

Although they sounded a lot different, freedom songs bore some similarity to rock 'n' roll: both were the music of the young, both were considered transformative music that could be a force for change in society, and both emerged from the interaction of black and white musical cultures. In the case of freedom songs it was the merging of folk and other songs of the primarily white labor movement with that of gospel. When these two groups began to coalesce in the 1940s and 1950s as the African American church became the nexus of the civil rights movement, freedom songs emerged. This process can be seen in an examination of the origins of the most famous freedom song of all, "We Shall Overcome."

The progenitor of this famous song could have been "I'll Overcome Some Day," written by Charles Albert Tindley, one of fathers of modern gospel, in 1901. It also has a resemblance to a gospel hymn, "If My Jesus Wills," which was composed in 1942 by Louise Shropshire, the leader of a Baptist choir and a friend of several leaders of the civil rights movement, including Martin Luther King and Fred Shuttlesworth. There are several mentions of songs with similar names being sung at union meetings as far back as 1908, when the February 1909 *United Mine Workers Journal* reported, "Last year at a strike, we opened every meeting with a prayer, and singing that good old song, 'We Will Overcome.'"[11] (This could have referred to Tindley's 1902 gospel song.) While the song did not emerge again in the gospel field until 1942, it was mentioned in accounts of union activity in the 1930s and 1940s, although we cannot be sure it was the same song as Tindley's because the words and tune were not reported. Thus by the end of 1945 several versions of "I Will Overcome" (or "I'll Overcome") were current in the gospel repertoire, while on the South Carolina picket line, Lucille Simmons and other striking tobacco workers were singing a slower version of the song as "We Will Overcome." Its secular origins can be traced to the union movement's growing appreciation of the power of music in advancing the cause. "We Shall Overcome" was published in 1947 in *The People's Songs Bulletin* under the direction of musician Pete Seeger. Seeger believed that the song had been passed on to Zilphia Horton, the music director of the Highlander Folk School of Monteagle, Tennessee, an adult education school that trained union organizers. Zilphia was an ardent collector of both black and white labor songs, and she probably learned the song from tobacco workers from the Carolinas who had come to Highlander. Zilphia taught it to many folk singers, including Seeger, who included it in his repertoire, as did many other activist singers, such as Frank Hamilton and Joe Glazer, who recorded it in 1950. Sociologist Guy Carawan was taught the song at Highlander, and he brought it to workers involved in civil rights activism. It appeared in the fight for union rights in Tennessee in the 1940s and became associated with the civil rights movement from around 1959 onward. "We Shall Overcome" was heard at the end of every demonstration or meeting in Birmingham in 1963, and it continued to be heard throughout the 1960s as the counterculture took to the streets. John Lewis remembered singing "We Shall Overcome" in a jail cell: "A fantastic, just a moving thing. I will never forget that. You had the fear, but you had to go on in spite of that."[12] When the Student Non-Violent Coordinating Committee rushed out a collection of over seventy songs of the Southern Freedom Movement in 1963 — collected at picket lines and demonstrations — it was entitled *We Shall Overcome!* Pete Seeger, Joan Baez, and Bob Dylan sang the song at rallies, folk festivals, and concerts, making it widely known not only in North America but all over the world. Protestors sang it in Northern Ireland, South Africa, and communist Eastern Europe in their own struggle for freedom. It continues to resonate in the Deep South's racial politics. In 2003 Leeds High School removed "We Shall Overcome" from its marching band's repertoire after complaints from parents. The superintendent said, "The focus should be on the music of the times rather than events in society."[13]

Long Hot Summer

In January 1963 George Wallace took office as governor of Alabama and set the tone of his administration in his "Segregation Forever" inaugural speech. The battle lines had been drawn. Up to this point the spotlight had been on Montgomery and the bus boycott, but this was to change that spring when Dr. King arrived in Birmingham. Activist Ed Gardner remembered that the local news media would not give the movement any coverage when they tested bus segregation in Birmingham, and five hundred of them went to jail, but there was hardly any mention of it in the press or on radio: "They acted as though nothing was happening. Just a few rabble rousers was agitating and the town was quiet."[14] King took a room in the A. G. Gaston Motel and addressed meetings in the Sixteenth Street Baptist Church just around the block, which could hold hundreds of people. The marches began at the steps of the church and continued across Kelly Ingram Park, where Bull Connor and his policemen were waiting.

What happened next is not really local history but American history writ large and televised. The demonstrations in Alabama became a symbol of the civil rights struggle and were watched all over the country as television cameras and radio microphones penetrated into the recesses of the segregated South. The photographs of young children being attacked with police dogs and firehoses were reprinted in newspapers around the globe. The world was listening to the inspiring words of Dr. King, but it also heard the freedom songs shouted out by the protesters as they marched or were dragged to jail. The tradition of a cappella singing was so strong in Birmingham, and so well established in its churches and schools, that it naturally turned into a vehicle for protest. In the tradition of blues players and folk singers making up new verses to old tunes, freedom songs were there to be improvised, their words changed to reflect changing circumstances. Choir leader and broadcaster Nims Gay: "Now when Dr. King came I was the first director of the movement [Alabama Christian Movement for Human Rights, ACMHR] choir... I wasn't directing the choir for fame. It was for something that we needed to help us rejoice while we suffer... They [Bull Connor and the police] would come curse. Sometimes, in stress, a song would come to you like 'I ain't gonna let nobody turn me 'round. Turn me 'round. I'm gonna keep on walking, keep on watchin' walking the freedom way!' And they'd turn it around and say, 'I ain't gonna let Bull Connor turn me around. I'm gonna keep on watching'... like that old Negro spiritual used to say, 'Walk together, children, don't you get weary, there is a great meeting in the promised land.' See, that is where that came from. Songs like these helped us to get over the hill humbly that we were trying to get over... Sometime when you are burdened, a song will uplift you. It will give you strength!" The photographer Bob Adelman, on assignment for the Congress of Racial Equality, remembered, "There was a lot of singing, because it gave us courage." People were getting beaten up on the street. Parents saw their children arrested. Nims Gay: "Anything worth having is worth suffering for. We would work all day and then come home and come to church and the children would go out. I had four of my children in jail at the same time. What they did, they'd carry them out there at Rickwood Park [baseball stadium] and put them out in the field out there because the jails were filled up . . . just because a man wanted to sit down and drink a cup of coffee. That is where it all started . . . once you are at the lunch counters and all that."

Gospel music became a potent force in the civil rights struggle in Birmingham. Nims Gay remembers singing over seventy nights in a row during that fateful spring: "Everything we did, there was a song to it." And although many came to sing in Birmingham's churches, the voices that many remember were those of Dorothy Love Coates and the Gospel Harmonettes. They were at the peak of their career, producing some of the outstanding gospel recordings of the decade. Evelyn Hardy, a pianist with the original Gospel Harmonettes, said, "Dorothy was one of the greatest gospel composers," a view shared by Nims Gay: "Dorothy Love Coates right now is the foremost gospel writer the world has right now! She has written over three hundred songs . . . like so many songs, like 'Ninety Nine and Half Won't Do' . . . The Harmonettes, they went around the world. In fact they sung some of everywhere overseas . . . Yeah, Birmingham has always been alive when it comes to music, but there are always the grand voices of Erskine Hawkins and all those guys, they had to leave Birmingham to get a start . . . So many of the gospel singers, they had to leave home to get a start, to really get a foundation, but it is all said and done, Dorothy Love, she never left! She has never left home. She go around the world and come right back home." Coates refused to cross over into the commercial mainstream: "They told me that I had to stop singing gospel and cross over to make a dollar. I wouldn't do it. I decided to stay with my Maker." "I can't sell out," she told Anthony Heilbut. She remained in Birmingham during its troubles: "On nights I'd sing for the people, days I'd work for the white man" — taking part in the demonstrations, and serving her time in jail. As one civil rights worker remembered: "Mahalia sang for us on the weekends. Dot was there every day."[15]

The mass demonstrations in Birmingham continued through the summer of 1963. The black radio stations played their part in rallying teenagers to the struggle, despite the policy that their broadcasts contained "no
discussion of political or racial questions." Shelley Stewart: "I used radio
not only as an entertaining medium, but an educational medium . . . Black
radio stations owned by whites, which even today, they don't want news,
you didn't have news! White owners felt that blacks did not want news . . .
White stations felt that you shouldn't get involved in problems of voting
registration, anything of that nature. I did just the opposite! I became very
fiercely involved in every aspect of it." Shelley the Playboy and Tall Paul
White rode the airwaves with encouragement and coded exhortations to
join the marches. The hundreds of young men and woman who marched
in the demonstrations relied on the radio for information. When the historic decision was made to use schoolchildren in the demonstrations at
the end of April, the deejays spent much of that week talking on air about
the "big party" to be held on Thursday at Kelly Ingram Park. Every black
high schooler knew what this meant. In this way the civil rights movement
exploited the technological infrastructure created by the popularity of
rock 'n' roll.

As the long, hot summer of 1963 dragged on, more journalists and television reporters converged on unhappy Birmingham. Ed Boutwell acted as a
part-time reporter for the national press and television, and he often filmed
the demonstrations as they wound their way from the Kelly Ingram Park.
He usually joined in and marched with his friends in the gospel community. Often clad in steel helmets, members of the press dodged stones and
tear gas on downtown streets to capture the most important news story of
the decade. Bob Adelman saw "a brutal hatred. It was a war. Birmingham
was one of the last battles of the Civil War." Shelley Stewart found himself
literally in the middle of the conflict: "My studios were located at WENN.
We were at the corner of Fifth Avenue and Fifteenth Street. The motel, the
A. G. Gaston Motel, was next door. Kelly Ingram Park was right across
the street. My record store was at 1607 Fifth Avenue North, which faced
Kelly Ingram Park. Shelley's Record Mart. That record store was where I
broadcast during that period, out of the window I could see it . . . Many of
the Andy Youngs and the other civil rights [workers] . . . the white walkers

or the T. C. Vivians . . . people met me in the back of the store many times. Martin Luther King Jr., who I knew very well and he knew me well, we were on a first-name basis. I was involved in that! I was involved in dealing with the radio aspect. To motivate the children to get the hell out of school and hit the streets. Yes, I did it!"

After weeks and weeks of conflict the city of Birmingham repealed its segregation ordinances at the end of July. The record producer Johnny Sandlin summed up this critical juncture in segregation: "And at that time, believe me, the people that I knew, you were kind of raised that way, but after a while it didn't make any sense. Once you started thinking and especially when you realized your favorite musicians and artists, or most of them, are black." Segregation did not make sense to a generation of rock 'n' rollers who heartily embraced black music and musicians. Nor did it make sense to club owners and booking agencies who depended on African American talent. Nor did it make sense to the music industry aiming to sell records and guitars to everybody, nor to the retailers downtown who were dependent on customers of both races. Yet outright opposition to segregation did not make much sense either, in terms of personal safety and economic advancement — if you did not get beaten up by the Klan, the City of Birmingham could always take away your business license, a tactic that was used repeatedly against black businesses. There is a saying among Alabamians of a certain age that it was great to be black on a Saturday night, but it was not going to last through Sunday morning. The musicians who had black colleagues traveling and playing with them were breaking the law. The retailers who served black customers could not afford to be seen socializing with them. The kids who bopped to black bands at fraternity parties were likely to forget their integrated entertainment once the show was over. As Brian Ward points out, "The racial violence that scared the city . . . served as a salutary reminder that it would take rather more than youthful biracial enthusiasm for Elvis Presley and Little Richard to bring down Jim Crow."[16]

Judge Robert Cahill remembered that teenagers in Birmingham in the 1960s were in "a very segregated society: you didn't see blacks, and segregation didn't merit thought . . . You had a social plane or a political plane where you had everybody publicly either contesting the civil rights programs or fighting [black] people going into Woolworth's or what have you. Then you had the music and most of the kids during that time probably had no opinion on race relations . . . I don't think that color meant as much to teens as maybe it did to the adults . . . I don't think that any of us had strong feeling—maybe a lot of us did after we got out of high school and into college. Probably many of the students had maids who were black or yardmen that were black and many of them still do . . . Even though you had white music and black music I think the kids here in the '60s they liked the best [music] whether or not it was a black or white band that was playing. I don't think color meant as much to the teens as maybe it did to the adults . . . I think that the key was that the teenagers were not out in the streets fighting for civil rights. They probably were not even thinking about it. It [the unrest] had not crossed the mountain [from downtown to the affluent suburbs], but they were listening to the music and they would go down to Newberry's, which was a downtown department store with a big record-buying area buying the music just as the black kids were buying too. They were buying it down there too. They had these little stalls in there with the 45s where you could listen, and everybody did it."

Many Birmingham teens loved black music and admired its stars. They also remembered their servants fondly: "I know people who will talk about their maid as a second mother." But the friendly interaction with maid or yard man did not extend beyond the quiet homes in leafy suburbs far from the historic drama unfolding downtown. The only newspaper in the world that did not treat the demonstrations as big news was in Birmingham. Comfortably numb teenagers agreed with their parents that the conflict downtown was the work of the outside forces who were upsetting the "southern way of life." The difficult decision to publicly take sides risked economic or violent retribution. Club owner Bob Cain looks back regretfully: "There were some very good black musicians that were in town. I really questioned whether I could mix and match like it is being done today and maintain the popularity. A lot of people were just not ready for that at that time. I never dared to take the step and be the first one. I can think of two or three guys that are excellent, that I would have loved to have around. It was just at the time where it was not the thing to really do. I would love to be doing it now. Just to be able to put musicians together and not worry about that."

The promise of rock 'n' roll was euphoric but not political; it created a world of interracial daydreaming—desegregation in the privacy of one's bedroom or college dorm but not on the streets, where it mattered. Birmingham's high school rock 'n' rollers had found out that attitudes about race were a big part of the generation gap. As Ed Boutwell noted, "There were a lot of people my age who were just quietly standing by with their heads in their hands, wringing their hands, let me say, because their parents were raising all this racist, white racist thing." Yet sitting quietly standing by was keeping Jim Crow in power, and it was this attitude of white liberals (including Birmingham's musicians and music lovers) that was a barrier to racial equality, as Martin Luther King pointed out in his *Letter from Birmingham Jail.*

Birmingham's high schools illustrated the schizophrenia of race and music in Alabama; they were hotbeds of unrest that were providing many of the troops fighting the battles for and against segregation. Reverend Fred Shuttlesworth of ACHMR called for the integration of Birmingham's schools after the Supreme Court's *Brown v. Board of Education* decision (1954), but when he tried enrolling his child at Philips High School in 1957, he was severely beaten. The threat of desegregation often led white students to boycott classes and take to the streets to taunt and attack their opponents. The National States Rights organization visited Birmingham's schools to promote and coordinate protests against integration. Robert Cahill: "We were separated from this [racial conflict at John Carroll High School]. In fact, we had one incident where they put all the senior boys in front of the school because in one of the schools in West End they were having a riot and they were fearful that the students were going to come to our school to get us to leave and join them in their riot, but I don't think any of us had any real strong feelings." Bob Corley recounts a musical tradition at Woodlawn High School (when it was all white) that unashamedly used blackface in the fine old Alabama minstrel show tradition. The Warblers put on their minstrel show every year, and had done that as far back as anyone could remember, yet at the same time Woodlawn was full of aspiring rock 'n' rollers who were doing their best to emulate their black idols every weekend.

The more the violence continued, the more segregation did not make sense to many liberal whites in Birmingham, but the more dangerous it became to stand up against it. The climax came in September 1963 with the senseless murder of four young girls in the bombing of the Sixteenth Street Baptist church — an act of brutal and calculated violence that was reported worldwide. Speaking for that music-loving generation of the 1960s, Robert Cahill said this "shattering experience" brought to an end all those rock 'n' roll hopes of one nation united under a groove: "Maybe we lost our innocence there. It was the worst thing that could ever happen . . . Everyone stayed in their homes, no one went out! I remember the mayor was on television and he was crying. The National Guard was brought in, there were soldiers on downtown streets and there was a lot of rioting in the black areas . . . I think that the children of the '60s were robbed of their innocence by outside forces that we had no control over. Kids in the 1960s were just going to listen to the music, black or white, and they would have gotten along. The church bombing just kind of shattered it . . . The civil rights movement caused us to maybe grow up more." Condemned by Martin Luther King as "one of the most vicious and tragic crimes ever perpetrated against humanity," an attack as inhumane as this could not be ignored: "Many people just kind of went into their homes and said, 'We don't know what to say.'"

Now that Birmingham was acknowledged as a center of racism in the United States, shame was now the overriding civic emotion there, in the words of Diane McWhorter. In popular culture "Birmingham" became the accepted shorthand for violence and hate in music, poems, films, and concerts. At the Woodstock Festival at the end of the '60s, Ritchie Havens made reference to "the Birmingham war." John Coltrane composed "Alabama" in outrage over the bombing in October 1963. John Lee Hooker started his "Birmingham Blues" with "I ain't going down to Birmingham by myself . . . get me a plane, and fly over Birmingham / Drop me a bomb, keep flyin'."[17]

CHAPTER SEVEN

The Beatles Are Coming!

ooking at the first sixty years of rock 'n' roll in Birmingham, nothing can match the impact of Beatlemania on the bands and their teenage audience. It transformed the world of popular music and inspired the creation of countless new groups. As Ed Boutwell said, it was the difference between night and day and nothing was quite the same after the Fab Four conquered America. The year 1963 was a very bad one for the city, and like the rest of the nation, Birmingham's youth took the assassination of President John F. Kennedy especially hard. He had talked to them of hope and empowerment and made them feel that they had a special part to play in the coming decade, but this vision ended in violence in Dallas. Richard Manley remembered that the two months after the assassination was "a sad, scary time for thirteen-year-olds like me."[1]

Then came the Beatles. First were the brief clips on the nightly news showing the screaming girls, and then "I Want to Hold Your Hand" was released and there was no escaping it. Ed Boutwell: "'I Want to Hold Your Hand.' It was gigantic! The Beatles rock was classy: pop music with a rock 'n' roll beat to it. Beautiful stuff! Pretty. But that isn't rock 'n' roll." Their record company, Capitol, mounted a huge publicity campaign to prepare American audiences for them. Five million stickers were distributed with the message "The Beatles are Coming!" No one including the Beatles and their management could have anticipated the wild scenes when they arrived at the newly named Kennedy Airport in New York in February 1964. "At the airport you could really feel that something important was happening," said one of the thousands of fans waiting for the Beatles.[2] From then on the pandemonium and media blitz was so immense that a new word was coined to describe the frenzied months that followed: "Beatlemania."

The Beatles entered the mainstream of American entertainment through the same technological gateway, and in the same explosive manner, as Elvis Presley. People had grown close to their television sets during the winter of 1963/1964 as the nation sat glued to their screens during the drama that unfolded in Dallas. The Beatles made four appearances on *The Ed Sullivan Show* in February 1964. The first appearance garnered the largest television audience ever counted up to that time and hit American teenagers right between the eyes. Guitarist Jay Willoughby of the Newboys and Willbillies: "I was like four years old and as you can tell it is like a Beatles museum around here. I was about four or five the first time I saw them and for some reason I just went berserk. I thought it was the coolest thing that I had ever seen in my life. I more or less decided then that was what I wanted to do." So did millions of other kids, sitting transfixed before glowing screens. Many were immediately and totally captivated from the first time they saw them. Bob Cahill: "Yeah, oh yeah! I thought that it was great! I was personally a little offended by the hair because, well, the rock 'n' roll days for me was where everybody wore the same color suits and you had your hair slicked back and short. And here these guys looked like they needed a haircut."

The Beatles had a special appeal to the young. Guitarist Rick Kurtz: "I guess I would have to start with the Beatles. I got my first Beatles album when I was in the second grade, *Meet the Beatles*. Jay Willoughby: "The Beatles had such a big influence on me. I love the songs. I love the melodies. I basically did not own a non-Beatles record until I was probably twelve or thirteen." Marc Phillips of Hotel: "I started taking piano lessons when I was eight. The Beatles came out and I had to be a Beatle you know, it was just one of those things. I wanted to grow my hair long, play the guitar." Guitarist Wayne Perkins: "I mean, I started playing when I was six years old. Got really serious at age ten. I knew then what I wanted to do, and I sort of really practiced my heart out 'til I was about fourteen or so. My interest in music was from listening to records. I was big into the Beatles and all that." Doug Lee of Dogwood and Hotfoot: "I guess like most of us our age, it probably had more to do with the Beatles than anything else. I guess I had picked up a guitar and started learning a few little things. Then when the Beatles busted loose, it was like everybody else had to learn to play and had to take steps being in a band . . . I guess the whole Beatles thing is what really got me started." Bobby Horton of the folk group Three on a String: "I basically started playing in grammar school, I think in the fourth grade. I started with the trumpet . . . when I graduated from the eighth grade I got a banjo. I saw my grandfather, so that meant I had to play banjo too. I borrowed a guitar from somebody and I just started playing on that. Then the Beatles came to America and I got hooked on that. Then I played rock 'n' roll." David Burke of Lost in the Mall: "In 1962 I got a snare drum and a cymbal. I was six years old . . . I started out, I guess, when the Beatles hit the scene, and before I played, of course. The Beatles are the one."

Charlie McCulloh was impressed with the effect the Beatles had on their female fans: "Well, like most people my age, the spectacle of forty thousand wet-pantied women screaming at the Beatles was not lost on me. I started playing guitar in high school like everyone else and played in high school bands." Jim Burford: "The Beatles were big back then, and that was probably one of the main reasons that I started playing the guitar, because I thought that if you could play the guitar you could get some pussy." Many of the young men who picked up guitars had girls on their mind and the Beatles proved beyond any doubt that being a musician had sex appeal. The young Bryan Price lived next door to some "great-looking girls . . . so even at that age I knew, Wow, these are great-looking girls, because every day they are out in bikinis laying in the sun! I remember one day for some reason we go into their bedroom to hang out, I walked in there and there were life-sized posters of the Beatles, those big huge closet doors and there were like two guys to each door . . . I had no idea who they were. I remember them laughing at me and thinking, God, if they like these guys well enough to put them up on their door, this must be okay."

There was something about the Beatles, their sound and the way they looked, that struck the young as different. John Hall felt their music was "amazing, not like anything I had ever heard before." Jeff Tyler: "The Beatles blew the world wide open with their music." Asked to describe his music he replied, "Hopefully mine, but it does have a lot of Beatles in it." Rudy Johnson: "The songs that really impressed me were anything the Beatles did because of the harmonies. Harmonies that just tore me up! I mean, it was just amazing."

The continued popularity of their songs, many beloved, some immortal, has maintained their influence on young musicians. Orenda Fink and Maria Taylor met in the 1980s while attending the Alabama School of Fine Arts in downtown Birmingham: "She saw me playing guitar in the common room at school and said, 'Let's start a band.' We were doing stuff that sounded kind of folky. We are far from that now, but that's how we started. I think that is how we cultivated a lot of our harmony . . . We all listened to the Beatles from day one. We still listen to the Beatles every day." Charles Arndt of Plaid Camels: "I would say the Beatles was always a huge influence just because it was my favorite band and it was everybody's favorite band." Judy Ranelli of the indie bands the Ticks and Vacation Bible School: "When I was in high school I listened to a tape of *Rubber Soul* and *Revolver* so much that I memorized the key of every song . . . I knew every song by heart. I could dream those songs."

The Beatles never played in Birmingham, and probably never wanted to because its recent conflict was well reported in England; this was one of the places strongly linked with segregation and violence (like Dallas, Texas) that they expressly wanted to avoid. While hardly anybody in Birmingham had heard of the band at the time of the *Ed Sullivan* broadcasts, some local musicians had already got the word. Tommy Roe often played Birmingham and Muscle Shoals from his base in Atlanta, and had toured with the Beatles in England and got a firsthand glimpse of the devastating effect they had on audiences. Johnny Sandlin: "I remember being over at Muscle Shoals and hearing about it. At that time, Tommy Roe, that guy from Atlanta . . . had been to England because he had that big hit record, and he was telling everybody about that band over there, and I remember there were some ads in *Billboard* at the time, and it just had like this haircut and it said 'They Are Coming' or something. It was a real big build-up to it. So we were all real curious about it." The Beatles' juggernaut picked up speed in 1964: two American tours, which brought their music in person to over 350,000 people, four top-selling singles, and the wildly popular film *A Hard Day's Night*.

In 1964 and 1965 their music dominated radio, and the mayhem of their concerts was widely reported in the press and seen on television. At first they played the big cities, but subsequent tours brought them into the Midwest and South, and this raised expectations in Alabama that they might make an appearance there. Cathy Fievet and her friends were typical fans. They walked along the halls of John Carroll High School singing 'I Want to Hold Your Hand,' and went home to bedrooms plastered with pictures of John, Paul, George, and Ringo. Cathy was not the only one praying for the Beatles to come to Birmingham. A performance from the greatest rock band ever meant a measure of recognition for a town that had become tired of being the whipping boy for segregation. The Beatles brought joy to their fans in Birmingham and also offered a hope of redemption for America's most segregated city: a hope that at least its cultural excommunication could be reversed.

Brian Epstein had created an image for the Beatles that stressed their working-class backgrounds (even though it was not quite true), and their public appearances reinforced their image as ordinary kids just like those in the audience. The more American teenagers got to know their idols, the more they realized that they were not that much different from them. Fans in unfashionable cities like Birmingham learned that Liverpool was far different from the mythical London portrayed on PBS's *Masterpiece Theatre* or in Broadway hits like *Mary Poppins*. Beatles fans in Birmingham felt a special affinity for Liverpool and their famous sons: "We thought of Liverpool as a dirty coal town like Birmingham had been in the past." Aspiring musicians recognized a little bit of themselves and their own experiences in the lives of the Beatles: "I saw them as working class, working class like me . . . They had a little band that got big."[3] This was true. The Beatles had begun as a garage band, jamming for fun in their bedrooms (few British houses had garages) and then playing small clubs and parties, just like the hundreds of guitar bands in Birmingham. While Elvis came across as a magnificent loner, the Beatles had always been a group, a union of four equals in which the sum greatly exceeded the parts, and their example took hold of the nascent garage band movement of the early 1960s and led to thousands of new bands being formed in their image. Doug Lee concluded: "But I don't think I had any notions about what a musician was until the Beatles thing exploded and being a musician was cool." Greg Hassler of Beat Feet summed it up: "The Beatles did it! You got to do it like the Beatles!"

Forbes and Nuncie's were doing frantic business, and so were the guitar teachers, whose lessons were booked from early morning until late at night. Every band made up a business card — a band card — with their name, an idea of the music they played, and a contact phone number. These were given to prospective clients, bar owners, girls, and anyone else who might be interested. At Forbes Piano store downtown "there was a row of show-cases on the other side where the guitars and all that other stuff [would be] and there was another row. You could bring your band card in and they would tape it to the glass from underneath. Nuncie's did the same thing too. There were cards all the way around, and I mean, there had to be at least two hundred to three hundred in Birmingham at that time. There were garage bands everywhere," remembered Frank Ranelli. Guitar music was being made all over the city, by the Rockin' Rebellions, the Distortions, Rooster and the Townsmen, the Hard Times, the Wild Things, the Indi-viduals, the Jerks, the Rubber Band, the Companion Band, the Strangers, the Reflections, the Brood, the Gents, the Vikings, the Torquays, the Wild Vibrations, and hundreds more. Many of them went through several name changes. Doug Lee started playing in a high school band called the Lobos: "We looked [the name] up in a Spanish dictionary, but then we changed it and this was the same basic group of guys that changed from the Lobos to the Odd Number — we used that name for a long time. Bunkie Ander-son has still got an Odd Number card! He used to have it up on the wall at Highland Music with a bunch of others. Then the next name we used was the Mourning Fog." Jim Burford: "Hell, there were a thousand bands all over." Ed Boutwell recorded so many of them that he has lost track of all their names. Even in the twenty-first century, the diligent collectors of Birmingham rock records are often surprised by discoveries of new groups that were previously unknown.

Rooster and the Townsmen were formed in 1963 in Birmingham by Charles "Rooster" Gallagher and Ricky Hester. They were joined by Gary Quattlebaum (bass), Tony Ardovino (drums), and Al Pinion (organ) and had a brass section of Durwood Bright, Steve Yessick, and Bruce Russell. Horns also played an important part in the sound of the Torquays, assem-bled in 1964 with Dale Aston on vocals and lead guitar, Steve Salord on sax, Eugene Hayes on drums, Wendell Colbert on bass, and Barry Bicknell on trumpet; and in the Rubber Band, formed in 1965 with Johnny Townshend on vocals and sax and John Wyker on trumpet.

During Beatlemania only the Beatles and their sound could satisfy American teenagers. Motown Records had supplied a great deal of material for the Beatles and some of its performers lost part of their white audience to them. Singer-songwriter Alice Bargeron: "I was really, really into the Beatles. When I was very young I was into a lot of the Motown stuff. I went from loving Motown to loving the Beatles as a kid, then went into the British wave — the Dave Clark Five and that kind of thing . . . It's funny though, certain bands that I will hear now and I would remember loving them and now think that is cheesy, I cannot believe I liked them. But I will put on the Beatles and think, this is the coolest stuff that I have ever heard." As American bands scrambled to reassess their music in the light of the success of the Beatles, more English groups — Gerry and the Pace-makers, Herman's Hermits, the Searchers — arrived in the United States. The Liverpool sound was in and British groups were cool. American garage bands now cultivated the Liverpool Sound and the distinctive "mop-top" haircut, along with anything else which might associate them with the Fab Four. Mac Rudd: "David Keller had this group called the Preachers. I recall one time when David and a deejay named Steve Norris set a scene at the airport in Birmingham and the Preachers came walking off an airplane with those wigs on just like the Beatles and they tried to gather a crowd there to greet them as if they were the Beatles."

Birmingham's garage bands were wondering if they should start sound-ing like the Beatles. Clearly the tried-and-tested instrumental formula — always popular with guitar bands — had no place in a music scene now heavily slanted toward harmonies and catchy lyrics. The Premiers were one of the most popular local bands at the time, but they could not handle those Beatles harmonies, said Pat Thornton. So they stayed with their be-loved R&B songs by Bo Diddley, Jimmy Reed, and Lee Dorsey. But they found that their audience wanted the Beatles. Nowadays Thornton laughs and says, "The Beatles put us out of business!" Many local groups had also been following the route of rhythm and blues, turning it into a harder and brassier version of the watered-down sound of the British groups. But with the advent of Beatlemania they found themselves, in the words of Ed Boutwell, "chopped off at the knees ... The Beatles wiped us all out," and they did it very quickly. What the listening public wanted was more melody and romantic sentiment in the lyrics. Birmingham bands responded with a softening of their sound, an embrace of pop tunes, more harmonizing, and the purchase of Beatle wigs. They even went out and bought the equipment the Beatles popularized. Ed Boutwell: "All those bands started buying those amplifiers [Vox AC15s]. They were horrible-sounding amps: low power, funky toy speakers in them. But that was how the Beatles sounded."

Most Birmingham bands incorporated some Beatles songs in their playlist, and some of them, like the Rockin' Rebellions, recorded a cover of a Beatles song ("Run for Your Life"). Many of them, such as the Hard Times, formed by Michael Melton and his brother Ronnie with some of their friends from Woodlawn High School, practiced their harmonies, and others moved into lush production numbers, backed by strings, just like the Beatles had done. Of all the Beatles soundalikes in Birmingham, probably the Torquays came closest to duplicating the Liverpool Sound. They took their name from a town in England. Their "While I'm Away" took the basic idea of "All My Loving" — a song for a girl left behind while the singer was on the road — and added the basic two-part harmonies and backing vocals, which immediately conjured up the Beatles. When Lennon and McCartney began to stretch their songwriting to cover more abstract and imaginative themes, the Torquays followed them with songs like "Pineapple Moon," with its nonsense lyrics and psychedelic sound, which brought to mind the influential *Sgt. Pepper's Lonely Hearts Club Band* LP.

Some Birmingham bands underwent personnel changes as the direction of their music changed. The Ramrods lasted until 1964, when three members joined with some musicians from the Webbs to form the James Gang. They moved from a stripped-down guitar-and-drums sound to a lusher, romantic sound, with strings backing up the vocals. The Counts had played all over the state and considered themselves pretty good musicians, and like other garage bands who played R&B, the Counts were not too impressed with the Beatles, as Ned Bibb recalled: "When we first heard the Beatles, the Counts were very successful with their horns and all. We didn't think much of the Beatles when we first heard them. We thought that they were way behind us in time. They played everything in easy keys.

We appreciated their harmony at that time. We had never heard anything like it. We sung a few background things, but never harmony. We didn't really appreciate it or think much of their musicianship until later on. They were tremendous and their songs were tremendous."

Like many British rock bands in the 1960s, the Beatles had got their musical education from listening to American records, such as the hits from Motown and Stax. Their 1964 repertoire spanned Chuck Berry, the Isley Brothers, the Miracles, and soul singer Arthur Alexander. They heard something in Alexander's music that moved them, and they covered several of his songs, including "Anna (Go to Him)," "Soldier of Love," and "A Shot of Rhythm and Blues." This latter song was probably on Paul McCartney's mind when he described the debt the Beatles owed to black music —"your B sides, all the shots of rhythm and blues" that inspired them. The African American guitarist Eric Dover talked about his influences: "Any one of the Beatles, they were classic. They ripped things off, believe it or not. Everyone has kind of ripped off everybody, so it is kind of a moot point." As a teenager "I moved to Birmingham and played in various cover bands and played acoustic duo stuff with some friends. We would do Beatles songs and Simon and Garfunkel and Kinks and that would be for little or no money." The Counts spoke for many Birmingham bands when they said, "We didn't like much of anything unless it was a black artist," but by 1964 the Counts — for all their musical accomplishments — had begun to sound outdated and the band was dissolved. Ned, Bobby, and Robert started the Distortions, added Zach Zachary on keyboards, and tried as hard as they could to sound like the Beatles: "The Beatles had a tremendous impact on the Distortions. They were the cause of us becoming the Distortions." They started to grow their hair in the distinctive mop-top style, and Ned tried his hand at writing a Beatles song. "Can You Tell" had the familiar harmonies and some chord changes that he liked from "She Loves You."

Rock and Roll as Big Business

The Beatles proved to the record companies that rock music was not going to peter out as quickly as all the other teenage fads. It not only grew more appealing and more profitable during Beatlemania, it also became institutionalized, part of the fabric of American social life instead of being just a teenage diversion. In the 1960s more businesses were using live guitar bands to attract young customers. Department stores, amusement parks, and record retailers were hiring garage bands to promote themselves. Loveman's Department store put on a "youth week" bringing in Freddy Cannon and the Gants as the main attraction and backing them with two local bands, Rooster and the Townsmen, and the Rockin' Rebellions, who also played for fashion shows depicting "The London Look." Frank Ranelli: "Before school started every year, Loveman's and Pizitz downtown used to have these big deals for going back to school. It was kind of the deal where you get the kids down there to shop and get their parents down there to shop for school clothes. They would book up-and-coming bands. I remember going down there and they would play a concert on the second floor." The British Invasion was good for all number of businesses and it was taking rock music out of the armory shows and smoky nightclubs and placing it on Main Street USA.

Downtown Birmingham in the 1960s had several entertainment venues along Twenty-First Street, known as "The Strip," and a grouping of hotels for the convention trade between Second and Fifth Avenues, known as "amusement alley." Most of them are gone now: the Bankhead, Thomas Jefferson, Molton, Guest House, Downtowner, Essex House, Tutwiler, and City Center. Each of them contained lounges where the obligatory and much-maligned lounge acts grooved around pianos. The old Parliament House on Fourth Ave South had three such lounges for "our parade of stars," and across Twentieth Street were restaurants that featured live music, such as Michaels. The Starlight Lounge was a large venue opposite the Federal Building, with seating for about 180 people. At weekends during the football season it was so crowded that customers would dance on the tables — "football weekends you couldn't get in." Bryan's Lounge on Fifth Avenue North claimed a special link to Birmingham, England, during the heyday of the swinging '60s. It advertised the longest bar and the largest dance floor in town, with Wayne Woodard and the Apollos providing the music. Bryan's hosted a miniskirt contest every Thursday, and in keeping with the spirit of the times, the shortest skirt naturally won. Watching half-dressed women was a major pastime of the adult audience downtown, and striptease was an important fixture in the bar scene. When the *Birmingham News* carried an article on life after dark in the city, strippers were included along with postal workers, policemen, and janitors. The Boom Boom Room, the Pussy Cat a-Go-Go, the Patio Lounge, and Gulas's Blue Note on Fifth Avenue competed for "the hottest strip act in town." Scantily dressed girls could also be leered at in the Inn Club on Third Avenue and Fourteenth Street, and they all performed to live music.

There were venues known for their good music and relaxed attitude toward teenage high spirits, such as the Kaleidoscope Club in Bessemer (1629 Fourth Avenue North), the Upstairs Club at 117 Twenty-First Street North downtown, and PJ's across the street from the Parliament House. The Five o'Clock Club (on Second Avenue and Seventeenth Street) was named for the late hours it stayed open; downtown entertainment went on all night during the 1960s, with venues often advertising their music lasting from 9 p.m. to 3 a.m. Bob Cahill: "I can remember one night at the Five o'Clock Club and we were in there listening to a band, I think it was a black band, and the police came in. Well, we were underaged, and all of sudden my buddy Mike said, 'Grab a towel: we are washing dishes.' His daddy owned a restaurant, and I said 'Why?' and he said, 'The police are here!' So the owner comes back and asks us very quickly why we are here and we had to tell him: 'Well, if you want to go to jail for letting minors in here drinking, then turn us in. Otherwise let us wash dishes for free!' So when the police came, he escorted us out with our dishrags."

The longest-lived and most popular downtown music venue was the Cane Break established by musician Bob Cain in the mid-'60s. Starting out as the Bob Cain Club on Morris Avenue, it had moved uptown to Fourteenth Avenue at Nineteenth Street North by the end of the decade. The Cane Break dominated entertainment downtown for much of the 1960s: "It was just fun. It was one of those things where we were in the right place at the right time. Everything just seemed to fall into your lap. I had my choice of all the better musicians who came through town. I got to call all the shots musically and we would basically play to the crowd. We played dance music to the crowd and it did not really matter to us as long as the performance was good, what style of music it was." Bob Cain kept a core of first-class musicians around him: Kenny Wallace on bass, Wayne

Brown on guitar, and Barry Gilmore on drums, and over the years numerous local musicians played for him. "I guess in that span of time, there must have been thirty different musicians that went through the band," Cain recalled. Although Bob Cain's first love was rhythm and blues, the group knew every popular song around, and no evening would go by without several renditions of "A Bowl of Butter Beans," a song about southern culture and food loosely based on "Just a Closer Walk with Thee," a familiar gospel tune. Gary Sizemore: "Bob Cain opened the Cane Break. It was the hot club, packed all the time. That's where the Alabama football team would go after the games. He had a good band."

The music might be down-home, but the atmosphere was formal — the standard in downtown Birmingham in the 1960s. "Coat and ties are in order" announced the Cane Break's adverts. But Beatlemania was bringing some changes into the entertainment industry. Rudy Johnson: "When the Beatles came along the music changed so drastically after that, for young people the generation gap hit like tremendously! Because my dad and my folks were going down to Bob Cain's and the Cane Break and all that stuff... They were really into nightclubs, and they were doing the Dean Martin–type deals while I was sitting at home listening to the Beatles." Wayne Perkins: "Well, Bob Cain had everything nailed down, but he wasn't appealing to younger audiences, and you know, people were getting turned on to Hendrix and Cream and all this and he is into a 'Bowl of Butter Beans,' you know."

The popularity of the Beatles made teenage guitar bands more marketable, and amateur musicians could expect to take home much more than the five to fifteen dollars a night that was the going rate established in the 1950s. Pat Thornton: "I earned $140 a weekend, more than my dad did working a whole week at U.S. Steel." Frank Ranelli: "I was working at the grocery store and all, and then I quit that too because I was going out weekends and I was making maybe $75 to $100. You could not make that working all week. Minimum wage was like $1.40 then. So I went to Nuncie's and bought a brand-new set of drums." There was money to be made all down the line, from singing the songs to writing them. After high school junior Dan Penn made $700 for writing a song that Conway Twitty picked up, he decided: "It's either the music business or nothing. I went to Florence.

I knew Rick Hall had a studio, and he asks me to write at $25 a week. So it's writing songs for Rick Hall, or working at Vernon's garment plant for $40." Bluesman Topper Price remembered how the money improved after Beatlemania: "I was with Johnny Winter and he signed [a record deal] for $600,000 and that was totally over the top! Steve Miller signed with Capitol for a $30,000 bonus, biggest bonus that had ever been paid anybody . . . There was a lot of money it, and you are talking about the Beatles."

Radio stations were playing more rock music than ever. WVOK and WYDE competed with WSGN to be the major rock destination for listeners in Birmingham. Both had very popular high-profile disc jockeys: Dan Brennan and Joe Rumore at WVOK and Dave Roddy and Doug Layton at WYDE. At the end of the 1960s there were at least ten AM stations in Birmingham and five new FM stations: WAPI, WVSV, WCRT, WJLN, and WBRC. There was more broadcast time as several of the smaller AM stations extended their operating hours. More radio stations meant more sponsored shows and live broadcasts, and more disc jockeys competing to break new records from local groups. There was such an abundance of live music in Birmingham that the radio stations began to sponsor "battles of the bands," reviving a tradition that went all the way back to the big band era of the 1930s. Boutwell Auditorium would be booked for a day, and guitar bands would play from early in the morning to late at night. Usually around twenty garage bands competed, and each played three songs. The voting was not very scientific; Duke Rumore would cup his ear as he leaned forward to catch the crowd's applause and make the important decisions. The field was whittled down to three bands, then two bands, and finally a winner. Steve Lowry's band was called the Echoes: "They had this all-day marathon, where twenty bands played three songs apiece. This was at the Opporto Armory." The Echoes made the final two, but eventually lost: "Years later they told me. The final two points that made the other band win instead of us, was they had matching outfits and we didn't. We were just devastated." For the winners the prize was not merely some cash and bragging rights over the other bands, but the opportunity to move on to larger regional competitions, local television shows and perhaps a contract with a record company. Rooster and the Townsmen won a memorable battle at Boutwell Auditorium that was sponsored by WVOK. Frank Ranelli of

the Wild Things: "We threw our name in the hat and we drug ourselves
down to Boutwell one time for WVOK, and they had a battle of the bands
and they started like at 10 that morning. The damn thing went on all day
long, and we were the third to last band. We hung out there all day long.
The last band to play was Rooster and the Townsmen and they won . . .
They won all this equipment, and I don't think they even got any money,
and they won a recording contract."

Instead of sponsoring small shows at local auditoriums, the local radio
stations were getting involved in promoting much larger affairs headed by
nationally known acts. WVOK led the way with its "Shower of Stars," which
began in 1961 with a show that included the Everly Brothers, Brenda Lee,
and Johnny Tillotson. WVOK formed a circuit with its sister stations in
Montgomery and Florida and took the Shower of Stars around the Southeast. A show that had started with twenty or so people in its studio for a
live performance was now held at Legion Field. Such was the popularity
of the "Showers" that at least half of the fifteen thousand tickets for each
performance were purchased even before the bill was finalized. The 1964
Shower of Stars reflected the British Invasion with a bill that could only
have worked in the 1960s: the Rolling Stones, the Beach Boys, and the
Animals.

Local bands battled it out for the best gigs and the most exposure. The
Southeast Battle of Bands went on for three weeks at Oporto Armory and
the Rockin' Rebellions won. Ross Gagliano started the Rockin' Rebellions
around 1966. Henry Lovoy was the vocalist and behind him were Rick
Fortenberry and Ronald Barbee (guitars), Ross Gagliano (drums), and
Donald Barbee (keyboards). Henry: "Out of sixty-seven bands we won first
place and Dan Brennan of WVOK played our new record and asked if we
would be on the Winter, Spring, Fall, and Summer Shower of Stars Show,
which were rock 'n' roll shows playing at those intervals. We played with all
national acts of America and England." The Rockin' Rebellions shared the
bill with the British band the Who during their first, and legendary, tour of
the United States. The Who's presence in Alabama was literally explosive,
with fireworks ignited on stage and in Birmingham hotel rooms by the
Who's maniac drummer, Keith Moon.[4] The Rockin' Rebellions were in
awe of the Who, and playing with them was something they would always

remember. The sales of their new record "Any Way the Wind Blows" kept building as they traveled around the South. They saw their record race up the WVOK chart, cheek to jowl with the latest Beatles or Beach Boys hit. "Any Way the Wind Blows" ended up selling over twenty-five thousand copies — no mean feat for a local band in the 1960s. The radio stations in Birmingham compiled their own hit charts, combining local groups with national acts, thus bringing the jubilation of rock 'n' roll success to a garage band. This was one of the ways in which radio gave teenagers a sense that they were part of the rock 'n' roll movement rather than just being mere listeners. A popular record by a local group — one that you might have seen or one that might have someone in it you knew from school — could individualize the listening experience and make it especially memorable — the way the Hard Times' "Let Love Come Between Us" seeped into the memories of the summer of 1967.

The Great Beatles Boycott

The closest the Beatles came to Birmingham was a performance in Atlanta during their third American tour in 1965. Sharon Fisher, her mother and her brothers, and other lucky Beatles fans with tickets drove over to Birmingham's greatest competitor and the outright winner in the struggle to become *the* city of the New South. In 1950 the population of these two cities was almost the same, at around 330,000, but from then on Atlanta pulled ahead dramatically. The city "too busy to hate" was growing rapidly, and the Beatles concert was held in the impressive new baseball stadium built to house the newly acquired Atlanta Braves — Atlanta was now in the major leagues. (Birmingham's Barons had left town, and the historic Rickwood Field would not to return to the Southern League until 1981.) Sharon was seated near the third base line, where she could clearly see the backs of the Fab Four. The sound of thirty-five thousand screaming fans was something never to be forgotten. Sharon was in tears: "It meant a lot to me, the Beatles performing for me," which shows how intimately the Beatles connected with their fans.

In 1966 came the rumor that Memphis was scheduled on the next Beatles tour. The news spread rapidly as it was passed from one Beatles fan to another: they were to play two shows in the Mid South Coliseum on August 19. Tickets were only $5.50. Seeing the Beatles, live and in person, was a monumental event. Larry Fivert saved his money, waited for hours, and finally got the treasured tickets in his hand. As a visually impaired person, he could not see the Beatles, but he loved the music and had learned how to play some of their songs on his guitar. His sister Cathy — in the best spirit of elder sisters — got her tickets free from a relative who won them on the radio and drove to the show in her brand-new Ford Mustang, while Larry took the bus there and back on the day of the concert — a pilgrimage to see the Beatles. Frank Ranelli had a chance to go to the concert but turned it down. He didn't want to go, but his father insisted: "So I went. I would not take anything for the experience now … When I got there the whole place was packed and the whole concert you could not hear anything: All those girls screaming!" Frank came home and decided he had to play in a band. For two long hours before the Beatles came on stage, the teenage audience "shrieked and screamed" through the hapless opening acts. One hundred policemen and a four-foot-high fence guarded the stage. Cathy sat seven rows from the front, right below John Lennon, and realized that her prayers had been answered. Yet she was growing more and more uneasy at the screaming frenzy of the girls around her. She could see the Beatles but hardly hear them. Her brother was seated way up high in back of the auditorium. The screaming and fainting continued throughout the performance. Cathy found it a sobering experience; she loved the Beatles but was uncomfortable at all the hysteria; she remembered that she could hardly hear herself think, let alone enjoy the sound of the Fab Four just a few feet away from her. Nevertheless, she and her brother went home that night convinced that this had been one of the highlights of their 1960s.

Just before the band left England in the summer of 1966, John Lennon was quoted as saying that the Beatles were more popular than Jesus Christ. He later retracted this statement, and nothing more was heard about it until a few American radio stations picked up the story. Chief among them was Birmingham's own WAQY, "Wacky" Radio, which starred Tommy Charles and Doug Layton after they left WYDE. They took the credit for "blowing the whistle" on Lennon after they read the interview in the American publication *Datebook*. They were part of a wave of denunciations that spread across the Deep South and led to thirty radio stations banning the Beatles' records from the air. Tommy Charles and Doug Layton fanned the flames, calling on their listeners to stand up against "a group of foreign singers that strike at the very basis of our existence as God-fearing patriotic citizens" and to bring their Beatles records and souvenirs to fourteen collection points around the city to be burned or shredded. This was not the first time for an organized boycott of records in the South; Louis Armstrong suffered one when he dared speak out against the opposition to the desegregation of schools at Little Rock in 1957.[5] Deejay John Ed Willoughby, one of Charles's longtime associates: "The Beatles incident did come up, and has been the most exaggerated... and I know what an opportunist Tommy was... Charles knew better than anybody. Stir it up! When Lennon made that statement, which I really don't think meant we are bigger than Jesus Christ... but what I am saying is, they took it to mean that Lennon said it with arrogance. Like he was proud of it... But Charles jumped on it: 'Oh, this guy thinks he is bigger than Jesus Christ and all that.' I don't know that he was the first, but he was the first to say 'Let's bust up all their records, let's burn them, let's do this, let's don't play another Beatles record' and all that!" Many adults now considered the Beatles subversive. Porter Landrum: "Back then with the conservative attitude of the country... even my parents thought that the Beatles were a communist prop to derail the morals of American youth; and when you go back to listen to it, it was love songs, peace, love, harmony, and happiness." Beatles fans often had a hard time in Christian families, who resented the ungodly influence exercised by four scruffy musicians. Ken King's mother cried when she realized she had lost her baby to the Beatles. Significantly, the attack on the Beatles was not just aimed at their ungodliness but was also directed against foreigners, "anti-Americans," a thread that was being subtly followed in the *Birmingham News* when it announced the rise of new American pop singers as a welcome sign that the British Invasion was over. "The Band That Changed Everything" had many enemies in a town that hated change.

Tommy Charles had little reason to view the Beatles favorably. When "I Want to Hold Your Hand" was first released, he had panned it and rashly predicted that the band would never make it. He was wrong, and his own career as playboy crooner naturally suffered as the Beatles became popular. Charles and Layton had made their reputations on being "characters" and built their radio show around their banter — "joshing," as the newspaper put it. Much of the humor on the Layton and Charles show depended on double entendres about sex and profanities — "totally tasteless" was how they later described their show. The "fantastic Beatles boycott" brought them a lot of publicity, and again focused international attention on the city. In England BBC television news ran a story about people in Birmingham, Alabama, burning Beatles records and made reference to the Nazi book burnings of the 1930s. Grinning louts burning Beatles records, books, and paraphernalia in America's Deep South produced disturbing images that took their place next to photographs of the same sort of people beating up civil rights agitators. The images of the "Great Beatles Boycott" appeared in newspapers all over the world and on television. They have been incorporated into the video history of the Beatles, which often identify them as occurring in Birmingham, but the most widely used photographs of teenagers burning Beatles records were taken in Waycross, Georgia. People who were there remember that Beatles records and merchandise was burned in Birmingham, but there was a note of farce in the boycott; WAQY radio had paid for the offending Beatles material to be shredded, but the man in charge of the shredder refused to put any vinyl records in it because they might damage the machinery. As WAQY had a very weak transmitter — "it was like a 50-watt-bulb station," said John Ed Willoughby — only a few people close to the station could have heard about the anti-Beatles campaign; so the "Great Beatles Boycott" operated largely in the imagination of the deejays, yet it was added to the history of Birmingham the 1960s without any further examination — Birmingham's reputation was enough to condemn it.

As the day of the concert grew near there were fears that there might be ugly demonstrations in Memphis. Brian Epstein was worried that John Lennon might be assassinated, and so was John. The Beatles had told the English newspapers, "We've got to go and get beaten up in America," but they only faced a quiet demonstration of a Christian Youth rally and six members of the Ku Klux Klan outside the Memphis coliseum. Firecrackers thrown from the crowd during the show caused a great fright on stage, but the music went on. Many radio stations had already dropped their ban on the Beatles, a wise decision during a major American tour, especially after the stations had been picketed by angry fans. The "Great Beatles Boycott" ended with a whimper. Eventually Tommy Charles and Doug Layton magnanimously accepted the "apology" of the Beatles, which was never made because the Beatles and their management had no idea who they were and did not care whether Birmingham, Alabama, liked them or not. It was soon business as usual at WAQY, but the Beatles were so upset with the harassment they received on this tour that they never went on the road again.

The boycott also had an impact on the Birmingham music scene. The music promoter Don VanCleave estimated that the fallout from this incident was so damaging that it dissuaded other touring bands from playing Birmingham for at least a decade. Rudy Johnson agreed: "We never got any type of music in Birmingham, well, you know, Tommy Charles was burnin' Beatles records. I mean, that kind of shit was happening in Birmingham . . . I'll tell you a profound revelation for me: The first time that I ever felt like that I was becoming an adult was when Tommy Charles was burning the Beatles records because I thought, 'How biased and bigoted that is!' And I thought even if that man [Lennon] had said that, how could they deny music that is so great?" Like many other musicians in Birmingham, Wayne Perkins and Rudy Johnson had no doubt why Charles started the great Beatles boycott: "He got nationwide on that. He got national coverage! That is what I am saying. It was publicity for him! That is what it was and it is a damn shame that we are known, that Birmingham is known today, because when you see things about the Beatles and you will see Tommy Charles. They actually show it on these things [television documentaries]. And it is a shame." Doug Layton: "Ask that motherfucker why he burned those Beatles records and ruined anybody coming to town for ten years."

Another piece of bad press had kept Birmingham locked in 1963, maintaining its reputation as America's most hateful city. During the 1960s it was "bad to be from Birmingham," in the opinion of French Forbes. When Michael Gadilhe's family went on vacation, they did not tell people they were from Birmingham, and his father even took off the Alabama license plates when they traveled up north. A small city in Alabama now had a serious image problem that stretched across the globe. Many in Birmingham considered this unfair in view of the other racial incidents that had occurred in other parts of the country. Wayne Perkins: "And we catch most of the grief for the civil rights bullshit because of Bull Connor turning the dogs and the hoses loose. I remember all that, but there was Mississippi, Arkansas — I mean, there was a whole lot of shit going on! . . . It was everywhere, we just got the brunt of it."

CHAPTER EIGHT

Birmingham and the Counterculture

The 1970s brought a gradual relaxation of racial tension in Birmingham. There was a new, more accommodating city government, and more holdouts took down their "whites only" signs. The passage of the Civil Rights Act made massive resistance to integration illegal, but not impossible. The municipal auditorium in downtown Birmingham began to accept integrated crowds for concerts, although blacks were seated on the floor and whites occupied the balcony: "So we could watch them dancing and having fun below us." The threat of desegregation and the unrest of the civil rights struggle had led many to join the "white flight" to the suburbs, and this left few live music venues downtown. The Cane Break continued to be popular, and there were always some after-hours drinking clubs. Musician Marc Phillips of Hotel: "In the Bob Cain era — there was not a lot of live music in the city." Wayne Perkins: "Not a whole lot of people wanted to go downtown, unless you were like down there already. The UpStairs was a place where you went after everything else shut down."

For the clubs catering to African Americans in the black business district downtown, and in the communities of North Birmingham, Ensley, and Bessemer, it was business as usual. The bloody struggle for civil rights had poisoned race relations in Birmingham, but the intoxicating sounds of R&B continued to push a steady stream of teenagers into black venues. Fifteen-year-old Steve Lowry was allowed to stand in the kitchen of the A. G. Gaston lounge while Cannonball Adderley and Booker T and the MGs played: "There couldn't have been more than a half dozen white people in the whole place." Listening to R&B acts was an education for a young white musician: "Joe Tex. I remember standing three feet away from him one night. I was mesmerized. I used to steal inflections and vocal licks from them. They were the best singers on the planet. I loved Sam and Dave and became obsessed with the whole Stax thing. I knew every Speed King bass drum pedal squeak that Al Jackson ever played." Steve Lowry went on to play all over the country, and when he did some work for Weather Report he met up with Joe Zawinul and told him: "I saw you with Cannonball Adderley. It changed my life. I had never heard music like that."

If you were adventurous you could hear the mesmerizing beat of Bo Diddley at the A. G. Gaston Motel, right next to Kelly Ingram Park. Or you could drive out to bottle clubs on Highway 78 and hear Rufus Thomas or Booker T and the MGs — two leading artists of the Stax stable in Memphis. It wasn't always comfortable. Ed Boutwell remembers, "The black people were looking at me like I was an idiot for being there." But there were good reasons to be there; "Oh, it was fabulous! It was wonderful. And you know what? Their PA system might be a little guitar amp with a little bitty speaker and that was all. The singers were singing at the top of their lungs. I think that is where the soul sound came from. No PA: projection!"

There was a generation of black entertainers from the early days of rock 'n' roll who were still out working every night. You could go out to the Madison Night Spot on Bessemer Highway and hear Little Richard, or enjoy Ray Charles singing at the Blue Gardenia. Bunkie Anderson went to the Eldorado Club, "and I saw James Brown there and B. B. King back when they were young and mean and lean." Larry Wooten went to Diamond Jim's: "It was in North Birmingham, you went past the cemetery up on the hill and it was back in there . . . It had a black band, Tina and something else, but they were good. Big John used to jump down on his knees and get on that bass! This was one of the best bands that you have ever seen! Terrible Tina, she had the big blond hair like Tina Turner. She would get down on the floor with that wig . . . She did some funky things on that stage. But man, she was hot! It was a hell of a band."

By the end of the decade there were some integrated jazz combos playing in Birmingham. Ona Watson: "I even worked a little bit for Bob Cain, and I would be the only black kid in there and he would let me sit in with him." Bunkie Anderson and his friend Glenn Wood: "Glenn and I were the only two white guys that played in black bands and all of that was going on [the civil rights struggle], and I never had one incident. I mean, it was great. Black and white bands never really started playing out, but you know white bands always backed up black singers and groups." Club owner Tom Baddley: "But when Morris Avenue came that kind of changed in that more bands from outside came. That was the first time I recall that a lot of black bands came in." Foxxy Fatts: "There were some other ones that played on Morris Avenue. That was the first time that I really recall some mixing then, which was good."

Beatlemania is usually remembered to be the domain of affluent white teenagers, but there are plenty of African American baby boomers in Birmingham who loved their music and can remember the lyrics to many of their songs. Everyone was covering their material, from middle-aged crooners who smothered them with lush orchestration to very young folk singers who picked out the notes of their favorite Lennon-McCartney melodies on their new acoustic guitars. The rise of the Beatles as creative artists accelerated the pace of change in the popular music business, and Birmingham's garage bands were playing a more diverse range of rock 'n' roll, which was now splitting up into subgenres as the size of the audience grew. The suffix "rock" was now being applied to a broad range of popular music: folk rock, psychedelic rock, hard rock, country rock, and so on.

African American popular music was coming under the same pressures that were altering the face of rock 'n' roll — the imperative to be real, to mean something more than entertainment and be more relevant to the times. The music was changing — becoming more self-conscious and blacker. In the aftermath of the civil rights movement there was a return to authenticity in expression and away from the commercialization and popularization of black music of the early 1960s, which reeked of exploitation by the white-run music business. Brian Ward points out that this feeling was one of the lasting legacies of the civil rights movement, which had given a radical, self-conscious makeover to the self-image of millions of southern blacks. Motown, the voice of "Young America," was replaced by a voice that was more worldly and less polished. "Soul," in the African American vernacular, stood for sincerity and realism, and authenticity was at the heart of soul music, with its emotional, gospel-based vocals in front

of tight, funky guitar and horn sections. Musicians who had once looked
to Motown and Jimmy Reed for inspiration were now listening to James
Brown and Odetta.

Soul had sprung up in that musically fertile area of North Alabama, Mississippi, and West Tennessee. It was as much North Alabama as Memphis
music. It was another amalgam of black and white culture as musicians
plundered each other's stuff. David Hood reiterated a point made by many
of his contemporaries when he said that constant interaction between blacks
and whites in Alabama increased familiarity with each other's music.[1] Dan
Penn also stressed the intimacy of black and white music in rural Alabama
when he talks about the influences in his songwriting. That soul classics
like "The Dark End of the Street" or "Do Right, Woman" were written
by skinny white country boys like Penn and Chips Moman shows how
much the races were grounded in each other's music. They might not have
thought of themselves as country, but it was evident in much of their playing, because they had heard so much of it growing up in Alabama. "They
may not like it, but they can't help but get some of it through osmosis,"
said their colleague Spooner Oldham.[2] Arthur Alexander and Percy Sledge
said they heard white singers before they heard those of their own race.
Alexander was inspired by a great number of country vocalists like Eddy
Arnold and Rex Allen, and even professed admiration for Roy Rodgers
and Red Foley.[3] Some critics have used the term "country soul" to describe
the music coming out of North Alabama in the '60s, which indicates a level
of musical interaction. It worked both ways: Otis Redding was inspired to
write "Dock of the Bay" after listening to the Beatles' *Sgt. Pepper* album.

Soul had an irresistible appeal to white players in Alabama who had
grown up with gospel. Kevin Derryberry was in a church choir: "The youth
choir and on up. I used to love listening to the Beatles and all the Motown
stuff... I loved Elton John and Billy Joel, and I seemed to always be able
to play that stuff because I really love soul. I love black R&B and in a way
it kind of went with Billy Joel. It does not sound black and R&B but he
kind of is, in a way. Deep down inside, he loves that too. We all do. Everybody does. It goes back to that." Soul found fertile ground in Birmingham,
Alabama, with its years of admiration for R&B and its multitude of horn
bands. When Doug Lee joined the popular band Days of the Week in 1970,

he noted that many of the bands playing in the late '60s and early '70s had horns: "Most of them had horns . . . They had an R&B approach. Horn bands were much more prevalent then than now — You can't afford to pay that many people [now] . . . That was the only time I ever really played in a horn band, and that is an exciting thing, because that is a big sound! When you hear those trumpets and everything coming at you! That is a real exciting sound." Days of the Week was led by vocalist Buddy Causey, an outstanding blue-eyed soul singer. It went through many incarnations and employed many musicians, but it usually had a three-piece horn section.

Although the fame of Lennon and McCartney encouraged many garage bands to start writing their own songs (which often sounded a lot like songs by Lennon and McCartney), the bread and butter of the garage bands was always covers, and the growing popularity of soul records in the Top 40 naturally brought them to this music. Doug Lee: "We played a lot of covers, like everyone else we played whatever was popular, pretty much. AM radio stuff, basically Top 40 music. Sam and Dave." When Rick Byrd returned to Birmingham from California in the late 1960s, he found a music scene awash in soul covers: "What people were into here was soul music and I had not been exposed to that in California at all. So when I got into a band here, they were doing Sam and Dave, 'Shake a Tail Feather,' and I don't know what else." For the Birmingham listening audience, soul was it — the real thing, the music that moved you. "That is what I thought music was all about," remembered Michael Gadilhe. "It was real, with a passion, those real tight groups, and it was music you could dance to." The young men who played the Alabama, Florida, and Georgia college circuits knew that whatever the current radio favorites were — the audiences still wanted to dance. Henry Lovoy recognized that the all-important frat boy audience still wanted to hear "rocking songs by Chuck Berry, Bo Diddley, James Brown, and Arthur Alexander" regardless of the current fads in pop music.

The Counterculture

The pressures for authenticity in rock music, and the growing need to be relevant as well as fun, affected the outlook of Birmingham's garage bands in many different ways. While the horn bands embraced soul and R&B,

the country players and acoustic duos looked elsewhere for their inspiration, reaching back into the past to embrace folk and traditional country
music — that is, country music not polluted by electric guitars, drums, and
Nashville commercialism. Folk music enjoyed a boom in the late 1960s. It
was easy to play and had a pedigree enhanced by its adoption by the civil
rights movement and its growing role in the opposition to the Vietnam
War. As the war escalated, the resistance to it took on the strategy and
tone of the fight for civil rights. The demonstrations were again broadcast
into every American home by television, and "We Shall Overcome" was
now being sung by affluent but disaffected college students from Berkeley,
Columbia, and NYU.

The war in Vietnam had become a divisive issue in American society by
the mid-1960s, and the introduction of the draft brought it uncomfortably
close to many young men. In 1966 Jefferson County was asked to increase
its manpower targets from 55 to 170 recruits a month. Now college kids and
married men without children were getting their papers. Ned Bibb: "I was
going to UAB at the time and none of the guys that I knew was gung-ho
about the war. UAB had four grades you could receive: A, B, C or F. We
would sit and sweat waiting for the test scores to be posted on the doors.
They scaled the grades, and there was always some brainy little girl that
would throw off the curve. If you didn't maintain a C average you were
gone." Loveman's department stores advertised a special deal from their
photographic studio: "Send a portrait to your serviceman," and way back
on page 5 or 7 came the first faint reports of opposition to the war. Many in
Birmingham were appalled at another campaign of civil disobedience. The
Birmingham News took a somewhat hysterical tone: "Lawlessness of racists
and peaceniks can destroy society and system of United States," it claimed.

Again protest songs filled the air as music became a vehicle for dissent,
and again the roots of these songs were in folk music, representing the non-
commercial, real voice of the people. The Lowenbrau in Homewood was
the center of the folk scene in Birmingham. It was packed with people
listening to songs of protest and flouting the age limit for alcohol consump-
tion. Ned Bibb had left the Distortions and got a job backing pianist Jack
Harris there. The place had become a hangout of the Southside crowd, as

Ned put it, which meant hippies, folkies, and layabouts from the old houses that clustered at the foot of Red Mountain from Five Points to Highway 65 South. They were listening to the songs of Joan Baez and Bob Dylan and taking part in the singalongs. "The Vietnam War was going on and folk music began to catch hold. I went to work with Jack Harris at the Lowenbrau House. We were bringing home wads of money . . . I was making more money than I ever made in my life," remembers Ned.

Country music was reclaiming its place in rock 'n' roll. Country rock began on the West Coast and quickly spread east. It was a favorite in Birmingham in the 1970s. Doug Lee: "I had always been a big fan of the country rock that came out of L.A. in the late '60s: Buffalo Springfield, the Byrds, and Moby Grape, which was a San Francisco band. I always really liked that stuff, and next to the Beatles that was what I liked the best." So did his friends Tom Fox and Doug Tinsley. They formed Dogwood to play the music of Crosby, Stills and Nash; Neil Young; and Poco. Although this genre of rock 'n' roll was created in the special atmosphere of the West Coast, it had relevance to fans in the Deep South, where country music had always had a strong following. What bands like the Byrds, Poco, and Buffalo Springfield accomplished was to mix the sounds of country with rock instrumentation into a relevant new hybrid; Buffalo Springfield's "For What It's Worth" became one of the iconic songs of the counterculture.

The emergence of a youth counterculture in America was supported by new music and fashions. The look of rock 'n' roll players had always been important because the appeal of the performance depended heavily on the spectacle. The first rock band that Doug Lee ever saw was the Counts: "I will never forget it. I saw them at Gardendale Community Center. I was about thirteen years old, and they were probably fifteen or sixteen years old. I can't recall what they played. Just hits of the day. I can't even remember. I don't remember what it sounded like. I just remember seeing them. The visual part was just like 'Wow!' I don't remember anything about the sounds." Although no one can deny that the Beatles were great musicians, their look, carefully created by Brian Epstein, was a big part of their appeal, and the fashionable clothes they wore helped create an aura of newness and modernity. One teen who watched them on *Ed Sullivan* noted: "They were so unusual-looking because they had their little suits on and they had their long hair."[4] Dressing up to play had always been part of the musical profession, and rock 'n' roll brought a whole new dress code for young musicians.

Whereas geographic location and high school affiliation had once defined Birmingham's garage bands, the late '60s saw identity conferred with musical styles and fashions. They had all started with the formal attire expected of professional musicians — suits, ties, short hair — but quickly moved into rock 'n' roll stage outfits: brightly colored mohair suits, silk smoking jackets, and ruffled shirts. Larry Wooten remembers the Ramrods: "When we first started playing we wore black pants with a red smoking jacket... We sold those and it seemed like we went to a blue ruffled shirt... Anyway, Mike Morgan was with Rooster and the Townsmen and they bought our smoking jackets." Then the popularity of the British Invasion made musicians buy new stuff: "Beatle jackets" with no collars, straight-leg pants, roll-neck shirts, and black leather "Chelsea" boots. Steve Lowry of the Echoes: "We had houndstooth English-looking mod rocker suits [sic] and the Beatle boots." The Distortions wore "Beau Brummel" jackets, bright shirts with huge flapping collars, and black Beatle boots. As psychedelic music and dress became fashionable, the garage bands changed their attire yet again. A photograph of the Rockin' Rebellions in the late 1960s reveals them in flowery shirts, bright neckerchiefs, satin jackets, and embroidered waistcoats — the latest in the psychedelic look. "Flower power" became an important element in this style, in fabric design, accessories, and motifs. Stage clothes had come to reflect music identities: The "bad boy" bands in Birmingham wore leather jackets and jeans, "junk and Goodwill clothes." They played R&B and hard rock —"blood and guts," in the words of the Distortions' Bunkie Anderson. They could be identified by their long hair, dirty jeans, and hangdog expressions. On the other hand, the bands from Mountain Brook, such as Johnny Robinson's Ramblers, all dressed alike in preppy clothes and played mainly Beatles and Beach Boys songs: rock 'n' roll lite in the minds of their peers who had been moved by *Sgt. Pepper's Lonely Hearts Club Band* and bowled over by *Are You Experienced?*.

These iconic recordings of psychedelic rock brought some unforgettable moments to Birmingham's rock musicians. Rudy Johnson: "And then all of a sudden I hear stuff like Vanilla Fudge and then I hear Cream and Hendrix and Zeppelin and as things came along I was just eating it up . . . I mean, I was getting profound revelations right and left by listening to that stuff . . . The first time I heard Hendrix I just went totally nuts!" Rock musicians in Birmingham remembered 1967 and 1968 as the years that everything changed — especially the advent of recreational drugs as the required accompaniment to radical new music, literature, and film. Rudy Johnson: "My first experience with marijuana was in the summer of '68 and I was already into Hendrix big-time — the music was hot, and we were really into the music. I do remember the first time I smoked pot I was listening to Steppenwolf and I was laying . . . with my head between the speakers and I was so engulfed in that. I lost it completely! Yeah, drugs and music were part of the culture." Rick Byrd: "Back then . . . 1969, 1970, 1971, it was when everybody was starting to grow their hair long or had long hair. It was when people around here were starting to experiment with drugs. It was a couple of years later than what was going on the West Coast. A lot of musicians that I hung around with, we started experimenting with drugs and whatever we could get our hands on. It was pretty wild! I had friends in high school who were shooting heroin and stuff."

Some exciting new films played their part in pushing the envelope of perception. Wayne Perkins: "Drugs and music were part of the culture . . . the next thing that hit was *Clockwork Orange* and so I went to see that, you know, stoned. Then I went to see *Yellow Submarine* stoned. I was trippin'!" Teens in Birmingham were hearing about love and peace on the West Coast: "Back then it was such a new experience to us, and we were trying to identify I guess with the freaks and stuff in San Francisco. I went to Disney Land in 1967 . . . and we went to a gift shop and I bought a hookah . . . I brought that back, a friend of mine that was in Vietnam sent us back some marijuana. So we put some wine in my hookah pipe . . . It was real pretty, real ornate. So I had some dope. It would kick your ass too, boy!"

The clothes, the louder volume of rock music, and its provocative attitudes were strongly influenced by the British Invasion, beginning with the Rolling Stones, who followed the Beatles to America in 1964. The Rolling Stones were named after a song by Chicago blues legend Muddy Waters, and they liked to think of themselves as blues purists. They also presented a surly demeanor that made the Beatles look uncomfortably conformist. The British groups that followed the Beatles to America had longer hair and dirtier clothes and harked back to that air of rebellion that had made rock 'n' roll so appealing in the 1950s. The Rolling Stones caused a stir when they first played Birmingham's Legion Field in their first tour of the United States. Steve Lowry was there with some bandmates: "They brought the Rolling Stones out in a Brinks truck because all the radio stations were talking about how the guys were from another planet. They were terrible, yet they were incredible. They weren't in tune and they were probably stoned. Brian Jones was the first one to come out. He had on eyeliner and I have never seen that on a man. I thought that was cool, but I didn't know why. I looked at the drummer and said, 'We got it — this is it for life.'" When the English band the Pretty Things played the Lyric Theatre, backing the Hullabaloos, they really caused a stir: "The Pretty Things were a biker band and were really rough-looking. They had leather wrist bands and really long hair. The Hullabaloos had really long hair."

Yet there was little musical rebellion to be heard in Birmingham's garage bands, who played in a much more repressive environment than the touring English groups, whose misbehavior in the United States was well reported. So when the Distortions covered the provocative Rolling Stones song "Let's Spend the Night Together," it was renamed "Let's Spend Some Time Together." When several members of the band were sent home from school because their hair was too long, their friends and fellow musicians jumped to their defense. Ned Bibb: "Robert and Zach got kicked out of school for their long hair. They went to court. Their mamas went to court about it. The court ruled that the school would have to accept them with long hair. I would imagine that it [the Hair Rally] was to raise money for their legal fees." "The Big Distortions Hair Rally" was to be held at City Auditorium. When the concert finally went on (at the Cloud Room), it included most of the big names of the local music scene: the Rockin' Rebellions, the Hard Times, the Vikings, the Torquays, and This Side Up. The program stated "Parents Are Invited," so the tone of the event could not have been too confrontational.

The growing prominence of the "longhairs" in the media naturally attracted more young people to it, who might not have had strong political views until the Vietnam War changed their minds. Nonconformity was becoming attractive to many young people in Alabama, and they signaled this change by growing their hair and listening to rebellious music. Becoming an outsider in one of the most conservative communities in America was pretty easy. Long hair, opposition to the Vietnam War, and consuming hallucinogenic drugs became the new definers of youth culture, and each one of them was associated with popular music. Long hair had become an obsession in '60s America. When bands came to Birmingham, one of the first questions asked them in press conferences was: "How long did it take you to grow your hair? Is it real?" As much as the Ku Klux Klan ranted about the threat of black music on white morals, hair length was probably the most contentious point in the interaction of rock 'n' roll and Alabama society. Ned Bibb remembered, "High school was very strict. One of the worst things you could do was grow your hair." Growing one's hair was as much a statement as a fashion, and everybody in Birmingham knew those individuals who first took the step. Most were musicians, as Bunkie Anderson remembered: "There weren't but twelve of us in Birmingham, and we all played in bands . . . I got beat up for having long hair . . . Two guys pulled me out of a phone booth and put me in the hospital because I had long hair and shot them the bird . . . With long hair, you didn't go to a certain bar. There were places that wouldn't feed you if you had long hair. White, green, black, it didn't matter if you had long hair. Everybody hated us." Long hair managed to offend a broad cross section of Alabama society, and it often led to a confrontation. Steve Lowry was attacked by some football players who forcibly cut his hair with a penknife. It is hard to believe now that some people who watched the Beatles on *The Ed Sullivan Show* were offended by their long hair — but by the end of the decade it would have been considered respectably short.

The proponents of civil rights, pacifism, communism, drugs, and a free-love lifestyle were all grouped together under the umbrella term "hippies" and were suspected of all sorts of abhorrent and subversive behavior. Naturally, the hippie lifestyle had its own unique music: unstructured, free flowing, and with songs about drug busts, free love, and getting high. Birmingham had its hippie bands; one was called Brass Buttons and had long-haired Marc Phillips as vocalist. Their band card had "Button Power"

printed on it, reflecting the fashionable term "flower power," which was
used to describe the pacifist movement. Fred Dalke started a band in 1968:
"And it was called Lovin' Way. And I think that's probably . . . to the era
in the late '60s — it was getting into the flower children, and the names of
the groups was changing, so I named the band the Lovin' Way." Of course,
"hippie" was a loose term that covered many ills, but in Alabama it was
always derogatory. Rick Byrd was a guitarist in Dogwood: "That second
version of Dogwood started playing at the Hill Top Lounge in Calera. We
were playing some original stuff, but a lot of Top 40 country. They called
us 'the hippie band!' They had go-go dancers in there. They had this girl
on the corner, with a black light over her, and fishnet stuff behind her." A
band led by the vocalist Buddy Causey that started as Days of the Week
was renamed Daze of the Weak and was described by Bunkie Anderson
as a hippie band. Other players in the band included Doug Lee, Tom Fox,
Jimmy Little, and Philip Stratton. On one memorable night in Tuscaloosa
they opened for Big Brother and the Holding Company, backing up Janis
Joplin in an evening of psychedelic music.

The Southside of Birmingham was the place to enjoy the hippie lifestyle with its coffeehouses, neighborhood bars like Joe Bar at Five Points
South, and head shops, which sold drug paraphernalia. In the 1960s it had
become one of the cultural centers of the city, with at least two theater
groups, and several bookstores, record stores, restaurants, and bars. What
had once been one of the most attractive and affluent neighborhoods of
the city spent much of the twentieth century in decline, and as a result,
the sprawling Victorian homes that had anchored this residential suburb
had fallen into disrepair. But this lowered the price of accommodation —
a large six- or seven-room house could cost as little as one hundred dollars
a month. This attracted many young people to the area, including artists,
poets, writers, and musicians, which gave the Southside its somewhat seedy,
bohemian flavor. Although the hippies shunned many of the conveniences
of affluent middle-class America, they still needed the essentials of life:
coffee, tie-dyed T-shirts, records, and rolling papers. Several head shops
sprang up to meet these needs. Wayne Perkins remembered, "Then the
Macos built the Purple Mushroom over there [downtown]." Rudy Johnson: "I had a head shop. Yeah, and I actually sold posters, black lights, roach

clips, and just all kinds of stuff: tickets, clothes, T-shirts . . . In 1971 or 1972 I bought a pet shop down in Tarrant and I changed the name of it from the Fish Wharf to Yellow Submarine. I painted me a big sign with a yellow submarine from the Beatles." The Angry Revolt in Homewood gives an idea of the political outlook of these retailers. Steve Handle and Ronny Seitel ran the Corner Stone head shop, a place where you could not only buy pipes, posters, incense, and clothes, but also hang out and enjoy coffee and a snack. At the back of the premises — which were derogatively called a "hippie joint" by the police — was a small area for listening to music. Steve Handle brought in local folk singers and rock groups until complaints about the noise closed the business.

Music was the glue that kept the counterculture together, from the coffeehouses in the Southside to the free concerts in Avondale Park. Larger crowds and louder music lay behind the trend for increased amplification. A photo of Chair playing a concert at Avondale Park Amphitheatre in 1970 shows them dwarfed by stacks of amplifiers and speaker cabinets. By the late 1970s and the popularity of free outdoor concerts, the amphitheater at Avondale Park had become a favorite location: "Another place that was very popular that Black Mountain used to play was Avondale Park at the amphitheater. A lot of groups used to play out there. I think they would do the gigs out there on Sundays. Ask some people about Avondale Park — it will start bringing memories back. There were always good crowds out there."

CHAPTER NINE

The Muscle Shoals Sound

Although the recording had always been central to success in rock 'n' roll, the ascendancy of the Beatles made it even more important, as both the means of production in popular music and the font of creativity for musicians. Americans first heard the Beatles playing pop music, but the boy band evolved into a more serious musical quartet with each long-playing record they released. Acquiring a Beatles album either as a Christmas gift or as a purchase was always remembered. Musician and promoter Rudy Johnson: "Rumore's Record Rack downtown was the place to go get records. And you have to remember at that time we didn't have Kmart or any of that stuff. I remember I got *Beatles 65* for Christmas, that was one of my Christmas presents, and I listened to that until I wore it completely out! I should have gotten three." *Sgt. Pepper's Lonely Hearts Club Band* launched thousands of overproduced records, justified millions of hours of recording time, and produced career-changing epiphanies for many in Birmingham's garage bands. After WVOK played a song, Rudy Johnson set off to buy the album: "I heard one song and I don't even know, I think it was *Sgt. Pepper's Lonely Hearts Club Band* . . . I borrowed money from the guy who was in the car with me and drove all the way to Homewood and had to hunt down Rumore's Record Rack and I got one of two copies they had." This was such a revered album that its producer, George Martin, became a celebrity in his own right. Guitarist Wayne Perkins grabbed his chance to meet the great man: "I got to meet George Martin at Muscle Shoals Sound for just a minute, I don't know, five or ten minutes, and it was just amazing! He is such a gentleman . . . The genius was there with McCartney and Lennon and Harrison and all of them, but he helped them on."

The goal of every garage band in the pre-Beatles era was to get a gig at an armory show, but after Beatlemania success was measured in records, which were now more than just as a tool to market the band, but a measure of its creativity. As a rock band in the post-Beatles era you had not arrived until you had a good record, and the bands are remembered today primarily through their hits or the prestigious labels they signed on. Fred Dalke: "This Side Up was a group that came out in 1968, in the late 1960s, and This Side Up was a local band, and they won a national competition for Capitol Records, and they got onto Capitol Records, and they were a local band out of Birmingham. They never gained national prominence, but they were a very good group, a real good band." Steve Lowry: "The seminal band of that period, the first band to ever get a record deal, a single, a fan club, was the Distortions ... They got an ABC Records deal and went to New York to sign it."

The example of the Beatles brought many more customers to Birmingham's recording studios. Ed Boutwell branched out on his own when he acquired some professional tape recorders: "First I had two mono machines, then I got a 2-track. I had the first 2-track in Alabama. It was an Ampex 351, and then I went into business in my bedroom making commercials ... Then along came rock 'n' roll! ... My studio was a garage ... Every little band in Birmingham, the little garage bands would come to my garage." As Beatlemania gripped the youth of America, the flow of guitar bands into Boutwell's studio became "a mighty stream. There were a couple [of other recording studios], but I was the only one who was really set up in a way to handle what they did ... I used to get so mad at them and I would say, 'Turn it down. It is distorting.' They would say, 'Yeah, great!' I would go, 'But it isn't clean.' I loved it!" The recording studio was replacing the radio station as the place where young musicians would go to learn their trade, network, and socialize. Ed reassured their parents: "Your kids are not driving around Birmingham drinking. Your kids are young entrepreneurs; this is something they love and it is a business and they are making money."

Homer Milam was still running his studio, Artists Recording, which concentrated on gospel; and Heart was still making many jingles and recording some rock groups and country and gospel singers. Ed Boutwell and Neil Hemphill both established new recording studios in the mid-1960s.

Both started as small-scale operations established in the homes of these entrepreneurs, but with the boom in garage band recording their businesses grew rapidly and they moved to larger facilities: Boutwell relocated to an old church building in English Village and Hemphill established the Sound of Birmingham Studio in Midfield. They were followed by Prestige Studios. When they entered the business around 1965, Kenny Wallace and his partner Rick Mayes were offered Milam's studio, but the equipment was old and they could not raise the purchase price, so they bought recording equipment and established their Prestige Studio in Irondale. At the same Al Hemrick was constructing Alabama Sound recording studios in Homewood. Hemrick had tried to start a recording operation in Nashville, but after suffering rejection there he decided to build his own studio in Birmingham: "He operated it for probably just a few months and at the time it was the state of the art, it was the most elaborate, most luxurious [if you use that word] studio around town," remembers Kenny. Eventually Kenny and Rick bought the studio and started recording in 1968. The Matose Brothers had a studio in an old icehouse on Oxmoor Road. Rick Byrd and Black Mountain recorded there in the late 1960s and early 1970s: "It was one of the nicest studios in town. I think Delbert McClinton may have cut his first album there. Black Mountain recorded a good bit of stuff there, and later Locust Fork recorded their album there in the late 1970s." Birmingham's recording studios had never been busier, and they were putting their money into larger facilities and multitrack recorders. Two-track recorders were soon replaced by 4-tracks, and then 8-tracks, just like the Beatles were supposed to be using (it was actually two 4-tracks joined together). Despite the great technological leaps in sound recording in the 1960s, success was still measured in hits, and it was one massive hit in 1966 that transformed the recording business in Alabama.

The Hit Recording Capitol of the World

The studios in Muscle Shoals had been always an option for Birmingham bands from the early 1960s. Muscle Shoals is a few hours north of Birmingham, close to the cities of Florence, Sheffield, and Tuscumbia. Musically it sits between Memphis and Nashville, thus its musicians grew up between the two poles of blues and country. As Scott Boyer pointed out, "There was a lot of interplay between the three areas . . . I am sure it was a matter of them growing up listening to that music, and that is what they learned to do, just listening to it." The rich musical heritage of North Alabama was a fertile ground for the interaction of black and white culture that produced some outstanding musicians as well as two influential record producers. Rick Hall was a man remarkably like Sam Phillips in taste and ambition. He started playing the fiddle in country groups in the 1950s, moved into rock 'n' roll with a band called the Fairlanes, and had some success as a songwriter. When Hall decided to set up a recording studio in Florence — Phillips's hometown — he had to come down to Birmingham to get some of the equipment — "three cheap mikes and a little mixer, and we began the task of putting together demos of new tunes, and everybody was writing them. I was writing. Billy [Sherrill] was writing. Tom [Stafford] was trying to write. All of a sudden the big time had hit Muscle Shoals."[1] Hall's strategy was to feed into the music center of Nashville, so he bought songs, made demos, and cut master recordings that he hoped he could market in the musical metropolis just a few hours up the road. And like Sam Phillips a decade before him, he cultivated local blues and R&B artists whose music he admired and whose masters might be purchased by independent companies like Vee-Jay or Chess in Chicago. It was Rick Hall who first recorded Arthur Alexander, whose records made a deep impression on the Beatles and the Rolling Stones. After every big recording company in Nashville rejected "You Better Move On" because it was "too black," Dot Records finally agreed to release it. In retrospect it was probably its blackness that gave it such appeal in Europe and caught the attention of blues-smitten listeners like John Lennon and Keith Richards. The record was a hit, and Rick Hall used the profits to build a better studio, which he dubbed FAME (Florence Alabama Music Enterprises). This was the beginning of the Muscle Shoals sound, but there were also other hit records that helped build FAME's reputation. Johnny Sandlin: "Rick, the way I heard it, he started the studio to do country music, but he had this success with Arthur Alexander right off the bat, black artist, and then Jimmy Hughes comes along with the song 'Steal Away,' which was a big hit." "Steal Away" (1964) owed a lot to gospel, and with some energetic promotion work by Rick and Dan Penn it became a national hit (number 17 on the *Billboard* chart). These hits convinced Vee-Jay Records to sign a national distribution deal with FAME Records, and it also provided a vital boost of self-confidence for Alabama's pickers and producers. Tom Stafford had always reassured them: "Yeah, you can do it, we gonna get us a hit record." Muscle Shoals legend Dan Penn: "Tom Stafford had said, 'We can have hits.' I didn't believe that, but he did, and then Arthur Alexander proved him right."

Rick hired his session players from whoever was hanging out around the Shoals, including Johnny Sandlin: "They're weren't a lot of guitar players in [the studio], so I had a guitar and I was dependable and I was sort of backup guitar player for a guy, Terry Thompson, who is dead now, but a great guitar player. Rick would use two guitars on a lot of things and I would end up playing on some for him. We usually did demos, and if they made it to a record it would be upgraded to union scale, which was just unbelievable money." Hall continued to develop Alabama musicians like Clarence Carter and several Birmingham garage bands that drove a few hours north to try their luck. Rick Byrd: "Well, Black Mountain went up there when I was in high school. I did some demos that Barry Beckett produced. We did maybe eight or ten of our original songs up there and it was pretty neat. Dogwood also went up there very early . . . We went up in a studio and some of the first, not the first but some of the early studio stuff I did was with Dogwood on steel guitar up in Muscle Shoals." In 1963 the Ramrods went into the Baldwin Recording Studio in Woodlawn, Birmingham, and recorded two original songs that impressed Rick Hall enough that he took them up to FAME Studios. To the disappointment of the Ramrods, "Night Ride" was released not on his well-known FAME label, but on "R and H," a brand that he had just started: business was taking off at the Shoals. The Counts spoke for many garage bands in Birmingham: "We felt like we had to get out of Birmingham if we wanted to cut anything any good. We had plenty of good options, Heart, Prestige, Boutwell, and others. We had perfectly good recording studios in our hometown. I thought that going to Muscle Shoals might help us. They had really started to produce some good artists up there."

The Rockin' Rebellions began recording almost immediately after they formed. Henry Lovoy: "We recorded our first record at Boutwell recording studio called 'By My Side,' which I cowrote with the keyboard player Donald Barbee. It got airplay on WSGN, and boss disc jockey Dave Roddy made it number 37 on the Hot Top 40. I guess you could say we were on our way. It got us a lot of gigs all over Alabama, Georgia, Florida, Mississippi, and Tennessee. We decided to make another record, but we wanted something major, so we went to FAME Studios in Muscle Shoals with Rick Hall. We recorded 'Any Way the Wind Blows,' a song written by Frank Zappa [and engineered by Jimmy Johnson]." "Any Way the Wind Blows" ended up selling over twenty-five thousand copies — no mean feat for a local band in the 1960s — and "a year later Duke Rumore introduced us to an independent producer named Eugene Lucassey of Memphis. He was the man who had Sam the Sham, who had a song out called 'Wooly Bully' that was a national hit. We signed with Mr. Lucassey and got to record at Sam Phillips's Sun Studios in Memphis. We recorded a tune by Paul Craft called 'Would You Like to Go Somewhere with Me Sometime' [in November 1967] which made the national charts and played all over the Southeast. We got to play many more rock 'n' roll shows for many more stations from Tennessee to Florida and from Mississippi to Georgia." Birmingham bands were picking up fans outside Alabama with the wider distribution of their records. The Distortions had their biggest hit, "Behind My Wall." Fred Dalke: "It came out in 1965 and made it to number 1 on all the charts locally, then it went to Smash Records, a national label. Smash Records picked that up, but it didn't make it nationally. Maybe it didn't have the promotion behind it, whatever, but it was a very good record." According to their producer, Ed Boutwell, it sold between twelve thousand and fifteen thousand copies.

Soon Rick Hall was doing so much business that he farmed some of the work out. Norala Sound Studios was far from being the main attraction at Muscle Shoals; it had been set up by the young deejay Quin Ivy, and it stood across the street from his Tune Town record shop. He handled the jingles and demos that Rick Hall was too busy to attend to at FAME. One day Percy Sledge came in with a song written by two members of his vocal group, the Esquires. Sledge worked as an orderly at the Colbert County Hospital and had never made a record before. Although his roots were in gospel and R&B, Sledge was also a fan of some of the new country artists like Charlie Rich and Kris Kristofferson. The song was rewritten for the studio and entitled "When a Man Loves a Woman." The session was as low-rent as you could get at the Shoals. The backing musicians were just a few players who hung out at the studio. The song was laid down on two mono machines joined together to make a 2-track, with only one chance of overdub because of the drop in sound quality in rerecording. The horn section, which was added later, was wholly out of tune, which did not really bother Jimmy Johnson, the guitarist who engineered the session, because Percy Sledge was singing out of tune as well. But when Rick Hall heard the track, he immediately picked up the phone and called Jerry Wexler of Atlantic Records in New York.

The first great soul hit record — a low-quality recording created almost by accident in a far outpost of popular music — represented the spirit of rock 'n' roll magic. Yet it managed to connect perfectly with listeners all over the world, and it still does. This was the record that put Muscle Shoals on the map in the music business and drew musicians and producers to North Alabama for a decade after its creation. It was a wonderful advertisement for the potent mix of musical talent found in North Alabama and its seamless integration. Jerry Wexler, who had plenty of experience dealing with racial discrimination in the North, found that there were more bonds between the races in the South: it wasn't ghettoized, it was checkerboarded. Outside the studios it might be tense, but inside it was different. Dan Penn thought "the studio was a great hideaway from all that."[2]

The rise of Muscle Shoals as a recording center reversed the traditional migration of talent out of Alabama, from W. C. Handy to Sam Phillips. Black musicians had been hurrying out of Alabama since Reconstruction. Now they were coming back — somewhat reluctantly, but they were coming. Wilson Pickett was born in Prattville, Alabama, then moved to Detroit with his father and started singing in a vocal group called the Falcons. He went solo in 1963 and came to the attention of Jerry Wexler. At first Wexler had Pickett record at Stax Studios in Memphis, but he then decided that FAME might be a better option and asked Pickett to return to rural Alabama and Muscle Shoals. Dan Penn, who was at the airport to meet him, noted that it was "real redneck time" during that period and that Pickett nearly backed out of the deal when he saw people picking cotton as the limo sped him to the studio. But he found the atmosphere at FAME Studios cordial, and it facilitated some of his greatest hits: "Land of 1,000 Dances" and "Mustang Sally." Atlantic brought gospel singer Aretha Franklin to record in Muscle Shoals after several years of disappointing results in studios in New York. Dan Penn: "We didn't really know who she was when she walked in, but it was a special day." The songs that she cut in Alabama in 1967 were some of the best of her career, including "Respect" and "I Never Loved a Man (the Way I Love You)," and they established Muscle Shoals as the hottest place in the country to cut a record (even though a lot of the record was overdubbed in New York).

When Arthur Conley asked, "Do you like good music, that sweet soul music?" all the world said yes. "Sweet Soul Music" was just one of the hit records coming out of Muscle Shoals, and it now had the confidence to call itself "The Hit Recording Capitol of the World" on traffic signs and billboards. In the words of session men Travis Wammack and Roger Clark, there was "a music explosion" at Muscle Shoals, with around nine studios working full-time, and cutting "five albums a week was nothing." The final and to many the greatest affirmation of North Alabama music came when the Rolling Stones arrived in 1971 and cut several songs for their "Sticky Fingers" album, including the classic "Brown Sugar." Gerald Hallerman: "I mean, it was just unreal. What was going on in the Tri-Cities and with Muscle Shoals and the recordings was absolutely beyond the realm of anybody's imagination. I mean, some of the greatest people in the world are coming to Alabama to play. Who would have thunk that?"

A few successful singles turned Muscle Shoals into a magnet for musicians all over Alabama, from Dan Penn in Vernon to Chuck Leavell in Tuscaloosa. Business was good and the musicians' network drew guitarists, songwriters, and record producers to North Alabama. Wayne Perkins in Birmingham heard from his friend Eddie Hinton that there were openings for session men there — the musicians who played behind the singers, making up the rhythm section. Wayne: "He said, 'What are you doing?' I said, 'Well, nothing.' He said, 'You know they are looking for a guitar player at Muscle Shoals?' I said, 'What?' He said, 'Quin Ivy Studio. That's where I am working now. You interested?' I said, 'What are they paying?' He said, 'A hundred dollars a week.' I said, 'I'm your guy!'" Session men were the journeymen laborers of the studio, the quiet men who played whatever

was asked of them and then packed up their gear at the end of the day and
went home. They had to be versatile; you could never tell what would be
needed in a session. When he got to the studios, Wayne was given a stack of
records that ranged from the smooth jazz of Wes Montgomery to the soul
of Joe Tex. He had to learn them all and be ready to reproduce the sound
at a moment's notice. It was the session men who created the Muscle Shoals
sound. Dan Penn: "Rick didn't know nothing either. We were all hungry. It
was the people, local people, who made it. They all came from the area, all
local boys." They were not flashy, in the opinion of Wayne Perkins and Scott
Boyer, who played with them. The latter recalled: "Well, to me it was a kind
of swampy, understated thing. The Staple Singers' 'I'll Take You There' is
a perfect example . . . Roger [Hawkins] actually hits the snare drum maybe
twice in the whole song . . . so that when he gets to the end of the verse and
they are going to the next section he goes [*snap*] and it just knocks you back
into your seat because he is not doing it all the way through the song. So that
to me was part of the Muscle Shoals thing was a way of understating everything so when you actually hit the snare drum it would have more impact
than it would as if you were hitting it all the way through." Boyer also made
an important point about the professionalism of the session men: "I will
tell you what: those guys did not fool around! They are very serious about
what they do . . . They don't drink when they are playing; they want it to be
good, and that is why it always is. It is because they make it a point to be sure
that it is good." The Muscle Shoals sound came out of the mix all thick and
smoky, like the air over a swamp, and this provided the inspiration for their
nickname "The Swampers." Wayne Perkins: "Me and Barry Beckett go back
a long way . . . I've done a ton of stuff for Barry. We worked . . . I mean, we are
swampers. I'm a swamper, he's a swamper: Jimmy Johnson, Roger Hawkins,
and David Hood. That is the Muscle Shoals swampers . . . The name came
from the back of that Leon Russell album called *Leon Russell and the Shelter
People*. Ronnie [Van Zant] got it off there."

The Swampers surprised the cream of 1970s rock musicians — ranging
from John Hammond Jr. to Rod Stewart — who walked into the studio
expecting a funky group of soul players and instead found a bunch of po-
lite, short-haired, white guys in clean jeans and button-down shirts. David
Hood told this story to Topper Price: "Rod Stewart called up Jerry Wex-

ler and said, 'I want to go record with those cats, that rhythm section in Muscle Shoals, man! I want to do an album with them.' So Rod Stewart and Jerry Wexler walk into the studio, and . . . me and Roger and Jimmy Johnson and Barry Beckett were out in the studio setting up our stuff, and Rod Stewart looks over to Jerry Wexler and goes, 'These guys are white!'" But nobody complained when they started to play. As Topper Price said: "They did not sound like the real thing, they *were* the real thing! Without a doubt!" Lynyrd Skynyrd acknowledged their skills in "Sweet Home Alabama": "Muscle Shoals has got the swampers, an' they been known to pick a song or two." True to the laid-back atmosphere of the Shoals, the Swampers took their fame in their stride and treated playing with the Rolling Stones or Bob Dylan just like any other session. Mike Lawley: "The best part of Muscle Shoals was back in the days when they had the old small building on Jackson Highway. That was when Traffic was there, Steve Winwood. The musicians that would play with these big names never acted like it was that big of a deal. They would say, 'Yeah, we recorded with Traffic today and drank a few beers with them over at the house, no big deal.' They did not realize what a big stir these guys caused outside of here. It was like a fishbowl to them. They just wanted to be treated as your regular guy." When Mick Jagger was asked about the Rolling Stones' experience recording at the Shoals, he made a point of stressing the relaxed atmosphere and ease of working there.

People in the music business were talking of a Muscle Shoals sound. Johnny Sandlin: "The sound was very distinctive. A lot of it, I guess, is in the echo chamber. That was one of Rick's secrets. He built this chamber, and it was just distinctive. You could tell when that record was cut at FAME if you were listening that closely." Other record producers saw something beyond the technical capabilities of the Shoals. Ed Boutwell gives a lot of credit to Rick Hall and the other producers at the Shoals: "It was just wonderful what they did. Rick was the daddy of it all and they, like I said, [made a musical] amalgam. They took these extremely adept — they were white, they really were white musicians — and took them and played tracks for mixing them with black singers . . . but the sound was not developed by black musicians, no no no. It was developed by Rick and his rhythm section and that is it. Point blank! They developed that sound and the musicians — it was extremely rare to be a black picker up there. It was not that they were not talented, it was just that this was the staff band that Rick had developed and they could play this big fat sound."

The rise of Muscle Shoals as an internationally recognized recording center had an immediate effect on the music scene in Birmingham, which lost the best and brightest of its musical talent to the studios springing up around Florence and Sheffield. It lost guitar players, some of the best in the region, including Wayne Perkins, who left for a steady job at a studio owned by Quin Ivy called "Quinvy's"; piano players and producers like Barry Beckett, who came from Birmingham but relocated to Muscle Shoals; keyboardists and arrangers like Chuck Leavell, who went to school in Birmingham and played in local bands; drummers and percussionists; songwriters like Scott Boyer; and record producers like Johnny Sandlin. Fred Dalke left for the Shoals in 1976 to try his luck as a songwriter: "I am proud of that. A songwriter for two years . . . In '76, when I signed in Muscle Shoals, see, I wrote rhythm and blues stuff, more rock 'n' roll . . . I had songs that were published and recorded, never got that number 1, never got me a hit. But it was an experience. It was fun." All of these talented people might have made Birmingham their base if not for the pull of the Shoals.

Birmingham still had its recording studios, but few local bands wanted to record in them even though they had superior equipment. Ed Boutwell had moved up to a 4-track recording machine in the early 1970s, which made his studios one of the most technically advanced in the region, but he preferred to stick to producing jingles and recording gospel: "I was recording a lot of black gospel. That was my favorite thing to cut." He recorded all of the local garage bands and many of the leading lights of southern rock: "I cut a lot of it! I cut Allman Brother stuff back when they were the Allman Joys." Boutwell's main business was in jingles, "literally thousands of them . . . I specialized mainly in doing jingles because you got paid the minute you gave it to them . . . I actually got paid money, whereas all the rock 'n' rollers were scrounging up as much money as they could and pay to have records put out and they rarely made a dime." Producer Kenny Wallace: "First of all, the rock [business] was usually younger kids, and they are not settled, and they don't stay together as long . . . Usually the groups don't stay together and they did not have any money . . . In those days it might have cost two or three hundred dollars to come in for a couple of hours and record and get three hundred records or something like that. Maybe four or five hundred dollars. So it wasn't a lot of money, but there was just no market there to specialize in that . . . There was not that much going on with rock groups. Country and gospel has always been the main thing as far as our studio." Birmingham did not have the business connections and the infrastructure to market the pop and rock recordings made in its studios. There were plenty of local labels but no nationally based company: "Well, we really were not a recording center. There were no record companies here to produce and constantly push because you had to have publicity to have success. They [the bands] had no way out. They would cut a record and they might sell a thousand or two thousand records and that's it. But they were heroes in Birmingham. They were our guys!"

The number of hits produced in Muscle Shoals is a matter of great pride for local players. Fred Dalke: "Hundreds of gold records. They had approximately 220 gold records recorded out of Muscle Shoals Alabama: Aretha Franklin, Wilson Pickett, Sonny & Cher, Rolling Stones — you ever heard the song 'Brown Sugar'? That was recorded in Muscle Shoals." Players and producers in the music industry always gravitate to the studios that produce the hits. Kenny Wallace: "That was kind of what happened in Muscle Shoals. They got a rhythm section that was really good and those guys really worked well together and Rick Hall was the producer and he knew how to get things done too! They just developed a name really quickly that was a great song and these groups get that sound. So labels started to send their artists there. Pretty soon pop artists and rock and country and all kinds were doing it."

Overwhelmed politically and economically by Atlanta, "The Showplace of the South," unlucky Birmingham was now dwarfed musically by "The Hit Recording Capitol of the World" in its own backyard. Both Atlanta and Muscle Shoals had benefited from a level of racial harmony that could never have occurred in Birmingham in the 1960s. It is hard to imagine that an African American like Arthur Alexander or Percy Sledge — a bellhop in a local hotel and a hospital orderly, respectively — would have been allowed to walk into a studio and cut a record in Birmingham, or even have the courage to do so. Muscle Shoals protected its reputation for tolerance and continued to draw African American talent to record at its studios. When musicians from the Shoals went outside the tri-city area, they found an entirely different atmosphere, especially if they came to Birmingham. Arthur Alexander stayed in the car when the other guys went into a restaurant downtown and soon found himself surrounded by an ugly mob. They backed off when they were told that this was *the* Arthur Alexander: "The funny thing is that these same guys who were buying my records wanted to kick my ass."[3]

Birmingham did not have the creative forces that powered Muscle Shoals. Dan Penn: "Rick Hall was the difference. You didn't have those people in Birmingham . . . They didn't have a Rick Hall." There was magic in the Muscle Shoals studios. As Wayne Perkins maintains: "It's still there, it's still in the walls!" But the point was that it was not in Birmingham, and at the very moment when the vagaries of popular music gave central Alabama its greatest opportunity to exploit its musical talent, much of its vital creativity had relocated a hundred miles or so to the north.

CHAPTER TEN

Southern Rock

One strand of rock 'n' roll which emerged in the late 1960s marked a high-water mark of southern prestige in American popular music. Southern rock could never be a precise term, and there was little agreement among musicians about what it was defining. Many Alabama-based musicians strongly disliked the label, especially when it became nationally known and many bands were categorized as southern rock as they got on the bandwagon. Johnny Sandlin, who played with the Allman Brothers and also recorded them, favors authenticity and thinks the term should apply to southern musicians living in the South: "I guess I don't like the term 'southern rock' myself, because to me it conjures up later bands that were I guess derivative of the Brothers." For Sandlin, "the bands I consider southern rock are Lynyrd Skynyrd, Charlie Daniels, both great bands, and later Molly Hatchet." Journalist and radio broadcaster Court-ney Haden described the sound eloquently in Birmingham's *Southern Style* magazine: "Not quite rock, more than a little roll ... typified by laconic vocals, a foggy bottom and lead guitars which sear but do not scorch."[1] Mu-sicians agreed that there were similarities in the music, "a lot of common threads," but many do not see a separate musical genre in southern rock. They see a community of musicians: all raised the same way, "listening to the same music ... going to the same churches." Muddy King of Slick Lilly: "It is a southern attitude more than anything. It is feeling kind of relaxed and low-key and not being someone out of New York, which is fast-paced ... You could actually kind of be yourself. That is more of the southern thing, and the music really means something to you as opposed to trying to impress everybody else." Carl Rouss: "The South! The blues was born here and it is ridiculous for a band from here sounding like it is from somewhere else. It wouldn't be real!" Yet southernness could be conferred on the righteous by acclamation of their talent. Muscle Shoals session men Roger Clark and Travis Wammack were mightily impressed with the singing of Tom Jones, who came over the monitors "like the voice of God." "He sang like a southerner," commented Wammack, giving the Welshman the ultimate compliment.

Southern rock sounded southern because of the blues and country influences, but where southern rock ended and country rock or the new "outlaw" country began is anyone's guess. David Scott played in several bands in the heyday of southern rock: "I used to think that Birmingham was a real happening town. But you would have to learn how to play country. I am talking [in 1996] about twenty years ago, when country was not cool like it is now, because a lot of the style of music which was southern rock is now country, contemporary country. The Allman Brothers helped to do that."

Southern rock became recognized as such because of the marketing carried out by record companies. Capricorn Records did the most to put it on the map, but the company's founder, Phil Walden, pointed out that the company's motto was "Support Southern Music" rather than "Support Southern Rock." Rock 'n' roll was a southern music that had been quickly appropriated by the Empires of Sound and shifted to their corporate recording studios. Phil Walden, like Sam Phillips and Rick Hall before him, parlayed a group of local musicians into a national music scene, but he kept control of it. Walden came from Macon, Georgia, the home of Little Richard, James Brown, and Otis Redding. He got a foothold in the business by managing Otis Redding. When the singer died in 1967 all seemed lost, but then Duane Allman appeared and Walden took over the management of his band. Walden was ambitious, and with Jerry Wexler's support, he formed Capricorn Records. Walden set up his recording studio along the lines of the studios he had worked in at Muscle Shoals, using session men to make up a house band that would back up the performers. Naturally he recruited some of the session men he knew from Muscle Shoals, such as Johnny Sandlin, who went down to Georgia and eventually realized his dream of producing albums. Walden's new label might have been a front for Atlantic, but he made the most of the opportunity, capitalizing on the success of the Allman Brothers Band by signing more bands with a similar sound and pouring his profits into making Macon a center of music production. At its height, Capricorn Records had twenty-seven acts on their books, which covered everything from old-time country to jazz fusion.

The 1970s was the southern rock decade in Birmingham: the bars and airwaves were full of music by the Allman Brothers, Lynyrd Skynyrd, Wet Willie, and Charlie Daniels. In North Alabama, Patterson Hood remembered it was everywhere. It was best enjoyed live — played by bands who toured constantly and who loved to play, even without payment. Southern rockers were especially accessible to their audience, and if you were in Birmingham at the beginning of the 1970s you could enjoy a night of Allman Brothers music at the Oporto Armory for only three dollars, or at their outdoor concert at Avondale Park for free. The Allmans put a lot into their shows, playing powerful music "that would blow you away," in the words of Michael Gadilhe, and they played a lot of them: twenty-five to twenty-seven shows a month in the early days, and a total of three hundred shows in 1970. During the 1970s you could see them from the cheap seats in the Municipal Auditorium or right up close in a club downtown. Steve Lowry walked into the Crazy Horse Bar on Morris Avenue, and there was Duane Allman playing guitar "sounding like John Coltrane on a Stratocaster." At one well-remembered performance in the Birmingham city auditorium, the police stepped in as it got close to the 11 p.m. curfew. Randy Holzman of the Generic Band: "They had a strict curfew that you had to stop playing then! And the Allman Brothers were in the middle of playing 'In Memory of Elizabeth Reed' and all of a sudden someone pulled the plug and the curtains got drawn. You heard all sorts of scuffling out in front of the stage, and I believe it was Duane Allman that came out and said, 'We have to shut down. We extended [beyond] our curfew, but the police say we can play one more song.' And the Allman Brothers came out and did like almost an hour's version of 'Whipping Post.' I'll never forget that. It was fantastic!"

Southern rock conformed to a code for dress and performance, just like all rock 'n' roll genres. Like the old-time musicians of the previous generation, they conspicuously displayed signifiers of southern life, but instead of overalls, fiddles, and skillets, they toted cowboy hats, electric guitars, and bottles of bourbon. Southern rock musicians were self-conscious in their southernness, draping themselves with the Confederate flag and often wearing clothes associated with the Old South, such as the hats worn by Confederate troops. The battle flag of the Confederacy was often hung behind them on stage, and the image could be seen all over the audience. Many of their album covers featured the Rebel flag as it became an identifier of southern rock. Even the California- and New York–based record companies hung out the flag for record release and signing parties of their new friends from the Deep South, and it might be that the ubiquitous Confederate flag was as much the work of the marketers and promoters as the musicians themselves. But the large Confederate flag that hung behind Lynyrd Skynyrd in all their concerts was a strong statement of allegiance, along with their rendition of "Dixie" that began the show.

The southern rock concert was fashioned to present the same image of both musicians and their audience: tough, dedicated, hardworking stiffs who had a tendency for drunken rowdiness but always got the job done and, most important, had an inordinate pride in their southern roots. The name of .38 Special's breakout album, *Wild-Eyed Southern Boys*, says a lot about the stereotype, and a glance at the cover reveals the essential visual identifiers of girls in hot pants, crushed beer cans, pickup trucks, and Cadillacs. Southern rock concerts were much more than performances. When the Allmans played the Fox Theatre in Atlanta, the bottles of Jack Daniels and smoldering joints of marijuana were passed around the front rows of the auditorium with the seriousness of a ritual. Southern rock was steering the heart of rock 'n' roll back to the Deep South and making people feel good about being southern.

The Blues Revival

The southern rock sound leaned heavily on the blues for its songs, and the country and rockabilly influences stood out in the sound of guitar or fiddle solos — Gregg Allman estimated that the ratio was six parts blues to one part country. Ironically, these significant blues influences emerged not from the musical heritage of the Deep South but from a bunch of pasty-faced musicians from far across the Atlantic. After the Beatles, the touring groups who caught the attention of young southern musicians were products of the blues revival in England: the Rolling Stones, the Animals, the Pretty Things, the Yardbirds, and the Who. High school groups that had jumped onto the British Invasion fad were slowly drawn to some of the lesser-known but much more serious British bands. Rick Byrd was in a high school guitar band: "What we were doing with the group out there was sort of covers. We were just in the seventh grade. We were doing the Rolling Stones, Beatles, and some Kinks. We would do maybe some Yardbirds and the Animals." These latter two bands were inspired by American roots music and greatly admired the mythical bluesmen they read about on the back of their LPs of reissued recordings. All the garage bands in Birmingham played Chuck Berry and Bo Diddley songs along with covers of soul hits, but they had very little contact with the blues. Radio was the one outlet for blues, but even the black stations in Birmingham rarely went beyond the current hits of R&B. Wayne Perkins: "The only blues that we were exposed to as the general public, the only access we had to the blues was anything that was popular on the radio. It had to be something that was popular on the radio and like in the Top 40, *Billboard* stuff that we would hear." If you searched the AM frequencies at night, you might be able to pick up some blues from distant cities. Larry Wooten: "I started listening to a black station out of Nashville that played black music — on a clear night you could pick it up just like it was in town — and they played nothing but blues and rhythm and blues . . . There was also a station out of New Orleans." Much of the blues was transmitted in Birmingham by records. "Well, the first record I ever owned," Wooten continued, "was a 45 that a friend of mine bought me in 1957, March of '57, called 'King Bee' by Slim Harpo [a record that also influenced the Rolling Stones, who covered the song on their first LP]." Like many other garage bands, the Ramrods played both blues and danceable rock music: "It was a different type of music than you would play at Duke's [Duke's in Dixieland Sock Hop] because of the dance, the bop the local kids did. It was more rhythm and blues than blues. So we would drag out more of the rhythm and blues stuff for there, and a lot of these other places wanted rock 'n' roll. So we would drag out our rock 'n' roll."

Love of the blues was passed from musician to musician. Wayne Perkins: "This is where I bumped into Darryl Carl and we did our marathon jam session all night. Took me back to his place and we played all night! I was a puppy and he was showing me some stuff... The blues, he was one of the first guys that turned me on to that. Oh, it was heavy!" Then came the neo-blues bands of the British Invasion, whose blues-inspired music got heavy airplay and whose albums saluted the great bluesmen of the past. Jimi Hendrix more than any other musician showed how rock 'n' roll could build on the blues. His concert in Tuscaloosa in 1968 marked a turning point for many Birmingham guitarists. Wayne Perkins was one of them. He thought that Jimi Hendrix opened up the blues to white musicians. Blues was, in his words, "pretty much a black and white issue up until 1967, but Hendrix busted that thing wide open! I mean, he played the blues, but it was psychedelic blues, it was a lot of things. He sort of opened up a can of worms to let you know there was other things out there."

The British Invasion had a profound influence on young musicians in the South. Inspired by the British admiration of their own southern culture, they examined their roots anew. Although southern rockers essentially followed the British blues revival bands back to the blues, they made it their own, because it was their own. It took an outsider like Jerry Wexler to grasp this important difference — southerners were grounded in the blues "in a more significant, intimate and real way than the British bands."[2] The blues the British revivalists played was old and new at the same time. It sounded new because of the louder volume and the higher levels of distortion and other electronic effects that were being dialed into the sound, but the feel of the songs and their lyrics pointed back to a more traditional music. The blues was reemerging as something that had meaning and resonance in the modern world, especially in the confusion and soul-searching of the 1960s. The upsurge in interest in the blues, folk, bluegrass, and other traditional music was all part of a generational movement back to authenticity in popular music.

Southern guitarists were mightily impressed with the innovations that Englishmen like Keith Richards, Jeff Beck, and Eric Clapton had added to the blues, and when they saw their idols play it came across as the most exciting rock 'n' roll they had ever heard. In Florida, Ronnie Van Zant saw the Rolling Stones perform and dreamed of creating an American version of them. He formed a high school band called the Noble Five, which covered songs by the Stones and Yardbirds. This was not the Florida of sun-kissed beaches and blue water, but the Florida of piney woods, swamps, and dirt roads — ideal territory for the blues. The blues revival was booming in Jacksonville: Duane Allman, Dickey Betts, Ronnie Van Zant, Allen Collins, and Gary Rossington were all playing there. Duane Allman and his brother Gregg grew up in Florida and started garage bands in high school, and when the British Invasion arrived, it inspired them to form the Allman Joys. Johnny Sandlin pointed out: "No, they were very much the opposite of what you would think. They were very English. The whole thing was that they were doing Yardbirds stuff, they were doing like real Top 40, very lightweight stuff. They would do some typical covers, a few Jimmy Reed things that . . . all the cover bands, well, all the bands used to play that. But it was more of the English thing that made them so different, but they would take a Yardbirds tune and do it better than the record." Much of this improvement was the work of Duane Allman: "He was playing a [Fender] Tele[caster] with a Vox distortion that was clamped onto the guitar, and when it came for the Yardbird sound he would hit that distortion booster and work the volume control where it would sound like the guitar was being played backwards."

Although some southern rock bands used fiddles as lead instruments, the wailing, overamplified electric guitar was the musical signature of the genre. The guitars of southern rock had a distinguishable chunky twang, especially when they were Gibson Les Pauls, the guitar of choice, amplified through stacks of Marshall amps — an English product favored by the bands of the later British Invasion. Southern rockers also used pedal steel guitars, which gave the sound an unmistakable country ring, and often used slides on the guitar frets to tinge their notes with a wailing, metallic hue. Terry Powers: "Then I heard the Allman Brothers. I heard Duane play that slide and I went out and bought me one. I have loved it ever since." Duane Allman was a powerful influence on Birmingham's guitar players and was held in great esteem. David Scott spoke for many of them: "Oh my god! Well, he is a genius." Musicians like David are full of reverential stories about Duane Allman: "My cousin Malcolm was playing with a band . . . and they recorded a couple of singles up in Muscle Shoals. So my cousin Malcolm was doing this little guitar riff, and he said this guy who looked like he just got out of bed with scraggly hair, these weird-looking chops [sideburns], which turned out to be Duane Allman, came out and said, 'Hey, man, if you play this riff like this instead of that, I think that it will fit the song better.' So Malcolm did it, and it did fit the song better."

In his introduction to *Southern Rock Opera*, Patterson Hood waxes nostalgic for the glory days of southern rock: "When it was okay to turn your three guitars up to 10." This was time of loud guitars and long solos. Flutist Libba Walker: "I always liked guitar players and soloists and that is who I caught [borrowed] solos from. We used to criticize people whether or not they played solos too long or too short or if they did not say anything. We did that kind of thing in the '70s. I don't hear that anymore, but that was a big thing if you could make a solo peak. One person I thought could do that really well was Duane Allman: he was the boss." Duane's "big, fat, chunky guitar sound" proved to be especially popular on radio, and this exposure pushed southern rock into the mainstream as "real" rock 'n' roll in the 1970s.[3]

The guitar, its relationship with the player/hero, and its ability to evoke deep emotion was one of the central pillars of southern rock. When Alabama musicians go over the sacred ground of the greatest players from the state, it is rarely in terms of any other instrument than the guitar; whatever name they throw out — be it Eddie Hinton or Wayne Perkins — it is always from the small pantheon of virtuoso electric guitarists. Seventy years earlier, they might have discussed the merits of celebrity fiddlers, but Elvis and rock 'n' roll changed all that. Ray Hoaney of the Birmingham-based band Warm was highly regarded. Doug Lee: "Warm was a great Alabama band. One of the greatest bands ever! One of the greatest guitar players ever: Ray Hoaney." Hoaney received the highest accolade you could get in southern rock. David Scott: "After Duane died, Gregg was at a club where they were playing, and after hearing Ray play twice, he came up to him and said that he was the closest thing to Duane that he had ever heard." Like the bluesman before them, southern rockers valued virtuoso guitar playing that marked their long apprenticeship and professionalism — there was no room for amateurs in this music. The rise of the guitar hero, epitomized by the career of Eric Clapton, fitted nicely into the aesthetics of southern rock and gave opportunities not only to lead guitarists, but also to record producers like Buddy Buie, who saw that there was gold in those guitar solos.

Birmingham's Southern Rockers

Naturally there were numerous young musicians in Alabama who were drawn to the British blues revival and then to southern rock. Guitarist Wayne Perkins had been involved in music since age fifteen, playing in several high school bands and a gospel group led by Tommy Walton, and working as a session man in Bob Grove's recording studio. He joined up with Don Fields, Joe Goody, and Roy Stanley to form Colours, which played Beatles and Stones material and got gigs around Huffman. Then came several bands under the name of the Vikings: "We stayed with the popular stuff, we did some Beach Boys . . . we could do the Hollies." By sixteen he had made some records with the Vikings and got some prestigious gigs, including one with a player who had a major hit with "Wooly Bully": "We ended up playing this gig with Sam the Sham at Jacksonville State University . . . We were sound checking and he was supposed to show up and he never showed. I mean, like we were all freaking out . . . Everyone is pacing the floor and like twenty minutes before the gig he comes strutting in there . . . Sam come knocking and it's just 'Guys! Settle down! Look at this shit: it's just three chords.' So he showed us all his material in twenty minutes. He said, 'Just watch me' and we did! We were freaking out, but he came on and took all the money and left! I said, 'Mmm, so that is how that works.'" Wayne was attracted to the British neo-blues movement: "The British Invasion pretty much was heavy, and then we later started, I did, started dealing with the blues and stuff and listening to that stuff. I heard Howlin' Wolf and I said, 'My god. What is this?'" Of course the term "blues" is subjective: one man's blues is another's rock. Davey Williams told bluesman Johnny Shines, a friend of Robert Johnson, "Man, I opened for [John Lee] Hooker the other night [at the Old Town Music Hall on Morris Avenue], and he goes 'Oh, Hooker, he got all them boys in there playin' rock 'n' roll. He ain't playing the blues!"

Johnny Sandlin started his career up in Huntsville, first playing in the Mark V (or Five), a band made up of Rick Hall's studio musicians, with Dan Penn doing the vocals. This was no ordinary high school combo, but a group of seasoned musicians — they had backed Arthur Alexander when he cut "You Better Move On" in FAME Studios: "It is probably the best band I have ever played with, and it was like when I was eighteen and I've been real lucky." Dan Penn: "The Mark V played a three-hour set, we played at Alabama and Auburn . . . All we did was R&B, that Beatles stuff was an insult, we were too blues for that!" The Mark V went down to Florida and then re-formed as the Men-Its (and later the Five Minutes). In Panama City Johnny met up with Eddie Hinton, who had been play-ing in the Tuscaloosa area with a band called the Spooks ("very politically incorrect," said Johnny), and Eddie joined the Men-Its, which had Johnny Sandlin on drums, Paul Hornsby on keyboards, and Fred Styles on bass. As the Five Minutes worked the Florida Panhandle and Daytona Beach clubs playing R&B and soul. Johnny Sandlin: "We were just kids! We were all eighteen, nineteen years old, and Eddie was just starting to develop that huge voice that he ended up with, you know, and we were still doing covers. We would do the whole James Brown *Live at the Apollo* [album], the '62 thing. We would do the whole thing, cape included!" Perkins and San-dlin hung out with the Allmans, started to grow their hair long like them, and accompanied them to little all-night dives in Daytona Beach to hear some real rhythm and blues. They played together, drank together, and often bumped into each other in the lucrative college market around the University of Florida campuses, equal to the concentration of gigs around Auburn and Tuscaloosa, and along the numerous bars on the Gulf Coast. These were the "drinkin' n' fightin'" joints that musicians like Hank Wil-liams had played in the 1940s and 1950s. As Duane Allman said: "There's a garbage circuit of the South, man. You make about a hundred and fifty dollars a week and eat pills and drink."[4]

When the Men-Its broke up, Sandlin and Hornsby joined up with Gregg and Duane Allman to form Hour Glass. Johnny Sandlin: "It was the whole soul thing. It was Ray Charles stuff, Otis Redding, no originals. In fact, that was just unheard-of, you know! Nobody ever thought to do that, I guess, or it was never even discussed . . . Yeah, by this time the blues was real heavy. By the end of the Hour Glass era, the British thing, we had gone from that and gotten back to the roots and I was always more into the blues, the R&B part of it, and when Berry Oakley got in, Berry was very much into the Chicago blues, the electric Chicago blues."

Alabama musicians like Larry Wooten were graduating from rock and R&B to something more substantial: "My early love I guess was 'Rock and Roll [Music]' by Chuck Berry because he was heavy guitar, which I liked, but I grew out of rock 'n' roll and started liking blues more . . . You wanted the real thing — not that Elvis was not real, but you wanted to hear straight from his roots." The Ramrods played a fair number of popular R&B songs: "About the time I got out they were doing stuff like Freddie King and stuff like that. Instrumental stuff. There was a song called 'Hide Away' that had become popular . . . That is when I got out, and I didn't really like rock 'n' roll anyway by that time. I was so much into the blues."

The blues not only provided the inspiration for their music but also for the life of a musician. Eddie Hinton, Duane Allman, and Dan Penn didn't just listen to the blues, they lived it. Hinton was already gaining a reputation among Alabama pickers as the most talented guitar player of them all. Steve Lowry: "He was a magnificent guitar player. He used to do things on the guitar . . . He would bend up and down on the strings. Eddie had this kind of funky slithering way. Keith Richards would give five years of his life to be able to do it that way . . . Nobody ever played like Eddie. He was simply out of this realm . . . A lot of great musicians would be stone intimidated when he came around." Eddie Hinton was the master of the blues, a white man who played and sang like he was black — the personification of white conceptions of the blues. If you listen to his records he sounds a lot like Otis Redding, sometimes more Otis Redding than the man himself. Hinton lived the life of the bluesman to the full — wandering, carousing, drinking. "Some friends of ours went over to this house where Eddie was. It was in the middle of winter. They go in the living room, and there were newspapers piled up everywhere, and Eddie was under them. There were beer cans everywhere. It was tragic." Hinton's rejection of the commercial side of music was one reason why his fame never spread outside Alabama and why he is held in such high esteem by blues aficionados today. A close friend of Otis Redding and Duane Allman, Eddie Hinton's playing inspired them both. Musicians from the Shoals tell the story of Otis Redding's wife playing Hinton's records to her children to instruct them on the finer points of blues and soul. This story might be apocryphal, but it does reflect the importance of acceptance by African Americans as the credential most sought out by southern rock musicians in Alabama.

In 1967, when Hour Glass got tired of being in California and trying to get a record out, they came back to Alabama. They played around Birmingham, where Wayne Perkins saw them at the Opporto Armory, and then went up to Muscle Shoals to lay down some tracks at FAME Studios. When Rick Hall listened to Duane play on these tracks, he told him to pack his bags and move to North Alabama. Duane Allman made an immediate impression when he strolled into FAME Studios. For one thing, there were his hippie clothes and amazingly long hair. Johnny Sandlin said this of Duane and his brother Gregg: "They were the first guys I had ever seen with real long hair, and they were just striking. It was shocking! They had this shoulder-length blond hair, and they were both very thin and you knew that they were going to be stars!" But the look was nothing compared to the reaction when they started playing: "Oh! Like the best we'd ever seen, and Gregg was such a great singer too. I mean, I couldn't believe it." Duane's first job was to lead the rhythm section behind hot-tempered Wilson Pickett, but it was a match made in heaven. Allman had the nerve to tell Pickett to record a Beatles tune, "Hey Jude," and to everyone's surprise Pickett agreed and the record was a hit — North Alabama soul reaping the dividend of all "those shots of rhythm and blues" previously exploited by their British admirers.

Johnny Sandlin noted the country influences in the Allman Brothers: "Dickey Betts's influences . . . seemed to be very heavily on the country side. Where Gregg's were more on the blues side, and Duane's was from just everywhere! He listened to everything . . . Duane had a lot of jazz influences, Dickey more of the country and swing influences, but they could play that stuff. A lot of other bands could play southern rock as it is now . . . but I don't think they could play jazz. The Brothers played jazz. They would go into a jazz thing and go anywhere and they would be together."

Duane Allman used several session men from Muscle Shoals when he assembled the band that would be known as the Allman Brothers. He had played with drummer Jaimoe Johanny Johanson and Berry Oakley in Muscle Shoals studios. Scott Boyer had met up with drummer Butch Trucks while they were attending Florida State University. Like many Birmingham musicians, Boyer was attracted to folk and folk rock — another musical strain that went into southern rock. Boyer was inspired by the Beatles and by Bob Dylan and was also drawn to the "protest songs" of Phil Ochs — "the protester's protester," as he put it. He played in several guitar bands, "and David [Brown], Butch, and I got together and it was right when Lovin' Spoonful and the Byrds had done [Dylan's] 'Mr. Tambourine Man,' and they said, 'You know, if you know all these Dylan songs, and we know how to play rock 'n' roll, then we could get ourselves a folk rock group together and be nailing all this folk rock stuff' . . . during the summer vacation of '65, '66, we went down to Daytona looking for a gig, and that is when we ran into Gregg and Duane Allman down there. I met them. They helped us procure some work for the summer in a club in Jacksonville where we were the house band seven days a week. The name of the band was the Bitter Ind. We were together for about three years, and we even had Gregg and Duane in the band for a while." While primarily attracted by folk and country, Scott came under the influence of his bandmates: "Gregg and Duane and Butch and David and I used to go to this black club in Daytona that was a sleazy little dive, but it had a blues band in there. There were four guys, and I think two of them were blind, but it was just — they played the blues! Little by little I got into the blues. I discovered myself that there wasn't a whole lot of difference with some of this folk music that I had been playing." When the Bitter Ind went to Miami to record some tracks for Vanguard Records, they changed their name: "So for some weird reason we named it the Thirty-First of February: it was the psychedelic age, and names didn't have to make sense . . . well, this was pre–Allman Brothers when we did this stuff . . . We cut some demos and Vanguard for some unknown reason turned us down . . . Oh yeah, and I mean, 'Melissa' was one of the songs that was on there. There were some great tunes on there . . . so about six months later the band sort of broke up . . . and they started to have jam sessions in the park at Jacksonville and the Allman Brothers came out of that."

The Allman Brothers Band was formed in Jacksonville in March 1969, as Duane Allman brought in his brother Gregg, along with Dickey Betts, Berry Oakley, and drummers Jaimoe Johanny Johanson and Butch Trucks. Most unusual for a southern band, the Allman Brothers were integrated — Jaimoe was African American. Audiences in Atlanta and

Birmingham were especially struck with the level of integration in the band and the well-known association of Duane Allman with African American musicians: "He was a white guy who played for Aretha Franklin; everybody was whispering about."[5] The Allman Brothers started as group of musicians jamming together in Jacksonville and continued this practice when they moved to Macon in May 1969. Many of their early concerts were free, including one memorable afternoon in Atlanta's Piedmont Park, which many of their fans consider the turning point in the history of the band. The first two Allman Brothers albums only sold around fifty thousand each, but their live recording at the Fillmore East (1971) captured them at the height of their powers and converted even the most jaded rock critic. George Kimball in *Rolling Stone* magazine reviewed this record and concluded that the Allman Brothers were "the best damn rock 'n' roll band this country has produced in the last five years."[6] The Allman Brothers were invigorating rock 'n' roll by mining American roots music and returning to the old values of 1950s rock authenticity; southern rock was essentially nostalgic for rock's mythical past of virtuoso playing and implied rebellion. As Phil Walden pointed out, "The new music from the South connects with the old music from the South. It's a very honest, very powerful connection."[7] The Allmans came across as working musicians rather than rock stars. The southern rock ideal was to be real rather than artificial. Patterson Hood wistfully points out, "Rock stars today aren't half as real."[8]

Being real was a reaction against the bloated showmanship of 1970s arena rock and the larger-than-life aspirations of other forms of popular music, such as disco and heavy metal. In the 1970s the size of the show and its audience was growing rapidly, along with the financial returns of playing. The performances and their stars were growing more self-conscious as the stadium concert entertained an audience of thousands with music, pyrotechnics, and increasingly elaborate staging. Rod Stewart, Boston, Foreigner, Kiss, and the other great stadium bands played the newly built Birmingham Civic Center (created by means of a successful bond issue in 1970), where the music (sometimes mimed) took a back seat to the lighting and outrageous stage costumes. The cult of personality in rock music reached its highpoint in the 1970s with performers like David Bowie creating dramatic alter egos like Ziggy Stardust when their own were not large enough to fill the huge stages they played. Southern rock went back to the basics just when audiences were recoiling from highly commercialized and overpackaged music; it took them back to the days when the musicians were not much different from the people in the audience and certainly did not act different. They wore the same clothes and smoked the same cigarettes. They eschewed the flamboyant and elaborate stage shows that were becoming the norm. Duane Allman made the famous point that musicians were paid not to dress funny but to play music. Southern rock came across as real rock 'n' roll: based in the mythological past of the bluesmen and truthful to the heritage of the 1950s that valued directness and honesty over artifice and stage craft. Southern rock reflected the duality of the South: traditionalist in outlook and sentiment, yet at the same time modern and forward-looking. The hippie clothes the Allmans wore were the height of fashion in the late 1960s and early 1970s, when it was cool to be scruffy and unkempt. The guitars they preferred were the classics — Ronnie Van Zant sings in "The Banker" that all he has in the world is a 1957 Les Paul (a Goldtop, worth around eighty thousand dollars today). Yet their amplification was top of the line, and the effects they used were at the cutting edge of electronic technology.

The New, New South

The more hits on Capricorn Records, the more bands were attracted to Macon, which was fast becoming a regional music center. Atlanta — the hub of Georgia music and the largest club scene in the state — also benefited from the rise of southern rock. Buddy Buie made the most of this opportunity. Born in Dothan, Alabama, he hung out in Ed Boutwell's studio in Birmingham to learn about record producing. After moving to Atlanta, Buie put together a band called Classics IV, which contained two musicians from Alabama — J. R. Cobb and Dean Daughtry. In 1968 they had a major hit with "Spooky," which helped bankroll Buie's ambitious plans to set up an independent studio on the lines of those he had studied in Alabama. He recruited several members of Classics IV to work as session men at his Studio One complex just outside Atlanta, in Doraville, and these made up the aptly named Atlanta Rhythm Section. The band had strong connections with Atlanta, and their "Champagne Jam" was not only a successful recording but also became a self-affirming concert experience that reflected the newly found, and somewhat bewildering, affluence of the New South's great city.

Atlanta was pulling ahead of all its rivals in the New South in terms of its economic development, global outlook, Yankee entrepreneurship, and lively bar scene. Its population grew in the 1960s, while that of Birmingham dropped by over 10 percent, as "white flight" took many from the city into the suburbs. The most segregated city in America had now been comprehensively overtaken by a city allegedly too busy to hate. Atlanta was now busy having a good time and enjoying its newfound wealth. Its vibrant music scene drew bands from all over the South, including Lynyrd Skynyrd, who moved up from their base in Jacksonville. And like many other emerging southern rock bands, Skynyrd looked to Muscle Shoals to make their first records and learn something about the process of turning their music into a salable commodity. After making a few demos at Quin Ivy Studios in 1970, Lynyrd Skynyrd teamed up with producer Jimmy Johnson at Muscle Shoals Sound to produce some impressive recordings, which brought them to the attention of MCA, a major record company. Before moving out to Los Angeles in 1974 Lynyrd Skynyrd cut two songs at Buddy Buie's Studio One in Atlanta. The first was "Free Bird" — a song that became a tribute to Duane Allman and ended up as an homage to Ronnie Van Zant. The second was called "Sweet Home Alabama." Van Zant had a good feeling about this song: "We got it down real fast . . . It's always the ones you get down fast that make it."[9]

The Allmans had demonstrated that it was possible for a southern band to break into the big time of rock 'n' roll without selling out. The successes of Rick Hall, Buddy Buie, and Phil Walden showed that Sam Phillips and Sun Records had not been an accident of history but steps in the direction of southern autonomy in the music business. Southern entrepreneurship had finally caught up with the music. A decade earlier, success in popular music had always been accompanied by a move to the Northeast and a contract with a major record company. This was no longer the case. As Johnny Sandlin concluded, the Allman Brothers were the first band to break out of the South, achieving the goals of all professional musicians without having to relocate to the commercial centers of the North or West. Dickey Betts remembered: "Everyone in the industry was saying that we'd never do anything out of Macon," but they stayed put, and this impressed all those other southern musicians who looked up to them.[10]

CHAPTER ELEVEN

Opportunity Knocks

The rise of southern rock increased the value of southern musicians, especially those who could play blues and rock while looking the part of the unreconstructed rebel — pretty easy for scores of Alabama rock guitarists who had been inspired by the same records, played the same joints, and had bought the same guitars as the Allman Brothers. As a consequence of the growing prestige of Muscle Shoals and Macon, Birmingham musicians suddenly found out that their skills were in demand nationwide. Although Macon claimed to be the capitol of southern rock, its players were drawn from all over the Deep South, especially Alabama. Bunkie Anderson recognized a community of players in southern rock: "They were from Tuscaloosa, but they lived here and they played the bars here and they were all part of an interchangeable group that made a big impression. I mean, they were players." The same players who hung out at Muscle Shoals and Macon also went to Nashville or Atlanta or Birmingham or Jacksonville to play gigs. Like their blues forefathers, southern rockers were highly mobile and connected to a network of musicians rather than to any one geographic area.

The commercial success of southern rock greatly increased the self-belief and the expectations of many guitar groups from Birmingham; if the Allmans and Skynyrd could make it to the top on the tried-and-tested formula of playing the blues within the context of electrified rock 'n' roll, then the door was wide open for every boogie bar band in Alabama. Everybody knew that several guys from Dothan had established themselves in Atlanta in top-flight bands, that more than a few musicians from Tuscaloosa had made the big time, and that pickers from Muscle Shoals were known and respected all over the world. In the 1960s Birmingham bands had to twist and turn themselves into musical styles that were imported, either from the two fashionable American coasts or from Britain, but in the 1970s they could be fashionable by just being themselves and playing the music they had always played, the music of home. It wasn't like the formative influences and musical experiences of southern rock were secret; they were common all over the South. For musicians in Birmingham, this was a special time. Tony Wachter: "I have always felt that if you sent a demo tape to somebody, if you have a Birmingham, Alabama, return address on it, that it was like, 'Yeah, sorry!' And I hate that! I think that it because of the civil rights. The stigma . . . you can go anywhere in this country, and tell people where you are from, and every time they look at you like, 'Birmingham?'" But now a Birmingham address was an advantage.

Just like Elvis Presley and the Beatles in previous decades, the Allmans set the direction to be followed in music, attitude, and look. Kevin Derryberry: "I listened to the Allman Brothers and I just loved Gregg Allman because of the blues. I grew my hair long like him . . . [Duane Allman's influence] had a lot to do with it [the sound of the band Telluride]. We have always had a slide guitar player in our band." The success of the Allman's ensured that they took over the mantle of the Beatles as the most copied band in Birmingham. It wasn't just the music; it was also the way the records sounded. After forming the Bluedads, Doug Royale and Ben Elkins approached Johnny Sandlin to produce their first record: "I got my *Brothers and Sisters* album out and said: This is the guy we have to get right there."

The high profile of southern rock brought many talented musicians back to Alabama. Wayne Perkins returned home with his two friends Tim and Steve Smith after touring the United Kingdom and playing the famous Cavern Club in Liverpool, as Smith Perkins Smith. Wayne Perkins had a long list of recording sessions to his credit and was good enough to audition for the Rolling Stones as a replacement for Mick Taylor. Keith Richards thought he was an "incredible player — he was as good as Mick Taylor, if not better."[1] Smith Perkins Smith naturally went to the Shoals to record, and when the members of Cowboy went up there, the engineers played them back the tapes of Perkins's band, Scott Boyer: "And it is like, I want to go home: I don't want to do this album, I don't want to ever play

again. I give up. I quit! They sounded so good." Wayne turned down an
offer to play in Lynyrd Skynyrd in order to join his brother Dale in the
band Alabama Power: Dale Perkins on drums, J. J. Jackson on bass, and
Gregg Straub on keyboards — all veterans of local rock bands. Terry Powers played with them for a few months: "We had a good solid band. Rock
'n' roll."

The typical performance in the 1970s was a show built around one act
rather than the long bill of stars that had been customary in the first decade of rock 'n' roll. This brought more money to the musicians. The Allman Brothers started by playing for free, and then a few hundred dollars a
night, but by 1973 they were charging a hundred thousand dollars for one
performance. Gradually this affluence trickled down to the cover and bar
bands with regular gigs. Tony Wachter remembered that from the mid-'70s
onward a band could make seven hundred dollars per weekend playing in
clubs in Birmingham. Ben Trexel played in a cover band called Joker, which
cleared about eight hundred dollars for a long weekend.

As more bands marketed themselves as southern rock, the demand for
suitably southern musicians increased accordingly. Hundreds of phone
calls were made to Alabama, Georgia, and Florida to enlist friends and
acquaintances in new bands, to recruit session men, or to join bands on
tour. A friendship or even acquaintance with one of the Allmans was often
the chance to move up in the music business. Duane's generosity was legendary, whether it was giving away one of his guitars to a twelve-year-old
fan or promoting the careers of his friends, such as the recording contract
he arranged in 1970 for the Jacksonville-based band Cowboy, put together
by Birmingham natives Scott Boyer and Tommy Talton after the Bitter
Ind broke up in 1969 and Gregg and Duane went on to form the Allman
Brothers. Cowboy also featured Tommy Wynn on drums, George Clark
on bass and Bill Pillmore on keyboards. Cowboy's repertoire covered
the gamut of rock but with more than a hint of country and jazz. One
can hear Poco or the Nitty Gritty Dirt Band in the songwriting of Scott
Boyer and Tommy Talton, especially the beautiful harmonies. Scott admitted: "The band Cowboy really backed in. We were a bunch of hippies,
you know what I mean? We wrote good songs and we could sing pretty

good, but there was me and one other guy Tommy Talton, [who] were the only two guys that could really play." The story goes that Duane Allman burst into Scott Boyer's apartment one morning at eight and demanded to hear the band play. Once he was satisfied with their sound, he fixed them up with Phil Walden (who also claims to have auditioned them in Scott Boyer's bedroom) and Cowboy were signed to Capricorn, making their first album, *Reach for the Sky*, in 1970 in Macon. Walden also arranged for them to open for the Allman Brothers on tour — one of the best gigs in the business in the early 1970s.

Many more Alabama musicians benefited directly from their association with the Allmans. Paul Hornsby played guitar and organ in Hour Glass, one of the precursors of the Allman Brothers Band, which had also included Johnny Sandlin. Hornsby then went to play with Southcamp back home in Tuscaloosa. On piano was another local player, Chuck Leavell, who had played in several Birmingham-based bands in the 1960s, including Care. Sandlin, Hornsby, and Leavell got the call from Phil Walden. Sandlin: "Capricorn at that time was in the works, but there had been no Capricorn releases yet. Phil was building a studio, and eventually I talked to Duane and Phil called me. I had met him while I was doing the solo stuff for Duane [at Muscle Shoals], and Phil had given me a chance to put together a studio band for this studio in Macon, which I did, and moved there." Sandlin's session men produced the demos for Walden's R&B acts, one of whom was Johnny Jenkins, who had once employed Otis Redding as the singer for his band the Pinetoppers in Macon. Sandlin went on to produce Johnny Jenkins's album *Ton-Ton Macoute* (1970), which was the second album Capricorn released.

Sandlin and Hornsby produced records for Capricorn. Sandlin mixed the Allman's *Eat a Peach* and produced the great *Brothers and Sisters*, but it was Leavell who got the opportunity of a lifetime. After some sessions with the Allman Brothers, the bemused eighteen-year-old was asked if he wanted to be in the band permanently, taking the place of the deceased Duane Allman, who was killed in a motorcycle accident during the making of *Eat a Peach*: "Hell, yes!" was his reply. "I was a kid from Alabama and all of a sudden I'm in this big group." Leavell went from playing in bars around Tuscaloosa to touring all over the world, adding another chapter to the "poor southern boy done good" story that was driving Birmingham musicians forward in the 1970s.

There were lots of ways to make money from southern rock. Scott Boyer wrote a song called "Please Be with Me" for Duane Allman while he was working for Capricorn: "I was living out there playing for Cowboy, wondering where my next pack of cigarettes was coming from, and I got a phone call from Johnny Sandlin. We would play jokes on each other, and he called up and went: 'Guess what? Eric Clapton just recorded one of your tunes!' I said: 'That's not funny, man! I am totally broke out here. I don't even have money for food. I don't know where I am going to get my rent' . . . and I hung the phone up." A little later Phil Walden called and confirmed the good news: "I was like, 'I'll be damned' . . . It was a rags-to-riches thing in a way. My first check was for like about ten thousand dollars, I think . . . compared to having nothing! Compared to having to play at Grant's Lounge for fifty bucks a man just so you could have enough money to eat, it was a big deal. I was driving a 1951 pickup truck [one day] and I was driving a brand-new Jag [a 1963 Jaguar XKE] the next!"

Many southern rock bands were forming in Birmingham. Chair was put together after the Rockin' Rebellions split up in 1968. Chair was Glenn Butts (guitar), Jim Liner (bass), Donald Barby (keyboards), and Henry Lovoy (drums and vocals). They could play blues, R&B, southern rock, and also songs by the Band, keeping the music of the Old South alive in the New. Rick Byrd thought highly of them: "One of the best Birmingham bands, in my opinion, that has ever been around was a group called Chair. Fantastic band! They probably had the best feel of any band I have ever heard. They used to do a bunch of the Band's material, 'Cripple Creek.' I would go hear them whenever I could." Another of Rick's favorite bands in the 1970s was a four-piece called Warm. Its foundation was the guitar virtuosity of Ray Hoaney. It had Ray Greene on guitar and vocals, and their drummer was Mike Bruce. "They played a lot of original material," Byrd recalled. "Played the clubs around here. They played the Crazy Horse . . . Warm, without a doubt, was probably one of our favorite groups to go hear."

Dick's Hat Band was formed in the 1970s by Ross Roberts. It combined rhythm and blues with the Memphis sound of a large horn section, producing the kind of good-time soul music that was so popular in Birmingham's bars and clubs. While many guitar bands were formed to take advantage of the popularity of southern rock, others followed the neo-blues movement all the way back, such as the aptly named Blues Band, which included Topper Price, Wick Larson, and Harold Floyd. Topper grew up in Mobile, and even then, Pam White recalled, he had "big-city ambitions." This meant moving to Birmingham. Susan Collier first heard Topper play with Scott Boyer and the Convertibles at Hoppers in Five Points.[2]

Dogwood was formed in 1971 around Don Tinsley, Doug Lee, Tom Fox, Mark Smith, and Rick Kurtz. Lee, Fox, Smith, and Little had all come from Buddy Causey's Days of the Week. Causey went in the Homestead Act, and their singer John David Harris joined Dogwood. Doug Lee: "It was almost like we had just swapped singers, and of course the bands could not have been any more radically different: although it was the same core group of people, we launched into a completely different direction. I had always been a big fan of the country rock that came out of L.A. . . . the L.A. and San Francisco bands. Next to the Beatles, that was what I liked best. It was that sound that was exemplified by the Buffalo Springfield, and then Tom Fox loved that sound, and then we met up with Tinsley, and he was very much influenced by that sound. We were just disillusioned with what we were doing, with personal problems between us and Buddy, you know? We were getting more and more serious about it and wanting to try to write some stuff." Dogwood had a real country flavor when Rick Byrd played the pedal steel guitar, and they also had excellent vocalists who could sing together in close harmony. Rick: "They were very influenced by Poco and all that country rock material . . . Since I had been playing steel guitar and they were doing country stuff, I said this might be a good mix, so they asked me to join the band. In fact, the first or second time that I ever played the steel guitar in public was with Dogwood." They felt at home sounding like Poco or the Eagles, but they could also duplicate the harder Allman Brothers sound, especially when they recorded at Capricorn Studios in Macon, where Paul Hornsby produced their albums. Dogwood was an important band in Birmingham, not only because of their close musical association with the Allman Brothers, but also because their personnel went on to play in other bands such as Locust Fork and Telluride. Rick Byrd pointed out, "It is funny how all the bands intertwine and are re-forming over the years."

When Dogwood broke up in 1976, several of its members formed Hotfoot: Doug Lee, Mark Smith (bass), Dale Robbins (drums), Mark Peterson (steel guitar), Beverly Owen (acoustic), and Eddie Bosman (vocals): "At that point country rock had exploded. You had the Outlaw thing with Willie and Waylon going and of course the Eagles . . . Country rock was really big with the college-age people at the time, and it was very much the right thing at the right time. We would pack the clubs out! We would really draw big." Locust Fork was formed in 1974 in Tuscaloosa in the middle of the southern rock boom, and in 1975 they brought in several members of the now defunct Dogwood. They started with Dwight Williams on bass guitar, Bill Marshall on guitar, and Kent Peterson. Dwight Williams: "Locust Fork, when we first got together, we were almost exclusively Allman Brothers stuff. We would play an entire night and we would not play anything but Allman Brothers and Marshall Tucker, not a song." They played fraternity parties and a circuit of bars around Tuscaloosa, Birmingham, Auburn, and Mobile. So did Black Mountain, which "leaned towards Mountain, Deep Purple, Yes, and Led Zeppelin. Not really heavy metal, but a harder rock type of material, with more of the screaming type vocals." Rick Byrd and Ross Roberts played guitar, Joe Breckenridge (bass), Kenny Sutton (keyboards), John McNam (drums), and Wes Cummings (vocals).

Like many of their fellow Birmingham musicians, Locust Fork spent a lot of time in Macon, where they were sometimes joined onstage by Gregg Allman and Dickey Betts. A music scene was developing in this sleepy Georgia town under the wings of the Allman Brothers. Johnny Sandlin recalled working in the Capricorn Studios: "We had a good little studio band. And it was the Allman Brothers band that was there, and Duane and the rest of the band would come by and help out, you know. It was very much a great music scene there! It was like music twenty-four hours a day!" Duane Allman was at the center of things at Capricorn: "Looking back at the situation, Duane was the leader of the whole thing — he was the reason all the people were in Macon, the younger people, the people that weren't just into the R&B."

Black Mountain was also attracted to Macon, playing wherever they could get a gig and hanging out at Capricorn: "Black Mountain was sort of in and out of that studio. We were trying to get Phil Walden's brother, Alan Walden, to pick up the group and push us. We were actually playing a good bit in a lounge over in Macon, Georgia, called Grant's Lounge. Back then, around '70, '71, Gregg Allman sat in with us. Dickey Betts sat in with us over there and we got to know some of the guys from Wet Willie because they were recording at Capricorn Studio. There was also a group called White Witch that was recording there . . . One afternoon at Grant's Lounge, some of the guys from Wet Willie and us got together. We jammed for a couple of hours . . . There was a restaurant there that we used to eat, called the H&H. Apparently one of the cooks was named Elizabeth Reed. But maybe I just made that up. The hotel we would stay at was the Central. Basically the people who stayed there were band members, hookers, and people who were after hookers. Dr. John was running around there one night with White Witch and I don't know . . . Anyway. Let me get on with the story. I love this kind of stuff!" The rise of Capricorn was attracting bands from all over Alabama. Wet Willie was formed in Mobile around the talents of Jimmy Hall. Often described as blue-eyed soul and the most soulful southern rock band, Wet Willie had several hits on Capricorn.

Yet of all the groups formed during this time, Telluride was the quintessential southern rock band of Birmingham. "Birmingham's own Telluride" became a favorite of the college and bar crowd during the 1980s and 1990s. Anthony Crawford: "We loved the audience! These guys have stayed in touch with their fans, and right now these guys have the fans. That is what music is really all about. It is playing your music for fans, and these guys were able to access a fan club that they have built over the years. Coming to the Telluride twenty-year reunion, it was awesome to see those guys, but they are still a band after twenty years, and that is like being in a marriage." The band started to come together in 1976, when guitarist Rick Carter moved from Selma to Birmingham: "When I came here I hooked up with Moose Harrell and Jim Liner. Jim was playing with a band called Dogwood at the time. That was with Don Tinsley, and you will see how all this stuff runs together. That is pretty much when we started Telluride

and its roots ... Then we got Robert Churchill [drums], who was from
Montevallo, who knew Jim Liner and all the Dogwood people. Roger Bailey played piano ... After '77 we traveled and started playing our first jobs.
Then as time went on and about the latter part of '78, Roger quit." Anthony
Crawford joined the band, and when bassist Jim Liner left he was replaced
with Scott Walker. Kevin Derryberry joined in 1980. Derryberry first saw
them in Auburn when they were all living in an old house together. He
joined them in 1980 to make a five-piece band: "So I called up Rick Carter
and I said, 'This is Kevin, I noticed you all did not have a keyboard player
last time [he saw them play], and this is what I want to do. I want to play,'
and they had all just decided to quit their day jobs and just do music ...
so we discussed it and Rick said that he could not pay me. They all lived
together in one apartment, and they only brought in thirty or forty bucks
apiece sometimes. So I said, 'Look, I have maybe a month or a few weeks
left on my unemployment.' He said that they wanted me: 'We want you to
come jam with us.' I said I would do it for nothing, and if my time runs out
and you don't think that it is working, then, like I said, it is no problem."
Another important addition was guitarist and vocalist Anthony Crawford,
who brought some folk influences to the music. During their many years
of playing in Telluride, several musicians came and went, but the core of
Carter, Churchill, and Derryberry stayed constant.

Kevin "So we started playing, and it started working, and I was young
and a lot better-looking than I am now: dumb, and what age I was, but the
girls liked me! We would draw a lot of them and the money started to get
better ... Girls on the first four rows. I mean, all girls, and then behind
them would be all guys. That is what music is all about ... That is what
it does. It brings people together." Rick Carter: "We were not mad about
anything. We were just all having a good time. The music reflects it too,
especially what we played ... that kind of Poco/country rock. You know
that good-time, almost bluegrassy kind of thing." The band's influences
were clear. Rick Carter: "Duane Allman. Oh god, yes! He was huge. Most
people might play an Allmans song, but unless you go and hear Telluride,
well, we might do about thirty of them. It was a huge impact." When Telluride went to Muscle Shoals to record in 1980, they wanted the Brothers'
sound on their first album, "which was produced by Johnny Sandlin, who

produced all the Allman Brothers' stuff. He produced all their stuff like *Brothers and Sisters* and all their big hits." Kevin Derryberry revealed the power of the Allman Brothers mystique: "Well, we thought we got this guy [Sandlin] interested. We were in heaven. This is the big time. Our hero, the Allman Brothers producer, is going to produce our record! We thought we were cool."

Southern Rock Values

Telluride personified the southern rock credo of paying one's dues, starting at the bottom with nothing — no money, no gigs, no recording contract — and working their way up by touring and practicing and learning the business the hard way. As Kevin Derryberry pointed out, "That was all I wanted to do. But it was such a learning thing. It was such a growing thing. The whole starving artist." The history of Telluride — living together in a broken-down house with nothing but each other and their music, playing together all day and then jamming with other musicians all night, traveling on the road for years before they felt good enough to go into a recording studio — is the same as many southern rock heroes. Kevin Derryberry: "We rehearsed for about six months and only played two gigs. We had a house where we all lived. Put up egg cartons all over the walls. It was the middle of a neighborhood. Families everywhere, but we were the rock band that lived in the neighborhood. Cops were there every night, 'Turn it down!' Women! The atmosphere, beer cans everywhere, everything you would expect a rock band's house to look like. It was always: 'What's that smell?'" Rick Byrd on Black Mountain: "The band lived out in a house on Center Point in a sort of nice residential area. We had pretty long hair and it was upsetting to the other people. They called the sheriff a couple of times. One time it was because we were outside with our shirts off on the roof. I think we got evicted from that house. We weren't really troublemakers, but if I look back now, I wouldn't want those guys living next to me and my family." Doug Lee describes the beginning of the band Dogwood: "So we put together this new thing together that was based in Montevallo. Didn't know what to call it there for a while. We nearly starved to death putting it together. Most of us at that point were living in an old farmhouse outside of Montevallo that was just outside a little community called Dogwood, an old falling-down . . . farmhouse that had been built in the 1800s, and we moved into it and had our first real taste of living on our own . . . We were living off, not the kindness of strangers, but the kindness of parents and other people like that. Students, friends, girlfriends, people would bring us food and just sacks of groceries and we would scrounge, but we made it through! I lost twenty pounds that summer . . . We were writing, we were doing it, yeah! We were writing a lot of stuff. A lot of the stuff was group written, and we worked countless hours . . . We worked really hard at putting this thing together, and real visions of stardom in our head! We used to sit up at all hours of the night around in the living room after we would get through rehearsing, and we would talk about when this happens and when that happens." After a career of pleasing audiences for over twenty years, Rick Carter stressed the importance of hard work: "We worked harder than anyone can imagine. We had no day jobs, we played music for a living. Sure, it was sixty-seven dollars a week, and six of us lived together, but we believed. We were a band, an unbreakable circle. The same musicians turned up at all three hundred–plus shows a year because we were once again a *band*."[3]

Playing live was the be-all and end-all of southern rock. Johnny Sandlin: "I mean, all the Capricorn bands were like road warriors. They all did well in taking the music to the people." At this time it was not unknown for a band to travel from Birmingham to Florida for a paying gig, even playing as far away as Key West and then driving home on the same night. The more ambitious bands looked even farther away, to the growing music scene in the Southwest, especially Austin; or to the big college circuit in North Carolina and Virginia. Rick Byrd got a job in Dennis Yost's Classic IV band out of Atlanta: "We played all the way from Key West to as far north as Maine." Touring had never been this important to rock 'n' roll, and it stood for the paying of one's dues in southern rock. While instant fame and fortune via a hit record remained the talisman for many in rock 'n' roll, making it in southern rock could come only after hard years on the road.

Life on the road brought the experiences that were incorporated into the songs and the mythology of the band. Transportation was always a problem because musicians usually put their money into their instruments, not their cars. The trials and tribulations of the road were the same for all players whether it was acid rock or bluegrass: engines caught fire, radiators overheated, exhaust systems fell off, or the highway patrol stepped in and brought the whole adventure to an end. If the transportation held up, there was still the boredom of being confined with all the other band members for day after day with nothing other to do than look out of the windows or squabble. Scott Boyer remembers a tour that took his band from Georgia to California, "we would start in Macon, go through Alabama, Louisiana, Texas, New Mexico, up the California coast into Oregon and Washington, and then come back across through Arizona and Colorado and St. Louis." They played about forty gigs in a two-month haul and traveled about ten hours most days. Boyer ruefully recalls being crammed in a Ford station wagon with seven other guys: "Oh yeah. I was learning how to feel the blues! It was part of my education there, I guess. It was rough! Sometimes, sometimes it was great, but a lot of times it was rough."

Accommodation, if you were lucky, meant cheap motels with sheets smelling of disinfectant, and cockroaches running amok in the bathrooms. If the band was short of money, accommodation might mean pleading with strangers to sleep on their couches or floors. Some bands became adept at crashing in other peoples' living rooms and stashing their sleeping bags behind couches or under tables. Rick Byrd: "There would be bodies all over the floor. It was just sleeping bag mania!" Many times they just slept in the van. Food was not that important, but drink and drugs were the fuel that kept many bands on the road, combating boredom, lifting performers when it came time to play, and acting as a general anesthetic to all the troubles and inconveniences of the tour. Drugs were the downfall of Black Mountain. Rick Byrd: "We would go over to Macon and play for a week or two, and then just sort of travel around playing where we could. One of the guys in the band was selling some dope to the townspeople . . . Apparently the sheriff's department found out about it . . . It turned out that the man did get busted and put an end to the band pretty quickly."

The mythology of the bluesman — a hardy, free-living traveling man both blessed and cursed with talent — was especially attractive to rock musicians in the 1960s and 1970s, who were becoming much more aware of their status and the power of their image. Duane Allman and Eddie Hinton represented the guitar hero in the same mold as Robert Johnson and those legendary blues players that went before him, and then way back to the tricksters and bad men of West African folklore. They began to identify as much with the image of the bluesman as the music — not the reality of being an itinerant musician in the Deep South during segregation but the fantasies imagined years later in the comfort of one's practice room. They moved closer to the blues' preoccupation with the lives of its practitioners and were drawn into a self-conscious representation of the bluesman told in the first person: "I don't own the clothes I'm wearing / I got one more silver dollar... no they ain't gonna catch me, no / they ain't gonna catch the midnight rider," sang Gregg Allman in one of the group's most famous songs, articulating the desperate journey of the outsider in the same way that Robert Johnson sang about hellhounds on his trail. Yet the Allman Brothers were now flying from stadium to stadium in their personal jet and succumbing to the pressures of fame and fortune, while they were singing "I was born in the back of a Greyhound bus, rolling down Highway 41."

The world these itinerant southern musicians traveled was made part of their songs: smoky bars, dingy motels and forlorn gas stations, and "women and whiskey and miles of road." Lynyrd Skynyrd sang of groupies in hotel rooms ("What's Your Name, Little Girl") and dangerous encounters in juke joints ("Gimme Three Steps"). They wrote about southerners like themselves and the places they had seen on their travels — not the rebuilt New South, with its affluent suburbs and technology parks, but "the forgotten South," in the words of Patterson Hood of the Drive-By Truckers: the South of trailer parks, truck stops, and shotgun shacks. The Allmans and Lynyrd Skynyrd liked to say that they were writing about, and playing for, the "common people," but the musicians they described were romantic, turbulent figures, never too far from danger. And like the legendary bluesmen they idolized, Duane Allman, Ronnie Van Zant, and Eddie Hinton all lived short and tragic lives. The most important value was to be real: to reflect the truth of who they were in their songs. Jeff Carlisi (of .38 Special) said this of Ronnie Van Zant: "When he wrote, he wrote out of his heart and mind and his soul... That's how genuine the songs were to him." Donnie Van Zant paid the ultimate compliment to his brother: "He was real, you know?"[4]

They sang about the trials of playing in rowdy bars with chicken wire strung across the stage to protect the band. Rock Killough: "They really did have chicken wire on stage from the stage to the ceiling. Beer bottles was the problem. I always thought that if you really wanted to get to somebody in a place where they have chicken wire, bring some peeled boiled eggs and some real ripe tomatoes. The chicken wire acts as a slicing device." Rock Killough tells a story about the bouncer at the Wooden Nickel, an off-duty policeman called George, ejecting one of the audience who "tore George's shirt completely off! He [George] was standing there with his sleeves in the back, he reached into his back pocket and pulled out a little slap [black]jack, and just casually laid it upside this guy's head, right about his temple and went *tap!* This man went to sleep immediately! I mean, he fell like an oak! *Bam!* They drug him out the door and threw him out in the gravel parking lot and came back in and locked the door." The smaller clubs in rural areas where country music was favored were among the most dangerous places to play. Rick Byrd: "I would play and sit in with just pure country bands. I am talking about heavy-duty redneck bars! Where people got shot and there are fights. They probably could have used some chicken wire."

Southern rockers on the road told stories about attacks by outraged boyfriends, cars broken into, equipment destroyed by jealous locals, or waking up in a motel with two underage girls and their father beating on the door. When Ronnie Van Zant sang: "I'm telling you son, well it ain't no fun, starin' straight down a forty-four" he was describing one of the occupational hazards of touring in the Deep South, and many of the road stories told by Birmingham musicians hinge on the introduction of firearms into the narrative. Kevin Derryberry: "We played at this one club just outside Selma called the Saloon. It was bad ... It was all this country stuff there. You know, the sticks ... We had to play some country just because we were out where they tote guns. One night I was in there and a fight broke out and I have never seen so many guns in my life! I ducked under the organ and I just kept playing. There were sawed-off shotguns, sawed-off rifles, just everything. Women were beating each other up. Ripping their clothes off! But we did not quit playing! We just kept on playing. I was hoping that organ would stop that bullet."

Musicians on the road had to be resourceful, as cunning as the tricksters on the folk ways of the Old South. They had to outwit rapacious club owners, avoid confrontation with the audience, and often talk or play their way out of trouble. Telluride played a high school prom in Grove Hill, Alabama: "We finished playing and wanted to go have a couple of beers and it was a dry county so we picked up a couple of little girls from there and we drove over to the Mississippi line. This was a Friday night. It had been raining, and so we see this place down in this little valley, almost. Right by the river on the Mississippi line. You had to walk through mud to get to it, and it looked like a shack, but it was built on stilts because of the river. So we go up these rickety stairs. This was just like a movie like *Roadhouse* or something. There was this guy at the door dressed up like Yancey Derringer . . . the gambler hat and he has a pistol stuck in his belt . . . So we go into this old roadhouse and there is this band up there playing. A bunch of rednecks just exactly like you would see on television . . . The bartender starts talking to us and we tell him that we are musicians and the drinks start flowing and the party starts getting to the next level. So the guy comes up and says, 'Would y'all get up and sit in with our band?' If you had any teeth there you were probably like the mayor. So we got up there and right then, the first thing before we started playing, Kevin says, 'Look at this, man, look!' I looked over at the guy's keyboard and there is this pistol up there on the keyboard. So we got up there an' just started playing and just kicked these people's butt. They were just jumping up and down! The first thing we played was 'Sweet Home Alabama,' so they were just going nuts, just crazy! We were having the best time in the world, and the guy from the door got up onstage and grabbed the mike, saying, 'Ladies and gentlemen.' Started talking about how good we were, and we are just standing there, and he said, 'We have got us a band here and we want y'all to come back! What's the name of y'all?' I looked up on the wall because we did not want to say our name, and they had a velvet picture of Willie Nelson up there. So I said, 'The Velvet Willies.' He said, 'The Velvet Willies!' They gave us a couple of bottles of tequila and about ten or fifteen dollars for gas money and we rolled out of that place and I have never laughed so hard."

Jackson Highway articulated the value of touring in their own story: "After paying their dues and coming together as a group, they went on the road . . . Road touring has helped them mature as a group." It was only after they had overcome the challenges of this "rough road" did the band enter the recording studio.[5] Facing the challenge of the road was stressed in the histories of many southern rock bands. The road experience was seen as something that would build character, develop musical skills, and provide inspiration for songs. As Kevin Derryberry summed up over two decades of playing: "We made it because we did not all end up in jail."

Coming Home

Despite their fatalistic concern with doom and danger in a chaotic world, southern rockers kept a soft spot in their heart for home. In the South-land the sky was always blue, and the Allman Brothers' "Blue Sky" sums up the traditional view of a mythical southern homeland: a slow-flowing river ("don't worry where it's goin'"), church bells, sunshine, and a country road. Much of the nostalgia for the Old South imagined a pastoral, peaceful place that people compared favorably with their new high-pressure lives in big, impersonal cities. Southern rock was continually looking wistfully over its shoulder to a better, earlier time while it pulled up its britches and prepared to march into the bright lights of the future. Patterson Hood (the son of David Hood of the Muscle Shoals rhythm section) is the latest in a long line of Alabama musicians to confront the duality of "The Southern Thing," a region that wants to move forward but is also yearning for what it has left behind. The New South revisited the same dialogue between old and new, traditional versus modern, even if the modern South did not meet the highest standards of the American Dream. In "Doraville," the Atlanta Rhythm Section lovingly describe this rural suburb of mighty Atlanta as "a little country in the city," and conclude: "It ain't much, but it's home."

Randy Newman's "Birmingham" is equally assertive in its southern pride and affection for home. It is a song about a blue-collar worker who is content with his lot: "Got a wife, got a family / make my living with my hand, I'm a roller in a steel mill / In downtown Birmingham . . . I work all day in the factory / That's all right by me." The chorus, "Birmingham, Birmingham / The greatest city in Alabam', you can travel cross this entire land / But there ain't no place like Birmingham," reflects the boosterism which went all the way back to Reconstruction, but with a bit of irony. When he came to City Stages in 1996 Newman was asked about his reasons for writing "Birmingham." He said that when he wrote the song in the 1970s everyone he knew hated Birmingham, but he figured that there must be someone, somewhere, who liked living there.

There was little doubt in the minds of southern rockers as they traveled farther and farther away from Alabama. Just like the minstrel and blues players before them, these musicians often yearned for home in their music. Many songs in their repertoires dealt with the adventures and pitfalls of traveling, and being on the road might be a thrill, but it also meant separation from loved ones at home. The more musicians traveled the world during the halcyon days of southern rock, the more they missed home. "We used to get so lonesome for the South," said Johnny Sandlin. Playing with Gregg and Duane Allman along with Paul Hornsby and Mabron McKinney in a band called Hour Glass, Sandlin felt as though he was in the big time: "We were kinda doing that rock star thing, well, that was the idea that we would end up that way . . . We signed with Liberty Records and moved to California, which was a real culture shock . . . We made two very mediocre albums; we weren't happy in California, being from the South. We never really adjusted that well to being there, even though we were there almost two years."

Although the bluesman myth had the hero enjoying a girl in every town, most of them in the 1970s had girlfriends, wives, and families at home. Being in a band was a bit like being in a marriage, but at the expense of other family commitments. Keith Harrelson, on the road with hard-living, hard-rocking Telluride, was struck by how much the band members talked about their wives and girlfriends back at home, and noticed how much time they spent on the phone to Birmingham. This was expressed in one of their songs: "As he drove into the city, there's two things on his mind / The show he has to do tonight and the girl he left behind. Then they'll get to the show and they'll go on the stage / The lights and the crowd will just take him away." It was no wonder that musicians looked forward to returning home. Rick Byrd: "I was getting tired of being on the road, and my girlfriend had shacked up with somebody else." Telluride's song "Birmingham Tonight" tells the story of a band on the road and the emotional return to the city. Kevin Derryberry: "And one night I was whacked out of my mind on something and I wrote 'Birmingham Tonight' at my apartment on the Southside on the piano . . . I thought I had something. I did not know at the time. I played it for the drummer's girlfriend, and she fell in love with it. I played it for the band, and they were like 'Ehhhhh! That's sucky!'" But Johnny Sandlin liked it and it was added to their first record, and Birmingham radio played it all the time; it became a local hit in 1980. After a grueling tour on the Gulf Coast, the band was driving home on Highway 65 one cold December night. As they could see the lights on the horizon that signaled that Birmingham was near, they turned on the radio and heard their song: "I'll be in Birmingham tonight, if you can forgive me and say it's all right . . . to get back to into your world 'cause I'll be in Birmingham tonight." More than a few tears were shed; there really was a Sweet Home Alabama.

CHAPTER TWELVE

The Morris Avenue Boom

The rise of southern rock coincided with a new sense of pride in the South that was emerging as the region began to enjoy an upsurge of economic growth. When Charlie Daniels sang "The South's Gonna Do it," the lyrics could easily be applied to much more than the success of Capricorn Studios. After years of painful transition, the southern economy was moving forward as it engaged other businesses outside of agriculture — not the heavy industries envisaged by architects of the New South, but a more varied mix in a service economy that encompassed finance, research, and health care. Higher prices for oil, gas, and agricultural products helped provide the jobs that attracted many workers to the Deep South. As the old industrial base in the North, the "Rust Belt," declined, new industries in the South, the "Sun Belt," were on the ascent, fueled by lower costs and nonunion labor. Internal migration took workers from Rust to Sun Belt, so its population increased, and this led to more representation and more electoral votes in Congress. In 1976 Jimmy Carter of Georgia became president — the first southerner in the White House since Woodrow Wilson. His fellow Georgian Phil Walden played an important part in his campaign for president. The Allman Brothers, Charlie Daniels, and Wet Willie all played benefits for Carter, and later some even got invitations to play at the White House. Jimmy Carter was the first presidential candidate to employ his connections with the music business in his campaign: "My name is Jimmy Carter and I'm running for president. I'd like to introduce you to my friends the Allman Brothers." Many Georgians might not have liked him, but he was a favorite among southern rockers, such as Chuck Leavell: "It's going to be good to have a country boy running the nation. It's nice to have a guy who cares about the music and who has grown out of the South."[1]

Southern rock and the Democratic Party were riding a wave of enthusiasm for southern culture — from cheese grits to banjo music. Nowhere was this optimism clearer than in Birmingham, the founding city of the New South of iron and coal, which was now diversifying into corporate services, communications, and health care. The city looked and smelled different. Once it had been impossible to see the railroad reservation from Fourth Avenue North because of the smoke, but now Birmingham was becoming cleaner and greener, leaving the soot and its grimy past behind it. University Hospital was growing impressively, and so was the newly created University of Alabama at Birmingham.

While Birmingham's new industries looked to the future, its entertainment looked back to a distant past of folk song, hillbilly music, and Confederate pride. One significant piece of urban redevelopment in Birmingham underlined this sentimental rediscovery of a southern musical past. When Randall Oaks described the new club he was building as part of the development of Morris Avenue downtown he said: "When a person visits Oaks Street, he will feel as if he has walked into history."[2] The history in question was certainly not the 1960s, or even the 1950s or 1940s, but further back in time, when memories of southern uniqueness were reassuring rather than shameful. The "Old Town" created on Morris Avenue was part of a plan to revitalize Birmingham's downtown, a plan that was distinctly modern, but the cultural experience at its core came from banjo bars, recreated speakeasies, and traditional folk and bluegrass music.

Morris Avenue was one of the oldest parts of the city. Running directly next to the railroad lines, it had been built as a commercial center where goods were taken from the railroad cars and delivered to retailers. In the late 1960s there were two or three clubs on Morris Avenue that hosted live music. Rudy Johnson: "Now Morris Avenue did not get hot until the late '60s. You've got to remember that it was '68 at least, '67 or '68, because during the mid-'60s the only thing you got was the armories, Shower of Stars, and the skating rinks, and then there was the Up Stairs. It was on the other side of town and we had to drive. Not a whole lot of people wanted to go downtown." Jimmy Watson, owner of Midnight's Voice, told its story: "It was located between Second and Third Avenue on Twenty-Second Street. It opened July of 1973: we really wanted to have a hippie bar. In '73 there was not that much to choose from in Birmingham. We had the opposite kind of a scene from the Cane Break. It was just a new place in Birmingham that you could go and just hang out, shoot pool, play Foosball... We started getting some recognition from the bands and all, so after that we kind of started running it as a music bar. We were bringing bands through, and we have a lot of people come in on Monday and Tuesday nights... Weekends were dead because everyone used to go home, or at least they used to." The early 1970s were, to Watson, "a transitional period, and all the old neighborhoods went to hell too. A lot of the neighborhoods like the old steel areas out there. I mean, Ensley used to be real nice. It was real safe, too." Morris Avenue had not changed much in the twentieth century, but it was pretty run-down when the revitalization project began in the early 1970s.

The first businesses to build on Morris Avenue were Victoria Station, a large restaurant modeled on boxcars and cabooses, and Oaks Street. One of the founders of the club was Dave Goodwin: "The purpose of the club was good clean family fun. It was divided into three parts. You had the Grape Arbor, which was suited for fine dining. You had the banjo parlor, which was the peanuts on the wooden plank floors... The other motif was kind of 1890s [the old-fashioned "speakeasy" bar]. So there was a lot of history... Mayor Sibels came down and drove the first nail in for the construction" while workmen were busy tearing up the wooden floor of the old Davis Wholesale Grocery building in August 1974. Randall Oaks promised that the fun would only end "when you're tired of singing Dixie, reliving the ideas of the grand 1890s and you're full of beer and peanuts."[3]

Goodwin: "I have some musical background... and was playing guitar and banjo, Flatt and Scruggs and all that stuff... That was a period when bluegrass had enjoyed a resurgence and I wanted to... just try and promote bluegrass music." The folk revival of the 1960s brought bluegrass to the attention of many young players in Alabama. Terry Ryan had started in a garage band, but then "in the '60s was when the folk boom hit, the early '60s and Peter, Paul and Mary. I was a Ted Mitchell Trio fan myself and... Pete

Seeger and Bob Dylan. All that was happening, and I kind of left the Epics and started singing with my brother Jerry . . . We did folk music. I played classical guitar, and he played banjo and steel-stringed guitar and in those days you could, two guys in a Volkswagen with some instruments and a fair repertoire could go play those little folk houses." Birmingham's little folk house was the Lowenbrau: "In that summer [of 1965] we did a Sunday night Hootenanny thing . . . Emmylou Harris used to come down to the Lowenbrau and do a Sunday night thing . . . We had a lot of fun in those days. Yeah, we would stand in the back and just sing and pick and have a good time. When she would sing and perform we would all go 'That girl's good!' . . . We were doing folk, and we started branching to a little bit more of bluegrass . . . and we got introduced to that mountain style of music, and then we progressed little by little into bluegrass. Bluegrass started coming on in the late '60s and early '70s, and then it was popular, really popular in the early '70s! The first movie to have influence was *Bonnie and Clyde*. They used 'Foggy Mountain Breakdown' in that, and that really set banjo picking up front." Glenn Tolbert mentioned several influential albums: "There was 'Will the Circle Be Unbroken' . . . Earl Scruggs, Mother Maybelle Carter, Jimmy Martin . . . just good ole down to earth tunes . . . That was like three of them I think . . . plus the fact in '72, you have got the movie *Deliverance* that had Burt Reynolds and they did 'Duelin' Banjos.'" Terry Ryan: "I will tell you how popular bluegrass got at one time: *Bonnie and Clyde* had a theme song that Flatt and Scruggs played, 'Foggy Mountain Breakdown.' The movie *Deliverance* had 'Duelin' Banjos,' and college kids got into it big-time." Ben Burford: "It was the kind of thing the hippies were into. They were into anything that was different . . . Before then I guess people would think, 'Bluegrass? Man, we are an urban city! We are modern. We don't want to listen to bluegrass.' But the hippies came in and said, 'Hey, I like that sound!' So they would listen to anything . . . around that time some of the most popular stuff was bluegrass and country-tinged stuff." Jimmy Watson: "The Southside was the only scene around. Then there was Morris Avenue but it did not last long at all. It ended real quick. Well, the Showboat was down there forever, and the Crazy Horse, before they started to develop all the rest. There was somewhat of a bluegrass surge back then. It was somewhat of an alternative music to the disco. There was the Front Porch String Band that used to play there, sometime before they used to play at Oaks Street on a regular basis."

The newfound appeal of bluegrass prompted many folk players to form bands. Red, White and Blue Grass was made up of musicians from around Birmingham: Grant Boatright, Ginger Boatright, Dale Whitman, and Dave Seabolt. They played at Oaks Street regularly. Claire Lynch grew up in Huntsville, and there she met her husband Larry and became interested in traditional southern music: "Well, the folk boom was big in the '60s, and out of that came a renaissance of old-time country music, including blue-grass. The college movement was really big back then, and the fact that it was all acoustic, it was just really hip to us. We thought that was cool!" The banjo player Selwin Blakely joined them in a bluegrass band called Hick-ory Wind with several other students at the university. Claire's pure, high voice gave the band a distinctive sound that complemented her husband's guitar and mandolin. When Hickory Wind got an offer to be the house band at Oaks Street, they changed their name to the Front Porch String Band and began a career that lasted into the 1980s. Glenn Tolbert: "So they started playing at Oaks Street on Morris Avenue. I remember taking my mom there . . . She loved good ol' bluegrass music. She liked to buck dance to 'Cripple Creek,' a tune that Earl Scruggs played on the banjo. I remem-ber taking her, and her riding down there with me to Oaks Street, like on a Tuesday night, and this was like the '70s when we are talking about. I remember the place Oaks Street being packed with people you couldn't hardly get in the door down there. Not on a weekend, bear in mind, but during the week!" Claire Lynch: "We were all still hippie. There were still longhairs and a lot of longhairs got into it, but there was always a mixture. This is the interesting thing about bluegrass. Everybody from granny to families with children and longhairs . . . It is a sort of blending together of all different ages . . . I think we were a sight to see, a sight to behold. We were okay. I mean, we weren't fabulous by any means. It took a lot of years to get good, you know! . . . The audiences were there to have a good time: they were partying, and yet they were attentive for the most part. Al-ways attentive, the food was good and they participated. They would clap their hands, yell, and they would get up and dance. It was fun! It was good fun music!"

Several musicians played in the Front Porch String Band: Allen Watkins and Herb Trottman on banjo and Terry Campbell and Andy Meginniss on bass, but Claire Lynch remained the voice of the band and continued with a successful solo career when the band disbanded in the 1980s. Herb Trottman started playing in clubs when he was seventeen or eighteen: "It is sort of funny, but the folk music boom, all that stuff, gave a lot of legitimacy to a lot of people who liked old-time and bluegrass music that were in college and stuff, but it let them be interested in music without having to go and be in a sort of revivalist or something... The three brothers I knew were the Spawlding Brothers — we played mostly at Shakey's Pizza in Roebuck for a couple of years... They would play five nights or four nights at Oaks Street, and that was the mid-'70s." Bluegrass also found a place at another new club. The Wooden Nickel was a converted convenience store on the Southside, a bare rectangular room with a stage at one end and a nasty toilet at the other. In its early days it booked country and southern rock bands as well as R&B and jazz combos. Renegade, Hotfoot, Just Us, Central Time, and Oakley Hill and Telluride all played the Wooden Nickel. But you could also hear playing there the bluegrass of Glenn Tolbert and Cross Country, and the blues of guitarist John Hammond.

Terry Ryan's band, Wheat Ridge, broke up around 1974, "then George [Sanders], Dave Seabolt, and I got together and formed Cross Fire, and that was the group that used to play down at Oaks Street. That was when Morris Avenue was in its heyday... We would play at Oaks Street from 9 [p.m.] to 1, and then we would stay up and party... We did that every night, just about, and at the end of two weeks, that was all we could do just to walk around... When Morris Avenue was beginning to collapse, or whatever happened to it, I joined Three on a String in the fall of 1977 and that was [his brother Jerry] and Bobby [Horton, banjo player]. Mark Weldon, Andy Meginniss, and me." This was not strictly a bluegrass band, as they played a variety of country and folk music. Three on a String played all over town, but they took over the stage at the Lowenbrau in Homewood. "The Lowenbrau, of course, Three on a String was ruling the city at that time as far as the folk/bluegrass market went. They were just packing them in at the Lowenbrau and Cadillac [Café] and everywhere they went, and still do! Oh, yes, they have a following. It is almost a cult!" Glenn Tolbert: "They would have a line of people waiting to come in, waiting for the other people to get up and come out. It was so crowded in there that there wasn't anywhere for them to sit." Terry Ryan talks of the high when a group of musicians connect with their audience, and how effortlessly the band can "make them dance all night . . . I think that is why Three on a String has been so successful . . . Birmingham wants to clap their hands, party and have fun, and be entertained . . . Three on a String kind of spoiled everybody, because nobody could keep up with their brand of comedy and their brand of showmanship: [imagining a dialogue between a musician and a typical pair of customers] 'Don't you all do funny songs? Don't you do a show?' 'Well, no, I pretty much just do music.' 'Oh well, all right. Are you ready to go, Martha?'" Glenn Tolbert remembers seeing Terry Ryan with "the crowd right in his hand . . . There were times when you could have heard a pin drop when I was up there picking with Three on a String. Not because I was there, but just because people would pay total attention to what they were doing . . . They are all incredible musicians and entertainers, but they are real good about getting the crowd to where the crowd seems like they are on stage with them and they are a part of the family, so to speak."

Players like Glenn Tolbert got their first important exposure from being invited on stage: "I had been a guest of Three on a String for the first time. So we hit the stage, he called one song off, and I would say 'Let's get it!' and from there on, I mean, it was just like magic." The camaraderie of bluegrass brought a mix of musicians, young and old, and festivals were the ideal vehicle to bring them and their audience together. Festivals became an important showcase for bluegrass music in Alabama. The Horse Pens 40 park (about a ninety-minute drive north from Birmingham) started in the 1960s as a nature park and performance venue (Emmylou Harris played her first gig there in 1964). There Warren Musgrove created the first bluegrass festival in America. It attracted the best-known names in old-time country: Doc Watson, Ralph Stanley, Lester Flatt, and Ricky Skaggs. Glenn Tolbert: "Actually, Three On a String gave me my first chance playing at Horse Pens 40. I played with them at the very first bluegrass festival at Horse Pens in May of 1973, and we picked a little bit . . . I remember one time in '74, it was so muddy up there that everybody was just sliding all over the place, walking from one end to the other, and they had to be careful not to slide into the guitars and things like that. There have been more parking-lot pickin' sessions up there than you can imagine! They just had a wonderful festival in general . . . I always had fun pickin' when I would play on stage during the day, but at night it is like there is electricity in the air. I don't know if it is because you couldn't see the people that were cheering for me or what, but at night it was just like . . . I mean, I have played nights up there in October when it was so cold that I didn't know if I was going to feel my hands moving when I got on stage. And you get up there and the crowd gets behind you and they love what you are doing, you can't help but do things that you didn't know you could do. One thing I have found out about bluegrass people is that most of them are not out there listening to you to be critical of you — they are out there to listen to you because they enjoy you."

Folk music was an important part of the Morris Avenue experience, yet it was not the only entertainment in town that looked back to Birmingham's musical past. Big band jazz had largely died out in the aftermath of the war, but one jazz fan decided to get into the nightclub business to bring jazz back to Birmingham. Jerry Grundhoefer had no prior experience running a club when he opened Grundy's Music Room on Twenty-Third Street North in 1978. A player himself, he and his wife Bernie wanted a place "with a nice atmosphere and music." Grundy's provided a showcase for the abundance of jazz talent in Alabama (much of it coming from the music education programs in the state), and also brought some of the great names in jazz to the city: Laura Washington, Maynard Ferguson, Buddy Rich, and the (reconstituted) big bands of Count Basie, Tommy Dorsey, Woody Herman, and Artie Shaw. Although Grundy's was the only all-jazz music club, jazz could also be heard at the Courtyard, which was opened by George Babakitis on the Southside, and Diamond Jim's downtown. Gatsby's on Morris Avenue was another place to listen to jazz. As Gatsby's, then Great Gatsby's, and finally 1776, it showcased Ray Reach and his trio every weekend from 9 in the evening to 3 in the morning. In the 1970s Birmingham had a thriving jazz scene with several venues, and three or four radio stations playing jazz.

Birmingham's Bourbon Street

Randy Hunter is not the only musician who gets "a little starry-eyed" when he talks about the club scene on Morris Avenue in the mid-1970s: "And if you know anything about Birmingham now, you just cannot believe that it is true." The redevelopment of Morris Avenue took several years, and by 1976 some people in Birmingham — including Dennis Washburn, the influential entertainment guide of the *Birmingham News* — were wondering if it was worth all the money.[4] Randall Oaks thought that the "backbone of success" would be local patronage but that the key to its growth would be visitors from all over Alabama: "Tourism will be our biggest money." And so it was. The musicians who played there saw an unusual mix of old and young, wealthy and not-so-wealthy, locals and out-of-towners. Ben Trexel remembers seeing working- and middle-class people, college kids and college dropouts in the audiences, which were drawn from both the affluent suburbs over the mountain and the less prosperous city neighborhoods: "People came from Mountain Brook and Hoover as well as Pinson and Gardendale," he recalled.

Opposite Oaks Street, at 2120 Morris Avenue, was the Cobblestone, a popular venue for southern rock that changed names several times, from the Pussy Cat a-Go-Go to the Crazy Horse. It was one of the oldest and best-known music venues in the city. Rodney Davis of Buttermilk: "We played a lot here in Birmingham at what was then the old Crazy Horse on Morris Avenue. Actually, it was a go-go club from the '60s, and they had go-go dancers in cages, you know — it was above the bandstand. That was probably the only rock 'n' roll club at the time [early 1970s] when there was hardly any clubs. There was a club downtown called the Inn Club. There was a place in Roebuck called the King Club. There was this place in Five Points called the Boom Boom Room." Gary Sizemore: "The Five o'Clock Club was on Second Avenue and Seventeenth Street. That was when people came downtown. I named the Pussy Cat a-Go-Go, did a song about it. It belonged to Gus Gulas, on Morris Avenue. They had a good-looking blond dancing in a cage — she'd been married to Gus for only a month! Joe Namath's was two doors down. It was the latter part of the 1960s, when people started to move from downtown."

The Crazy Horse Saloon, according to Fred Dalke, "was another big place, down on Morris Avenue. The Crazy Horse was *the* place, and we auditioned. We worked a lot of lesser clubs at first to get tight, to get a repertoire of songs, and then we auditioned and got the Crazy Horse. And that was the place to be playing in Birmingham in the late '60s." Wayne Perkins: "Gatsby's. I never played Gatsby's except jammin' with people, but I played the Crazy Horse under three or four different band names. We were the Vikings at one point — Randy Carmichael, me, and Eddie Mantie. We won a couple of those [battle of the bands] there." Ben Burford: "We played the Crazy Horse a few times, and that was the only place down there we played. That was when they had the cages and all that stuff . . . but originally when the Crazy Horse started out, you could drink underage there if you were clever enough." Rick Byrd: "See, at that point in time, we are talking about '74, the main place in town for Dogwood, I want to say the Crazy Horse." By the end of the decade it was called Dillinger's, and six nights a week it offered local music and cheap drinks: twenty-five-cent draft beer, happy hours, and ladies' nights. Those were the days.

The other clubs on Morris Avenue were the Sho-Boat (or Showboat), the Odyssey, and the Old Town Music Hall, which had an old fire truck in the middle of the club. Kevin Derryberry: "It was a cool place, and we opened for Delbert McClinton and Poco there. REM played there. Right down the street, Alabama was playing. They had their own club, but we [Telluride] was kicking their butts. We had lines out of the door, and they wouldn't have any. So I guess they had the last laugh on that one!" (The highly successful country band Alabama was based in Fort Payne in North Alabama, but had their own place on Morris Avenue.) Telluride would often get together with Hotfoot and play gigs together. Doug Lee: "We used to do this thing, 'The Hotride with Telluride and Hotfoot.' We worked up a set of material together, and we would book a week at the Old Town Music Hall. Telluride would play a set and Hotfoot would play a set . . . then the last set was both bands together, and that was a lot of fun! And boy, you talk about drawing some crowds. Oh man. We would pack that place out!" Randy Holzman of the Generic Band: "Morris Avenue had so much charm. The cobblestone streets, the peanut factory, and you would go down the street and there was actually a gay bar down the end of the road."

Morris Avenue was drawing so many people that other clubs opened close by. Diamond Jim's, a restaurant and music club on First Avenue North and Seventeenth Street, was run by Millie Wathen and her son James Cobb. Diamond Jim's attracted a broad cross section of the Birmingham music scene, encompassing blues, folk, soul, and rock with performers like Backwater, George Law, and Crosswind. Envisaged as a saloon re-creating the Gilded Age, Diamond Jim's was stuffed with antiques and other treasures like the ornate doors from the old Tutwiler Hotel. Two blocks up, the L&N Cafe on Nineteenth Street and First Avenue had a full schedule of local and regional acts. Rick Byrd: "A lot of groups played in there and it was a restaurant during the day and we would put plywood up on the check out counter and on the first booth. It was all you could do to get people on the stage. We would actually sing through the stereo system. If you had the mic you just sort of put it through the stereo. That place. It was just happenin'! A lot of people around here would remember the L&N Café."

Morris Avenue also had dance clubs. The Morris House Disco, which promised "wild disco action every night," and a large hall called the Sho-boat and a gay bar called Bell's at the end of the street. The popularity of disco hurt the earnings of musicians. Dwight Williams of Locust Fork spoke for many of them when he recalled, "It was real threatening to us . . . It was a kind of phenomenon. We had to deal with it and of course we hated it. Number one: disco did not have bands. And number two: we did not play any dance music. The fraternity parties we played, people would come in and bring chairs and sit down. Nobody danced. All of a sudden the dancers were the stars. The crowd was the star." Jimmy Watson: "Disco came in during the '70s and that was some of our biggest competition . . . because the people that were coming to the bars to hear live music were going [off] to shake their ass at the discos. Karaoke, I do not understand that either. That is just beyond me. Disco is still pretty damned big." Terry Powers was in a rock band called Snakebite: "It was myself, Jimmy Linear, and Allen Byars . . . it was a good-sounding group. It was the best trio I ever had. We packed that thing [Kimberley's] out for a year and made that place a lot of money. Then after that, my wife and I bought Scandals downtown. We actually got the old Shooters and I was going to put Snakebite in that little club. The acoustics sounded so bad that we just could not do it, so what we did was hired a bartender that said, 'Café Deville is about to shut down for a month, you need to start spinning dance music so you can get a crowd.' We did it and it worked. We were there for four years. I had my guitar under my bed and did not touch it for over two years."

Disco had already established itself in dance clubs before it was ever called disco, but with the release of the soundtrack to *Saturday Night Fever* in 1977 it rapidly took over the charts. Marc Phillips: "It was the height of disco. It was just awful, because *Saturday Night Fever* had the first twenty slots on any chart that you opened up. It would just be 'Staying Alive,' you know." Dancing was one of main reasons that R&B and rock 'n' roll had been so attractive to young people in the 1950s, but southern rock and heavy metal were not meant to dance to and disco filled this void. There were several disco venues in town outside of Morris Avenue, such as the Lighthouse on Nineteenth Street N. and First Avenue, and Flanigan's in the Village East shopping center.

There was something for everyone on Morris Avenue. Telluride jammed with Dickey Betts and Friends, which contained a lot of the Allman Brothers band, and Kevin Derryberry remembered "Chuck Leavell actually had to use my keyboards." Wayne Perkins: "There wasn't a lot of mixing goin' on back then [in the '60s], you know? We didn't see any black people when we would do the armories and all that . . . No they didn't come out, man! But we started mixing in like on Morris Avenue and then you would run into some players and you could get up and jam with 'em and make 'em sit up straight, you know, if you could hold your own you were cool." Several big-name touring bands, such as Buckingham Nicks, Stevie Ray Vaughan, and Poco jammed in the Cobblestone after their performances at the Civic Center and gave a few local players a night to remember. Southern rockers would play with jazz musicians and more than one country picker tried his luck in a full blown rock 'n' roll band. When the bluegrass great Vassar Clements joined in a jam session with his fiddle, he surprised the assembled players by starting into "Satin Doll," a jazz standard from the 1930s.

The fun began on Thursday nights with the infamous beer busts and continued through the weekend. Traffic slowed to a crawl while the crowds milled around in the street because the sidewalks were full with tables, chairs, potted plants, vendors, loudspeakers, and amplifiers. Although the

1960s usually get the credit for the sex, drugs, and rock 'n' roll decade, in Birmingham it was not until the mid-'70s that hedonism reached its peak. Rick Carter: "So it was more acceptable to go out and get shit-faced and drive around in your car. I think there was a lot more of the party spirit in those days than there is now . . . This is a lot more conservative now. In '76 and '77 when we first started playing down here at the Wooden Nickel. It was balls to the wall. It was as crazy as shit. It was pretty much the climate of everybody." Rock Killough: "Pretty hot! Oh yeah! Every club was full . . . it was a busy place. Morris Avenue was a busy, busy place! Cobblestone streets and all that . . . A car load of young people went down there and one of them had a rock . . . well, somebody threw a rock and it went through the window into the hall . . . They hollered something and then drove around. When they came around again this partner of Duke's [owner of the Old Town Music Hall] had a .357 magnum. He ran from the office to the other end by the fire truck, out the door with this gun up like this. Everybody was stunned. Ran out in the street and went *pow, pow, pow!* Right down the middle of that crowded street . . . they were two hundred people there watching him run and hollerin' 'I'm gonna get you sons of bitches!'"

Each weekend would find the bars and restaurants packed to capacity: "It was pretty hot. Every club was full." Pioneer MTV veejay Alan Hunter found Birmingham "such a hot musical place, Morris Avenue. So being very nostalgic about it; when I came home from college it was a hotbed of musical activity. Anywhere from Three on a String to Hotel to jazz. It was just, and all musicians will say the same, it was just a great place to be playing music live and playing original music." Marc Phillips: "You would drive and there would be a restaurant, and like a little place to buy peanuts, and then there would be a jazz club, and then there'd be a rock 'n' roll club, and then there was a dinner theater, and then there was a magic bar and then there was a show club, with a show band doing floor shows and that kind of thing, and there was a country band and it was just all down one strip, it was really amazing. And a couple of rock 'n' roll bars, a bluegrass place. I mean, you could just hear anything and do anything, you know, and it really was a great time for the city." Randy Hunter: "For two or three years in 1977 to 1980 on Saturday night there would be ten, eleven, twelve clubs happening at one time . . . at the other end there were a couple of discos and there was the Showboat which had the big bands. They were the best places to dance in the world. It was just like Bourbon Street but not quite as crowded and not nearly as gross." Ed and Fred Foster: "We had a sandwich shop, open during business hours, we had a little table outside on the sidewalk. We would be open 9 to 5 then from 6 till 2 or 3 in the morning, Oaks Street, Morris Avenue would still be going at 2 or 3 in the morning. Morris Avenue was the happening place, just like Atlanta is now. You had Victoria Station down the road, 1776, the Showboat. We did a lot of dancing, the kids nowadays don't dance. Back in those days there was music in the air." As Claire Lynch remembered: "There was a lot of music and a lot of musicians" in the city at that time. "It was very novel, it was fun. Underground Atlanta was happening then too, but it was a real hot spot too and it was a similar type situation. Old town streets just lined with clubs . . . I think the Morris Avenue era was sort of a high point in the musical scene." Ken Talley of Garden of Eaton: "Back then the music scene was, there was music everywhere! Everybody that had some kind of entertainment, there were a few places that had disco music or deejays, but everybody had a live band." Lee Bargeron: "You could walk down Morris Avenue and have five or six different places to go in and hear different kinds of music. When we were in Hotel we did a ballet thing with the Birmingham ballet, and the symphony was booming, more clubs were booming." Twenty years later people remember the Morris Avenue as the time of "music really being the driving force in this city." Marc Phillips said that Morris Avenue was "the best thing that ever happened to Birmingham."

Cover Bands

The Morris Avenue scene created a boom in live music that meant more income for musicians. Rick Carter remembered that there were probably only a dozen full-time rock bands at the time and they were booked continually. The great thing about Morris Avenue from the musicians' viewpoint was that the gigs lasted for more than one night; bands could get contracts to play four or five nights in a row at the same place, and take in hundreds of dollars a week. The popular bands who played weekdays in addition to weekends could make as much as $2,000 playing from Tuesday through

Saturday [adding in their tips]. Homestead Act would start on Tuesday night and play through to Sunday early morning, and pull in from $1,800 to $2,000. Even if they only played two weekend nights, they made $600–$700, according to Tony Wachter.

Although southern rock held sway in Birmingham in the 1970s, most music venues offered some sort of rock nostalgia with cover bands which journeyed back to the beginnings of rock 'n' roll. Just like bluegrass and disco, old-time rock 'n' roll got its boost from a popular movie. Ben Burford: "See, *American Graffiti* had come out and was just hugely popular and people were suddenly getting real interested in the '50s, but kind of kicked it off because people became real conscious of '50s and '60s music. So when we first started off [Chevy 6] we did a '50s show, we would dress up and slick back and all that. At that time there was only one other band doing that and that was The Cadillacs . . . So we started out doing more '50s and early '60s, and that kind of began to shove the '50s aside . . . we tried to move on up into the '60s and we are still trying to move up into the '70s . . . All I want to do is what people want to dance and party to. If you can't dance to it, I don't think it is much fun." Chevy 6 started in 1974 with Ben Burford, Brian Smith (bass), Mike Grayson (keyboards), and O'Neil Smitherman (drums). Ben: "You have got people with integrity and then whores like me! But you know it is true, I've whored myself out for years, but it is what most people want to hear. We have even, at times, tried to throw in some original material that I wrote and people would just look at us . . . We tried to do Top 40 at one time . . . so we learned a set of Top 40 music and we did it okay, but it pretty much sucked because people didn't want to hear that. They just wanted to hear oldies . . . There was always a place for what we did and I don't know if they considered it unique or else it was the little brother that everyone liked. So we were able to coexist with disco, country, and new wave. We just rode the thing out doing what we did no matter what the main trend was." They carried on for decades, delivering those classic rock songs "with so much enthusiasm" that J. R. Taylor paid them the ultimate compliment In 1987: "Funny that a bunch of old men often come the closest to re-creating genuine rock spirit in this city."[5]

While many cover bands were formed to relive the highlights of the 1960s, some concentrated on reproducing the music of only one famous group, a practice which began with cover bands of the Beatles. You could hear sets of songs from the Beatles (Crosswind), the Rolling Stones (Shelter), and the Grateful Dead (Bud Greene) without having to pay for an increasingly expensive concert ticket. Homestead Act was a good example of a successful cover band: they played restaurants, clubs, fraternities, private parties, debutante balls, political rallies, and country clubs. It was a money-making Top 40 band; the goal was not to reach the top of the *Billboard* charts but to make a living for each of its members, who shared around six to seven hundred dollars for playing two weekend nights. It was formed in 1974, with Doug Lee, Alice Bargeron, Mac Rudd, Tom Fox, Tony Wachter, and Mike Reed. Over the years about fifteen to twenty different musicians played in it. There was a lot of money in paying oldies. It was said that Dick's Hat Band would not appear for less than eight hundred dollars. Many cover bands played only weekends so that their members could keep their day jobs and play for some extra money. One of them was Hotfoot, a country rock band with members having full-time "straight" jobs. Rick Ranelli of Born Guilty pointed out the appeal of cover bands to musicians: "We made more money playing oldies. Always."

Bar crowds wanted the same old songs that they knew the words to, or a new song that everyone had heard on the radio and liked. One musician had no illusions why his audience was there: "All they want to do is get laid. They could really care less about the band." They weren't going to sit still and listen to the music. Rock Killough told this story about playing one night with Marc Phillips: "I saw a lady hit him upside the head with a pocketbook one night down there and it about knocked him on his ass . . . So after a sixteen-song set we would do a break. Then they [the audience] would all talk and get a bit out of it. We started back and he started quietin' them down and this lady had been in there and had been drinking for a while. She was pretty well oiled and she was mouthin' off on him and he said, 'Right, go ahead, leave, that is what you need to do. If you are going to talk, then you go.' She said, 'I don't go to a beer joint to be quiet!' *Whack!*"

Top 40 was now dominating radio programming; many radio stations played only the hits on the *Billboard* charts, and working musicians in the bars and clubs had to do the same. Rock 99 ruled the airwaves in Birmingham, with a playlist that included Marshall Tucker, the Outlaws, Allman

Brothers, and Charlie Daniels. Although Top 40 was definitely a deroga-
tive term among musicians (advertisements to recruit personnel for bands
often carried the warning label "no Top 40"), it was the best way to make
money and keep playing: "That was the thing to do," Porter Landrum and
Doug Royale said. For Birmingham musicians, and probably for musicians
all over the country, the choice was brutally simple: "Either you play cover
music to make your car payment . . . or you write original music and you
starve." The other option was a day job, but Doug Royale found this option a disappointment: "I got to where I was tired of all these drunks and
playing. I just got burned out. So I got me a real job and I quit and got real
depressed. I was like, 'God, this real job stuff is a lot worse!' Once you grow
up giggin' and all, I have always been depressed if I have not been giggin'
somewhere. If you have New Year's Eve go by without a gig, oh man! I
talked to Topper about that one time. He said, 'Oh yeah, if you ain't got
a gig on New Year's Eve, you are sinking low.' So that is just the way it is.
It is almost like a thrill, and it is almost like a curse at the same time." So
he went back to covers, and this is what many local bands did during the
days of southern rock, for, as Anthony Crawford of Telluride concluded,
"Nobody wrote originals back then!"

The heady successes of southern rock tempted many local musicians to
dream of quitting the cover scene to record their own material and escape
from playing the same old southern rock favorites in a bar. Ned Bibb: "One
of the guitar players in the Cadillacs tried to learn 'Sweet Home Alabama.'
You had to know that song or you couldn't get on stage. I hated that song."
Rick Byrd talked about the Dogwood philosophy: "We are going to play
what we want to, and if you don't like it you can just go. Just go somewhere
else! We pretty much had a pact that we would never play 'Sweet Home
Alabama.' For some reason. We would die before we would play that song
or 'Free Bird.' Now when I hear 'Sweet Home Alabama' in the last couple
of years, it is really a pretty damn good recording!" A lot depended on the
venue and the sort of audience it brought in. Rick Byrd: "There was club
called Rocky Raccoon's that was on Seventh Avenue South. That was a
great place! Good place to play. Good place to jam. Play original stuff. The
crowd was definitely into not wanting to hear Top 40 stuff." Doug Lee remembered: "The only time I did many original songs was in the Dogwood

era, in the early to mid-'70s. That was sort of a creative peak for me without a doubt . . . other than that, most of the bands that I have been in have been pretty much cover bands. An original song or two here and there . . . but it was in Dogwood in the early 1970s when we started really trying to concentrate on that and got stars in our eyes and thought we were going to be successful . . . We got closer than a lot of people do. We had some pretty good people in our corner in that band. Big-time record producer and big-time management and all, and it didn't happen, but we had our chances!"

Hotel were attracting such big crowds at the Cobblestone that they too began to get stars in their eyes. Hotel began as an acoustic folk group, playing Poco, Buffalo Springfield, and Crosby, Stills and Nash, and then evolved into Tumbrell Hotel. They worked all over the city in the early 1970s, from Joe Namath's bar downtown to the Round Table on Green Springs Highway. Marc Phillips: "We were a house band there for the longest time, just stayed there for ever and ever . . . Bob Cain was playing downtown in the Cane Break during that time frame. There wasn't a lot of live music in the city . . . I can remember during that same time that draft beer came to town, I mean, there wasn't any such a thing as draft beer in Birmingham . . . It was in the '70s. Early to mid-'70s. From the Round Table we wound up at the Cobblestone on Morris Avenue, and during that time we started playing a lot of university gigs at Alabama, Auburn, Birmingham Southern . . . We went to the Cobblestone, and that was during the Morris Avenue boom . . . And it was during that time, around '76 or '77, is when we got our record deal."

Hotel was acclaimed as the most musically accomplished band in town. Gerald Hallerman: "Tommy Calton when he was with Hotel . . . Tommy is one of the best players that I probably ever heard in my life. I do not care who you are talking about. I think that if you talk to musicians that know him . . . he is in a class by himself." Lee Bargeron: "In fact, I think that is one of the things that probably got us the [record] deal was that we had a really good base of support in this region, and I think the record companies looked at how well you did on your own as far as building your own following." Their sets at the Cobblestone included much of their original material sandwiched between covers of songs by Elton John or the Doobie Brothers. At their peak they could command fifteen hundred to two thousand dollars a night and bring in three to five thousand dollars a week. Their instrumentation was heavy on keyboard rather than guitar, and the songwriting of Marc Phillips and Tommy Calton spread the band's material over a broader range than just rock 'n' roll. The influence of Steely Dan — one of the most progressive rock bands of the 1970s and 1980s — can be heard in their music, which contained many references to jazz and more complex constructions than the two-and-a-half-minute pop song. The group grew larger and eventually comprised Tommy Calton, Michael Reid (guitars), Michael Cadenhead (drums), George Creasman (bass), Marc Phillips, Lee Bargeron (keyboards), and also Tim Townley, Jim Papard, and Mark Smith.

Hotel did some demos at the Sound of Birmingham Studios that attracted the attention of the record companies. Lee Bargeron: "We did our first single with Mercury Records, which was 'You'll Love Again,' and that charted into the *Billboard* Top 100, but we did not get an album option, and so we shopped some more and got hooked up with a label called Scotti Brothers. Scotti Brothers had been an independent promotion company that would take product from other record labels and promote them and get them going. So they started their own record company, and they were distributed through Atlantic Records. Scotti Brothers liked the product and signed us up, but Atlantic wasn't that interested, so they did a separate distribution deal with MCA Records." Marc Phillips: "The record company did not even call for an album, they signed the band for a 45 release . . . it was a one-record deal, and they put it out there to see what happened, we just got nowhere with it, and the record company did not support it all . . . and we got out of the deal and, sure enough, he [the producer] signed the band to Scotti Brothers and then they farmed us out to MCA and we wound up having five *Billboard* singles [hits], I mean, you just couldn't believe it. We started touring after the release of the first album [*Hotel*] and we were on the road. And then the second album was called *Half Moon Silver*. We started doing major shows at that point. We quit playing the Cobblestone." Lee: "We toured for about a month with the Little River Band, and we did a tour with Hall and Oates. We did a lot of one-night shows where we were the opening act for people like Toto, Atlanta Rhythm Section. We did coliseum-type rooms. We were really well received . . . Most of the time we were called back for an encore. It was a taste of the big time and to hang with the people who are in the big time . . . Things started really going well for Hotel. It was because you just felt like, apart from being young and having all that enthusiasm, that youthful enthusiasm, you felt like you were on the threshold of something big. Then reality hits you and you know all the facts, that this is a business, and it is not just going out and making the music and becoming a star overnight . . . I think it was the Little River Band that wanted us to keep going with them on the tour, but we couldn't. As a front act you don't make a whole lot of money, and we just couldn't economically do it. It wasn't feasible, and we asked the record company for maybe a couple of thousand dollars so we could get up into D.C. and New York and into some major markets, and they wouldn't spring for it. So we couldn't do it. That was when we realized we were on our own."

Marc Phillips: "I believe we had five *Billboard* singles, five charted singles—'Hold On to the Night,' 'You'll Love Again,' 'You've Got Another Thing Coming,' 'Half Moon Silver'— maybe that was it, maybe it was just four. The highest we ever made it up the charts was number 54, and that was 'You've Got Another Thing Coming.' Oddly enough, we had an incredible response from this city. Totally unexpected, because you know the hardest place to make it is in your own hometown. The grass is always greener on the other side . . . but radio just embraced us here: WSGN was huge, AM radio was huge, WERC, they were all playing our records. It was one of the first Alabama groups to really do anything on the national level. I don't know of anything that happened from a rock 'n' roll standpoint prior to that." Lee Bargeron: "I think we kind of got lost in the shuffle. We had two singles off the first album made it to the Top 100. We got very little promotion from the record company. 'You've Got Another Thing Coming' made it to like number 58. I think that was '79, and then we did a second album that had two singles in the Top 100, and we released a third single, which was the only song we didn't write. It was a song that was kind of forced upon us by the record company. They liked the song, and we rewrote it because to us it was just a little bit cheesy . . . and they released that, and it was the only one that we had that was released that didn't make it. Didn't chart at all. It was kind of a bittersweet victory . . . It was our way of almost saying, 'We told you so! Let us write the material. We know what sounds good for us.' Our enthusiasm was waning a bit. We kind of realized that we were getting lost in the shuffle. For one thing, during the first album we were up against *Saturday Night Fever*, which was controlling the top ten to fifteen spots on the charts. Disco was coming in and it was just taking over. Plus we were kind of between MCA thinking promotion was Scotti Brothers' job, and Scotti Brothers was thinking that it was MCA's job. Nothing really got done . . . We started going back to the club jobs that we had been doing . . . We got out of our record deal because we felt like it was just holding us back more than anything. The record company really wasn't interested in us."

The music business had become larger and more competitive. Promoter Michael Trucks: "It has grown up and become a business. In the '60s and early '70s it wasn't a true business in the sense that we call business in this day and age . . . It has grown up from a business that was a few million [dollars] in volume to billions in volume . . . Remember that from '69 through to '72 we were dealing with a lot of underground stuff. Hendrix was underground, Cream was underground, the Grateful Dead, and it was all alternative life styles, counterculture, love-ins, you know what I am saying. But then the music grew up from a lot of standpoints . . . I think a lot of things grew up there, and the music became a more central focus and mainstream American life as opposed to something that was part of the counterculture that someone from mainstream America looked at with just passing interest."

CHAPTER THIRTEEN

Decline and Fall
The End of Southern Rock

With southern rock enjoying nationwide popularity, business was good for Birmingham's recording studios. The Sound of Birmingham and Boutwell were full of work, and several new recording studios opened in the 1970s. Polymusic was formed around 1977 by Randy Hunter, Mike Panepento, and Dan Whiteside. The Bates Brothers began their studio in a garage in Fairfield, and after building the business recording gospel, they moved to Hueytown in 1979. The studios were working full-time: Record after record was cut, mixed, mastered, released, and shipped. Some of them were meant for national distribution; others were done just for the fun of it. The Front Porch String Band started thinking about a record "during the Oaks Street days, and we started branching out to these festivals and we noticed that the bluegrass tradition is that everyone has their own record table . . . You sit behind the record table and you sell your records, so we decided that we better make one. Larry's mom and dad gave us a thousand dollars and we did the whole album top to bottom — *Smiling at You*, it's out of print. Thank God! So we recorded that one at Ed Boutwell's and put it out ourselves. I started my own publishing company and my own record company [Front Porch Records], and I learned a lot about copyright laws. It was a real valuable experience. I guess we sold about a thousand of them eventually, and it helped support our habit." *Smilin' at You* was released in 1977 and was followed by *Country Rain* later the same year: "We did another album, and we did the whole thing from top to bottom in six hours! Top to bottom! It was really much better than the first one, which we labored over." In 1981 the Front Porch

String Band released a self-titled, nationally distributed album by the independent Rebel Records, while Claire released her solo debut, *Breakin' It*, on the smaller Ambush label.

Telluride moved into recording in easy stages. Their first effort was a single recorded in 1980 at Boutwell Studios. Anthony Crawford: "We had our own record company. We started our own. Lizard Head Records. Everything us! We dealt with a couple of record companies. It was like you give up your soul, you give up control. We did not want to give up control. We never got a manager because we didn't want anybody tell us what to do. We just wanted to play music." Then they went to Polymusic Studios and recorded a six-song EP under the direction of Mike Panepento. Still without major-label backing, they recorded an LP at Boutwell in 1983. *Stand Alone* contained ten original songs and one cover. It was an impressive debut that signaled Telluride's shift from country rock to mainstream rock 'n' roll. Two cuts from the album, "Smile" and "Turn Up! Your Little Radio," received a lot of radio play in Alabama. After five years of performing, the members of Telluride hoped that "Stand Alone," one of their signature songs, which often opened their set, would get them noticed outside the South. Kevin Derryberry: "So we were pluggin' away and we wanted to put out a record. That was our dream! We wanted to make a record. Everyone wanted to put out a record." Their ultimate goal was "having a major record deal, a national concert tour and making a video," a dream common to many southern rockers. Even a local hit, a self-produced record played on Birmingham radio, could bring considerable financial rewards. After their hit "Birmingham Tonight," Telluride found their average club attendance boosted from around one hundred to over five hundred.[1]

Making the record was the easy part; getting it played on the radio and placed in record stores across the country was much harder. Telluride discovered this when their record came out. Kevin Derryberry: "Everyone went out to the record stores and asked for it, and nobody had it. We showed up the next day with boxes of them. 'Could you take this record? This is our new record.' So it all kind of worked out. From that point on we were on a kind of an upswing for years. We had our second album come out. We had made a lot of money playing. A lot of people used to come out and see us. We spent a ton of money on our second album because we thought we knew what we were doing, but we did not. We blew a lot of money... It was basically overproduced. They had five thousand guitar tracks on it. Nothing off of it really did that well on the radio. Our third album [1984] had 'Let Me in Tonight' on it... When 'Let Me In' came out, we did really well with it. The only problem with our third album was that by the time that it got out and hit the radio, CDs had come out. I think that if we had out it on a CD, we would have done a lot better. We did not, though, and by the time we got the album out we did not have the money to spend. It was brand-new technology. It was beyond our heads."

During the 1970s record producers and radio programmers saw southern rock as rough-edged but essential rock 'n' roll that might turn the clock back to a simpler and more profitable times. When the big record companies thought of Birmingham and Alabama, they naturally concentrated on southern rock and the Muscle Shoals sound. They came, checkbooks in hand, to sign up authentic southern rockers. Several major record labels looked over Alabama Power. Propelled by Wayne Perkins's driving guitar, they were as accomplished a group of rock musicians as you could find. In 1978 they signed a record deal with Capitol. As is often the case after signing a contract with a major label, the band was re-formed and renamed Crimson Tide. They went to Los Angeles and recorded at Capitol's high-tech studios, which had accommodated stars like Frank Sinatra and the Beach Boys. Cowboy recorded five albums for Capricorn, all of which were well received, and the band went on to tour with Gregg Allman in 1974. They recruited blues singer and harmonica player Topper Price in 1977. Everything pointed to Cowboy joining Capricorn's other bands in the charts. Local band Cross (with Buddy Causey, Mike Lawley, and Dennis Guley) signed a record deal and went to record at Muscle Shoals. Dogwood worked in Hemphill's Sound of Birmingham Studios with Glenn Wood, and at Capricorn Studios with Paul Hornsby, who had produced a couple of albums with Marshall Tucker. Doug Lee: "The goal from day one in Dogwood was to get into the studio and make records."

Alas, these recordings came to nothing; not one hit came out of Birmingham or from a Birmingham-based rock band in the 1970s. Many of them achieved regional hits, but only Hotel came close to national exposure. For all their years of work — rehearsing for hours every day and then playing for five or six hours a night, releasing two albums and numerous singles — Hotel never did make it into the *Billboard* Top 10. Marc Phillips: "We didn't get a lot of support from the record labels, ever. So whatever success we had, I really feel it was on the merit of the music and the band, whoever came to see the band; it was just word of mouth. We never broke out of the Southeast, even though Dick Clark played 'You've Got Another Thing Coming' on *American Bandstand*. It still just wasn't enough ... We came out with the second album, and it didn't do as well as the first, and we had no tour support and were on the road opening up for whoever was doing well at the time ... We'd do a show for $300, open up for Toto for $300 to $500, and it would cost us $700 to get to the next gig. So we were $200 in the hole, and the next gig would be $250 and it would cost us another $600 to $700 to get to the next job, so we'd be $700 in the hole. And by the time it was all said and done, we were thousands and thousands of dollars in debt. And it's finally just: you gotta quit. We've got to come home, we've got to pay off some debts, we've got to pay off lawyers, we've got to pay off managers and agents ... The record company eventually dropped us, and we tried to get back in the record business, but we didn't know how. And we couldn't do it alone."

Ironically, the only number 1 record that Birmingham claimed in the 1970s was not southern rock. Anita Ward was a soul singer from Memphis who had been taken under the wing of a local record producer named Freddie Knight. Her recording of "Ring My Bell" on the Juana label hit the jackpot in May 1979. It has been a disco favorite ever since. Legend has it that "Ring My Bell" was recorded in Birmingham, and people still talk about that one moment of fame for the city's music scene. Knight started as a singer and got involved in record production. He moved to New York and recorded R&B songs for Mercury and Capitol Records, but with little success. He then came back to Birmingham and recorded a song written by his wife at Sound of Birmingham Studios. Stax Records of Memphis picked it up and made "I've Been So Lonely for So Long" a hit in 1972. His friend and business associate Clinton Harris: "Fred Knight and I started a small label [Juana Records in 1975]. Fred is from here. We used to live next door to each other in Bessemer. He had always been in the record business. I joined on as a wanna-be ... We were distributed by TK Records out of

Miami. The president of the company was Henry Stone. We had a couple of his songs on the Controllers [a group Harris managed], like 'Somebody's Gotta Win, Somebody's Gotta Lose.' That was their biggest record." Lenard Brown of the Controllers: "We never recorded an album here [in Birmingham]. Not one. At the time there was not the proper facilities here when we started recording. When we signed for TK Records at the time we started out, the very first record was 'Somebody's Gotta Win, Somebody's Gotta Lose'—that was our very first gold record. We did that at Malaco Records in Jackson, Mississippi . . . Frederick Knight was producing at the time, so this is where he wanted to record it." Clinton Harris: "Finally came Anita Ward with the song 'Ring My Bell.' That was the number 1 record across the country. We were distributed by TK Records and they supplied us with the studio. Malaco Records was also there. We used the studio in Jackson, Mississippi. We would cut the artists there and then ship them to Miami . . . I guess that it [Juana Records] lasted about seven years. It struggled and pained. Freddy did not have consistent hits. He had a record that went well, then he would go three or four years before he would have another hit . . . He was a good writer. 'Ring My Bell' was published by our small label. That was during the late '70s and early '80s, when the record industry kind of died. That was the time of the disco era. The company that we were dealing with, TK Records, went bankrupt. We did not get a lot of money from sales of 'Ring My Bell.' When they went, we went." Several of Knight's songs were put on a compilation made in 2006 by Chicago deejay John Ciba. *The Birmingham Sound: The Soul of Neal Hemphill* has tracks from Sam Dees, Ray Reach, and Wayne Perkins. Some good songs, but not a Top 40 hit among them.

The failure to meet the southern rock expectations of the 1970s put a lot of pressure on Birmingham's bands, and few of them survived the decade. Cowboy broke up in 1978 after a dispute with the record company. Hotel disbanded, and so did Chair, Hotfoot, Cross, and Crimson Tide. Local bands who had worked so hard to achieve a breakout hit found their records languishing on the discount shelves of local record stores or out of print, their best-known songs now only a memory.

To make matters worse, the Morris Avenue boom turned into a bust. There had always been the problem of convincing people to come to downtown from the outlying suburbs, and what was uppermost in the minds of those coming over the mountain on Friday and Saturday nights was their personal safety. Being in the heart of downtown, with all its attendant crime problems, made some visitors to Morris Avenue apprehensive. But for Ed and Fred Foster, who ran Fred's Leather Shop, one of the few retail businesses on Morris Avenue, there were no problems: "We worked there late at night, we carried a pistol, but we felt safe there! There was only one shooting there. We had a mascot — a rat, a gopher rat . . . He would stand on his hind legs and beg for food." Nevertheless, the street was gaining a reputation for rowdiness. David Goodwin: "Robberies, vandalism, that kind of thing. When word catches on about things like that, it affects your business . . . You know we were by the train tracks. Unfortunately, there was a lot of panhandling." Then somebody was stabbed in the doorway of a club. Doug Royale: "And it was all over the news and everything! That really — and I mean, I was there — shut down Morris Avenue . . . The other thing that hurt Morris Avenue was the change in the drinking age [from eighteen to twenty-one]. We were there, and it was just packed every night of the week and then right in the middle of our gig, they said, 'Well, twenty-one.' It cut business way down, and then with the stabbing there were no more gigs." David Goodwin: "For a lot of reasons it went from Oaks Street, to Broke Street, to Croak Street."

The end of Birmingham's Bourbon Street mirrored the decline of southern rock generally. Some of its audience was bled off by a resurgence of pop-oriented country, and some preferred to listen to slicker, easier-listening rock 'n' roll. Rock Killough played with a band called the McKnight Brothers, whose influences went from Little Feat to Ry Cooder: "We had a hard time playing country joints because we weren't country enough, and we had a hard time playing rock joints because we were not rock enough." The rise of Top 40 country — in part the consequence of the success of the film *Urban Cowboy* — tended to enforce the lines between rock and country, putting pressure on bands to make their allegiances clear. But Top 40 country was quite different from old-time country music. Rick Byrd: "I was just playing the honky-tonks down there doing just Top 40 country. Playing from 9 until 4 in the morning six nights a week. Trying to make a living! They ended up firing me because they said my steel guitar was bringing in too many rednecks. I laughed in their faces and said, 'Fine. I'll see you later.'"

The identification of southern rock with southern musicians worked against Birmingham bands in the 1980s. Johnny Sandlin thinks that the brand was hurt by the stream of bands that followed the Allman Brothers but were nowhere near as accomplished as the original. Marc Phillips of Hotel classified their music as pop rock, but "people expected us to be southern rock, and I think it worked against us, because we weren't an Allman Brothers. All that southern rock 'n' roll was coming out of the South. Then here comes this band from Alabama: 'It's got to be southern rock.'" Doug Lee explained the decline of Dogwood: "The heyday of southern rock, and that's what people expected us to do, but we didn't do it. We didn't have an Allman Brothers sound, we didn't have a Marshall Tucker sound, we didn't have a Lynyrd Skynyrd sound . . . because a lot of our stuff was real rock 'n' rolly! Real raw-sounding rock 'n' roll, and we sounded nothing like any of the southern bands who were having so much success at that time, and that is what people expected us to be." Southern rock continued to define bands from Birmingham until the end of the century. Damon Johnson: "Coming out of Birmingham and playing in Utah, you are a southern rock band! You are obviously a southern rock band because you are from Birmingham and you have long hair and blue jeans, so you are a southern rock band!"

Southern rock rose and fell in time with Capricorn Records. Success had inflamed egos and led to conflicts within the company and its stable of bands. Johnny Sandlin: "The whole thing where people start out and there's this common goal and they are working together and as money becomes bigger and bigger various factions start breaking apart . . . It was just kind of disintegrating there, and Phil had gotten involved in politics. Jimmy Carter was running for president and a lot of the record company's energies went into the Jimmy Carter campaign. But the whole thing just kind of fell apart."

Southern rock stars like Lynyrd Skynyrd and Charlie Daniels still continued to score big hits, but the *Billboard* charts were taken over by country pop, electronic dance music, and the alternative groups like Blondie and the Police. The popularity of highly produced and polished recordings, and

the growing influence of synthesizers, all combined to make southern rock
sound definitely old-fashioned by the end of the decade. Most important,
it was no longer cool with college-age kids. Talking about Telluride and
Dogwood, Ben Burford observed: "Those bands were huge, and even the
frat rats were into country at that time." But times change very quickly in
rock 'n' roll. Doug Lee remembers playing at Richard's in Atlanta — one
of the biggest venues for rock in the South. After a set of country rock, the
manager told him: "I really liked your band, but I can tell you right now,
you have picked a hard way to make it in the music business with what you
are playing!" One member of a southern rock band put it bluntly: "We all
looked like a bunch of rednecks." Southern rock did not die in Birmingham; you could still see the Charlie Daniels Band at the large Oak Mountain auditorium, or experience the spirit with a bar band like the Georgia
Satellites, but the gravy train had come to a halt. A lot of musicians went
back to day jobs and cover bands. By the end of the 1970s Capricorn Records had filed for bankruptcy and Eddie Hinton was living on the streets
of Decatur, Alabama. Disappointment had replaced New South optimism.
Bunkie Anderson: "Well, I don't know if Birmingham was a big deal. To
me, 99 percent of it was guys that played covers and made a few bucks and
went out and killed time and now are shoe salesmen."

Depression and Covers

With the decline of Morris Avenue as the premier entertainment district,
the action moved downtown to Diamond Jim's, Rocky Raccoon's, and Al
Pilkington's Cabaret on Third Avenue and First Street. Al's Crossroads
at Center Point became one of the largest venues in town for rock 'n' roll.
Doug Royale: "That was probably one of the highest-paid gigs in town,
because you had so many nights. A huge place . . . it was like 'Wednesday
beer busts at Al's Crossroads, featuring Crosswind,' and there would be
eight hundred people there every night. Wednesday night! Packed! We
were playing Top 40 rock. That was the thing to do! The latest hits on the
radio." The club scene in the 1980s was dominated by bands that played
covers: Telluride, Split the Dark, Revolver, Radio Berlin, the Newboys, the
Medallions, Mel and the Party Hats. Homestead Act was typical of them.

Alice Bargeron: "It was kind of the weekend party band. We played clubs, fraternity parties, country clubs, and pretty much anything or anybody would hire you to play. We would play all the time." Crosswind played Beatles music from 1976, "and we broke up in 1983 and played gigs the whole time!" remembered Porter Landrum.

In 1981 the club Louie Louie opened on the Southside. Jim Burford: "We put together a little group to open a bar because everyone always wanted to own a bar. The idea initially was, it was supposed to be like a beach club that they used to have in Atlanta. Basically a deejay played prerecorded oldies music, and that is the way it started. At that time it really did not have a stage, but it had a little risen area, and we got Chevy 6 to play in there one time, and then that was when we realized that we needed to have bands. It originally started out being oldies music like Chevy 6 plays, and then we fielded oldies bands from all over the place . . . We resisted having more of the contemporary bands like Telluride and those sorts of things, and then when we finally started having them, and it just got into a rotation that worked really well . . . The place was not big enough to have big-named bands, they wanted too much money to make it work and they would not play but only for an hour. You could not make any money with a big band . . . We never had anyone that was like a Nick band that played all originals unless they had some kind of name recognition. The Subdudes played a couple of times, and they had played City Stages, and everyone knew who they were."

Louie Louie soon established itself as the premier rock venue in town: "At Louie's you went to party. It was a party place. The club thing is all a matter of putting on cool, is what it all boils down to. Very few people ever came down to Louie's to listen to the band; they came to see and be seen. They were there to have a big time. People think that you are making all this money, and you are not. Particularly if you have a big up-front expense for a band . . . You have to sell so many drinks or else you have to do a cover charge. One of the reasons Louie's survived for so long as it did was because we never did guarantee the band anything, they would get maybe 90 percent of the door . . . From our perspective we did not have the risk of having to pay them. If the people came in to see them, well, fine; then they got the money and we sold the people the drinks." With a healthy ratio of girls to boys (5–1 in the estimation of Tony Wachter), it was no wonder that Louie Louie was so popular.

Playing in a cover band was not the dream that inspired young men and women to take up music, but live entertainment was suffering in the early 1980s. Rock stars were still stars, and the values revered in the 1970s and 1960s — authenticity and paying one's dues — were being submerged under glitter and gigantism: millionaire rock stars, huge stadium tours, long-playing albums that took years to create in the recording studio, and videos that cost a quarter of a million dollars to produce. But playing in the bars and clubs in Birmingham often did not bring in enough money to justify the effort. At the top end of the scale, rock 'n' roll had become a very big business. Michael Trucks: "So the one thing that has happened is that it has got to be more of a business. Bands have increasingly over the years demanded more and more money . . . That is where you see bands going out and saying 'I have got to have half a million dollars a night' or 'I have got to have a million dollars a night.' Unbelievable terms! As a concert promoter, it changes the equation a lot." Trucks joined with promoter Tony Ruffino: "Then the Civic Center moved here, and then he moved here. I guess the first show we ever did at that venue, in the building, was Kiss . . . We then shortly thereafter did a date with Peter Frampton . . . We sold out Kiss, we sold out Boston, we sold out Peter Frampton. I mean, it was a great way to get started. Those were the giant bands at that time." Gone were the days when the musicians set up their own equipment, or used a roadie: "The road manager was typically the guy that was a friend of the band that didn't play an instrument . . . slapping equipment around and if he wasn't doing that he would probably be hanging out at a surf shop . . . The lighting and sound were rather elementary to what it is now. A band goes out on the road and takes an accountant with them. He is not a musician, he is a guy from an accounting firm that settles shows. There are sound companies, there are lighting companies that are very sophisticated . . . Roadies now have engineering degrees . . . They are being paid salaries commensurate with an engineer, and there are pension funds, benefits, and all the issues that come along with a big business." By the end of the 1970s, rock 'n' roll was in the hands of global record companies, hugely influential agents, and stadium tours propelled by fleets of eighteen-wheelers.

At the retail end of this billion-dollar business were the megastores in the shopping malls. Matt Kimbrell worked in one of these retailing chains, called Oz, and was depressed that so many young people wanted to buy records that he thought were boring, mediocre, and outdated — stadium rockers playing the same old thing, or excruciatingly repetitive electronic dance music, or, even worse, boy bands so fake it hurt: "I remember thinking, man, they buy the worst crap here. The manager said, 'The first rule of the music business: If it smells, it sells.' And that's the goddamned truth." The lack of originality in popular music was beginning to hurt the bottom line. Sales of records and concert tickets were going down almost as fast as costs were going up. By the end of the 1970s the dollar volume for sales of concert tickets and recordings was down by more than 10 percent.

This decline continued through the early 1980s, when a recession followed an upsurge in energy prices, and this in turn affected the market for live music. Terry Ryan: "In the early '80s we were heading or were in an awful recession and unemployment in Birmingham was up around 16 percent, 17 percent! It was the worst since the Great Depression! Nobody had any money . . . Nobody could afford to go out, so nobody could afford to play and nobody could afford to run a place that catered to entertainment." Doug Royale: "There would be little booms, like Morris Avenue, and in 1983 I said, Man! There is nowhere to play. In this town this is no place . . . Everybody got a house band at that time. So there wasn't anywhere to play! So I looked in the paper and got a sales job." There were also significant technological and cultural changes in the early 1980s that hurt live music. Mac Rudd: "The drinking age [increase] hit us like a ton of bricks. The second thing came the DUI laws. People became more careful because of the DUI situation. It got very rough for a while especially on the [Gulf] coast and the tourist places where I booked a lot of groups . . . One of the biggest things in my opinion that changed the club scene — even more than disco as far as live music; disco had its impact big-time on live music — but movies you could rent. You could go rent some movies and bring them home. There was your entertainment. People that wanted to buy a six-pack of beer and bring it home and not worry about going out. We lived in a false economy where people did not have that discretionary spending money that we were supposed to have had, and instead of going out to nightclubs and spending a lot of money, they could rent a movie for two bucks, stay at home, enjoy themselves, and not have to worry about getting caught driving while drinking. So the club owners were saying that they could not afford paying for bands. The era of paying for the door came about, and it was the death knell of many groups, but for certain groups, very smart groups, it became extremely profitable. People like Telluride who in the beginning couldn't get paid for a job, had to play for the door, began to play all around and start a mailing list, and from that grew fans and fans and fans, and then Telluride did not want you to pay them. They wanted the door! Because it was incredibly big money for them. They were very smart." Jamey Hollingsworth: "Telluride, these guys who started when music was big in Birmingham and the bottom fell out, and they still here, still playing music. So that is what they want to do, but it is not the same. They are not making as much money, and it is a kind of a struggle."

The recession hit the bar business hard, and several live music venues closed their doors. Dan Nolen of Brothers Music Hall: "The economy went south. It was probably the third year of the Carter administration, and we looked at either trying to continue on and to try and borrow some money to save it ... The economy was in horrible condition — the interest rates were 22.5 percent to borrow money. We just said that a lot of the shows have not done well, the economy sucks, the landlords are impossible, these next few months do not look good, and neither one of us were willing to make a commitment to go any further in debt, and we just said: that is it." It was significant that Hotel, the band that looked likely to make it out of Birmingham in the 1970s, closed Brothers Music Hall: "Hotel. New Year's Eve 1981. That was when they were huge too. That night we had Hotel play for $19.81 tickets, all you could drink and it was an open bar. We did about a thousand people. The last night we were open we did $20,000."

People who moved to Birmingham from larger cities in the South in the 1980s were struck by the lack of entertainment and a parochial attitude toward culture. Aaron Beam moved his family from Houston in 1984 to set up a health care business with his partner, Richard Scrushy: "The atmosphere was sterile. There was not much of a music scene, as far as I was concerned. It did not jump out at you, and there were certainly no big-name bands that had a hit around. Anyway, there was not a music area in

Birmingham, we started to go to Five Points South, but there was not a lot going on in music at the time." According to the magazine *Trouser Press*, Birmingham entertainment was "dominated by middle-aged Bill Murray–type lounge crooners and monotonous quasi-authentic bluegrass bands."[2] The "terminal boredom" of the local music scene was blamed on repetitive Top 40 and classic rock radio and a never-ending stream of cover bands playing "Margaritaville" and "Sweet Home Alabama." Natalye Pond: "You have the older men and the powers that be, clubs that play nothing but live jukebox. You could go and hear the same thing at the Holiday Inn that you could hear at Gatsby's . . . If they wanted live jukebox, why don't they do a sound and light show and do disco?"

There was nothing much going on downtown, except for Grundy's Music Room and a rock 'n' roll club called Shutters on Twentieth Avenue South. Terry Ryan: "Nobody had any money . . . nobody could afford to go out, so nobody could afford to play." The bar business "fell off horribly, and with it went live music," said Tom Baddley. The payment for a night's work slumped: Matt Kimbrell was getting only seven dollars a night, and Eric Essix's combo was getting eight dollars each per night in the early 1980s. The conclusion of Tony Ruffino, one of the most powerful music promoters in the Southeast, was that "Birmingham was musically dead in 1984." People were asking promising musicians like Tony Wachter why they bothered staying there.

MTV and Big Business in Rock 'n' Roll

After a decade of raised expectations in Alabama, the only local boy to make good in the world of entertainment was more an actor than a musician. Alan Hunter was working in New York when he managed to get the job of being one of the five disc jockeys (or veejays) on Music Television when it first went on the air in August 1981: "I was in New York to be an actor . . . I auditioned a couple of times . . . There were a lot of people involved, a big television studio, there was the scurry and the hustle and bustle prior to an opening. You could feel that there was a lot of money. This was Warner Communications and American Express together in a company called WarnerAmex. So there were big dollars behind this sucker, and they were going to launch it in a big way . . . They needed a blond-haired nonregional kind of guy, slightly southern in demeanor. So maybe I just fit the demographic . . . I didn't quit my job as bartending. I was working at the Magic Pan restaurant. The day we launched I still had my gig as a bartender. At night I would go and tend bar at the Magic Pan. By day I would go and do television . . . There was not all that many videos when MTV came on. We played REO Speedwagon, Styx, Rod Stewart, and .38 Special [who represented southern rock] over and over, and it was just maddening . . . At that point we had about 2½ to 3 million households audience . . . When I left I think it was about 45 million." Michael Trucks: "I think the worst thing that has ever happened is MTV! I loved it when it came out, and now I think it is the worst thing that has ever happened . . . MTV is probably 60 percent game show, or some alleged 'real life' or some cartoon show." Chris Hendrix: "Oh god. Video killed the radio star. That's all there is to it. MTV hit and music went to hell. It ain't music anymore, it's package deal. How many units you can sell. How cool the T-shirts look." Natalye Pond: "It had no heart! Didn't make you feel anything, I can't even . . . I don't know. It was horrible!"

Music television upped the ante for a local band trying to break into the big time — now you had to have a video as well as a record — and it also gave the big-name bands more exposure in the smaller musical markets like Birmingham, edging out local music. Yet Birmingham bands still dreamed of breaking into the national entertainment scene. After the breakup of Hotel, "Tommy [Calton] and I [Marc Phillips] stayed together and formed the Calton Phillips group and from there we turned into Split the Dark. Other than just continue to write [music], it was a way to make a living, and it was a good band . . . We had to fall back into the cover-band syndrome after that. And then we got it to where we could do shows of our own original music again. And the one thing that I really wanted to do was not live off of the Hotel thing. I really wanted to continue with my career. And so Split the Dark wound up winning the MTV basement tapes [talent contest] and wound up getting turned down by fourteen or fifteen different record labels." One MTV viewer wrote to the *Birmingham News* that the exposure Split the Dark gained on national television was a boost to all live music in the city — indicating the importance of this type of recognition to Birmingham's vulnerable self-image — but fame was fleeting on MTV. Marc Phillips learned a lot from his experiences in Hotel and Split the Dark: "As a singer or some type of artist on a major label, you're no longer in competition with the people in Birmingham, you're in competition with the world. And you don't just throw anything out to the world, if you're interested in making it as a career. You've got to put your best foot forward, because it might be the only shot you get. It might be the only door that ever opens for you, and if they close it, you might not ever get back in again." He remains philosophical about his experiences: "I think that it just wasn't meant to be. Now that I look back on it, it just wasn't meant to be. If it was, I wouldn't be here — I'd be on some stage somewhere." "Authenticity," a by word for professionalism and integrity in the 1970s, was now outmoded, and "seems to have become a slang term for 'boring as hell.'"[3] Southern rock had raised the expectations of many local musicians, but in the end the sad reality was that "they just don't make rock stars out of bar bands from Birmingham."

CHAPTER FOURTEEN

The New Wave

While southern rock and disco dominated American popular music in the 1970s, a new wave of rock music had evolved under the noses of the record company executives, agent management, and radio programmers. Bands like the Sex Pistols and the Ramones might have played like amateurs (which they were), but the excitement they generated reminded some of the early days of rock 'n' roll, when a band could change your life. Not since the 1950s had popular music heard such an assault on the prevailing notions of how it should sound and what it was all about. Punks in Birmingham like Matt Kimbrell called into question the value system of southern rockers: "We were making fun of the whole thing... because in the 1970s everybody was so fucking serious... We're fighting against inertia and this fuckin' city's idea of what's proper... the same boring boogie bands or country rock rehash bands." For a new generation of Birmingham musicians, southern rock was the music your parents listened to. Guitar hero Tim Boykin: "I was familiar with American '70s rock. My parents listened to Lynyrd Skynyrd and I was really getting sick of it. When I saw these hairy self-important stoner guys with these puritanical attitudes, it was getting old. [Music critic] Lester Bangs made this big point that rock 'n' roll was not supposed to be this real musicianly thing where you sat around and practiced for years and years. He made this grand statement that rock 'n' roll was supposed to be the ultimate popular art form, because anyone could do it. That was it. When I read that, I decided I wanted to do it now. I didn't have to wait until I was twenty or whatever."

The new wave came to Birmingham on record, just like rock 'n' roll had done twenty-five years earlier. Independent record companies and record stores like Charlemagne Records on the Southside, and the Odyssey music store in Hoover, brought the sounds of the Sex Pistols, the Ramones, and Iggy Pop to the Deep South. Chris Hendrix was into heavy metal in the mid-1970s when he was living in Bay Minette, across the bay from Mobile: "I guess the fact that I was living in a really redneck place, I was looking for anything that was not what all those people were into. I was listening to all sorts of bizarre stuff, whatever I could lay my hands on ... The first thing I got, I found an Iggy Pop album, a copy of *Lust for Life* of all places at Woolworths, for $1.25 ... I found that and I thought, 'This is cool.' It was pretty radically different ... You could get just about anything at Charlemagne then. When Keri Echols worked there, he turned me on to things like Black Flag, Flipper, and Christian Death and I don't know what all. He turned me on to the Dead Kennedys, and I bought just about all of the early stuff there. If was not for those guys, there was a lot of the real hardcore stuff that I would have never seen ... At the Odyssey, Brad Quinn from Carnival Season got a lot of good thrash stuff too." Then he got hold of a cassette of the Sex Pistols' seminal album *Never Mind the Bollocks*. "Because I figured, I never heard it, but I thought, Well, if I don't like it can record over it ... And, you know, *whewwww!* Jeez. Man. As soon as I heard the foot-stomping and that hand-clapping, that first chord hit—I just went *aaaaargh!* I just about creamed, man. I said, this, this is the shit right here." What Natalye Pond heard in this record "was like someone had opened the door for me! I thought, music can be fresh and new and count."

Public appearances quickly followed the first punk records. Brothers Music Hall was the work of Dan and Seth Nolen, who established their first club in Jacksonville. When they moved to Birmingham, they formed a partnership with concert promoter Tony Ruffino: "Oh yeah, Tony was the big name back then—they were the gods. They were putting shows on at the Civic Center right when it was built ... I had seen some shows at Boutwell that they had promoted and they were just like the ones I [did], so I was really honored when Tony called me ... We decided that day that we would become partners and do something. We decided that we would start looking for a location and ... start doing something together where the concept was where I would be more in charge of the bar and I knew all the street-level bands. He was the established promoter and would get all the national acts. Together we would have an unbeatable combination. We did a fifty-fifty deal. Brothers was a neat old place. It burned down [much later]. We looked for a while at a location and ended up making a deal with that place. We remodeled it, sort of. It was a Gothic inside. The main music room had cathedral ceilings, and we built a stage at one end of it and had two or three different bars and a pool table area. It was tremendous." Rick Kurtz: "There was this place called Brothers Music Hall. It was like this big beautiful mansion that was hollowed out. It just had this beautiful stage and I guess it sat maybe twelve hundred to fifteen hundred people. I saw Elvis Costello there, the Ramones, the Police. That was probably the best place that I have been in."

When it opened in 1978, Brothers concentrated on local talent, such as Telluride, Alabama Power, and Locust Fork, but it also brought to town Stevie Ray Vaughan, Dire Straits, the Police, and reggae pioneers Bob Marley and Peter Tosh. "As things go, I think it was really way ahead of its time, and I think in retrospect it was definitely ahead of its time. You know Albert Collins played for forty people. Stevie Ray Vaughan played for about fifty people. Thunderbirds played for about the same. The Ramones ran it up to about four hundred, and Dire Straits sold out." The appearance of the Ramones at Brothers in 1979 was a seminal event in Birmingham's punk rock education. Dan Nolen was not expecting much of a crowd for this strange-looking crew from up north, but they came in droves — people in weird attire with outrageous, teased-up hair or shaven-head "mohawks." "It was like crock-sotted hair and leather, and you know it was just like this crowd that came through the door and we were wondering where these people were coming from . . . but it took me completely by surprise because the show did four hundred people and I did not know a face in the crowd." These fans had come from all parts of the state and also from Florida and Mississippi. They were desperate to hear this music. Elvis Costello was moved by the welcome he got from the crowd at Brothers: "They seemed starved for this kind of thing . . . They are not like kids in New York or London; they're still unspoiled down here."[1]

Chris Hendrix probably spoke for many punk fans he when admitted: "I really wanted an excuse for people to think I was even weirder." Tim Boykin said: "You didn't have to do too much to be confrontational — it was easy." Attracted to the outrageous music and attitude of the punks, alienated youth began to come together. Scott Boykin: "Later we met the guys that were going to be in the Ether Dogs with Tim. Just met them out somewhere — they just came up to us and started talking about music. It was a pretty small group of people at that time that were interested in that kind of music." Chris Hendrix: "I was just walking through the mall one day, just wandering around for something to do, and I ran into this guy named Bruce Hardy. He was wearing a homemade Flipper T-shirt that said 'Life Is Pretty Cheap' on the back. I ran up to him and said, 'Hey man, don't think that I'm weird or anything but where did you get that T-shirt?' He said, 'I made it myself.' I said, 'You're into Flipper?' He said, 'Yeah!' Two and a half hours later we are still standing there talking about stuff. We decided that we were going to form a band . . . None of us had any stuff . . . I had an acoustic guitar and that was all. They knew this guy that they hated that lived in Hoover and had a good electric guitar and amp. We were going to break into his house and steal it. But we didn't. I am very proud to say that we didn't."

Grossest National Product, GNP, began as Spike on vocals, Jimmy Starr on bass, Keith Patton on guitars, and Dougie Dune on drums. Scott Boykin joined them on guitar: "I basically just asked them if they wanted someone else to play guitar and they said yes. So I started playing with them." His brother Tim Boykin sang for them at one point, and later they added Chris Hendrix on guitar. "I was at the Odyssey music store in Hoover, flipping through records, talking to Brad Quinn, and he said, 'GNP needs a guitar player.' I was thinking 'Holy shit!' then he said, 'Yeah, I'm going to try out.' Then I thought, 'I can't fucking believe this!' . . . I bought a ninety-five-dollar Lotus [electric guitar] . . . I still have pieces of it, as a matter of fact — I smashed it. I didn't have an amp, but I had an electric guitar, which meant that I was one step away. I plugged it into my stereo . . . and I already knew how to play [Iggy Pop's] 'I Wanna Be Your Dog' . . . I told them I had already been to a bunch of their shows, I had an electric guitar, and I already knew 'I Wanna Be Your Dog.' I had been writing songs before I joined the band. I was ready to do it, the stuff they had, the stuff I had, any covers. I was ready to do it. Gung ho and away." GNP competed vigorously for the dubious honor of being the "worst band in Birmingham," describing their music as "drunk rock," "abrasive noise," and "loud,

LOUD." Chris Hendrix remembered the first time he played with them: "I was more excited than nervous. I realized that if I fucked up, they weren't going to think that I was a crappy guitar player. None of us really knew how to play. We were all kind of sloppy. It was just about getting up there and pounding it all out. We didn't worry too much about screwing up . . . I was ready to get up and be an obnoxious bastard in front of people. I wanted the calculated outrage . . . As long as we elicited an extreme reaction, that was why I was there. That was why I wanted to be in this band."

The other pioneer punk band formed at the end of the 1970s was the Ether Dogs. This started as Jerry Weldon and Mike Lewis on guitars, Will Platt on bass, and Al Naff on drums. Clay Jones had a guitar but could not play it, so he was given the microphone. Like all punk bands, the Ether Dogs went through many changes of personnel, but the most important addition was the teenage guitarist Tim Boykin. The Ether Dogs were straight-ahead "hard-core" punk, which meant guitars played at numbing volume and frantic speed. Chris Hendrix: "The Ether Dogs, they were just *whewww*. They were what any band who wanted to be a hard-core band in this city would aspire to be. Tim Boykin, the lead player, was sixteen at the time [he was fifteen]. He was better than any guitar player that I had seen. They called him the Kid."

While southern rock valued virtuosity and the paying of one's dues, punk rock was all about wanting to play rather than being able to play. Chris Hendrix: "I had this old red and white Stella Sunday guitar that my mom had gotten me when I was sixteen . . . It was actually kind of an awful-sounding guitar, but I learned how to play, more or less, on it. I had this old *Beatles Complete Songbook*, which is of course anything but complete. I was plunking stuff out of that. And then, you know, I started hearing all this other stuff. Once I heard the Ramones, I realized that these guys were just moronic enough, this stuff is just snotty-assed four-chord, I can do that. I might be able to do better than that. So I realized that you did not have to be some classically trained proficient guy like Rick Wakeman or just be some guitar genius guitar player to go out there and stomp." "I literally learned how to play on stage," said Judy Ranelli, and "we basically learned to play as we went along," admitted others. For southern rockers, the lead guitarist was only a step away from hero status, but for the punks it was a little different: "We needed to get a lead guitarist. Neither he nor I wanted to, so we were saying 'Well, you do it.' 'No, you do it.' They said, 'No, you're the lead guitarist!' I said, 'I don't know what I'm doing.' I had been playing for a year, and so I just played anything... After we were through, everybody came up and were really cool about it. That was what gave me the bravery to keep trying to do it instead of running off and going 'Oh, I'm too awful.'" With an audience of fellow punks to encourage them —"they screamed while we sang our songs"— some bands got completely carried away with the acclaim: "We were pretty serious about the music, tuning our guitars and such."

Natalye Pond, who made her living as a professional artist, started a band called the Colas with her husband and some of their friends: Natalye sang and played keyboards, Tim Pond played bass guitar, Mark Reynolds was on the drums, and Charlie McCulloh played lead guitar. "I played the Beatles, Rolling Stones, and the Kinks. I played all that stuff when I was in high school, and at that point I just did not want to play that any more and I wanted to do original music. There were also a lot of people around Birmingham that wanted to do the same. There was one problem, though, and that was that you could not play in any of the established clubs, at least not your own music. They only wanted to hear Top 40 music, and there were a lot of them, too. There were a lot of Top 40 bands that were around, though, don't get me wrong... Most of the time we would play for parties and things of that sort." They all wrote songs and the Colas' sound was "loud and raw," as Natalye described it.

The Invaders consisted of Bill Crow and David Parsons on guitars, Martin Ross on bass, and Mark Reynolds on drums. Deprived of favorites like "Sweet Home Alabama," the audience could turn nasty. "I almost quit right after we started," admitted Martin Ross. Judy Ranelli remembers playing an American Legion Hall in Leeds "with little girls standing on chairs sticking their fingers in their ears and screaming *Boo!* at us. So we got the power cut... They yanked the power on us and then they accused me of stealing a patch cord... and we drove away and I kept imagining a posse following us. These angry guys in cowboy hats. It was terrible. That was the worst show I ever played. Well, not the worst..."

Jim Bob and the Leisure Suits formed up in 1979. Matt Kimbrell joined with school friends Mats Roden (guitar and vocals) and Leif Bondarenko (drums), and later with Craig Izard on guitar. Mats: "My friend Matt Kimbrell and I decided we wanted to do an original band that was sort of punk rock–inspired, catching up to be really new wave. What we were seeing at the time was a lot of fast-playing all-night-long that was mostly covers instead of originals, so what we decided to do was mostly originals and as few covers as we could. So at the time clubs were not really into that. We had a lot of resistance because people associated punk rock with bad playing . . . There were three or four bands in the area that were definitely trying to do their own tunes. I think it kind of got the whole process started." Matt: "I started to play the clubs when I was fifteen. The scene back then was a lot tougher. It seems like there was only about five or six clubs . . . At that time the Wooden Nickel was not really happening yet, and there was really nowhere to play. We just bullied our way into the Old Town Music Hall . . . We then started playing at the Wooden Nickel and started getting our places to play, and that was real fun. The first gig we ever did, we opened for the Romantics, and the second one we did, we opened for the Ramones. After that we could at least tell people that we had opened for these guys." In his heartfelt tribute to Matt Kimbrell (who passed away in 2010), Ed Reynolds argued that, apart from Sun Ra, "the Leisure Suits were arguably the most revolutionary band to ever emerge from Birmingham" and "transformed the city's musical dynamic as they annihilated the barrier between audience and performer."[2] Their repertoire included perverted love songs ("I Want a Date with a Paper Plate") and satirical updates of Birmingham's garage-band past ("Panama City Bleach").

The shambolic beginning of punk music in Birmingham was a pair of "historic" concerts in June 1983. The first took place at St. Andrews Church on the Southside, near the UAB campus. It featured two hard-core bands — GNP and the Ether Dogs — along with Jim Bob and the Leisure Suits, who helped organize the event. Chris Hendrix: "I was talking to David Smith on the phone one day: he said, 'Man, there is a punk show with local bands.' Of all places, it was at the St. Andrews Episcopal Church. United Campuses Against Nuclear War was having a benefit . . . I went to the show, not really knowing what to expect . . . We went inside, there was a big cross on the wall in front. Bruce said, 'Let's go up there and turn it over,' but of course we couldn't, 'cause there was all this musical equipment in the way . . . GNP played first. They only knew five songs at the time. Three of the songs were covers, and at least one of them wasn't played right. They just did not care. They just stood up and pounded away. As soon as they started playing, this whole crowd of people just started thrashing. I was standing at the edge of the crowd thinking, 'I don't know about this.' I remember I was wearing the standard dog chain that was part of the uniform. All of a sudden I see Bruce Hardy. His hand just reached out, grabbed me by the chain, and yanked me into the middle of the whole fracas . . . I started slinging my elbows around trying to get the hell out. Then I realized, 'Oh, this is what you're supposed to do.' So I just stayed there and thrashed away. GNP quickly blew through their five songs. They were great in their horribleness. They were just up there blazing away." Scott Boykin: "I remember everybody was really psyched about that show and they had pictures of it and they were talking about it —'Ah man, it was so great!' It caused a big stir."

Tim Boykin: "People would just come out like they were going to see a car wreck or something. They would kind of say, 'Oh, there is a punk band playing. Let's go to see what will happen.' There was a lot of slapstick to the slam dancing back then." The second punk concert in 1983 was at Birmingham Southern College. Chris: "Delta Chi decided that they were going to have a fraternity punk rock show. Of course, it turned out semi-disastrously because they weren't expecting things like a lot of real punks to show up. The real punks had a lot more sense than the guys that were trying to be cool . . . That was GNP and the Ether Dogs, just those two bands. I remember that GNP was doing their theme song, which was called 'Cow Song.' Spike was handcuffed to the mike stand and blindfolded and was throwing himself around, screaming, 'Tell me, why do I go to school? I hate my teachers, they're so cruel. I am like a cow.' He proceeded to go over the edge of the stage [apparently high on LSD], which was about three feet off the ground, and land on the concrete floor. Head first. We were all thinking, 'Oh my god, he's dead.' So we were running up there saying, 'Are you okay? Are you all right?' He was just lying on the floor going, 'Ahhhhh.' The sound man was going, 'Oh my god, my microphone, my microphone!' It was chaos that whole night." The punks did not use the best equipment.

Chris Hendrix: "They said that they had a drum kit. It was a little bitty drum kit, not quite half size, kind of like a starter kit. It had fake brown wood-grain contact paper on the outside, to show you how much class they had. They had one 10-watt Fender amplifier that Jimmy and I both plugged into, because it had two jacks. We both jacked into that thing, turned it up all the way, and created some heavy scrogg, I got to tell you."

Punk performances were not meant to ingratiate the band with the audience; these musicians were not playing covers for tips. As Matt Kimbrell explained, "The whole thing was to rile people up and piss them off! That is what music used to be [referring to the early days of rock] — that is what you used to do with music. That is what all the serious music of the twentieth century has been, just to piss people off!" Tim Boykin said of the Ether Dogs: "At the age I was then, the music was very confrontational, we would actually get into scuffles with people while we were playing. I can remember at least one occasion where there were actually blows." There was a new etiquette for female performers. Natalye Pond admitted, "I was a screamer!" One disgruntled listener later described the Colas thus: "They're assholes and the singer is a dirty little whore with a big mouth."

Although some punk bands had political-sounding names like the Dogs of War, Chris Hendrix admitted that "none of us were particularly political. We just didn't like people. That was our big thing. Fuck the world." While the southern rockers could not wait to get into the big business of rock and cozy up to the multinational companies that ran it, punks were anticapitalist and antiestablishment: "People thought that of people who were into the punk scene because they didn't like anything else that was going on, [but punk] showed that they actually had a brain and weren't going to just sit back and suck up what was being given to them by the mass media." The Sex Pistols had the mantra "No future for you, no future for me." Chris Hendrix: "I don't know if we were ever that deeply serious about it. I still think sometime there is no future. Who really knows? So you might as well go out and raise hell now, because there is no telling what is going to happen. I think ours is more like a bleak outlook tempered with [whether we like it or not] a little bit of southern good ol' boy attitude of 'Let's just throw down and party.' If there's no future, let's just fuck off.

Who cares? You can sit around and have some illicit drinks and the like while listening to thrash music. Then you go out and vandalize things."

"The bar owners, we would approach them and [they would say], 'Well, original music doesn't sell.' They would ask us what covers we did. We didn't do covers. If we did, they would be very obscure... We were not going to regress and start playing covers, because why bother? Play a record," remembered Natalye Pond. Chris Hendrix said that he was sometimes the only audience member left in the room "because people would just walk out... GNP was, and even when I was with them, infamous for driving people away. They didn't know what to think of us. You were either an avid GNP fan or you would come and check us out and then walk." Asked if GNP ever cleared a room, he replied "Oh yeah. Oh yeah! We have cleared rooms. Oh, have we ever." Excluded from bars and clubs, the punks played in lofts and apartments. They played for each other. Tim Boykin: "The loyal ones showed up for every show. People noticed if you weren't there. Everyone was dressed in black with the white makeup."

In the do-it-yourself spirit of punk, Natalye decided to open her own club, the Cavern, in 1983. Charlie McCulloh: "Morris Avenue had fallen on some really hard times. Someone got shot there and it was big in the papers. At one time Morris Avenue had six to eight clubs that did really well... At the time that the Cavern started there was hardly anyone down there. In the middle of the night you could do anything that you wanted to, the police did not even go down there." Natalye: "I got the name of the Cavern from the Beatles biography... We wanted people to get the idea that was where they got their start. My mission was to do anything I could to get new music a start. To allow original music to get a foothold in the Birmingham market... It did not matter if it was country, alternative, or new wave or punk or thrash or hard rock. I don't care. If you played your own music, you could play here Thursday night." The bands invited all their friends and played for the money collected at the door. Natalye showcased Jim Bob, the Ether Dogs, Invaders, Beat Feet, Mood Elevators, GNP, Davy Williams, and LaDonna Smith as well as some of the big names in punk: DDT, Guadalcanal Diary, Black Flag, and the Circle Jerks. Bryan Price: "I would say the Cavern and that era was probably the best scene Birmingham ever had, period. That was probably the best scene." In 1984 Bob Carlton of the *Birmingham News* named it the best nightclub in town, announcing, "Punk rock finally comes to Birmingham!"

The Next Wave

The punk movement morphed into a broader category known as new wave, which according to Scott Boykin "is a little slower and a little more melodic, and new wave had a tendency to use effects, a lot of guitar effects, whereas punk is a little more distorted and more violent. There is some overlap, but GNP and the Ether Dogs and some of those bands, when I first started hearing them I was not used to listening to punk, it was almost like I could not listen to it. It was that extreme." The recording industry and the music press put it all under the umbrella of alternative music. When Natalye Pond opened the Cavern, "we went from having two or three bands that did their own music, to where I actually had about twenty to twenty-five to choose from." Carnival Season, formed late in 1983 or in 1984, replaced the Ether Dogs: Mark Reynolds on drums, Ed Reynolds on guitar, Brad Quinn on bass, and Tim Boykin on lead guitar. Scott Boykin: "Carnival Season was actually a kind of transition. They were actually consciously trying to do more of a glam rock kind of thing." Tim Boykin remembered: "The Ether Dogs just worked a riff and the singer screamed over it. It was very by the numbers. But then bands like Hüsker Dü came out, fast and really loud, yet they had lyrics and melody." By the mid-1980s some punk bands had mastered their instruments, and as Kenny Wright of the Dougs said: "It was really just like, pick up your instruments and learn how to play. I mean, we worked very hard. It didn't happen overnight, and we lived in a damn practice pad with no shower or anything, and we worked very, very hard. But we wanted to take it one step further and actually write good music. Beauty is in the eye of the beholder, but we feel that we came up with some really good music."

Jim Bob and the Leisure Suits disbanded early in the 1980s. "We tried desperately to survive, but it just did not work. We had a falling-out basically because we were too drunk to enjoy each other. Alcohol was a very important part of that band. Mats wanted to do his own thing, and we never did what I wanted to do in that band, which was doing a rockabilly band. They just wanted to be nutty and wear costumes and that sort of thing. That, however, evolved into the Primitons and the Ho Ho Men. I started the Ho Ho Men [in 1983], [with] Ed Blaze and Walter Kelly, and then we played one gig and it was such a disaster. One of the guys decided that he was going to play while on LSD. After that I decided that I did not want to play again. I did not play out again for eight months. Then we finally got back and played the Cavern. Our big shtick with Birmingham was being known as the worst band in Birmingham. We never practiced, and our whole gig was just getting out there and just being as terrible as possible, and people loved it. We had about ten songs and we would sit there and play them. Then we got us a real drummer, because Ed could not play too well. We got this guy named Ronald Parker . . . We got to be a pretty good band and almost gave the Primitons a run for their money. But they had records then, and we could not get a record deal. We just put out our own cassettes instead."

The other offshoot of Jim Bob was the Primitons, which emerged at Halloween in 1983: Leif Bondarenko on drums, Brad Dorset on bass, Tim Christner on guitar, and Mats Roden on guitar and vocals, and later Don Tinsley on guitar. The Primitons were more pop-oriented and brought in some southern influences such as country and rockabilly. Birmingham's skate punks were the Dougs. Formed in 1987, they consisted of lead singer Kenny Wright, bassist Steffan Wiggins, guitarist Tracy Hancock, and drummer Doug Benjamin. Then Tommy Little joined the band as drummer and they added Ricky Little and Chris Geridono. The Dougs had been inspired by GNP and Compound Fracture, basically because the Dougs couldn't play very well ("They were terrible!"). For every punk purist band like Compound Fracture or Intense Regret, there was one with more esoteric tastes. Vacation Bible School was formed in 1986 with Judy Ranelli, Anthony Hatfield, Rob Tasslin, and J. T. Farmer. J. R. Taylor described them as a "bizarre cross between Bad Company and the Dead Kennedys, with elements of pop melodies sung in a scalding shower." Barking Tribe, which grew out of Chain Gang, played an esoteric mix of punk rock and some half-forgotten sounds of the 1970s like Jethro Tull. Electric Circus was formed about the same time in the mid-'80s: "We called it earth metal — we were almost hippies but we still had rock and were totally punk-influenced." The Electric Circus started out as Chris Lowery (lead singer), Tiger Pike, Patrick Mchallen, and Greg Hassler, who came to them from Beat Feet in the early 1980s and basically taught them how to play. Tommy Little started playing drums in 1987, and soon after that Roman Glick and Johnny Epilito joined.

The major problem facing these bands was finding a place to play. Natalye Pond: "Birmingham club owners . . . they didn't want us around. They were very suspicious and sacred . . . You saw people with mohawks . . . It was just a new way to be afraid of youth." After the city closed the Cavern, punk bands migrated to a downtown retail outlet for expectant mothers called Storkland. Bryan Price: "That is where the Ether Dogs used to practice, and they started that whole thing. They started letting people come in and watch them practice, and before long it was turned into this . . . So we just started having bands and people would charge money, I guess, and yeah, that was a big thing. It was amazing." Judy Ranelli's parents owned the venerable nightclub Tuxedo Junction: "There was dust all over the place. There were these old tables with magazines from the 1940s on them." The space was rented out for parties and weddings, and at one party so many in the alternative music community "showed up and it was like, wow, a place to get bands and party." Thus the great shrine of jazz in the city became a center for punk rock, skank, and speed metal: Stevie Stiletto and the Switchblades, the Vomit Spots, Random Conflict, Neurosis, Caustic Outlook, the Headless Marines, War Zone, Mass Confession, GNP, the Dougs, Vacation Bible School, Random Conflict, and Monster Dogs.

The Wooden Nickel was fondly remembered as "basically a bikers' bar" in the 1970s. In 1983 Dan Nolen was managing a band. "They were called the Fits and I had booked them there to play . . . So I went down there and talked to George Drennan [the club's owner] and he said, 'Do you want to open it up for the weekend and have your band play? Hey, the beer is cold, the lights are on, have your band play and run it for three days.' That was in June of thirteen years ago, 1981. So he said, 'Here are the keys, you run it.' I told him I would run it for the weekend and we will talk on Monday. So I got my girlfriend at the time and a few friends to tend bar and work the door and we did three nights. We did that, and I then met with him on Monday, and we have had the place ever since . . . In a nutshell, the early years of the Nick; the whole deal of why I even had this band at the Wooden Nickel was because the guys that owned Louie's would not allow my band to come in, and I said, 'We will take a Tuesday night and some at the door' and they said no because we played originals. I could not get the band in any other bar so I went and put them there at the Wooden Nickel . . . There was no one at that time in the city that was going, 'Let's do original music.' So anyway I knew that there was an opening and I knew that there was a void because I was a band manager trying to get my band into Birmingham. Nobody really gave a shit about the music; all they wanted to do was make money. That is how it was at that point in time, or at least that is how it seemed to me. But once I got the keys to the place I said that I would do an original club for all bands, national or local. The place has enough of a reputation where I try and stagger it and mix it a good bit. I am really proud of it. It has helped a lot of talent and it has helped a lot of bands move along . . . It was the Wooden Nickel, and I was broke at the time, and I said I have to rename the place, and I said that we were going to be on the cutting edge of music, so I looked at the sign. So then it came to me to just cover the sign with white paint and call it the Nick . . . we have had our share of some of the great stuff that has gone on: Jane's Addiction, Johnny Winter, the Red Hot Chili Peppers, Faith No More, you just have to look at the wall down there. Mr. Crowe's Garden that turned into the Black Crowes played down there. Everybody and Wendy O. Williams played. I mean, I saw her punch someone. Soul Asylum, Black Flag — I mean, everyone has played down there."

The Alternative Scene

Chris Hendrix: "The prevailing attitude of the underground, no matter about the scene politics, or how obnoxious the backfighting ["Oh, you fucked my girlfriend" kind of stuff], even in the time of militant skinhead problems, there was still enough of a rebellious underground scene that hated all the pop bullshit." This emphasis on being different spread to other musicians. The Extras was formed in 1981 by Alice Bargeron: "That band, we pretty much started out doing what would now be called alter-

native music. It was called new wave then, but we did a lot of new wave
stuff, a little bit of original stuff, and real obscure covers... At that point
probably is where we got popular, I think. We still did some obscure stuff,
but we just found out that we could do a whole lot more." The Mortals
formed in 1981, with Lolly Lee, Mickey Nichols, Bruce Crain, Rick Kurtz,
Brian Owings, and Don Tinsley: "We played between the Nick and the
Old Town Music Hall. It was about half and half originals and covers...
We played a sort of female vocals, male vocals, Beatle-y new wave rock 'n'
roll... The Old Town had a really nice cross section of people. You had
mohawks and guys in cowboy hats to the ones in motorcycle outfits. It was
real wild. The Mortals were more of a straight-ahead rock 'n' roll band. I
liked that. I miss that band." The Mortals often branched out into new
territory, such as a ska version of the Beatles' 'It's Only Love.' Rick Kurtz
commented, "We were kinda riding on new wave thing... making a break
with what had gone before."

Another break with the past was the attitude toward recording. When
an interviewer once asked GNP if they had any plans to make a record, the
band members were taken aback, never having considered that option. But
as bands compiled a repertoire of original material over time and got some
confidence in their musicianship, they began to consider methods of saving
it. The tape cassette was the first step. Cassette players were everywhere in
the 1980s, in home stereos, portable boom boxes, clock radios, and cars. You
could record on cassette and use another recorder to make copies of it: "We
sold our cassettes and made more money than the Primitons ever made."
Jim Bob recorded some songs in Mark Harrelson's garage on a multitrack
reel-to-reel recorder. Matt: "That was a 45 recorded at 33 ⅓ with like five
songs in it. Then we went out and tried to get jobs. We were also making
our own records, which at that time other people were not doing — they
had done it in the '60s, but for some reason were not doing it at this time.
We started our own label [Polyester Records] and dressed up a 45. Well,
we dressed up an EP and an album." The Colas also released a single on the
Polyester label. Gregg Hassler: "We went into an icehouse, a literal icehouse
in Homewood on Oxmoor Road [the Matose Brothers studio], and we
recorded there... and we put it out and we got some place in Nashville to
press them, and we put our picture on the cover. We Xeroxed the cover: we

got the 45s in a white pack, so we put the Xerox copy over that and stuck it on the plastic sheet . . . It is pretty much routine that you have to come out with an independent, regionally released CD."

Carnival Season was of the first new wave bands to get a record contract. Tim Boykin: "First we put out a self-made 45. We were disappointed with the way that it came out. We had made a pretty good demo tape. We got a lot of response from it. We got a response from MCA Records — they paid for us to go and cut some more demos for them at Terminal Studio in Jackson, Mississippi. It was a terrible studio. I don't know why we were there; it was just an awful experience. MCA didn't sign us. Brad kept shopping with our demo and with What Goes On [a London-based independent company]. The guy from What Goes On in the States heard remnants of American punk in our sound. He compared us with MC5 and stuff like that. There was some conflicting agendas within the band as to whether we were going to be a lightweight pop thing or a heavy guitar band. I was the lead guitar player, and of course I wanted to be a heavy guitar band . . . They signed us and had a New York office. That was the first time that I had ever signed with a small record company. We made two records. The first thing we cut was a 12-inch EP, which we did over in Mississippi at Terminal Studio. We took Mats Roden over to Mississippi with us to produce. He did a fine job of production. We got a noisy but ballsy sound . . . He didn't try to mess around with anything — he just let us play. It was good for us. It didn't mess up what we were doing. We put out a 12-inch 45 with three songs on it [including "Please Don't Send Me to Heaven"]. There was no real major impact. It got a few good reviews and stuff . . . We did a full-length album in 1987. What Goes On released it. Tommy Keene produced it. He is sort of a cult figure in indie rock. This was recorded in Maryland at a slightly better studio . . . The recording came out okay. It focused the band on what we were . . . I was a complete bastard at that time we were making the record. When we got home, I was like, 'Well, it has been a lot of fun. See you guys later, fuck off.' The band broke up for a few weeks. Then we got back together, went to Maryland, and finished the record. It was very weird. I stayed as drunk as I could most of the time. The record did okay critically, but I don't think that it sold anything that would have ruffled any feathers. It did well in the States. I do recall an English reviewer — because I was totally doing my glam riffs, he felt that it was too contrived: jerk! The album was called *Please Don't Send Me to Heaven.*"

Carnival Season now had an indie record contract, a growing reputation outside Birmingham, and a loyal following at the Nick, but they were not making any money: you could hire them for only $150 a night. Brad Quinn's expectations of the record deal were not unlike those of many other rock 'n' roll bands, past, present, and future: "Hopefully, after this record comes out, things will change a great deal for us." Tim: "The final phase of the band, and that part of my adolescence coming to a close, ended in a full-throttle U.S. tour. We toured all across the country. We did like all the other bands that had been coming through here: We toured to support the album . . . I was in my early twenties . . . The gigs went well, but inwardly I was falling apart. I was starting to hear things. Our days were numbered at that point. Me and Brad were not speaking to each other in a van across the country. I was just thinking about how bad it sucked."

After the demise of Carnival Season, Tim Boykin had joined Barking Tribe, with Kerry Pate, Mike Callahan, and Skohti Hamilton. "They had done really well at the Nick and stuff. I knew the guys. They had been hanging around in loser bands through the '80s. They were a hundred-dollar [a night] band with good reason: they weren't very good. They had a buzz going on at the Nick, and they were in the process of cutting some deals with record labels, actually with a label called Rykodisc company, which is a big-money label out of Minneapolis . . . Anyway, I was on the road with Barking Tribe and I had fun playing with those guys . . . We didn't make any money. We were broker than we had ever been. Since I was sober, it seemed like I was working really hard. Barking Tribe made one album on Rykodisc. We also made a 45. The album was called *Serpent Go Home.*"

The Primitons also sought out an indie label. Mats: "We did a four-song demo and went up to New York and played a friend of ours' party and then got some really positive feedback on the tape really quickly from Slash Records, from Mitch Easter, who was producing REM at the time. We had met him through a friend who kind of inspired us to go ahead and try for it, and that ended up taking all my time in the 1980s, until 1990. We ended up putting out a recording on [the Boston indie label] Throbbing

Lobster Records [in 1985]. That did really well in the college scene . . . We put the record out and it got a lot of airplay on the college stations around the country like Atlanta. It also sold, I think, about five thousand units. We made it basically for three to four thousand dollars. We got to play a lot because of that record and got a booking agent in New York. We then toured the East Coast a lot, and it was really disastrous on the western tour. Then we got hooked up with an English label called What Goes On and put out a 12-inch 45 and a full-length album called *Happy All the Time* [in 1987]. That was not as well received. It was a much worse recording. But it had some great tunes on it. We played a lot . . . but the Primitons thing started to go down after the release of that album."

J. R. Taylor saw the establishment of the Primitons and Carnival Season on the same label as "a pairing of Birmingham talent that should have made the city a shining light of indie music."[3] Yet they had entered the same vicious cycle that had dogged Birmingham's best bands in the 1970s: relentless touring and fruitless attempts to get a song played on the radio. "The sad thing about Birmingham's music is that there has never been a college radio. I would see bands getting to a certain point and not having anything [a record] out and then not being able to get any airplay that would really help the following. We had a following here as much as anybody could. Once again, though, it was so frustrating to not get local radio play. By that point we had been through a lot of personnel changes, and Leif and I really had almost had it with each other. We broke up in 1990." The Primitons and Carnival Season could not stand the strains of touring, and in the words of Mats Roden, "everything blew up into a big indie mess."

New Wave Values

Alternative music was seen as a vocation. Fred Panning of Caustic Outlook: "We weren't trying to get rich, it was just part of a lifestyle. We did it because we enjoyed it and it was a way to party and live, and go on the road for five days out of the week." Chris Hendrix: "Once you discover what kind of stuff was going on, Black Flag or something like that, you want more. You get a little taste of it and you wanted more. The more you got into that lifestyle, it was just something that made you want to go overboard with it." Judy Ranelli: "I remember one time I went to the bathroom and there was graffiti . . . 'I saw Vacation Bible School and you didn't.' I was like, *Awwww!* I thought that was awesome. I wanted to take a picture of it." Chris Hendrix: "It is cool to have audiences, but that is not why we play. If I was playing for the thrill of the audience, for riches and fame, or to pick up chicks, I would have given up after the first six months. I would have just said, 'Fuck this.' Because I don't have riches or fame. I do have a little infamy, I guess. A lot of people know who I am. But I can't even get into the Nick for free. They don't give a shit that I am in a band. They charge me anyway. It's not like I get girls because I am in a band. GNP was one of the bands that repelled women at an unbelievable rate. We attracted teenage skate punks that liked to beat each other up for fun."

The '60s idea that music could create a community was still attractive in the '80s. Gregg Hassler: "We were a family — we are going to do this as a whole family. It was very family-oriented as far as the way we lived together and worked together." It was playing in a music scene where "everybody was friends. Everybody knew everybody. It was a pretty small group of people," in the words of Scott Boykin. Kenny Wright: "There was just this sense of unity. It was still kind of new, and everyone would hang out at the foun-tain [at Five Points], and there were fights now and then, it was all like skinhead-related. Everybody seems like they stuck together . . . It was just because we felt like outcasts anywhere else." Fred Panning: "When I first got into it, I didn't want to go to the fountain, because I thought everyone hated me. I thought it was silly and preposterous for me to be there at the time. I didn't know anybody . . . I didn't think of it in terms of a black guy hanging out with these people, because I had been in a white environment throughout all of grade and high school. It was nothing different for me. It was just a different group of people . . . I just wanted to hang out. But then I did start to dig the rebellion thing that was built into it. Where if you wanted to get a bad haircut you could. I was made to feel almost at home." Charlie McCulloh: "Everybody knew everybody or knew of everybody. I was just a really good scene. I really enjoyed it. There was a lot of good music and a lot of good people. There was a lot of talent as well. The Cav-ern went on and kind of lurched to a stop when there was so much work to keep it open for very little money because everybody that enjoyed alternative music or the new music did not have any money really. It was not one of those things where . . . guys would drive up in their Cadillacs with their girlfriends and spend sixty or eighty bucks an hour, you know. It was people like us counting out change to buy a beer."

The new wave established a new paradigm of success in popular music. When Jimmy Starr of GNP began contemplating relocating to the much bigger punk scene in Atlanta, the other band members turned him down flat: what was the point? The point, as Tim Boykin put it, was that "if you put something out at that time, it was just an art project. There was absolutely no money to be made in an indie band." The reality that framed alternative music in Birmingham was, "We knew we were never getting out of here."

The new wave did bring important changes to local music. As Charlie McCulloh said, the Cavern "should be remembered in Birmingham as the place where the first inklings of original music began . . . By the end of the 1970s, though, a lot of people in town started writing their own music." Mats Roden concluded: "We really changed the way that Birmingham looked towards original music." Scott Boykin: "The biggest overall difference is not so much the style of music that people are interested in or whatever has changed, but that people are much more willing to accept bands that play original music in Birmingham today than they were back then. So the reason so many doors were closed to us at that time was not simply the style of music we played, but the fact that we played original music and not too many people were willing to go out and hear original bands." Natalye Pond: "People were coming out, and they were coming out in droves. They would go to other clubs and say, 'Oh, live jukebox.' They would complain to the management and leave. That made a difference!"

The punks were the first to challenge the immutable gender rules of rock 'n' roll. Women had always played in rock bands, but mainly as vocalists or dancers in the background, and the permissive 1960s had not given women many opportunities to come onstage. The punks usually accepted women as equals and now there were more women on stage, playing guitar, fronting groups, and writing songs. Lolly Lee, Libba Walker, Judy Ranelli, and Jennifer Hensley were on an equal footing with men in the new wave — in terms of their musicianship, ability to consume alcohol, and the knowledge of music that defines the true believers. Natalye Pond: "So he was clueless and was a good guitarist, but he would come in and brag: 'Do you know anybody who is faster on the downstroke than me?' I said, 'Yeah.' He said, 'Who?' 'Well, Les Paul comes to mind.'"

The new wave was also color-blind, and this led to the first integrated rock bands in Birmingham: Fred Panning played with the Dougs, Milton Davis was in the Cast, and Jesse Suttle played drums in Working Mothers. The Working Mothers were Bill Kizziah, Jesse Suttle, Alan Helms, and Bryan Price, who recalled: "We played everywhere! We toured everywhere in the States but the West Coast. We would play the Nick, and then we would go out and we would hit Florida, Texas, Tennessee. We toured Canada, had a blast! Oh, man, we sold out the first two shows. Working Mothers did just great up there, and those kids up there buy the shit out of merchandise, man. You can make a ton selling T-shirts and albums. We made our own demo on cassette and we signed with this little label called Cargo, and they were out of San Diego, Montreal, and Chicago, and what they did was they just basically sent us the money to record." Their record, *Crush Me* (1990), did not storm the charts; nevertheless, the Working Mothers had demonstrated what a little initiative could do. Bryan Price: "I think we were one of the first to show people that you could be a shitty little barchord-playing-roughly band and do okay and not give a shit too . . . Well, it was funny with Working Mothers: man, after we did that, we started noticing bands around town popping up with black drummers and getting a little grungier because we had a little success and everybody was like, 'Oh.'" Punk and new wave were bending the rules. As Fred Panning remembered: "I was never made to feel different . . . I guess I was drawn into the no-rules thing, and I just did not know it."

CHAPTER FIFTEEN

The Next Big Thing

T he establishment of several new health care facilities in Birmingham created a surge of growth in the late 1980s which helped transform the national image of the city from that of polluted, hateful
steel town to a progressive research, communications, and health care
center. This was the New, New South of big corporations: HealthSouth,
Bell South, and AmSouth. They were creating thousands of jobs. Health-
South, for example, had about one thousand employees when it was established in the mid-1980s, and ten years later it employed forty thousand. As
Aaron Beam of HealthSouth pointed out: "A hospital is a tremendous economic phenomenon, a little city that needs everything from floor sweep-
ers to brain surgeons. We hired them all, but bringing brain surgeons to
Birmingham made its mark on the city." That Garrison Keillor's *Prairie
Home Companion* show, a stalwart of elitist, intellectual NPR, could sell out
in Birmingham — even in the middle of a rare snowstorm — reveals how
much things had changed. Ed Reynolds: "One show got snowed out...
He did one show in the snow, and people were walking downtown to the
Alabama Theatre." Michael Trucks: "As we change from a product city to
a service city, service meaning health-related as opposed to steel-related, all
of a sudden you are getting more people in, more cultures, etc. The perfect
thing is, go back ten years [to the early 1980s] and look at the restaurants
in Birmingham that were available. When I was growing up and I wanted
to go eat Chinese food, there was only one place to go and that was Joy
Youngs. I always remember that you got to eat at Joy Youngs and would get
these big fat yeast rolls, and I always wondered, what do these have to do
with Chinese food? Now you look at it and say, 'No, I don't want Chinese
food, I want Thai, I want Indian,' and so on."

Birmingham's national image was changing. Many were flattered to see their town described favorably in *USA Today*, and they took on a special pride in their new status as a "best-kept secret" where the Yankees would not find them. This took some of the sting out of the continual unfavorable comparisons with Atlanta, which had kept Birmingham in its shadow since the 1940s. Birmingham's population grew impressively in the 1980s, yet this figure of 755,580 could not compare with Atlanta's 3 million. Birmingham looked to the future. Richard Arrington, the newly elected mayor in 1979, and the first African American to hold that position, said: "We need in Birmingham something of which we can be proud."[1]

Two events in 1989 proved beyond any doubt that music could give Birmingham a sense of pride. The Rolling Stones' performance in 1989 during their Steel Wheels tour was a shot of self-confidence for the city. Ed Reynolds: "I remember the day the tickets went on sale for that, the first show. Birmingham was already in an uproar about it. I remember going down to my mother's office because supposedly they had these phone lines that you could camp out on a busy signal . . . We were down there all day trying to get through on those phone lines." The *Birmingham News* music critic Shawn Ryan was one of many who said, "It was the best show I saw that year . . . I mean, they were larger than life!" And he pointed to its impact on a city that felt itself a cultural backwater: it was "a very big boost in the ego for Birmingham to do that . . . there was a feeling here, because 'I was here and I wouldn't ever see the Stones' . . . It was like this validated the community . . . People told you that they went, they didn't tell you about the music. They just said, 'I was there!'" Twenty-five years previously people had been praying for another top British group to offer some chance of cultural redemption. Now the Stones had made good that particular dream.

The other event was the first City Stages outdoor festival, which successfully began a run of over twenty years as the foremost music festival in the state and a major attraction in the Southeast. Birmingham had proved that it could put on a show and that it was important enough to attract the biggest names in the entertainment business (with the help of Tony Ruffino), but there was not much being said about its own music and musicians. Coming in before Mississippi might have comforted Alabamians in the past, but now people in Birmingham had bigger aspirations. Surely there was somebody in the music scene who could do the city proud?

The search for the Next Big Thing in popular music business became part of the yearning for national recognition, something to be proud of in a city trying to escape its past. Musicians like Matt Kimbrell felt the pressures of "having some names. Birmingham has always struck me as — they wanted the big bands to kind of validate the social scene." Yet success in the popular music business was elusive and short-lived. Shawn Ryan: "Telluride had three albums out in the '80s and didn't do anything, ended up playing frat parties and sororities and clubs and making a very good living out of it, but the albums didn't help them out. In the '80s you had . . . all these bands had albums but it never went anywhere! . . . I have heard so many musicians say, 'God, if only I could just get an album out, from a major label. It doesn't have to be big, it doesn't have to succeed, but that I just want the shot.' I heard that twenty-seven thousand albums were released last year. What is your chance when you are one in twenty-seven thousand? . . . When I was a music writer for the *News* I would get seventy-five CDs across my desk per week!" The daunting statistics against success did little to dampen down hopes of a hit record. Doug Royale: "We were going to be the ones . . . the Birmingham band that actually did go national and do something and didn't just have a record down at Blockbuster for three months and it is gone!"

The Next Big Thing in popular music did emerge from a cultural backwater, an unfashionable, deindustrialized part of the country in the shadow of some prosperous neighbors. Nirvana came from Aberdeen, near Seattle, Washington, and like the Beatles and Sex Pistols before them, they changed everything in the business of rock 'n' roll. Their first album cost only $606 to make and did well enough to impress the David Geffen Company, who gave their indie label Sub Pop a distribution deal. *Nevermind* came out in 1991 and was soon selling a hundred thousand units a week. The single "Smells Like Teen Spirit" became the grunge anthem for the next wave of alienated youth. After only four months on the shelves Nirvana's *Nevermind* had sold 3 million copies. Michael Trucks pointed out, "The music industry is reactive, not proactive. The music industry waits for someone to become a success despite of the industry and then everybody jumps on it . . . All of a sudden a band breaks, I mean, breaks big! . . . and then there is a scene and there are record companies saying, 'Go to Seattle, see what else is out there! Go to Minneapolis, see what else is happening there!' . . . So it feeds off itself, bands break, record companies get interested in going to that city, and that buzz attracts other musicians to go to that city . . . and it creates a whole community, a really creative community." Talent scouts and record company A&R (Artist and Repertoire) men went out looking for promising alternative bands, and this brought some of them to Birmingham. Everybody knew that it only took one big success, one Next Big Thing, to raise up every other band in town. Rob Thorworth: "All it would really take, I think, would be for one or two bands to hit out of here! And then everybody is going to start looking because that is what happened to Austin, that has happened to Athens and Seattle. It just takes one or two bands."

Birmingham's alternative bands adjusted their sights higher. Rick Kurtz had decided, "I don't want to make a record for our friends again. I want a commercial record, one with radio-friendly cuts." Some of them were being courted by indie labels and booked by Southeastern Attractions. Expectations were being raised: "We can broaden our audience. Maybe we can quit our day jobs." After the Primitons broke up, Mats "pretty much took the next year off. Then I was actually leaving the music business and I ran into Carole Griffin at UAB while I was registering for some classes. We wanted to get together and jam, so we did. So we started playing with the same unit that was the Primitons. We wanted to do something that was different, with Carole as more of the focus of the group. She came in pretty much as being a backup singer. At the end of 1991 I think we had acquired Eric Audimus as bass player, so it was Carole, Leif, Eric, and myself. So right around Christmas of that year that we played as the Sugar La Las." Don Tinsley came in from the Primitons: "I was in and out of that band about five times for the next four years [1985–89]. I went in not playing keyboard and accordion and I left playing those things . . . In the end it kind of mutated into what became the Sugar La Las, and we would have anywhere from three to eight people in the band depending on what night it was." They would pull up in a long limousine outside Louie Louie,

bathed in the light of the Hollywood-style searchlights, and the band and
their entourage of dancers, dressers, and posers would make a triumphant
procession around the packed house. Judy Bowles remembered that seeing
the Sugar La Las in full swing was a bit like experiencing an Elvis concert
in Las Vegas with all the glitter and glamour.

Mats: "We developed an act, as it were, at the Nick. It then really solidi-
fied when we went to South by Southwest in Austin and played a showcase
there. We had a lot of response there from publishers and record labels, and
so we really got into this hard-core gang trying to get a deal playing all these
showcases all over the country: New York, Austin, Nashville, and Atlanta.
We played every showcase we could. We took the whole act, dancers and
all — it was really a nightmare in a way. We ended up getting a publishing deal, and we had a huge bidding war, I am embarrassed to say, but it
was over the band between six or seven publishers. We ended up with Peer
Music. Basically we had a $100,000 agreement for three records. Started
doing some demo work and got Mitch Easter to come in . . . So we signed a
deal and got $30,000 to do things and split up the money. It was all predi-
cated on these tunes that I had written, and so I signed them away for the
band. Then it just deteriorated for Carole and I and for the rest of the band.
We were just really burned out at this point because we had spent a lot of
time working towards these goals. Our personal relationship as well as our
professional relationship just really suffered. That is just the way a lot of
bands go. It just wears you out. Especially what we were doing, which was
exhausting but it was really fun. It was a lot of fun for me, but she split just
after six months of the signing of the contract. That was really devastating
for me and the band. It just left things really screwed up."

After the Working Mothers broke up, Price and Suttle joined with Tim
Boykin to form the Shame Idols. "When we put the Shame idols together
Tim was so frustrated with playing with people that it was just not any
fun to him anymore and it wasn't any fun for us doing this, because you
play with somebody that doesn't let you have fun or express yourself and
it just gets blah because the music business itself is going to knock your
butt around. So you start realizing, 'No matter what happens, I want to do
something I enjoy.' So that was our main motto in the Shame Idols, and
it still is today. It is like: let's get together, and if it feels good let's just have

fun, and if something happens, it happens; if it doesn't, who gives a shit?" Tim: "The reason I got into the Shame Idols was because I wanted a format. I had been in all these bands and I wanted to make a go at songwriting and making a living . . . There is money to be made in the Shame Idols. A few years back it was really weird and spooky. This is now where everything is so par for the course that everyone is cynical about it now."

The band made their first record after only six months, on a 4-track recorder in somebody's basement, and sent out the cassette to scores of independent record companies. They got lots of calls back, including Frontier Records, who were sold on a tape of a live performance at the Nick. Frontier financed a session at the studios of Conrad Uno in Seattle, the hottest record producer at the time. "Tim always knew, he was like, 'Man, we are going to be great one day if this guy Conrad could just produce us because I really think with what we want to sound like, and what Conrad gets bands to sound like, it sounds like it would work.' We are like, 'Oh yeah!' That was the sound we wanted! We wanted the driving guitar, the in-your-face drums." Tim: "It was terrifying when we went to cut the record. I guess it is because at some point a band becomes a band. We weren't really a band when we got on the plane, but we were on the flight home. I know that sounds corny, but that is how it happened. We felt like, oh, we really have to do this now . . . I had all these control issues like, 'Who is flying this plane? Who is making this album?' It was really weird stuff, but everything went great . . . We did that CD in five days. What is amazing is that there are fourteen songs on there, and do you know how many songs we did? Twenty-three in five days! We just walked in there and nailed it." The Shame Idols put out two records in four years. Tim: "One thing that is a feather in our cap is that we have two legitimate indie releases behind us already. If we do sign to a major label, they are not going to wonder what we are going to do. They are going to know what our stuff will be like; maybe it will be a little bit cooler with some extra cash . . . We have been scratching our heads for the past three years wondering why we are getting to do this. Our shit is in Spain and Japan now . . . We are supposed to be touring Canada soon." Bryan: "We came back to Birmingham and the immediate response was just unreal. It was just like for a while we were the darlings or something. It was funny! . . . It is like 'You ain't worth a shit here until everybody else from everywhere else tells people here that you are worth a shit.' That is just the way it goes. You are not going to get any radio play here until people from L.A. and New York tell them to play you. But we had all this media response here . . . You try and explain to people, 'Look, we are on a small label, it's not going to happen quite like that' . . . Artistically it is great! Total freedom! Both these CDs I will be proud of for the rest of my life. Downside, they don't have a lot of money for promotion. They are a small company. They don't have a lot of money to help you tour." The Shame Idols kept their day jobs.

When the major labels finally came to Birmingham to sign new talent, they were impressed not by a hard-rocking punk outfit but by an accomplished set of musicians who were as comfortable with jazz fusion as they were with rock 'n' roll. The Cast (previously Forecast) was drummer Mark Lanter, bassist Milton Davis, guitarist Glenn Butts, and vocalist Libba Walker, who fronted the band and played flute. They had signed to the independent record company Cameleon in 1991, which was then taken over by Elektra Records in 1992. Rob Thorworth: "They all of a sudden popped up, got a record deal, changed their name, changed their style of music from the Cast. I mean, just from a personal standpoint, yeah, I got tired of seeing bands like Vova Nova / the Cast. I feel like they should have stayed the Cast. They probably would have been huge if they would have stayed the Cast, but they started playing stuff like the Chili Peppers." On the face of it, Vova Nova had made it; a recording contract with Warner/ Elektra and the clout of the William Morris booking agency behind them. One commentator wrote: "You'll probably be hearing them on the radio and drooling over them on MTV." The band had played to many college audiences in the past, but now they found that the circuit had changed radically in the Nirvana era. Vova Nova's discs languished on the shelves of record stores, and soon the band returned to Birmingham and went back to playing the bars around the Southside.

Kudzu Records

As one of the leading booking agencies in Birmingham, along with Southeastern Attractions, New Era promotions had the "city all sewed up" (as

one musician put it) by the end of the 1980s. They opened the Five Points
Music Hall in 1994 in an old supermarket in the Southside. The cavern-
ous interior could seat about a thousand people. Greg Hassler: "The Music
Hall is looking at numbers, figures, and what is in the charts. If it is not in
the charts, he is not going to put it in that big club." The Music Hall filled
the gap between the clubs like Louie Louie and Zydeco (two hundred to
five hundred people) and the stadium venues like Oak Mountain Amphitheatre, where New Era staged the big names who came to Birmingham.
Conrad Rayfield: "We started a little management company . . . and did
a little record company which ultimately yielded a different kind of label
deal with Mercury [a label of the major Polygram record company]. It was
really a pure imprint deal." The experience of developing acts and signing
them to record contracts with larger labels had been unsatisfactory: "I got
my seat-of-the-pants education on how to shop a band with Split the Dark
and it formulated with failure . . . [but] we had acquired the fundamental
skills required to run a record company." Scott Perry returned to Birmingham from his job in New York to do publicity, and Michael Trucks helped
set up the company and handled the new label's legal affairs.

     The retailing expertise was in the hands of Don VanCleave of Magic
Platter Records, which had just won an award as the best record store in
America: "I just knew I wanted to open a [record] store. I had never been
in retail before. I didn't know anything! So that was ten years ago [Novem-
ber 1987] and we came in and did well. Learned the business and then we
opened the second about three years ago after the first one, and I started
learning a lot about the distribution side of things, and about the record
label side of things, and was really good friends with quite a few bands.
Became kind of an adviser to quite a few musicians, like Brother Cane,
and Rob from Gravy. We had a lot of musicians working for us, and I kind
of got the idea that I wanted to be involved with a management of a record
label side of things with bands. So that is where the whole Kudzu idea came
up. Jay Wilson, a really good friend of mine, and I kind of thought that
there was some local talent here that wasn't getting exposed very well on the
national front. Jay worked for Conrad Rayfield down at New Era management, and they managed Brother Cane and several other bands. So Magic
Platter and New Era management formed a partnership that was called

Kudzu Records, and I, at that time, brought Gravy into the fold. They were all employees here. Rob [Thorworth] and Jay Johnson both worked at the store, and I spent a lot of time nurturing those guys along. I had put up the money to record *From the Hip*, which was Gravy's first album, and we did it in a garage at John Scalici's house over in Mountain Brook, and I fronted the money for all that, and that is what I brought into Kudzu . . . and that went on to be our biggest-selling release of the three [records] that we did get out. Conrad and Jay found Catfish Jenkins playing at Zydeco. They were an Athens [Georgia] band that just happened to be playing here one night, and then Conrad and Jay already had the affiliation with Slick Lilly, and those are the three records we put out. We were not only going to be a record label, but we were also going to manage these three bands and totally manage their career. Things went pretty amazingly well at first."

Gravy was Rob Thorworth, Jay Johnson, and John Scalici. This blues-oriented trio started in 1992. Rob: "Basically I was playing solo acoustic at the time and I had been working on and off with a drummer that used to play with me in the Newboys: John Scalici . . . Jay Johnson had played bass in Jay Willoughby and the Town Criers. I forget if they were disbanding, but I remember them playing next door at Louie's and I literally sat down with him that afternoon for about two hours and taught him every song that I know . . . I had worked at La Paz [a Mexican restaurant] here and knew the people here and we had done a Christmas party for them and I had bartended for them . . . and they liked it and said, 'Well, we want you for the house band down here for the summer' . . . and so Gravy was formed officially and we went down there as a blues band. That's what they wanted, was a blues band, and that was what I had wanted to be playing. So we did three sets a night . . . We kind of eased ourselves under the wing of the [Magic City] Blues Society, and they kind of took us in and they helped us to get gigs and we started playing higher-profile gigs and we had come back as an all-electric band at this time. We were playing the blues and we were starting to write songs." After they signed with Kudzu Records, they went into Airwave Studios to record in 1994. Don VanCleave: "It was the very end of December [1994] when we got our first batch of releases out. We got Gravy out first because Don Alias of the Bear [radio station] got a Gravy song on the radio and the demand went through the roof! Over the Christmas of '94 we sold thousands of copies in Birmingham, and we knew we had something there. Then we released Slick Lilly and Catfish Jenkins in January of '95. So I pretty much left Magic Platter at that point and devoted myself full time to the Kudzu operation. We had a national distributor out of Denver [Encore Distributors] that was really good at getting the product into a lot of stores around the country, and we had accomplished some pretty amazing feats!" Kudzu would sign an imprint deal with Mercury Records giving them access to the marketing network of one of the major record companies.

Rob: "We had actual distribution through Kudzu and a lot of big things started to happen for us. We played with Koko Taylor, Buddy Guy, the Allman Brothers, and went on tour with Government Mule, and things were just popping for us and happenin' and happenin' and happenin' . . . There was this guy [radio deejay Don Alias] who was going to go out on a limb and start playing our record and he would call up Kudzu and he would say, 'Man, I have never seen a record react like this! I've got truck drivers calling me, I've got housewives in Mountain Brook callin' everybody, all the demographics are reacting to this song and I think if you were to get a little money behind you and if it were played on a national scale, these guys would blow out the water!' Well, obviously that never happened, but it was encouraging for me to think, 'Wow, my music is being played on the radio and it is reacting.' And we went from selling a few CDs from the stage to blowing out of them in all the record stores in town and shit started happening." Gravy sold a small but respectable number of records for an indie release (about fifteen thousand copies).

Slick Lilly was formed in 1988 as a rockabilly band with Carl Rouss and Muddy King, but evolved into a more bluesy, hard rock sound. Waddy Wachtel was involved in the production of their record *Rituals*, which was partly recorded at Airwave Studios. Don VanCleave: "We got Slick Lilly added to tons of radio stations! Had a number 1 single with them, and we did it all ourselves, unlike a record label that has a big staff of people all over the country. We were able to get [radio] programmers to add the song, and it was mainly Jay Wilson's relationship with these programmers . . . They picked his call up." Carl Rouss: "That disc was played, it peaked out at like eighty-one or eighty-two stations nationwide . . . It did make a small dent and it opened a lot of doors for us as far as getting better gigs." Muddy: "We went from playing small clubs to going to amphitheaters and hockey arenas and stuff like that . . . back then the Nick was really the only club [in Birmingham] that showcased original music back when I first started in '90 or '91." Carl: "So then we moved to Louie's, and that widened our crowd a lot . . . That was kind of a big step up. Then the Music Hall opened up and we moved up another level for that. QBQ booking agency out of New York . . . got us on the Ted Nugent tour. So we went from playing the Nicks of this world to like catching opening slots in theaters . . . and playing Oak Mountain–type places and bigger . . . Having a good booking agent is definitely a big part of it. It is just a matter of who is behind you and who is pushing it. It is about money, man! It's up to the music about 60 percent, but otherwise it is all about who is pushing it and who has got it to where people hear it and can appreciate it and would buy it." Don VanCleave: "We had a lot of initial thoughts that if we could get Slick Lilly to a point where they were getting significant airplay that a major label would swoop in and sign them, and we would benefit, we and the band would benefit financially from that . . . But we were having problems at that point realizing that we had a turntable hit with Slick Lilly. It was getting pounded on the airwaves, and that is not free! You have to spend a lot of money with consultants and radio people to make a record happen on radio. Radio programmers don't play a record just because they like a record."

Damon Johnson and Glen Maxey started playing together in Chyld in the early 1990s. Damon: "I came here in 1987 and played with Split the Dark. Shortly thereafter I met Scott [Collier] and he was playing in a band and we were all doing different stuff. Playing a lot of covers and stuff like that . . . I had the idea of starting a band that was all original tunes like in the beginning of 1990, and it went through this real twisted kind of metamorphosis, but we officially started Brother Cane, I guess you can say in 1992 . . . We did a lot of demos and got signed with Airwave [recording studio]." Conrad Rayfield took the band under his wing, but found that the A&R people of the record companies were not interested, "and the head of rock promotion says he doesn't hear a single [hit] song that he says could get played on rock radio and this is a rock band. So we just don't know if we are going to be able to make the record . . . So in our last-ditch effort I sent the tape to a girl named Tracy Douglas in Atlanta and . . . a guy at that company was the number 1 rock consultant. In other words, he consulted more program directors in rock radio than anybody in the United States . . . and this guy's nickname in the industry was 'Dr. No' because he hated everything, said no to everything . . . He listened to the tape, absolutely fell in love with it, so much so that he picked up the phone and called the head of rock promotion at Virgin and said, 'Buddy, if you don't release this record it will be the biggest mistake you have ever made, the first single should be "Got No Shame" . . . I guarantee it will go to number 1!'"

With a contract with Virgin, and a debut album (*Brother Cane*), the band toured the country in 1993. "For us, once we had the recording and we had the radio after the first record came out, but not here [Birmingham], and we did not necessarily play a lot here . . . We did do some shows off and on, but it was not like Brother Cane had built this following in Birmingham, Alabama, around Brother Cane. Everybody in the scene knew who we were individually, but it was not like it was that — we went elsewhere to get that stuff! We just happened to be from here. Well, I just mean once we got signed to a major label, they realized a record all over the country. So we were very fortunate that we had a song that started making some noise and it started in the Southeast and branched out from there. That was a song called 'Got No Shame.' That was the first single on the first album." Conrad: "So they not only got the song played, it became song of the year, and became the second most played song at AOR [Album Oriented Radio] for the entire year and number 1 for either seven or eight weeks. So that will give you an insight into how clueless these record companies are." Damon: "So what we have been doing since that time is trying to expand a core band, so the second record [*Seeds*], we had a song that did good for us too ["And Fools Shine On"]. So radio is important! There are a lot of cool bands like Vova Nova. Mats and those guys — the Sugar La Las. They rule! See, those and all the great bands. They just didn't at the time put out anything that found its way on the radio. As much of a fan as we are of live underground bands, we were never shy about our intent to go into mainstream. If getting on radio and MTV is mainstream, then we were absolutely going for it, man! We just were! That is what we were doing . . . It is like, well, man, do we want to play this really cool, whacked-out gets-us-off shit, or do we want to fuckin' sell records and play and ride around in a bus and do cool shows and you know: go for it! Hey, man, I want to sell 10 million fucking records, and you can quote me on that! And I have never not wanted to sell 10 million records!" Scott (from across the room): "I have never wanted to sell 10 million records. I am an artist!" (Laughter.) Damon: "I am so happy to see the deterioration of this alternative attitude that, you know, I give [Kurt] Cobain and [Eddie] Vedder their profits, man, because it is obvious that those guys never really wanted that, and that's cool, but it is kind of a drag to feel like I had to hide the fact that I wanted to be famous and wealthy and successful because of my music."

Conrad: "One of the things that we learned was that we always thought that once you got a record deal all the work as over, that you hit the gold roll, but it couldn't have been farther from the truth! It is almost like the poorest that the band is ever going to be is when they get their record deal, until they begin to really start getting enough going on at the radio to where the record company will give them some support." The band spent most of 1993 on the road. According to Johnson, from January 26 to December 6, 1993, the band members were home for only five days. They traveled all over the country and opened for Lynyrd Skynyrd, Van Halen, Bad Company, Robert Plant, blues bands, hard rockers, heavy metal groups, and all those in between. At each stop in the tour they put on acoustic performances at radio stations and record shops. They made personal appearances, signed records, and did everything the record company asked of them. Damon: "We have played every town in the country, twice! As far as I know, Brother Cane is the only band, R&B, rock, country, whatever, that is from Birmingham, Alabama, that is out there that the rest of the country knows about, and they attach Birmingham with the name Brother Cane." Conrad: "They had MTV on the first record and lost it on the second record, even though they had a song that did great at modern rock [radio] with 'Fools Shine On.' So this next [third] record ultimately will have to find a way to cross over out of the rock charts into modern rock, and for that matter ultimately maybe to the pop charts if one of the songs connects." Their no-frills, straight-ahead rock 'n' roll might have been a little out of fashion: "Alternative is the really . . . hip thing right now, but there's tons of fans out there that want to just hear good songs and good music."

274   MAGIC CITY NIGHTS

As only the second Birmingham rock band to break nationally (after Hotel), Brother Cane alerted the majors to their local music scene. Conrad: "There were additional bands that got publishing and record deals and things like that . . . and there is always a feeding frenzy that results from one or two bands that are signed out of a market. Really the big ground-swell of interest came about five years ago [early 1990s], and that is when a lot of A&R people started showing up here routinely because right on the heels of Brother Cane thing came the Sugar La Las and there were several other things that were happening during that time period that came close to getting signed. We managed a band called Slick Lilly that had a very prominent profile and got what appeared to be a serious deal." Don Van-Cleave: "Slick Lilly was getting some attention. We had a lot of big, big executives fly in to see Slick Lilly and nothing ever happened for them. They just didn't connect with these guys very well and they didn't get signed." Muddy King: "It was a ballsy attempt and a good attempt to try and make something happen, but there wasn't enough bands here . . . They are starting to write their own music. So I think that this is the biggest step and the most progress that people in this town have made."

Before long several Birmingham bands had snagged big contracts with major companies: Verbena, Remy Zero, Vallejo Brothers, and Little Red Rocket had once been delighted to play at the Nick but were now being flown to Los Angeles or New York and placed on major national tours. The Vallejo Brothers were formed at the end of the 1980s around A. J. Vallejo (guitar/vocals) and his brothers Alejandro (drums) and Omar (bass). Bruce Castleberry played guitar and sang, with Diego Simmons as the percussionist. In 1990 they won a "Battle of the Bands" contest and got studio time at Front Row Studios. Shawn Ryan: "Vallejo are doing very well; they are getting some attention. They are in Austin now. They have signed two records deals in a year. They signed with a real small label out of Chicago, IMI, and then got picked up by TVT, which is a bigger label out of New York. So they are making their march up . . . Vallejo might be the next one to make it, because they do have this Latino funk rock sound which is unusual. Santana meets 311 kind of sound." Their first self-titled release was in 1997, and this was followed by a year of intense touring, opening up for bands like Matchbox 20 and Los Lobos. Their second release for TVT,

Beautiful Life, revealed a more eclectic approach to their music with more emphasis on their Latin roots. A single, "Just Another Day," was a hit in 1999, and they made a deal (their fourth) with Epic/Sony to release their music on the Crescent Moon imprint label.

Remy Zero was formed around 1989 by Cinjun and Shelby Tate, Cedric LeMoyne, and Louis Schefano. They found it very hard going in Birmingham: "We literally could not get a gig, so we moved away . . . There's no real music scene, unless you are playing Lynyrd Skynyrd covers."[2] Admittedly their music "was quirky and sonically interesting. It just wasn't the stuff you play pool to. It wasn't the stuff you drink beer to." Aaron Beam of Louie Louie: "Good old southern boogie rock was easily the most popular live music — the bands that played original alternative music just could not fill a club. Take Remy Zero, for instance, they say that they could not get a club owner to book them at the time . . . The Remy Zero type bands did not draw enough crowd to book them. The people did not support original local music — they would rather hear 'Sweet Home Alabama' and that kind of music." Some of Remy Zero's contemporaries saw them as proof of the insipid local scene: "You are sitting in your living room in Birmingham, Alabama . . . You're in your early twenties. In the shadow of local Birmingham bands like Remy Zero you know you have got to get out." (This came from Virgos Merlot's press sheet.) Cedric LeMoyne: "We started making tapes, but only after we had a record company interested did we start to figure out how to actually be a band, how to play these songs live, how to get gigs. We couldn't do this in Birmingham so we had to move away . . . When we started the band we couldn't even get a gig at the Nick. We moved to Nashville because we couldn't play in Birmingham . . . There's never been any sense of a coherent scene or mutually supportive scene. I think that's one of the things that have held Birmingham down. No one wants to help each other out . . . But we got lucky. There were some people at Geffen and Capitol Records who were new at the time and they got interested. Then we started to get money to make recordings."

That old tormentor ambition was returning to take hold of Birmingham's indie bands, if only to find an appreciative audience outside Alabama. Leif Bondarenko, a drummer who had played in many bands, put it this way: "I'm glad to do a project that might have some legs and go out of this city. That's all any artist can hope for."[3] Remy Zero "got fully signed to Capitol and started moving around some more. We moved to New Orleans. It's a cool town . . . We finished the record and moved back to Birmingham . . . There are always these mergers, people moving around in the record industry. And like you get a new president at the record company. He will bring in his own stuff, his own bands, and fire the staff and drop the bands that are not already famous. We were one of the bands who had not released our record yet. So we got dropped . . . But we got lucky in that we had already made a lot of friends in the industry. Our tape got to a very important public radio station in Los Angeles, KCRW . . . so the person who ended up signing us to Geffen heard us through that and the deejays talking music to him. So he heard us, loved it, and came down to Birmingham to sign us. We got very lucky." Their first self-titled album was released in 1996. The band now had Gregory Slay on drums and another guitarist, Jeffrey Cain. Their second album, *Villa Elaine*, was released by Geffen in 1998 and attracted some attention. Several songs were used on movie soundtracks: "Prophecy" appeared in *She's All That* and *The Last Kiss*, and "Fair" was used in *Garden State* and *Fanboys*. When Remy Zero returned to the South to promote the album, Cedric LeMoyne found that "the music scene had changed a little bit. It was easier for more adventurous music to be played. This is post-Nirvana, the alternative explosion had started to happen . . . People are much more willing to accept bands that play original music in Birmingham today than they were back then [in the 1980s]."

Scott Bondy, Les Nuby, Daniel Johnston, and Carson Lamm formed a band called Volume. Verbena started in 1995 with Louis Schefano (drummer), Scott Bondy (guitar and vocals), singer Anne Marie Griffin, and Daniel Johnston on bass. (Les Nuby replaced Schefano on drums.) Verbena's sound evolved from pop to harder-edged alternative rock, and the vocal interplay of Bondy and Griffin nicely fit the idea of a commercial sound in the 1990s. After issuing several singles, their album *Souls for Sale* for the Merge/Setanta was released in 1997. Shawn Ryan: "Verbena might do it! They might be able to take the next step. It is a good little album and they are good live, except that have got that cold attitude towards the audience, but they sound good live."

Wish was formed by 1995 by lead singer Jacob Bunton. In 1997 they too received a major label contract — from Atlantic Records. With Bunton on lead vocals, Wish had guitarist Michael Swann (later replaced by Chris Simons), drummer Matt Finn, and bassist Carl Ray Hopper. As often happens with a big-label signing, they changed their name to Mars Electric after a sign Bunton remembered seeing a few blocks from his Tarrant home studio. The band recorded an album for Atlantic at Tarrant's Syncromesh Studios, but unfortunately the company dropped them before any tracks were released. This should have been the end of Mars Electric, but they gained the support of A&R man John Kalodner, who signed the band to Columbia. *Beautiful Something* was released on Columbia's Portrait imprint in early 2000. Columbia arranged for some high-profile touring in support of headliners like Stone Temple Pilots, Mötley Crüe, and Nickelback. Bunton: "It's the coolest feeling in the world right now, we could blow up and become absolutely huge, or we could flop miserably."

Virgos Merlot began as the Devine. Singer/lyricist Brett Hestla, guitarist Jason Marchant, and guitarist Ted "Deacon" Ledbetter released one CD as the Devine, *Victim*, but broke up shortly after. Hestla, Marchant, J. D. Charlton, Ledbetter, and bass player Chris Dickerson formed Virgos Merlot. On the basis of demo recordings made in the basement studio of friend and producer Jason Elgin, as well as a showcase performance at Orlando, Florida's House of Blues, in March 1998, Virgos Merlot was signed to Atlantic Records by A&R man Steve Robertson — a mere eighteen months after they formed the band. Their major-label debut, *Signs of a Vacant Soul*, was released in March 1999, and a single, "Gain," received a lot of radio play and made the *Billboard* Top 40. Jason Marchant: "A video is in the works. They [Atlantic] want to get rolling one step at a time. That song is really getting a good response. It's refreshing to hear your label say it's been easier to get airplay than they thought it would be . . . We've been traveling around, out west and in New York, and the buzz on Birmingham is bigger than people realize. Birmingham has a lot of good music, but a lot of people go to the clubs to see cover bands because a local band always stays a local band. In Orlando [where they relocated], that's different . . . Plus the bands have a tendency to bash other bands here, and to trash Birmingham because the people aren't supporting them. Truth is, the bands haven't given them a reason to be supported. That's why we have to give Verbena and Remy Zero a lot of respect, because they're doing it."[4]

Of all the new bands in Birmingham in the 1990s, the ascent of Little Red Rocket was the fastest. The band began as a duo of singer-songwriters Orenda Fink and Maria Taylor. With Louis Schefano on drums and Greg Nobles on bass, their Beatlesque melodies were strengthened with harder-edged guitar backing. Little Red Rocket were new and sassy and had a sound that had many A&R men reaching for their cell phones. In 1997 they signed to a mammoth seven-album contract with the mighty Geffen label. Orenda Fink: "We were playing in Nashville at the Nashville Extravaganza. Some guy in the crowd saw us and liked us. Within two months we signed a deal with him, which was kind of a developmental deal. It was a deal to go into the big record contract. Right now we are putting out our first album on an independent label. We are giving ourselves time to develop a little more. Our second album, which we will start recording in about four months, will be our big Geffen debut . . . Our new album [*Who Did You Pay*] has been out for three weeks. It is on college radio right now and is doing pretty well. It is on the Tim/Kerr label, which is based out of Portland, Oregon. They are going to give us some promotion and support . . . It is a nice happy medium between a major label and an indie label. We have been working with Geffen for two years and they haven't done anything. Geffen has numerous bands and we are low on the priority list." Maria Taylor: "I think that it is because major labels started to sign any band when the indie labels became so huge. All of a sudden they realized that these bands were not making the money as they had. They are a little more cautious now about scooping up the baby bands and throwing them into the big picture. They wanted us to develop more." Louis Schefano: "I did all this before with Remy Zero. It was with a major label and was a big deal. It was on Capitol Records. We were really excited. I was nineteen years old then. I was thinking, 'Oh God, this is the life.' Now we are just trying to sell records and get a career." A group that had only been playing for a few years out of school now had a contract with a major player in the entertainment business. Orenda Fink: "We are locked in for seven more albums. There is something in there [the contract] like: if you die we get everything." The contract with Geffen was talk of the local music community, and the band was acknowledged as the Next Big Thing. Conrad Rayfield: "The jury is out on Little Red Rocket, but their record has just released and they're having some success on college radio . . . The band has as much potential as anybody given the fact that they are with what I consider to be one of the two or three best record companies out there . . . I think they are going to do great, and I think they want for the right producer. They still have to develop musically. But they have a tremendous amount of potential."

At decade's end the pace was picking up dramatically for Birmingham's alternative bands. In 1998 Brother Cane's third record for Virgin, *Wishpool*, was released. The cover shot showed the band lounging in the Alabama Theatre downtown, a nice connection with home. They were being treated like heroes in publications like *Guitar Player* and were touring with alternative music headliners like the Foo Fighters and Smashing Pumpkins and living the rock 'n' roll dream. Damon: "I want big lights, big trucks, big PA, and lots of people! Lots of them, and I want it now more than ever I have ever wanted it. Because, I mean, we've got a nice chance, man. We've got a real shot! We are one of the lucky bands, man! Sometimes I think we are the luckiest of all those bands because the only thing that limits us is ourselves. It has taken a long time and we have been patient and hopefully this time next year . . . Brother Cane got to do a lot of cool things, to realize numerous dreams for ourselves, our friends, and our family, and even for the people and musicians here in Birmingham."

Verbena's *Into the Pink* was produced by Nirvana's drummer, Dave Grohl, which attracted the attention of Birmingham's media. The well-respected Grohl, whose alternative pedigree could not be better, was acknowledged as the person who "gets the most out of the band's sound," making this "the album that Verbena's fans, and the entire Birmingham music scene, have been waiting for."[5] Darin Powell in the *Birmingham Post Herald*: "The Magic City's own Verbena hits it big . . . Critics and music insiders hailing the band as the Deep South's answer to Nirvana . . . with favorable articles in *CMJ*, *Request*, and *Guitar Player* magazines and a three-star review in the most recent edition of *Rolling Stone*. The band is part of a wave of Birmingham rock performers who have been receiving national attention as of late. The band admits that being from Alabama sometimes makes them an object of curiosity, especially since they have chosen to remain here rather than moving to some place such as Los Angeles."[6]

Birmingham bands were now receiving a lot more attention in the national music press. *Rolling Stone* cited Verbena and Three Finger Cowboy in their list of bands to watch. Three Finger Cowboy was Ryan Kirby, Hunter Manasco, drummer Caleb Gentry, and vocalist Katherine McElroy Artist, who had once worked at the Magic Platter record store. Their debut album, *Kissed*, was underwritten by the Indigo Girls and issued on their Daemon label in 1998. The band went from playing the Nick for a dozen or so people to supporting the Indigo Girls on tour to audiences of thousands. Remy Zero's "Villa Elaine" was also a *Billboard* hit, and the single "Prophecy" was getting playing time on alternative radio all over the country. When Remy Zero returned to Birmingham in 1999, they came as conquering heroes and were billed as the next Radiohead. Dave Rossi, the influential programmer for alternative radio station 107.7 ("the X"), was planning an X-Fest festival that would bring Remy Zero, Verbena, and Virgos Merlot together to celebrate this impressive flowering of local music.

The ascent of so many promising new alternative bands was a source of pride among their fans and led to hopes that Birmingham might make up some of the cultural ground lost to its neighbors. Greg Hassler: "We need a flag carrying band to come out of Birmingham, but the thing of it is, the crowd comes around when they see it flocking. No one had carried the flag and taken it out and make a mark on the world like a Seattle band or Athens . . . we've got a handful of bands like we did in the early '80s, and that is all we have ever gotten up to. Each decade you have these handful of bands that are really pushing, and they push for the whole decade. Some are still pushing from decades before." The first decade of the new century was greeted with optimism. In 1999 Chuck Geiss wrote, "Birmingham may finally have something on which to hang its hat. Incredibly, that something may be music."[7]

CHAPTER SIXTEEN

Music and Community

W hen Birmingham was created in the late nineteenth century, the musical culture of the new community was not considered important because the city was intended as an industrial center. It had no history, no heritage, and no identity of its own. Industrializing North Central Alabama was part of a movement to modernize a region devastated by war and held back by antiquated social mores and inefficient agriculture. The New South was to be an urban, industrialized South that could compete with the great industrial centers of the Northeast, primarily in terms of production, but over time this comparison included the arts as well as sciences. Culture became an important factor in creating an identity for this "Eldorado of iron masters." "The Youngest of the World's Great Cities" needed credentials other than tonnage of pig iron poured or coal mined to be part of the New South. Birmingham was named after a world-famous iron-manufacturing center in England, and from day one, "The Pittsburgh of the South" was constantly being pushed and pulled into something else. Nearly 150 years later the community was still struggling with an identity; Mark Kelly of *Weld* wrote in 2013 that the attention Birmingham was attracting in the twenty-first century brought into "sharp relief" the one thing the city had lacked over the years: "a sense of civic identity, a unifying vision of who we are."[1]

All the people who came to the new community of Birmingham brought music with them: blues, work songs, spirituals, hymns from the nonconformist churches of Wales, old English and Appalachian folk tunes, and fiddle and banjo breakdowns, but some music was deliberately imported to provide status as well as entertainment. Low-class culture was easily available — it came in the backpacks of immigrants and on the wagons streaming into Birmingham, but high-class culture, especially symphonic music, required a calculated seeding and nourishment. Birmingham's growing middle classes, the professionals and managerial elite who might have had some misgivings about moving to a "sort of exaggerated coal-mining village," worked hard to establish a cultural life that belied their situation in a barren valley in Alabama.[2] From the earliest days it was proud of the music it produced and the talents it attracted to play its concert halls. Like New Orleans and Memphis, Birmingham saw itself as a "musical city": "There is no city more music loving than this, nor any community more dedicated to music."[3]

Birmingham's cultural identity stayed locked into comparisons with other great cities, but by the turn of the century its rapid growth justified some of the claims made by the New South boosters — the "heaviest corner on earth" was made up of impressive skyscrapers at the junction of First Avenue North and Twentieth Street. The cultural life of the city was also growing. The historian Ward Haarbauer calls the decade before World War I the "golden age" of Birmingham's theaters.[4] By 1910 the city supported ten theaters as well as several small movie houses. These theaters and cinemas comprised the downtown entertainment district, which stretched along Second and Third Avenues between Seventeenth and Twentieth Streets. People liked to talk about Birmingham's "Broadway" (Second Avenue). The golden age began with the construction of the Jefferson Theatre in 1900, an extravagant and sumptuously decorated venue that was intended to be one of the finest in the New South. Next came the Alabama Theatre. This picture palace was built specifically for motion picture exhibition at a time when the talkies were transforming the industry and its theaters. The building cost about $1 million to construct and had some of the most ornate decoration of any theater in the region.

When Birmingham celebrated its fiftieth birthday in 1921, the city took stock of its history and examined its identity. Its people felt that its industrial base had helped it turn away from the Old South and the values associated with it. A *Birmingham Age-Herald* article in 1922 argued that Birmingham was the most cosmopolitan of all cities in the South, a modern, forward-looking city with "nothing here of the easy-going complacency that characterizes so many cities of the South, where the ante-bellum spirit survives."[5] The Alabama Theatre fit this image perfectly. Promoted as the most "artistic" and sumptuously furnished theater in the South, it represented a validation for the city as a cultural center. When the chairman of Paramount Pictures, Adolph Zukor, chose Birmingham as the location for his movie palace in the New South, it meant a great deal to Birmingham's boosters, expressing, "louder than words, the confidence of investors in Birmingham and Alabama." The souvenir program issued on its opening day on December 26, 1927, made this clear: "A city that is the leading metropolis of the South now has the finest theater in the entire South."

The building of the Alabama marked the highpoint of the downtown entertainment. From 1900 to 1929, thirty-two theaters were built, and Birmingham had reason to promote itself as "The South's Best Show Town." The theater district brought "Broadway to Birmingham." By the time of World War I it had established itself as a major destination on the vaudeville circuit. When "The Smart Set" came to town in 1916, one of its promoters noted, "The city is full of performers."[6]

Birmingham's Music Festivals

After the boom in iron production in the first decades of the twentieth century died out, Birmingham spent most of the 1930s in depression and there was little development. Performers saw little reason to visit the city. The well-known swing bands from Birmingham spent the 1930s and 1940s on the road, and while everyone knew the song "Tuxedo Junction," the city was far from being an entertainment center. The war years saw a rapid increase in industrial production, but the emigration of musical talent continued — success in the entertainment business always meant leaving Alabama. Birmingham was considered a cultural backwater in the 1950s, and the bad press of the struggle for civil rights did little to change the city's poor image. But the newfound affluence of the New, New South pushed government and businesses to improve the image of the city and its culture. In the 1980s the State of Alabama embarked on ambitious plans to promote the state, its people, and its industry to the rest of the nation. George McMillan: "City Stages came into being in the summer of 1988. I was called by the Greater Birmingham Convention and Visitors Bureau and asked if

I would undertake to start a major music festival in Birmingham. I think their interest in me was the Alabama Reunion ... This was a campaign that Governor Hunt had in which he asked various communities to undertake special projects." The Alabama Reunion was built around a "Come Home to Alabama" campaign, designed to create a warm and fuzzy image for the state. Encouraging businesses, investors, and tourists to come to Alabama had significant economic payback, so the state government asked communities to come up with cultural events. George: "The governor contacted the Greater Birmingham Convention and Visitors Bureau. They thought, 'Well, hey, what can Birmingham do?' They thought of a music festival. I remember when they called, I told her that they had the wrong person, because I had never been to a music festival, I played no musical instruments. She said that she wasn't looking at me for my musical background, but she felt that I knew how to bring people together to make things happen ... We formed the Birmingham Cultural and Heritage Foundation, a not-for-profit organization under whose umbrella every year we have produced City Stages ... The goals were to give local musicians the opportunity for exposure, to highlight Birmingham's musical heritage, and to engage in an outreach, an educational outreach, that involved music." As one organizer said: "Our festival isn't just about the acts; it's about community."[7]

The overarching goal of bringing Birmingham's people together in a public event was not purely an act of good works. Anything that could change the negative image of Birmingham and Alabama was welcomed by government and also by the Birmingham business community, whose banks, medical institutions, and developers would benefit from a more cultured downtown. An outdoor music festival was a perfect fit for the twin objectives of building up the downtown and improving the city's image, and in this way City Stages became a surrogate for the ambitions of its new service industries.

Local and state government were not the innovators in creating community music events; they merely followed the lead of neighborhood groups and individuals who saw music as something more than entertainment. After the racially troubled decades of the 1960s and 1970s, community music became part of the "industry of reconciliation" (in the words of Diane McWhorter), which sought a different identity for Birmingham, an alternative to the image of the "Johannesburg of the United States," and one better suited to the prosperity and self-confidence of the New, New South. In the 1970s rock music had been experienced in smoky bars and rowdy clubs. Southern rock had dominated Morris Avenue and what remained of the Strip on Twenty-First Street downtown. In the 1980s it lived on in the form of cover bands that played the clubs at Five Points on the Southside. But as the club scene kept in tune with its college-age, frat-boy audience, the market for Birmingham's traditional music — folk, country, and classic rock 'n' roll — moved into public spaces.

In the 1980s live music became an important part of neighborhood activities, and many private parties evolved into public events. Urban revitalization and the industry of reconciliation had brought some new ideas about the uses of music in the community. From the Magic City Art Connection in Linn Park to the Southside Festivals, live music was to be the magnet to bring people together in a city once torn apart. The Southside Festivals began around 1983 as the brainchild of the Southside Action Committee, a grassroots group aiming to revitalize the area. In the words of Betty Bock of the Southside Action Committee the goal was to transform a scruffy and often dangerous commercial district into "a people place" where suburbanites and local residents could feel comfortable together. The streets were closed off around Five Points, and stages were erected for live music and other entertainments, such as puppet shows. All along the streets were food vendors and stalls selling crafts and artwork. For one Saturday every year the Southside came alive with music from bluegrass banjo players pickin' in parking lots to the Birmingham symphony playing in Brother Bryant Park. The festival discouraged drinking and unruly behavior in order to maintain a family atmosphere. New Orleans native Aaron Beam and his family decided to turn up, interested to see what a Birmingham music festival looked like, "so we naturally loaded our cooler with beer and went down to the Southside, found a place to park, pulled up our cooler to the street, got out a few beers, and in a minute a cop comes up and says, 'If you don't put that stuff away we are going to arrest you.' You could not drink in public. I heard that you could not drink a beer in your front yard."

While groups like the Southside Action Committee were organizing street fairs and festivals, and the police were keeping everyone sober, indi-

viduals were holding their own neighborhood parties. In 1985 Aaron and
Phyllis Beam held a traditional crawfish boil in their backyard with fifty
pounds of crawfish brought up from New Orleans: "It hit us in the face
come crawfish season that there was no crawfish in the restaurants. New
Orleans food was unknown then." The party was a success: "Oh, people
just loved it. I mean, people were just so excited about it, and for weeks
afterwards people would thank me for all the fun they had . . . and everybody was asking us when we were going to have another one . . . Richard
[Scrushy] had always, always wanted a band, you know, and he . . . and his
band, Proxy, played for the second one we had, and the people loved it."
Aaron found out that the music was the main attraction: "The formula
was for local bands, but then I started bringing in the Louisiana sound
that would go along with a crawfish boil . . . It has always been something
for everybody, all sorts of pop music." Michael Chandler is a physician in
Birmingham with an "emotional and psychological addiction" to playing
rock 'n' roll. His care of musicians has earned him the title Dr. Rock: "You
can never get it out of you, and sure enough, a few weeks later there you are
with a guitar in your hands . . . It is that uplifting fun part — that no matter
what else bad is going on in your day, if you are playing that night it gives
you something to look forward to. It is fabulous . . . Richard Scrushy and I
met and formed a band in his basement. It was just the two of us, and we
had a dream, he had a background similar to mine in music, and we had
always wanted to get back into it. So we started a band called Proxy. We
played almost a year, several jobs. We started the benefits for cerebral palsy
and all the good work that Richard does. He has since contributed millions
to his charities with his bands." Rock 'n' roll for charitable causes began in
the 1980s and has not looked back since then, with Live Aid and all those
other events, but this marked a major change from the for-profit rock 'n'
roll that went before it.

Music continued to be the main attraction at community events in
Birmingham. Aaron Beam: "All year long we would get people asking us
about the crawfish boil. People kept asking me, 'What about the Crawfish
Boil?'" So many people were turning up that the party had to be moved
to Sloss Furnaces, and it took more than one pickup truck to deliver the
three or four thousand pounds of crawfish consumed. Instead of one band

playing, there were several, including old favorites like Telluride and new bands such as Gravy. People began to look forward to the big party in April, which began the entertainments of summer — the street festivals, art shows, concerts, and open-air movies. Every get-together had a reason or a cause to support, which ranged from increasing awareness of the dangers of drug abuse to a mass tribute to man's best friend. This last event, Doo Dah Day, was another private party that started in 1979 and got bigger and bigger. In essence, it was an excuse for the city's dog owners to come together and parade down the meandering Highland Avenue while bands played, and merchants sold food, drink, and crafts. It was just one more party in a city that had rediscovered the joys of public entertainment, and hardly a green space in Birmingham did not host at least one musical evening over the summer.

All of these events experienced surprising growth. Betty Bock and her colleagues thought that they were being very optimistic in their expectation that a thousand people might turn up for the first Southside Festival. In fact, they sold out of everything by midday, and the police estimated that seven thousand attended. During the eight festivals held in the 1980s the attendance grew steadily to around thirteen thousand for each event. The Crawfish Boil was becoming so popular that people were selling the invitations to what was at that time a free private party. Aaron Beam: "It was getting really expensive because hundreds of people were showing up. Then I decided to do it for charity. I did it as a fundraiser for the Southern Dance Works. Charging an admission price of eighteen dollars, it was still a good deal, covering all you could drink and eat." The Beam Crawfish Boil went from a few hundred people in the late 1980s to thousands in the 1990s, when it was moved to an even bigger venue — the Birmingham race course, with the music temporarily suspended while the races were run. Aaron Beam: "I had the biggest lineup ever: Dr. John, Delbert McClinton, Warren Haynes & Government Mule, Sugar La Las, Proxy, and Grounder. We had two stages going on simultaneously. The race track Crawfish Boil was really ambitious. I could not believe they agreed to let me do it!" Doo Dah Day had started with a few dozen people and ended up with thousands filling up the green spaces from Forest Park to Five Points. No matter the reason for the event, you had to have live music. Aaron: "Club after club, all over the country, was closing because people were just not going out at night as much. Thus outdoor festivals were coming in — you know, it was a family thing. Nowadays the festival calendar is a very important venue for music in the good weather months." As Shawn Ryan pointed out, Birmingham musicians now found jobs in "an entirely new industry of festivals."

City Stages

In the planning for City Stages, George McMillan went to all parts of the community to drum up support: "The first year I probably gave ten speeches a week. I would go to a Methodist church club, I would go to this civic club and that civic club . . . I would say that there was some healthy skepticism . . . I certainly had to go out and convince people. I had to convince them that this community was ready. People said that you won't get blacks and whites or you won't get all these different communities to come together. It wasn't achieved immediately. For the first year or two, our audience was 90 percent white. Now [1996] we have a very healthy mix of African Americans, white Americans, and any Americans. City Stages has served as a melting pot for Birmingham. City Stages has brought people together and enabled people to rub shoulders with people they otherwise wouldn't be thrown in with. I think that people can't help but leave City Stages with a few less prejudices than they brought."

The first City Stages was in June 1989. It was located downtown around Linn and Kelly Ingram Parks and drew on local businesses and government for support — the public-private partnership that was fashionable in the 1980s. Put together on what would now be considered a shoestring budget of three hundred thousand dollars, it featured two main stages for rock 'n' roll — the Jubilee and Heritage Stages, which featured the headliners: John Prine, Chuck Berry, Travis Tritt, and Beau Soleil. The Alabama Folklife Stage presented traditional music, the Talking Tent showcased the spoken word, and there was also a Children's Stage. "We attracted thirty-eight thousand people . . . I was so happy after the first City Stages. I cannot describe the emotional joy of seeing people together right in the heart of the city center. They were enjoying themselves and felt great about Birmingham . . . The feeling afterwards on a Sunday night, knowing that you had played a role in giving birth to an event that was so positive for a city."

With increased corporate support the second City Stages was a much larger affair. There were three main stages, sponsored by Coca-Cola, Miller Lite, and the *Birmingham News*, respectively. There was also the Chubb Classical Music stage, the Alabama Folklife Stage, and the Talking Tent. The headliners were Bo Diddley, Marcia Ball, the Subdudes, Dr. John, Los Lobos, and the Commodores, but the majority of the performers were local acts, ranging from the blues of Topper Price and the Upsetters to the folk of Three on a String and the jazz of the Erskine Hawkins Band. Southern rock was represented by Telluride and Locust Fork, and the diversity of Birmingham rock music could be found in the Plaid Camels, the Cast, Vova Nova, Proxy, the Newboys, and Slick Lilly, which covered the gamut of covers, jazz-pop, and straight-ahead southern boogie rock.

Reaching the baby boom audience was the key to City Stages' success. Shawn Ryan: "It caters to baby boomers. The Coca-Cola stage is strictly what they call the 99 percent recognition stage, where 99 percent of the people will recognize the headline act on that stage ... [Jimmy] Buffett is number 1 and [James] Taylor number 2, but I was sitting there and the people behind me came in, and every time another couple came along it was: 'Hey! How are you doing? How are the kids? Where did you eat?' ... [Jimmy] Buffett is beach music for baby boomers. It takes you back to your trips to the beach on spring break, and that is what the Allman Brothers does — I guess it takes you back to you laying in the back of the pickup truck chugging Jack Daniels and all that stuff and smokin' dope." The boomers were also a major part of the audience for the stadium shows put on by New Era, Ryan recalled: "These New Era Productions at Oak Mountain [amphitheater] is very baby boomer. It is strictly for baby boomers and not college students ... I mean, look who is coming there. It is Bubbapalooza! They've got Lynyrd Skynyrd one show, then they've got Hank [Williams] Jr. the next show, then they've got the Allman Brothers. Three concerts in a row that are a redneck-a-thon ... Southern rock, especially for the South, is always going to be the region's comfort music, and it is safe and it is comfortable and it makes them feel good, and it is nostalgic. I get nostalgic listening to some of that old '70s stuff. A lot of the CDs I am buying now are remastered, reissued CDs of old '70s stuff. Whenever I listen to 'Can't Get Enough' by Bad Company, I still flash on my high school girlfriend and I breaking up!"

Shawn Ryan was not alone in reliving the 1970s in the 1990s, for the baby boomer audience could be relied on to come out and hear the music of their long-past but well-remembered youth. The affluent boomers were usually professionals, working in the business or medical communities, with homes and families. They brought their children to the show and also consumed food and drink and invested heavily in its merchandise. Especially prized were the VIP tickets, which gave the wearer visible status (as the ticket was on a lanyard) and access to the exclusive VIP sections, where there were separate restroom facilities (valued by wives and girlfriends) and shorter lines for food and drink.

One of the founding principles of City Stages was to give local music an outlet, and this goal eventually gave rise to the Home Grown stage. Local musicians established a hierarchy of the various stages, and ambitious rock bands could chart their progress by graduating from the Home Grown stage to one of the bigger corporate stages. But resentment soon built up as City Stages reached out for bigger names, and over time the Home Grown stage was often seen as inferior. Judy Ranelli: "The Home Grown stage for local artists, which I think is a disaster. It is a tiny stage . . . Why not give us a break? Putting us on these little stages, and I will never play City Stages again."

The organizers of City Stages had to please all the musical constituencies in Birmingham. The important heritage of gospel music and sheer number of choirs led to the establishment of GospelFest under the direction of Sarah Fuller and Martha Douglass. For the three days of the festival, Birmingham's choirs filled the First United Methodist Church. Joyce Cauthen had won a grant from the National Endowment of the Arts to put on a folk festival in Alabama, and it went into the first City Stages as the Alabama Folklife stage. The organizers decided that this should continue after the funding from the NEA ran out, thus the Alabama Sampler stage was established with corporate support. Birmingham's big band history was brought back in the form of the Birmingham Heritage Band, which was made up of many retired jazz musicians.

The establishment of a city stage devoted to world music was a significant step toward establishing cultural diversity in the festival. Many in Birmingham thought of world beat as just reggae until City Stages brought them music from West Africa in 1990 with O. J. Ekemode & the Nigerian All-Stars, one of the pioneers of Afrobeat, a fusion of African rhythms with funk, reggae, and jazz. In 1992 the new wave of West African music, mixing traditional songs with faster rhythms and Western instrumentation, arrived at City Stages. Kanda Bonga Man of Zaire, a leading exponent of *kwassa kwassa* dance rhythms, delivered one of the most exciting shows of the festival. His band played as loud and as fast as any rock group, inspiring the audience as well as his troupe of dancers, who shook and slithered across the stage. The next year one of Africa's greatest musicians, Tabu Ley Rochereau, came to Birmingham. The presence of so many world-renowned musicians did make City Stages a world-class music festival, and placing the World Beat stage and African village (where African crafts were sold) on the corner of Kelly Ingram Park, the great battlefield of civil rights, provided a symbolic act of closure. Shawn Ryan: "Well, you look at the World Beat stage, and whenever I go out there, there is a very heavy contingent of young white people out there, and I think some of it is love of music. I think some of it is being liberal . . . I think it means something to these kids." To see African musicians playing to an integrated audience on that historic spot made a powerful statement about a New South city trying to forget its past.

The big story about the second City Stages was the increased attendance. About a hundred thousand people came downtown, which was nearly three times the number that attended the first event. For the rest of the 1990s City Stages got bigger and bigger; more stages, more acts, and many more people. By the mid-1990s the total audience had grown to around 250,000, and about 25 percent of them came from a hundred miles outside the city. It was no longer "City Stages: A Birmingham Festival" but "City Stages, Birmingham's World Class Music Festival," an event that was reported in the region's newspapers, not just the local ones. The budget reached $2 million in 1997, supporting 270 acts on sixteen stages with the assistance of four thousand volunteers. In 1998 it was slightly larger, with 275 artists on twelve stages. This was a far cry from the original production of 65 acts on four stages. The 1998 City Stages drew a record 270,000 people to downtown. They had paid twenty-five dollars for three days of music, and most of them purchased food, drink, T-shirts and novelties. George McMillan: "City Stages has a significant economic impact on the city of Birmingham . . . I've seen estimates from as low as $21 or $22 million to as high as $38 million. This is in terms of our cash budget of $2.2 million." Its success gave Birmingham a cultural centerpiece, a selling point in recruiting professionals to Alabama, a valuable lesson in civic integration and something it could be proud of. Shawn Ryan: "It has helped Birmingham's image out there in the real world, a softening of Birmingham's image because City Stages is such a success . . . I saw a quotation from New Orleans about somebody [who] said it is the best music festival in the Southeast bar none, and that's from New Orleans!"

What started out, in Shawn Ryan's words, as hesitance rather than expectation turned into delirium. Don VanCleave: "City Stages is one of the most incredible festivals on the planet! Hands down, it is the proudest thing we can ever have." Foxxy Fatts: "It is the only thing you can actually go down to the heart of Birmingham and don't even realize that you are in Birmingham! No problems. People are together, laughing together, having a good time together, walking around, laughing, talking, no problems! It is like the whole weekend in Birmingham another state came in and played . . . The only thing I dislike about City Stages is the fact that they don't want to play local talent, which I feel like they should." Damon Johnson: "City Stages is the coolest, greatest thing that this town has! Great! You wish you could find some way to spread that around year-round. Some kind of way to make that a thing, but it is almost like people hold out for this one weekend in June where they get their yearly music fix and convince themselves that they are in the know." George McMillan: "City Stages has brought people together and eliminated some inferiority complexes about this community . . . It made a city feel good about itself."

The Festival Season

City Stages was one of the rare events that brought suburban dwellers to downtown, and without its reassuring presence every year the work of revitalizing downtown, such as the Discovery 2000 Science Museum, would not have moved forward at the same pace. Shawn Ryan thought the example of City Stages helped a lot of the smaller festivals along: "Nobody ever thought of combining music with an outdoor festival in town. There might be a little flatbed truck, but no serious stage built, solid, lights and that kind of stuff . . . Because of the success of City Stages, you had the infrastructure on how to do something like that. Where to get PAs. How to do vendors . . . People really didn't know how to do it." The smaller festivals experienced the same frenetic growth as City Stages, and from spring to fall, street parties and music festivals dominated social life in Birmingham. The festival season traditionally started with the Crawfish Boil in the first weekend in May and was followed the next weekend by Doo Dah Day. City Stages dominated the calendar in June, followed in July by the Midsummer Magic Festival and the Tuxedo Junction Jazz festival, in August by the Birmingham Heritage Festival and the Great Southern Kudzu Festival, and rounded off in the fall with the Birmingham Jam. The Birmingham Heritage Festival was geared toward promoting African American music. It was the idea of Larry Allen, who began the festivals downtown in 1991. He acknowledged the importance of City Stages in establishing downtown as an entertainment center: "They broke the ground for us and made the way for us."[8]

The benefits claimed for outdoor music were many. The application for a grant to fund the Function at Tuxedo Junction Jazz Festival in 2008 promised that the event would "promote and encourage tourism . . . educate youth and recognize the historical significance of jazz legend and Birmingham native Erskine Hawkins . . . and facilitate public health, consumer credit, home buyer and other educational opportunities." The Function at Tuxedo Junction got twenty-seven thousand dollars, but the Birmingham Cultural and Heritage Foundation (of City Stages) got seven hundred thousand dollars. City Stages' insatiable appetite for public money did not escape criticism. David Pelfrey in *Black & White* argued that close to a million taxpayer dollars justified asking whether City Stages had actually accomplished its declared mission as a "cultural and heritage festival and as a tax exempt organization that claims to disburse funds for local scholarships . . . with an annual budget that usually exceeds $2 million, [it] offered in 2005 and 2006 three music scholarships of $1000 for high school seniors. That's less than a fifth of what it spent on VIP hospitality in 2006."[9]

Most of the criticism aimed at City Stages was directed at the bill: local musicians felt left out of the festival as it sought big-name players, baby boomers complained about the vapid boy bands, and the thousands of high schoolers who filled up the festival wanted fewer oldies and more Top 40 acts. The high points of the City Stages programming, the headliners who closed Friday's and Saturday's program, were usually Motown and Stax superstars: Diana Ross, the Temptations, Ray Charles, and Al Green. There were grounds to complain that City Stages was way behind the times. For all its very black profile, hip-hop had a considerable following in the lily-white suburbs around Birmingham. Yet City Stages was locked into the African American music of the 1960s and 1970s, and it was some time before rap entered the festival. In an article titled "Rap at City Stages: It's About Time," a writer who called himself Sir Laurence pointed out that the rap artist Nelly became the first national known rap act to play City Stages, and this was in 2001. Sir Laurence admitted that rap did not fit the wholesome, family-oriented image of the festival but argued that many of its strongest adherents in Birmingham were young white suburbanites from over the mountain. "We seem to always be the last ones to catch on," he concluded.[10]

Despite all the criticisms from musicians and audiences, the rise of City Stages was met with pride. Whether it was hip-hop or symphonies, music was an important part of the city's self-image. When the Artists Series of classical music was threatened with closure in 1963, the *Birmingham News* argued that it had to be saved, along with "the reputation of the city of Birmingham."[11] The survival of the Alabama Symphony continued to be important for the city's self-image, and its demise hurt Birmingham's reputation as a cultural center. Mike Panepento: "One of the worst things that I find . . . is the lack of culture here. As a city losing the symphony was just one of the worst things that could have happened. I know that if I didn't live here now, there is no way you could get me here." Judy Ranelli: "The symphony thing was terrible, losing the symphony, and what a blow to Birmingham . . . They would gladly get another football stadium but could not understand why losing the symphony was horrible." This put more weight on City Stages to boost the city's self-esteem. It "has come to play a significant role in the way people in metropolitan Birmingham feel about their community... and represented Birmingham at its best," said Mark Kelly, highlighting the year-long cultural calendar of "festivals, concerts, exhibits" that made the city "a well-kept secret."[12]

Birmingham's club scene was also enjoying growth in the 1990s. The entertainment center of the town, and the prime tourist destination in the whole state, was Five Points on the Southside. Anchored by Louie Louie, the Mill, and the Five Points South Music Hall, the bars and restaurants of the Southside attracted thousands of visitors each weekend. During the football season the sidewalks were crowded with people as the bars overflowed and the party moved into the street. Lee Bargeron: "There was a point in time when Louie's every night had a crowd around the block waiting to get in." Ben Burford of Chevy 6: "Older people liked us, and at the time younger people thought it was pretty cool too. So we were able to transcend a lot of age groups. We would pack the place out... At Louie's we would have fifty-year-olds in there, nineteen to fifty easy. I mean, they would be in there shoulder to shoulder."

Spreading out from the Southside were more places to hear live music: Zydeco just up the hill on Fifteenth Avenue; Marty's on Tenth Court; the Back Alley and Blue Monkey Lounge on Cobb Lane; the Magic City Brewery on Fifth Avenue South; Flamingos on Highland Avenue; and the redoubtable Nick on Tenth Avenue South. On a typical weekend in January 1996, Warren Zevon played Louie Louie, Bela Fleck and the Flecktones were at the Five Points South Music Hall, the Goo Goo Dolls appeared at Boutwell Auditorium, Alison Kraus and Union Station put on a concert at the Alabama Theatre, and AC/DC brought down the house at the Birmingham Jefferson Convention Center. Shawn Ryan wrote about a "weird week" ahead at the clubs, when a "nuclear polka band" called Brave Combo was scheduled to appear at the Nick, and a jam band signed to Capricorn Records called Everything, with "elements of ska and punk," was going to play Zydeco.[13] Ryan took issue with those in Birmingham who continually wailed "Nothing's ever going on here" by pointing out that five local bands had released records in the last few weeks: the jazz scene was represented by Robert Moore, whose album *Wildcat* featured Cleve Eaton and Mark and Matt Kimbrell; country rock by George Scherer; singer-songwriters by Fischerelle; power pop by Roadkill Ballet; indie rock by Steve Hines; and reggae by Lost in the Mall. Local bands were making an impression on audiences at the South by Southwest music conference, a showpiece for the seven hundred up-and-coming bands that played the five-day event. In 1997 Little Red Rocket, Verbena, Vallejo, the Quinsonics, and Marlee MacLeod played there.[14]

Corporate Entertainment

Outdoor festivals kept in step with Birmingham's steady economic growth in the 1990s. Not only City Stages was expanding: the Beam Crawfish Boil attracted around twenty thousand people in 1996 and featured over ten live musical acts. The amazing growth of these events reflected the number of people in Birmingham with money in their pockets. Birmingham's population had gone from 558,928 in 1950 to 755,580 in 1990. The Sun Belt was booming, a southerner was in the White House, and the nation enjoyed peace and prosperity. The university and medical complex of UAB was now the leading employer in Alabama, and the "University that Ate Birmingham" was gobbling up the neighboring Southside. HealthSouth spent much of the 1990s buying out other businesses; the company's annual revenue rose to $1 billion by mid-decade, making it the nation's largest provider of rehabilitative care. It was now one of the great success stories of southern entrepreneurship. HealthSouth, which was now calling itself "The Healthcare Company of the Twenty-First Century," was a source of some pride in Birmingham. In 1995 CEO Scrushy announced that the company was going to build a new headquarters on eighty-five acres of land, containing a five-story office building, conference center, gift shop, and HealthSouth museum. Other Birmingham businesses were doing equally well, especially banking. The Birmingham skyline was dominated by a series of skyscrapers that marked a new era of prosperity, in much the same way that the "Heaviest Corner on Earth" symbolized the cast-iron boom at the turn of the twentieth century. The South Trust Tower, the corporate headquarters for SouthTrust Bank, was the tallest building in the state when it was completed in 1986. The AmSouth Harbert Center opened in 1989 with a luxurious mall on the entrance floor and a food court above it.

City Stages' aspirations grew with that of the city, and it was agreed that a world-class festival needed world-class talent. Yet these stars did not come cheap, and City Stages became reliant on corporate support to make ends meet. Because it was a not-for-profit operation, its growing debt was not initially seen as a cause for concern, but as that debt grew steadily in the 1990s, City Stages' organizers had to raise more money from the community and from corporate sponsors. By 2007 City Stages' corporate friends had retired $780,000 of the debt. The businessmen who bailed out City Stages had realized that sponsoring public entertainment could burnish their image. The management of HealthSouth had earned a reputation for innovative thinking, and they decided not to base their image building on the tried-and-tested print and broadcast media. Aaron Beam: "Health-South as a company stayed away from advertising in radio and papers, we went for supporting community events and charities. We felt it was important to be a good corporate citizen. There is a great demand for companies to support these kind of events, and it was a good way to advertise and get our name awareness out there." Richard Scrushy also wanted to associate the company with charitable causes and with successful sports, entertainment, and medical personalities: "By doing this HealthSouth's brand would become synonymous with success." HealthSouth's imprint could found all over the city, not only in libraries, day care centers, sports facilities, and conference halls but also in events, venues, and performances. Aaron: "One of the most successful things we ever did was those crazy water bottles, which we gave away at events. We started in the third year of City Stages giving away fifty thousand bottles at each event. I was traveling in Italy a few years ago and saw a guy holding a HealthSouth water bottle from a festival in Atlanta!"

Businessmen were beginning to appreciate the profit potential of sponsoring entertainment, not as an investment opportunity but as an entry to the lucrative youth market. Throughout the 1990s the corporate presence in American popular entertainment grew, with businesses with hardly any connection to music sponsoring concerts, tours, individual bands, and fes-

tivals. Public entertainment in Birmingham followed this process. By the
late 1990s all those private parties now had big companies backing them up.
The Beam family's crawfish boil became the Shaeffer Eye Center Crawfish
Boil. A competing crawfish boil, Mudbugs and Music, was sponsored by
Burr Forman, a powerful Birmingham law firm. In addition to the ever-
present beverage companies, this event also had backing from a retail store,
a decorating company, and several more law firms. At the turn of the century one could enjoy an "Original Coors Dance party" at Sloss Furnaces or
listen to a band play at the HealthSouth Plaza at Oak Mountain. Concerts
at UAB's auditorium, the Alyss Stevens Center, were sponsored by real es-
tate developers and insurance companies. In 2005 City Stages became the
Vines & Waldrep City Stages, named for its major sponsor, a law firm, and
in 2006 it morphed into the Waldrep Stewart & Kendrick City Stages,
presented by Lanny Vines and associates. The official program for the 2007
event had a page of sponsors' logos under the headline "We Couldn't Make
the Music without Them." Corporations now figured large in entertainment in Birmingham. Louie Louie was taken over by a franchised disco-
dancing operation, and the national chains of "Irish pubs," Ruby Tuesdays,
and TGIFs were eliminating neighborhood bars. Blockbuster, Camelot,
Coconuts, CD Warehouse, and other chains of record/video stores tried to
finish off the independent record stores. Even Doo Dah Day, that bastion
of neighborhood initiative, was soon attached to corporate sponsorship:
PetSmart and Banfield Pet Hospital now underwrite the event, along with
Piggly Wiggly supermarkets, Cahaba Cycles, Land Rover cars, and Norfolk
Southern railroad.

    As the leader of Birmingham's business community, HealthSouth took
the leading role in supporting local entertainment, and in the 1990s there
was hardly a festival or show that did not bear its logo. The HealthSouth
stage at City Stages was one of the major draws of the festival. Both CEO
Scrushy and CFO Beam were music lovers and each distributed Health-
South's largesse to the music community: buying entertainment venues
(Beam owned Louie Louie for a while, and Beam and Scrushy ran the
Rocking Horse in the Colonnade Mall), supporting local bands and musicians, and forming and promoting new groups, such as Haley Bopp (Beam)
and 3rd Faze (Scrushy). Richard Scrushy was a frustrated musician, and he

hired some outstanding Nashville session men and put together a country-rock band called Dallas County Line after his Alabama birthplace. Both of his bands played the HealthSouth stage at City Stages. He yearned to break into the Nashville music scene and got a contract with Polygram Records. Dallas County Line put out two albums and made a video. Scrushy also made a deal with Walmart to sell his record and played in several of their parking lots, where bemused rural folk walked past well-heeled Health-South executives who been persuaded to provide "purchased applause," while Scrushy — dressed all in black, with a pack of cigs underneath the rolled-up sleeves of his tee shirt — performed his song "Honk if You Love to Honky Tonk."

CHAPTER SEVENTEEN

The Curse of Tommy Charles

The new century was not kind to City Stages. In what some insiders called the greatest mistake made by the festival's organizers, in 2001 it was moved from its date in the middle of the congested June schedule to May. Unfortunately, rainstorms and cold weather ruined this three-year experiment, and the festival's debt crept up to nearly a half million dollars. City Stages' organizers then moved the festival back to June and scaled down the number of acts, but kept signing the expensive headliners — a move criticized by those who wanted a festival with local acts. City Stages was not the only festival in the Deep South or even in Alabama, and its success naturally drew many more music festivals into being and put more pressure on the organizers of City Stages to sign even bigger names. Although it enjoyed some successful years in the first decade of the twenty-first century, lackluster lineups of performers, higher ticket prices, and lower sales steadily increased its debt. The death knell of City Stages was the success of the Bonnaroo festival in Tennessee, which started in 2002 and grew alarmingly, attracting the best talent to Manchester, Tennessee, on the same weekend that City Stages was trying to entice them to come to Birmingham. Bonnaroo has a policy of not letting the acts signed to them play at events close to Tennessee, and this effectively cut off the supply of talent to City Stages.

The purpose of City Stages was to bring the city together and exorcize some of the past's nightmares, yet the stigma of the 1960s did not go away that easily. With so many other cities putting on similar festivals, Birmingham's checkered past, and the low estimation of its music scene, handicapped it in the competition for festivalgoers. Unlike New Orleans, Memphis, and Nashville, Birmingham was never known as a music town,

and this hurt in the regional marketing of its music festivals. Mike Lawley was not the only musician who argued: "There is our own sound but
people do not capitalize on it . . . We should claim it and take pride in it.
We should take a lesson from the people who do it. It works every time.
Chicago, St. Louis, Memphis, Nashville, New Orleans." Lenard Brown
pointed to a lack of a brand for local music: "Birmingham does not want
to promote what they have." Damon Johnson had the honesty to articu-
late a basic truth: "Let's call a spade a spade: Birmingham is not a music
town."

For those musicians who had left Birmingham for greener pastures or
were touring the country, the old reputation of Bad Birmingham could
never be entirely shed. Birmingham and Alabama still have a negative
image to outsiders. Muddy King and Carl Rouss found that audiences in
Los Angeles think Alabama musicians "are living in the woods, in a farm
somewhere . . . barefoot and pregnant!" Foxxy Fatts: "There is nothing in
Birmingham. It is a country-backwards town. That is what people say. I
hear this so much, man! When we go places and play sometimes, we were
in Florida one time doing a festival and we met these people out of Washington, out of New York. They could not believe that we were from here!"
Some musicians see coming from Birmingham as a disadvantage, prefer-
ring to stay vague about their hometown or just saying they are from Alabama rather than Birmingham. Charles Arndt of Plaid Camels: "I think
that Birmingham plays against you." The perception of Birmingham as
a "country-backwards town" is widespread, even in the Deep South, and
often makes an audience think: "He must be a country bumpkin 'cause he's
from Birmingham." Most important, the events of 1963 have still not been
forgotten, and as Alan Hunter said, "It could be that Birmingham just
plain has a tough time getting over the stigma of Birmingham." Eric Essix:
"I mean, it is so hard to shake, those images of the '60s . . . If you ever hear
anything about Birmingham or see anything about Birmingham on the
national media it is always that. You always see dogs or firehoses." Promoter
Stephen Knight: "A town that suffered so much during the integration
movement and really carries that burden, that mark, that scar. I mean, you
turn on the national news, and any story about Birmingham is preceded
by footage of [dogs and firehoses], the media eats it up! Anytime they are

going to retry those guys for bombing the church, it's all over the national media. I think that hurts us nationally. I've actually had bands, they call me in advance to get everything straight and ask, 'Look, we are a black band and we really don't want to have any trouble. Da da da ... we are a little worried, is everything going to be cool?' I am like, 'There's no roadblock on I-20,' so you still have people who fear it ... 'Eh, we don't want to go play that hick town.' A lot of bands will bypass Birmingham, but the audience in Birmingham is still extremely segregated. There are white clubs and there are black clubs and the whites won't go hear black music in black clubs, and black people don't come hear music in white clubs."

Susan Collier, the president of the Magic City Blues Society, faces the same problem when she brings bluesmen to Birmingham: "I have had more than one black musician ask me if there are problems here, will they be all right? Sugar Blue, when he came in, that was one of the first things out of his mouth: 'Am I going to be comfortable? Is it going to be okay for me to be there?' I said: 'Yeah, we have come a long way! It is all right.' And then for that to happen to Ed, I was like, I apologized for a day! ... Last year I had an experience with Little Ed, and Ed — there is no telling what his musical adventures have been, but he has no driver's license and I am sure he has been in jail a few times or whatever. So we left the Sloss Blast [a blues show at Sloss Furnaces Historic Site] ... and I was responsible for getting Ed back to the hotel. So I get in the car and we go down to the Best Western at University [Avenue] to go to the Steak and Egg to eat about 1 in the morning. We get in there and there are two black cops in the parking lot, and Ed got out of the van with a beer in his hand ... The minute we got to the door they stopped him! He was with a white woman, and I was with a black man, and these two black cops stopped him and asked him for his driver's license ... They harassed him for about thirty minutes, and I stood outside of the Waffle House with him, and I was almost livid, and I thought, 'These are your own brothers here,' and I could not believe the way they treated him! Finally they let us go, but nobody would wait on us, and I have no problem being in there with that black man, but nobody would even wait on us, and so we left."

The Magic City Blues Society reflects one aspect of the racial divide in Birmingham. Formed in 1993, it describes itself as "a nonprofit blues society in which our main purpose is to preserve the blues, promote the blues in Alabama, and present the blues to the community as a cultural form, and expose a lot of folks that don't get credit anymore as being the musicians that they are. We have not put as much effort into it, I think, as much as we should to find the old guys [blues players]. We bump into them here and there and do the best we can . . . and I think we have two black members [out of a total membership of around three hundred] besides the bands that are members! So it is just an ongoing battle. When I have been in symposiums in Memphis with the blues foundation, everybody deals with it. That is true. They deal with it all across the country. So that is not a southern thing! . . . It is white man's blues, period!"

Blues in Alabama might be white man's music, but jazz stays remarkably integrated with the tradition of musicians of both races sitting in and playing together. Unlike blues and rock 'n' roll, the jazz audience tends to be well integrated. Ona Watson was a student of Frank Adams and learned to play trumpet and trombone before switching to vocals: "I was never in the Commodores, but I played in bands that would compete against them . . . In Birmingham I played a place . . . the Eldorado Club. It was almost like a Blues Brothers–type thing, real dangerous. A guy would shoot up in the ceiling and everybody would duck." Ona was one of the youngest players inducted in the Alabama Jazz Hall of Fame: "I think that it is one of the greatest things that that ever happened to me." He opened his Music Room in 1997 in the dead zone between downtown and filled the void left by Grundy's Music Room (which closed in 1992). Ona's customers listen to jazz and R&B in a relaxed atmosphere: "I've got black people and white people coming in, and they don't sit on opposite sides of the room. They all sit together."

Unfortunately, Birmingham has not been able to escape the bad memories of the 1960s. Successive trials of the perpetrators of the Sixteenth Street Church bombings lasted from the late 1990s into the twenty-first century, keeping Birmingham in the news and the specter of 1963 alive. In the Capitol Records press release in support of Verbena, their hometown was depicted as the 1960s Birmingham, complete with the largest KKK chapter in the nation (untrue) and a sense that it was a miracle that a bunch of talented musicians could have escaped such an environment. Even minor stories, like an incident of racial discrimination at the local Shoal Creek golf course, attracted national media attention because it was in Birmingham. John Ed Willoughby: "What kind of image do we have? Everybody thinks of us as a bunch of rednecks down here, burning crosses and hanging people . . . Everybody has given Birmingham a black eye all these years."

Although Birmingham's residents were comforted to live in a city that they thought was a "well-kept secret," it was also "beset by a viciously innate inferiority complex" that probably started in the days of the New South and was aggravated by its reputation as "America's Most Segregated City."[1] Birmingham's inferiority complex is evident in its attitude toward its musicians. Natalye Pond: "I have known, my entire life, marvelous musicians in Alabama. And the fact that Birmingham club owners said, 'Oh, you don't count because somehow you are from Birmingham, therefore you are not good enough.'" There is a widespread belief that Birmingham audiences will usually only go and see a band that has made it in another city, anyplace other than Birmingham. Bobby Horton identified "a certain psyche about someone that comes from out of town. They are always better no matter what." Lenard Brown pointed out that Alabama is a place "that loves winners . . . I think they are open to new music as long as you are not from here." Doug Royale: "Birmingham has so many great musicians and there is no recognition!" Michael Trucks: "Birmingham has never had a great view of their local musicians. It has never gained a position of respect within the city. The local music scene has never been viewed as the 'in' thing. It never developed a feel like certain cities did, like Austin, Texas." This state of mind is an accepted part of the local music scene. As the *Black & White* 1999 Readers Poll concluded: "You're So Birmingham If . . . you don't go see local bands until they get signed."[2]

While City Stages struggled to break even, HealthSouth began to melt down. In 2003 it recorded $4.5 billion in revenue, but questions emerged about the veracity of its accounting practices, and Scrushy's sale of $100 million in stock before the company posted a loss in late 2002 raised some red flags. The U.S. Securities and Exchange Commission accused HealthSouth of inflating the company's earnings by $1.4 billion in an illegal process that had begun back in 1996. In some years, the company's income was overstated by as much as 4,700 percent. The FBI raided the corporate headquarters, searched through the company's records, and arrested Scrushy. The great HealthSouth bubble burst. The downfall of Health-South ended its investment in the Birmingham music scene. In the various lawsuits directed at Scrushy it was alleged that he had spent about a million dollars of the company's money promoting his all-girl band, 3rd Faze. The expenditures included flying the group around the country in the corporate jet and paying for breast enhancement. It was also claimed that he bribed Sony music's president with HealthSouth stock to give 3rd Faze a record contract. In his defense Scrushy and his lawyers argued that these entertainment ventures brought real value to the company's brand and that at the time they were considered effective marketing. In an article titled "Character Is Destiny: A Chronicle of Birmingham's Decline," David Pelfrey reflected on the hubris that characterized the economic boom of the 1990s and the rise and fall of Richard Scrushy: "Everything you needed to know about the aesthetic values of well-moneyed hicks — and far more than anyone wanted to know about Short Man Syndrome — was right there in one redneck package." Dallas County Line became somewhat of a joke in the Birmingham music scene. One of the "Top Ten Reasons to Think You May Have Been Over-Refreshed at City Stages" was "You're really looking forward to hearing Dallas County Line."[3]

HealthSouth was not the only corporate sponsor deserting City Stages as it got smaller and smaller. At its peak, the festival featured thirteen stages, almost three hundred acts, and performance areas over a thirteen-block area, but it was now reduced to about one hundred acts on six stages. Ticket prices had gone up to the point when you were paying as much for one day as you had paid for the whole three-day festival in the 1990s. The Great Recession that began during George W. Bush's presidency finished it off, as well as numerous clubs, bars, restaurants, and entertainment businesses. The year 2009 was a very bad one for many in Birmingham, and ticket sales for City Stages, which had been more or less constant for years, dropped by 50 percent. After a lackluster 2009 festival, George McMillan announced that the total debt had surpassed $1 million and that there would be no more City Stages. The Birmingham Cultural and Heritage Foundation filed for bankruptcy amid a flood of lawsuits and claims of corruption, nepotism, and waste on the part of the festival's organizers.

The Curse of Tommy Charles

The demise of City Stages was accompanied by more disappointments for Birmingham's Next Big Things; the boom/bust cycle of local bands attempting to achieve national recognition was repeated in the twenty-first century. Vallejo led many to believe that this might be the band to make it bid in the alternative world. Given their Hispanic roots and upbeat pop, they looked like "a present-day Santana," which would appeal to the alternative crowd. Vallejo's album *Into the New* was released by Sony in 2000. Rob Thorworth: "They went out to Austin for a year and they busted their ass and they soaked up, God knows what kind of music they soaked up out there. Good music! Better than here! We were out there playing and we went down the street and they were having their CD release party and they are playing in a thousand-seat room, and it is packed with people, and they are on fire, and they are a completely different band than when I saw them here in Birmingham. So there is something to be said about that right there. The irony of it is that they are not from Birmingham anymore! They are saying they are from Austin, Texas. It gives them more clock! You can't blame them. You are not going to say you are from Birmingham. Hell, we would go out and I would say we all was from Alabama . . . and you know Birmingham has a lot of derogatory connotations to it too. Bull Connor! That is what you are thinking when you say Birmingham." Unfortunately, *Into the New* did not sell well, and by 2002 Vallejo were releasing their music on their own label, Vallejo Music Group. *Stereo* was followed by *Thicker Than Water* in 2008. J. R. Taylor looked back at their earlier promise: "That could have worked out with them and Los Lonely Boys as the Beatles and the Rolling Stones of Latino rock. It's turned out more like the Del Taco and the Taco Bell . . . *Thicker Than Water* was a fairly mundane affair, sounding more like a decent bar band . . . It makes you wonder why Slick Lilly never made it big."[4] After a four-year gap, Vallejo released *Brothers Brew* in 2012. They were now marketing themselves as "one of the best pop bands from Austin, Texas."

Remy Zero's third album was released by Elektra in 2001. *The Golden Hum* was received well, and a version of "Save Me" was used as the theme song for the TV show *Smallville*. After releasing this album the band broke up, temporarily coming back together to play a few shows in 2010 in memory of their drummer Gregory Slay. Mars Electric broke up at the end of 2000. Three Finger Cowboy were disappointed with the low sales of *Kissed* (only about twelve hundred copies), and *Hooray for Love* (1999) was their last release for Daemon Records. Virgos Merlot disbanded after the unsuccessful release of *Signs of a Vacant Soul*; the band later re-formed without guitarist Jason Marchant as Virgos, which lasted until 2002. Little Red Rocket broke up after Geffen reneged on their record deal. Taylor and Fink parted ways with Schefano and Nobles, then moved to Athens, Georgia, and became Azure Ray. After releasing records for the small indie label WARM, they relocated again to the burgeoning music scene in Omaha, Nebraska, and the indie label Saddle Creek.

Brother Cane represented Birmingham's most successful rock band in 1998, having sold hundreds of thousands of records, opened for bands like Aerosmith and Van Halen, and toured extensively. The heavy touring continued as Brother Cane went on the road to support *Seeds*. From 1993 to 1996 the band averaged 270 dates a year, a punishing schedule that could not be continued indefinitely. Damon: "When we hit the road in '93 with a record under our thumb, we were clueless. We had no idea what to expect. Fortunately for us, we met some people on the road that were kind enough to sit down with us and go: 'Okay, look, you are going to burn out, people aren't going to play your songs, the record company is not going to promote it like you want them to, MTV is not going to play the video because you don't fit into their clique of the week.' We just thought, 'Hey, man, we love everybody, everybody is going to love us.'" In 1996 the band stopped touring and dropped from the public eye, "and everything shut down." They returned to Birmingham to recuperate and disappeared from the radio waves.

Praised by Shawn Ryan as "a solid, rocking album that some are calling brilliant," *Wishpool* represented Brother Cane's last chance to stay in the big time. Virgin needed the album to go gold, selling at least five hundred thousand copies, or they would drop the band. "You have got Brother Cane signed to Virgin. They are coming up on their third record and this is make or break time. I have talked to the guys in the band and Damon admits it, he said, 'If we don't go gold, we are probably gone!' Damon has thrown all the burdens on his shoulders. He is the singer, songwriter, he is the president of Brother Cane Inc. He told me, 'All the fucking bills come to me, man! I am the one with the ten thousand dollars on my American Express card that I have to pay off. I am the one who has to pay the other band members when the money comes to me from the record label, I dole it out.' So poor Damon has got all the pressure on him . . . They are hard rock, that is a really passé or out-of-vogue musical style right now. So I think that hurt them. MTV wouldn't play them, and without MTV these days you are pretty much sunk. The biggest difference now in the industry, which kills local bands, or any bands: in the '70s and '80s, I guess more than anything, a band could be a cult band and that would be okay. Now if you don't sell millions of copies you don't get a chance . . . You only get three shots! Three strikes and you are out, and that really hurt. There is no development of a band on the national scene . . . It may not be a disaster, it may just be a slow burn, slow burn, slow, painful, just dwindle away instead of a band in dissension that splinters the whole thing. They may just fade." *Wishpool* failed to go gold, Virgin dropped them, and Brother Cane broke up.

Slick Lilly continued to tour to promote their record on Kudzu. Don VanCleave: "We put them out on tours with Bad Company and some other bands." Carl Rouss: "We were gone for three weeks on the Bloodline tour and then we had like two or three days to wash clothes and hanging out and then we had to drive to Miami, and it would start from there, and then we worked our way up to . . . Chicago, and that went on for a whole 'nother month." Muddy King: "That is one thing, you cannot put out a product and not tour on it. No matter how much radio airplay is out there. That solidifies your fan base for the next record." Don VanCleave: "At that point it became obvious that Slick Lilly was not going to be picked up by a major label and that they were not going to sell a lot of records, and that we had a ton of records out in the marketplace that we were going to get back." That was it for Slick Lilly.

Gravy was going through the same arduous touring. Rob Thorworth: "And once again the road got really hard, from let's say September to December we were just poundin' it . . . But at the same time we were all our own tour support, which normally bands don't have to do, and we pretty much sucked our entire band account dry just supporting ourselves with gas and hotel rooms. Not to mention we were on a pretty hard road too, and I think in September of '95 we had done like twenty-six shows in twenty-six days. We were all about to rag out and kill one another, and John decided that he had had enough and he was going to split! We have been out there pounding the pavement from Texas to Virginia to Miami, and after four years we don't have a whole lot to show for it . . . I have busted my ass for five years to put this band to get it to what it was, and now I've got to start the fuck over! But you know, it is a hell of a way to make a living. It sucks! Unless you have, I have dreamt about this since I was four! So you've either got it in you to do it and make the sacrifices, or you don't . . . Right now I am trying to decide what the fate of Gravy is going to be. Probably going to lay it to rest. We have been after it for four years now and made a good bit of headway, but it is almost to the point where . . . we got out of the New Era management and Kudzu . . . As we were out on the road killing ourselves, shit was boiling up inside there and I smelled it all going down, and when John quit, not too far after that Don VanCleave bowed out of Kudzu . . . So I took the loophole [a "key person" clause in the contract, which gives the band the right to withdraw if a key person in the record company leaves] and ran with it because I smelled something going down. So about four or five months later they [Kudzu] closed up shop . . . So if you are not on a major label, you are not getting your record played. So the little guys like us don't have any hope."

And what of Verbena? They were Birmingham's vote for the band most likely to succeed with their Nirvana sound on *Into the Pink*. J. R. Taylor: "The album's production left Verbena with a generic alt-rock sound and, consequently, reputation, which was the last thing any band wanted at the end of the century. *Into the Pink* was a big nothing after years of hype. Verbena was set to become another remnant of changing times."[5] Scott Bondy: "When that last record didn't do well, it was the best thing that could have happened to us. I wouldn't want to duplicate anything that record represents." Griffin left the band as it slowly self-destructed. After four years — an eternity in the music business — the trio Verbena released *La Musica Negra* and disbanded after touring failed to capitalize for the single "Way Out West."

The end of Kudzu Records marked the end point of all the optimism and raised expectations of local bands in the 1990s, yet some musicians were wary of signing to them from the start. Bryan Price: "Jay Wilson, he helped with Brother Cane and he got Little Red Rocket their deal with DGC. He came to us a few times. All of us were like, 'No.' We would beat him up in a week because, to start with, the first thing you have to look at when he got involved with both of these bands, the first thing they did was to fire members of the band . . . He comes in and this guy is a money maker, which is great. I mean, it is a business: 'Yeah, you want to make money,' but if it is to get rid of so-and-so, and get so-and-so . . . There is no way. No one is ever going to tell me that . . . I mean, the Shame Idols' odds are stacked so high it is pathetic, but at the same time . . . I don't have to get up every day thinking, 'Oh, today is the day I have to make it. Today is the day I am going to get the call.' I think just us being older helped. We have been beat up. Do you know what I mean? Before we started the Shame Idols we had been around that bash-your-head-against-the-wall thing: 'Why haven't we made it? — blah, blah, blah.' So now our attitude is we are just so happy hanging out and creating what we create."

What had gone wrong? What had ruined these attempts to be the Next Big Thing? Was it a fickle music scene? Why couldn't local bands break out from Birmingham and be nationally known? Don Tinsley: "I have lived through four of five of them [music scenes], and they go in cycles. We have had some incredible bands from here and great musicians, and about every five years it dies and is a horrible death. Right now [1996], right where we are, there is a false boom going, and it is going to die horribly in about a year and a half . . . I think that everyone is going to be waiting around to see what else is up with music. I think that everyone is waiting for something different to happen . . . Bands are a product of their time. We live through a lot of changes." The popular music business was getting more competitive, and it was much harder to get a hit record. Michael Trucks: "And it is tough to say; it is all about timing. It is all in timing! If you look back, if a band like Brother Cane came out two years pre-Nirvana, they would have been right there with the Guns and Roses or something like that. But there is a distinct line with what happened to music pre- and post-Nirvana. Bands that were literally selling 4 million, I know of bands that sold 4 million before Nirvana, and sold 40,000 records after Nirvana. It is scary how that changes. Before Nirvana, what were known as alternative bands or college radio bands, boy, if they ever sold over 50,000 records, this is a giant hit! If we sell 50,000 records, we are doing good, but this went from 50,000 to 2 million records literally in a six-month time span."

Birmingham's musicians and business people all point to the lack of radio support for local music. Courtney Haden: "The lack of imagination from the very top down to the people who are actually working the microphone switches. The lack of willingness to take a chance on music and formats. The refusal to commit to backing local music and musicians." Ben Burford: "The state of radio here is just pitiful, and I don't know whose fault that is. We may be simpletons here in the South and in Birmingham." Opinions were pretty unanimous with Tony Ruffino's conclusion that Birmingham "has absolutely the worst radio of any [comparable] market size in America." Mats Roden: "The eternal complaint when we were playing Birmingham was that you could not get a song out, it is really hard to break in this market. It seems like there would be the right conditions to have some kind of radio simply with the colleges that are here in town." In the golden age of rock 'n' roll, radio stations would play records by local bands, but things changed in the 1980s: "You can't take a record down to 95 [FM, a radio station] and let them play it, they don't do that anymore." Libba Walker: "When I was first playing, radio was much more diverse, music was a lot more open-minded. You could turn it on one station and hear Led Zeppelin and hear Aretha Franklin right after that. There was no black or white radio or classic rock or country. Nobody knew how to label stuff so it was just like: 'This is someone new.'" After the 1960s Birmingham's radio stations rarely played local music and stayed well behind the times in their programming. Tony Ruffino said this about a deejay on Rock 99, the main rock radio station in Birmingham in the 1980s and 1990s: "When we did Pat Benatar, the Police and Dire Straits had all those great records, he would not play it. We had to go up to him and beg him. His response was 'Birmingham people do not want to hear that, they want to hear Marshall Tucker, the Outlaws, and Charlie Daniels.'" Tom Baddley's conclusion: "Oh, good god! Radio? What radio?"

The Suburban Love Junkies claimed: "We get airplay in other towns, but we don't get any here in Birmingham."[6] Although there were a few stations such as the WRAX or the Bear that routinely played music from local bands, radio as a whole in Birmingham has ignored local talent: "I think that is lacking here in Birmingham. There is no outlet! There is no radio out there for local bands." In the 1990s the concentration of American radio around a small number of powerful companies tended to edge out local music in favor of Top 40 playlists chosen by analysts in corporate head offices. Michael Trucks: "You have to realize that the majority of the radio stations, in fact all of them now, are owned by one or two big syndicates. Either Dick Broadcasting or Cox Broadcasting. You have got two companies that own all the stations." John Ed Willoughby lamented the end of the autonomous deejay in corporate radio: "Because they are ruining creativity, and not only on the front end with the musicians, but they are ruining it in the [radio] studio. The guys in the studio are all robots now. They are nothing but key punchers! They are time and temperature people. 'Hey, WSGN, it's 9:05 [a.m.] and 68 degrees,' and then they go to something else . . . They are killing radio, it all sounds alike, it is all jukebox!" Mike Panepento: "What Birmingham radio? It tends to be very corporate. If anything is going to happen here, you have to get the right person at the corporate level to get songs played — let's just use the word 'plugola' . . . What has happened is that radio has done exactly what music has done and has formatted themselves into corners . . . They don't get to hear new forms of music here, therefore they are less apt to accept them." When local stations like the Bear and WRAX 107.7 temporarily bucked the trend by playing alternative rock and focusing on local acts, there was an immediate upsurge in their record sales. Rob Thorworth: "I think the main thing that got us over the hump was we befriended Don Alias at the Bear and he started playing 'Junk Yard Man' and 'Change' on the radio and it reacted." WRAX became one of the highest-rated alternative radio stations in the country in the 1990s. Gary Weinberger of New Era — the largest concert promoter in Alabama — recognized its importance: "There are a lot of bands coming to town now that wouldn't be coming if WRAX wasn't playing their records."[7] Unfortunately, Don Alias's numbers went down and he was fired, and that was the end of local music on the Bear.

The popularity of alternative music had been built on the foundation of college radio. Although Birmingham had several colleges and a large public university — the leading employer in the state — it could never claim a credible college radio station. Conrad Rayfield: "What we really need, and I have said this all along, is a college station. We need that in the worst kind of way. Adult alternative or college station, either one would be wonderful. It is a major void." Ed Reynolds: "My complaint was always not having a college station here in town ... There is nothing local here as far as radio. These are just big company stations. There is no individuality or Birmingham flavor whatsoever." Cedric LeMoyne: "When we started the band there weren't any places we could play. There is no college radio in Birmingham. That kind of thing is unhealthy in other ways for a musical scene. Birmingham has five colleges in town and no college radio." Bryan Price: "The difference to me in the Tuscaloosa crowd and the Birmingham crowd is just unbelievable! You play Tuscaloosa, and this sounds snobby, but it just seems like a more musically educated crowd because they have college radio. They have heard bands that people here have never freakin' heard of."

The major record companies were usually depicted as the guilty parties in the stories of a local band's rise and precipitous fall. Michael Trucks: "The rock record business was started by guys that were real music people ... These record companies grew and now have been absorbed by international companies. They are really run by the lawyers and accountants, and that is sad ... They are not music people — they view the music as a product. We are selling widgets." Ona Watson: "I have a lot of buddies that have record deals but they are not in control of their careers. They have to play a lot of places they do not want to play."

Music professionals point to the lack of recording facilities in the city. Birmingham could not boast of a record label or studio that had created new stars, and the belief that Freddie Knight recorded "Ring My Bell" in Birmingham proved to be wishful thinking. After the demise of Kudzu, the city could not claim a record company with a national distribution deal. In the 1970s there was an abundance of musical talent in Birmingham, but "where we dropped the ball was not having adequate recording facilities at the time to put out a professional product. Most everyone went to Nashville or Muscle Shoals." Ed Boutwell's studios have been the longest-lived in Birmingham, but if you ask Ed what his most successful recording was, he will tell you that it was a jingle for Jack's hamburgers! He "rarely made a dime" from all those rock songs he recorded. Mac Rudd: "A couple of studios around town have really tried hard to make it on their own without having to go the commercial or jingle route. It just doesn't work... The studios have to keep their doors open, and jingles and voice-overs bring the dollars in. Musicians don't bring the dollars in, unfortunately."

Ed Boutwell was around at the birth of rock 'n' roll: "All the musicians were just in the middle of the development of all of it. There were so many people and so few positions of fame. There were only the Top 10 records and some of those things that would stay on the charts for months and months; the chance of you getting a record out and getting a hit on it [was slim]; you just had to keep cutting and hoping that one of them would be a hit and then you would be considered a great producer." Sixty years later there are a lot more bands competing for audiences and record contracts, but with the same Top 10. Rob Thorworth: "There is oversaturation and all of a sudden because of Hootie and the Blowfish, we have gone out there, every college guy with a damn ball cap on backwards is playing an acoustic guitar, and he is writing little Tom Pettyish pop songs, and there are a million of them out there!" Shawn Ryan: "Right now alternative is so, is getting real passé, and right now alternative is in the same set-up as rock and pop were in the early '70s. Where you have got thousands of one-hit wonders... The audience gets quickly bored with the band, and they play the shit out of them for a month, and then *boom*, they've gone! You can't do a twenty-year gig like Telluride, not anymore. Definitely not! You better hit while the iron is hot." Conrad Rayfield: "When I first got into the business fifteen years ago, one of the most alarming [statistics] was one out of every ten bands that was signed to a major label survived to make a second record. One out of every ten! Twenty years later the statistic is twice as bad. One out of every twenty! Sure, I get tapes constantly! We are flooded by them. A lot of quick-driven one-hit wonders. Worse than they ever were. That is the total function of MTV. Bands become totally oversaturated very early on. They develop big profiles via video, but they don't develop fan bases, and because of that there is no allegiance to the bands, the kids don't develop any passion, there is no mystique. The reason we went to see bands as kids because all you ever saw were publicity photos, and the idea of getting to see them in person was like rubbing elbows with the stars. Nowadays the airwaves are so saturated with them, and the video waves for that matter, you don't have a chance to develop that attachment. You get bored with them before you ever get close."

The pop music business in the twenty-first century is overcrowded, and the odds against a band making it get longer and longer every day. But could the reason for the lack of success of Birmingham musicians be something to do with fate? Could it be that an incident forty years previous had put a curse on local musicians, forever quashing their dreams of making it big and leaving town, and submitting them to a life sentence of playing "Sweet Home Alabama" in rowdy bars? Matt Kimbrell had no doubt about the real reason for all the ruined dreams of the 1990s: it was the curse of Tommy Charles.

A Town with an Inferiority Complex

In the twenty-first century the Birmingham Chamber of Commerce was so concerned about the city's low self-esteem that it put a million dollars into a campaign to sell Birmingham to its own people rather than to the outside world. David Adkisson pointed to the "hang-wringing and soul-searching over issues of image" and promoted the "Living a Dream" advertising campaign because "we felt the issue of self-image was more important than image."[8] Sam George of *Black & White* noted "an alarming number of Birmingham natives have a generally negative view of their own city."[9] Much the same could have been said about musicians' attitudes toward playing in Birmingham, because any band with ambition felt the need to leave town. Jamey Hollingsworth of Common Ground recognizes that Birmingham doesn't have much of a music scene: "I don't know what it is. It is impossible to say what the missing element is, and I don't want to sound real pessimistic about it because I love playing music here. But one thing that happens, people that really have talent here . . . that once they realize that they really do have musical talent, they get the hell out of Dodge!" Rob Thorworth put it bluntly: "I will tell you this, our main objective was to get the fuck out of here! Because I have seen so many bands . . . There is nothing here! I mean, there is nothing here! Well, I shouldn't say that,

Birmingham has been real good to us! I mean, we have sold four thousand records here, but if you know anything about the music scene . . . I mean, it took us a long time to pound our original music into people's heads and they finally picked up on it . . . But I think that is why we did well here, but you go into a bar now and a band, your crowds in general, and I think a lot of places in the South are reluctant to embrace original music. No matter what form it is in."

The imperative to leave town in order to be successful has been a constant for all of the twentieth century; bluesmen took the train north, vaudeville players attached themselves to touring groups, and jazz musicians left for better bands and bigger cities. Even garage bands routinely chose to record outside the city in the 1960s, and this helped establish Muscle Shoals as a recording center. Ned Bibb said of his band: "We felt like we had to get out of Birmingham if we were to cut something good." Jazz player Ray Reach: "I left Birmingham kind of feeling a little bitter about, well, if I am ever going to do anything in music, by golly, I have been told that all my life: 'You have to get out of Birmingham, boy!' 'Well, he must be a country bumpkin because he is from Birmingham, Alabama.' Still, Birmingham has that bloody nose that it got in the occurrences and the way the media hyped it in the '60s. That did not help things with Bull Connor with the firehoses on black people and all of that! But there is still the attitude of 'Yeah, Birmingham is still a one-horse town,' and in many ways it still is. It is still crippled by the good ol' boy politics . . . that is why the Lionel Ritchies move to L.A. and the Nat Coles and then on and on and on. You name all the folks that have risen to national and international prominence from Alabama, how many of them live here? Not many!" Nims Gay argued, "If you wanted to be able to branch out you had to leave here 'cause Birmingham, right now, is fenced in. Birmingham wants to be a hick town! They don't want to move out. They just want to stand in one rut, and it is not there. A city without a vision dies. Music without a vision can't go anywhere."

The successful bands who had left for bigger music scenes usually argue that they left because nothing was going on musically in Birmingham. As Vallejo and Little Red Rocket tactfully pointed out, "It's extremely important for an artist to be in a city that has a music scene," and there's "nothing better than competition."[10] Conrad Rayfield: "Vallejo has relocated to Austin and has really got something going... Happy for the band, and thrilled to see their success, but also realistically you have to acknowledge the fact that there is a direct correlation between them relocating to Austin and the success they have enjoyed."

Bands that made it in other cities always reminded local audiences that they had never gotten any support in Birmingham. The Drive-By Truckers built up an international audience with their mix of southern rock and roots music: "This band had a following in Atlanta and Richmond and even in Chicago long before it did in Birmingham. For six years the Nick would only let us play Monday nights," remembered Patterson Hood.[11] Damon Johnson: "We have absolutely felt a little frustration at times about our lack of profile in our own town... I say you can't blame the people, but then again you go on tour with a band like Van Halen and every show that you go from the East Coast all the way down to the West Coast, every show is sold out except one, and do you know what city that was? Birmingham, Alabama, and it was not even close to selling out." "They are the least popular here," as Conrad Rayfield points out. "Brother Cane sold more records than any other band, but in Birmingham nobody knows who they are!"

There is widespread agreement among local musicians that "Birmingham audiences suck!" Their opposition to original music, their inability to sit still and listen, and their perception of live music as merely the background for flirting and drinking has been chronicled by bands from every decade and genre. Alan Hunter: "Birmingham has the talent. The talent has moved away because they could not make a living or the talent has had to go and be trained in air-conditioner service repair person because it is hard to make a living... It just takes a certain youth base to make those things happen, and a college town will certainly make those things happen. I don't know why UAB does not provide a little bit of that... There are so many great musicians here, but I think that what has happened is that there has not been enough to come in and fill the shoes of those guys in the '80s that got burned. There are young people out there with original music but they cannot make it with it and I guess that reflects that there are people out there that do not have the desire to listen to anything new other than a pop song that they know." Birmingham's music scene is still dominated by covers. Bryan Price: "Oh yeah! Today you look at like, if somebody does a poll of your most favorite bands, I would say that four out of the top five are always cover bands . . . most bands do some type of cover stuff, I mean, like Topper and the blues, but for originals: it has always been the Nick or nothing. That is the thing about the Nick, people can cut it and they can get mad at it, but I mean, hey: if it weren't for the Nick, where else would everybody do what they do?" Ed Reynolds: "There are so few clubs to play. It just seems that everyone is fighting for those few nights, especially those weekend nights at the Nick . . . we have Zydeco, Five Points Music Hall, Louie's, but the Nick is just so much more open to new music than these other clubs are. It is the only place they will let you play. The hot spots in Birmingham are down in Five Points South, and that is the fraternity/sorority crowd supporting that kind of stuff. There is not much of an underground kind of thing going on in Birmingham . . . People have got MTV and cable and everything; if they go out they want to talk. While you are playing you just hear this constant buzz and chatter, and that kind of stuff drives me crazy. The audience have paid their five dollars and they have done their part . . . If they want to talk I can't hold that against them. I may want to scream "Shut the fuck up!' . . . But I am not going to do that because it is up to me to stop them talking." Rick Carter agrees that it is the musicians' responsibility to get the audience excited about the performance: "You don't see a bunch of jet mechanics sitting around saying, 'Wow, I wish everyone would be more into jets.'"

American Idol

The validation that Birmingham bands and their audience sought finally came from an unusual quarter — a televised talent show that became a national obsession. *American Idol* marked another British import and an invasion of sorts — not a succession of bands with the same haircut, but turgid talent shows where amateurs sang popular songs. The show opened in 2002 and soon garnered an enormous television audience. *American Idol* generated the same kind of interest that characterized the golden age of televised talent shows in the 1950s. In 2003 a Birmingham entertainer named Ruben Studdard became the second *American Idol* on a wave of local pride that included a line of T-shirts with the 205 (telephone area code for Birmingham) affiliation and a homecoming show at UAB. *American Idol* revealed how important local music was to Birmingham's self-image and how a few successes could make the city feel good about itself. Bo Bice placed second to Carrie Underwood in the fourth season of *American Idol* in 2005, and such was the excitement in Alabama that the governor declared May 24 "Bo Bice Day" (he had already declared March 11 "Ruben Studdard Day" in 2003). In 2006 Taylor Hicks became the fifth American Idol in one of the most-watched television shows of the decade, and this turned a spotlight on the city's music scene that it had never received before. The prestige of Birmingham as a musical city reached new heights, and calls were coming in from all corners of the country to hapless university professors seeking to know the secret of the city's musical genius. The Alabama magazine *Excursions* claimed that "winning *American Idol* is the equivalent of one of the state's schools winning the national championship in football."[12] There could be no greater accomplishment for Alabamians. The Birmingham Chamber of Commerce put together a double CD of the city's best-known musicians in the wake of the "inevitable" success on *American Idol*: "While New Orleans, Memphis, and Nashville got all the early buzz as southern music Meccas and then Austin and Athens, Birmingham kept quietly churning out world-class musicians decade after decade, year after year. But we really didn't stop to notice until *American Idol*. So pause and think about it. Why shouldn't we be surprised that all these 'idols' came from Birmingham?" The CD liner notes followed "Birmingham's rise to musical greatness" from the 1930s through to the triumphs of the 1980s, "drawing huge crowds to outdoor concerts by groups such as the Rolling Stones . . . City Stages set the benchmark for downtown music festivals nationwide" and provided more evidence of Birmingham being "so musically inclined." But the music on *American Idol* was stale and unoriginal, much of it a throwback to the soul and R&B of the 1970s; and at the same time that people were watching amateurs singing old favorites on TV, original music was hardly heard in the city's bars and clubs, especially after WRAX went under in 2006. The careers of the American Idols lasted only a few years and a few records before they disappeared from the headlines. In

2007 Studdard was dropped from his record company, J Records, and the next year Arista Records (part of the massive Song/BMG group) canceled the contract of Taylor Hicks, both because of poor sales of records. The party for Alabama's American Idols was over.

The search for the next Next Big Thing continued. Wild Sweet Orange was formed when Preston Lovinggood joined up with school friends Taylor Shaw and Chip Kilpatrick to form a literate, indie band with folk leanings. Soon the band caught the attention of the local media. Mary Colurso of the *Birmingham News* was convinced that this was the Next Big Thing, and her story about the local band "making waves nationally" appeared on the front page. All the local media were convinced that Wild Sweet Orange "Hits It Big." The *Birmingham Weekly* put them on the cover, and David Feltman announced that the "local wonder boys" were "on the verge of hitting the big time."[13] Their record *We Have Cause to Be Uneasy* was released by the indie Canvasback Records in 2008, they were booked to appear at Lollapalooza, and their song "Land of No Return" was featured on the TV show *Grey's Anatomy.* With a record label, a publicist, and a page on Myspace, Wild Sweet Orange was ready to start touring the country. An appearance on *Late Night with David Letterman* brought them before a national audience and convinced some in the music business that they were going to be the next indie sensation. In Birmingham there was no doubt: "People thought of us as millionaires," remembered Lovinggood, and their sell-out local shows were "love fests." But the band needed to sell lots of records to break even, and the declining economy hurt all record sales as well as concert attendance. Wild Sweet Orange played before enthusiastic audiences who knew all their songs by heart, but the band soon found out that very few of them had actually bought their record or paid for a download. The band sold about eleven thousand records, but they needed to sell over sixty thousand to stay on their label.

The failure of any band to make it on the national scene is felt by local musicians: Doug Lee: "Nobody has ever made it out of this town except for a few individuals. A group has never broken out of this town." Charlie McCulloh: "The best people in town, the people that have the drive and that have the chops, get out of town. The people that stay can make a good

living." Michael Chandler: "You have to get out of Birmingham to make
it in the music business."

Alabama's state tourism office bravely promoted 2011 as the "Year of Alabama Music," but with little to brag about. With City Stages a bad memory,
especially for those bands and retailers who never got paid, the two replacement festivals — Birmingham Arts and Music, and Secret Stages — carried on with obscure local acts playing local venues. When Mary Colurso
of the *Birmingham News* concluded that "a big deal, an extraordinary
occasion — was missing" in these events, she was hammered in an edito-
rial in *Black & White* that suggested she leave "this city that she so clearly
loathes."[14] But self-loathing was common in a city of cover bands and disinterested audiences. Conrad Rayfield: "There was a widely held perception
for a long time that if a band was from here they couldn't be happening." In
2012 Amber Ritchie was comparing audiences in Birmingham with those
in Atlanta and asking "What is it about Birmingham that lacks motivation
to attend concerts and discover new music?"[15]

There was little good news about Birmingham. In 1996 the EPA had
tasked Jefferson County, in which the city of Birmingham is situated, to
rebuild the sewage system. Years of incompetence and corruption increased
the debt of the county as it borrowed millions in a massive construction
project. The financial crisis of 2008 found the county $4 billion in debt
that forced it into bankruptcy in 2011 — the largest municipal bankruptcy
in American history up to that time. The county was left with the most
expensive sewage system in the world, massive cutbacks in services, and
outrageous water and sewage bills. Seventeen people eventually went to
prison, including the mayor and other notables, in a highly publicized legal
process. Once tagged with the title of the most hateful city in America,
Birmingham could now claim one of the most corrupt local governments
in the United States. This scandal attracted a lot of attention to the least
attractive aspects of the city: a heritage of government corruption, poverty,
bad schools, undermanned police, terrible roads, and uncollected garbage.
In the words of the *New York Times*, "Birmingham looked like a monu-
ment to urban blight."[16]

From that point on, every positive notice about Birmingham was seized

upon and "all of them greeted with jubilation," in the words of Mark Kelly.
In June 2013 an article posted online by AP and printed in the *New York Times* was entitled "Once Dying Birmingham Is Suddenly Hot." The
piece began, "It feels like Birmingham finally is emerging from the shadows cast by the ugly racial violence of 1963," but then went on to list its
"revival" since then: a minor league baseball stadium, some examples of
fine restaurants, an independent film festival, and a "thriving nightclub
scene." This is in direct contrast to the commonly held belief that the city's
music scene is "laughing-stock status."[17] Favorable articles published in
Forbes, Delta Airlines and *National Geographic Traveler* magazines, and
USA Today and features on NBC were widely quoted in Birmingham. Later
in 2013 an "All American City" award clinched the idea that Birmingham
had finally arrived. The local media joined onto the booster bandwagon,
applauding the progress of "a city so long beaten down by negativity and
mismanagement."[18]

The city's "innate inferiority complex" comes from a historic cycle of
raised and lowered expectations, and the music scene is a big part of this
process. In an article entitled "Birmingham's Broken Promise," Kyle Whitmire chronicled the cycle of raised expectations and eventual humiliating
failure that dogged the city on its journey to redemption, pointing out that
Birmingham, the "City of Perpetual Promise," was recognized as early as
1937 by George Leighton in *Harper's* magazine. Whitmire felt that Birmingham was prey to same curse as Sisyphus, "shouldering the boulder to
the top of Red Mountain only to watch it roll down the same side."[19] "The
serial failure of Birmingham to fulfill its promise," in the words of longtime city archivist and historian Marvin Whiting, is the one thread that
runs unbroken through the history of the city and its musicians.[20]

CHAPTER EIGHTEEN

Birmingham Music in the Digital Age

The music business changed so drastically in the first decade of the twenty-first century that the paradigm of success established by the rise of rock 'n' roll in the 1950s was made obsolete. The year 1999 was when Verbena, Little Red Rocket, and Remy Zero made all the local headlines, but it was also the year of Napster and the complete transformation in the way that popular music was marketed. The 1990s was the decade of the home computer and the Internet. In 1992 there were an estimated 2 million users online; by 2000 it had exceeded 100 million, and personal computers could be found in more than 50 percent of American households. In the early years of the decade, a desktop computer could connect, via a call-up modem, to the Internet, but it took such a long time to download a song in MP3 format that it was hardly worth it. Computer technology advanced so fast, however, that soon downloading a song could be done in seconds and the whole world of recordings was at your disposal if you did not mind engaging in a little Internet piracy.

The same computer that connected to the Internet was now powerful enough to become a home recording studio. Programs like Pro Tools made the home studio in the 2000s as good as professional studios of the 1980s, and this convinced the majority of musicians to go into the recording business, either as a tool in practicing and rehearsal, or as the end product of all their creative work. The availability of high-quality equipment at affordable prices pushed home recorders into becoming businessmen. Daniel Farris was one of them, and his Denial Studios opened in 1993. Since then he has worked with many local musicians. He recorded some of the demos that convinced the big record companies to sign indie bands like Little Red

Rocket, who also recorded their first album there: "We did it at a place called Denial Studios. It is the basement of this guy from Birmingham's house. His name is Daniel Farris. It was 24-track and he recorded it for three thousand dollars. We recorded fifteen songs. The mixing and the packaging cost three times that. The average song is three and a half minutes. We spent a month on it." Denial Studios is all digital, as Daniel says on his website: "I have never owned a 4-track [tape recorder]." There are a lot more bands recording in the digital era and many more studios, both the traditional complex of rooms, and the newer single-operator, computer work stations. Synchromesh Studios represents the former. Opened in Tarrant in the mid-1990s with ten thousand square feet of studio space, it has the latest digital technology as well as a 16-track analog (tape) recorder. In the 1950s you only had two places to record in Birmingham; now there are scores of choices — a studio for every taste and budget. Rob Thorworth: "We recorded the *From the Hip* album, we rented a damn drum machine and recorded it in the drummer's garage, and I had a million people come up and say, 'Man, that shit sounds better than a bunch of stuff in the studio!' Which was the whole reason we did it. We did it in a bunch of studios and we couldn't ever get the sound we wanted, and I said, 'Man, I could do this myself! Just rent some stuff.' We just have to experiment a little bit, and we did, and it ended up sounding great!"

Digital technology altered every part of making music, from drum machines to guitar effects you could run through a laptop computer. Doug Lee: "The things that have made playing live music different: part of it is technology. Back in the old days in the late '60s and early '70s we used these primitive PA systems, and then everybody went through a phase when they got these big, elaborate PA systems, high dollar. Now people are scaling back . . . You can put together a small PA system now that sounds like a million bucks." Learning to play a guitar has been simplified by a new generation of digital tools and crutches. The value of virtuosity, like everything else in music in the twenty-first century, has been devalued. Mike Panepento: "The skill level and performance level of musicians has dropped throughout the country and the world due to MIDI recording, computer-generated music. There is not as much skill." Nobody feels pulse of the garage bands better than music teachers. Ben Trexel: "None of the kids really want to learn how to play the guitar. They want to play the latest grunge songs, and they are easy to learn."

Digital technology provided musicians with the "digital audio workstation," enabling them to make their records at home and sell their music directly to their fans on the Internet. Justin Wallace of Fighting Meeces: "Macs [Apple computers] changed the music world for the better: you've got Rock Band [a game], the Internet, GarageBand [a recording program for laptops and an app for smart phones] . . . It's having a humongous effect. You get a decent recording program free with a Mac and then you post it directly to YouTube . . . Recording music in the home — making music more accessible — the music is there for the people . . . but the quality might be going down because technology makes it so easy." In 1999 Verbena had several sites on the Internet: some set up by fans, one by their record company, and one by the band members. You still had to phone in to hear a song, but the introduction of social media sites like Myspace gave bands the option to embed their music in MP3 form on their websites. At its peak in 2008 Myspace could credibly claim to have revolutionized the production and marketing of popular music. "Myspace changed everything," said Tyler Godsey of Bremen — more a musical collaborative of students with other career goals than a commercial endeavor of professional musicians. "We weren't much but a small band, but we could still play the Bottletree [the new indie venue in Birmingham] and put a music video on YouTube just like the big bands." Facebook, Myspace, Bandcamp, and all the other websites transformed the relationship between musician and listener. Bandcamp can "sell your music and merchandise directly to your fans," providing numerous formats for downloads, cover art, and liner notes. This technology removed the important intermediaries of disc jockey and record store. YouTube gave any musician with some experience in operating a digital video camera an alternative to the live performance and MTV video. David Byrne of the Talking Heads has pointed out that in the digital age there have never been more opportunities for a musician to reach an audience.

The Internet has helped fracture popular music into numerous niche audiences all connected through social media. It has also condensed space as well as time, therefore location isn't half as important when the Internet connects people worldwide, with no consideration of their origin. The powers that be are still situated in New York or Los Angeles, but the geographic origin of music has become less relevant as the Internet expands to every corner of the world audience and satisfies every taste. In the digital era of popular music, being a southern musician means playing music recognized as southern or reflecting a southern musical heritage rather than actually working in the South. The rapper Yelawolf, born Michael Wayne Atha in Gadsden, represents this new generation of southern musicians. He is based in Seattle, plays often in the New York area, and has record contracts with several independent record companies, such as Interscope Records, and his own label. *Trunk Muzik 0–60*, his fourth mixtape, was well received, but not supported by any gigs in Alabama. Nevertheless, his music is southern. His song "Pop the Trunk" from *Trunk Muzic* portrays life "among the meth labs and gun-blasted back roads of the South."[1]

Digital technology evened out the playing field in popular music and gave all ages and talent the same opportunity. Allison and Katie Crutchfield made their first appearance as the Ackleys at age fifteen at Cave9. The twins had started their own all-female band in the best spirit of the new wave: "We were really bad, we couldn't play our instruments."[2] Later the Ackleys were made up of two high school seniors, Michael McClellan and Carter Wilson, and two juniors, the Crutchfield sisters. Cave9 was as much a music commune as a club, giving a stage to underage, Christian, and alternative bands. Although there was a cover charge to get in, the atmosphere at Cave9 was so relaxed that you had to look for someone to pay. Aaron Hamilton of Cave9 helped the Ackleys make their records and put it out on his own House of Love label. The Ackleys played City Stages in 2006. A few years later the *New York Times* was calling their work "two of the year's best and most affecting indie rock albums."[3]

The rise of the next Next Big Thing from Alabama gives an example of how digital technology has speeded up the process of becoming a star. The Alabama Shakes started in Athens, Alabama, with the coming together of some high school friends. Lead singer Brittany Howard taught herself the guitar and used a MIDI keyboard and computer to write songs. A home computer was instrumental in the Shakes' first recordings. The plan was to build a recording studio in one of the members' house, but noise from a nearby railroad track forced the band to record a few songs for an EP in a small studio close by in early 2011. These recordings, including the song "You Ain't Alone," were posted on the Internet, where a fan who had been impressed by a live set in a Nashville record shop linked them to Justin Gage, who writes the influential music blog *Aquarium Drunkard*. Gage's positive review of the band circulated through the Internet, and he also emailed MP3s of "You Ain't Alone" to some of his associates, including Patterson Hood of Drive-By Truckers, who immediately arranged for the Shakes to open for his band. These Internet postings in July brought them to the attention of the music industry, and "all hell broke loose," according to their Internet biography. They were besieged by emails from record companies, managers, bookers, and fans. They got rave reviews from print and Internet media and a mention on National Public Radio. In October they traveled to New York and the CMJ booking agency's Music Marathon showcase for new acts. The *New York Times* music critic Jon Pareles gave them a glowing review, and this helped them get a record contract with England's Rough Trade Records as the Alabama Shakes. By the end of the year everyone from MTV to *Rolling Stone* was calling them the best new band in America. In February 2012 they started their debut national tour; in April their *Boys and Girls* album was released and they appeared on *Late Night with David Letterman* and many other important television venues; and in June they were headliners at Bonnaroo. By the end of 2012 they had broken into the Top 10 lists in both the United States and United Kingdom, had been nominated for three Grammys, had toured Europe, and were contenders for best album and record of the year. By 2015 the Drive-By Truckers were opening for them in music festivals. A *Guardian* article highlighted the rapidity of a rock band's rise in the digital age: "A few years ago, Alabama Shakes were playing covers in old folks' homes. Now, on the eve of their new album, they're the world's best southern rock act."[4]

Yet rock bands in the digital age have short life spans, and Andy Warhol's prediction that everyone would be able to enjoy a few short minutes of fame certainly rang true in popular music. Porter Landrum: "New Era told us that we were opening for Hootie and the Blowfish and I was like, 'Hootie who?' So then all of a sudden they went to the top of the charts and a year later they are hurting for gigs. See, here is Hootie and he is cool, and here comes his second record. His first record sold 9 million, but his second record sold 2 ½ million, and so now it is a flop." Doug Royale: "Everything is so short-lived now. In the old days, people like Fleetwood Mac, people would follow every album, couldn't wait for the next one. So a band could survive that long. Now it is a real short-lived thing, and it is just kind of the nature of the business. You have one band that is just the best band in the world and a year later, 'Oh yeah, I forgot about them.'" The Spin Doctors' career is an example of the speed with which a band can rise and fall. Their debut studio album, *A Pocket Full of Kryptonite*, was a smash hit in 1991, selling about 5 million records for Epic/Sony. They came to Birmingham and played the largest stadium venue. Their second album sold only 1 million in 1994, and soon they were among the local bands playing Doo Dah Day. Their third album only sold seventy-five thousand copies, and Epic Records dropped them in 1996.

The digital age has made it easier to form a band but has also aggravated the problem of saturation. In the 1970s and 1980s, when a band broke up that was it: you went home, maybe got a few gigs playing acoustic sets at local bars while you looked for a day job. In the digital age you just form a new band, make some more records in your home studio to release on your personal record label, establish a new identity on the Internet, and use a variety of social media sites to sell your music. After Wild Sweet Orange broke up, the members returned home. One correspondent to a website noted their change of fortune: "The lead dude, Preston, works as a temp in my dad's office for spare cash. Pretty cool."[5] But pretty soon they were making more music in new bands. In 2010 Preston Lovinggood put out his solo album *Sun Song* on his own label with local producer Taylor Hollingsworth of Dead Fingers. After Brother Cane broke up, Damon Johnson played a few solo acoustic gigs in bars on the Southside while putting together his new band, Dragonfly, with fellow Brother Cane member Roman Glick, Bruce Castleberry of Verbena, and Leif Bondarenko of L-Mo, the Cast, and Space Camp. He later replaced Tommy Shaw in Ted Nugent's band Damn Yankees after they re-formed in 1999.

In the days of the garage bands, joining a group was making a long-term commitment; you stayed true to your partners, worked hard to preserve the union, and avoided the temptations of playing with attractive suitors.

Charles Arndt: "It is kind of like being married; you zone together and you see the best and the worst of how people are. It will either make you or break you." Leaving a band was often remembered in terms of breaking up with a loved one. Judy Ranelli: "Breaking up a band is like a divorce — it's horrible." Rob Thorworth: "You go through more of that than you do with your actual girlfriend . . . It was kind of like, 'Well, this is my band and I am sorry you feel like that, but this is the way it has got to go.'" In the digital age musicians mix and match in a variety of different bands, each with their own identity on the Internet and a unique catalogue of recordings. Allison and Katie Crutchfield make up the Ackleys, but each has a solo project and also plays in other bands. The music of Orenda Fink and Maria Taylor appears under the names of several bands and in different formats. Professional musicians in Birmingham now play in numerous bands to make ends meet. Part-timers play restaurants, parties, and events as duos, trios, quartets, and solo acts — whatever fits the bill. Jamey Hollingsworth: "Something in Birmingham that happens which is a necessity right now . . . but it is like everybody plays with five or six different bands . . . everybody in order to make a living has to play with so many different people."

When rock 'n' roll appeared in the 1950s, the music could be enjoyed live in person, purchased as a record or heard on the radio. Sixty years later listeners can access music through ubiquitous mobile phones, laptops, tablets, and other digital devices. Alice Bargeron: "I think that music is very secondary to a lot of people. It is never 'Oh, that moves me.' I do not know if it is just the computer age and just the technology where everything is just so fast-paced. I do think, though, that technology has done so many wonderful things, but it has also hurt so many wonderful things . . . You have replaced the camaraderie between two human beings. You have replaced all the awareness of each other." Marc Phillips: "They don't get the concept of listening to music. Music is such a saturated art. It's in Walmart, it's in the dentists' offices, it's in the hospital waiting room, it's in your car. It's everywhere you go. It's on TV . . . So, it's a three-and-a-half minute format, or a four-minute format, or whatever the case may be; if you talk through it and you never listen to what it says, you don't hear it . . . Music is just an art form that I really feel is more than any taken for granted . . . because there

is so much of it. You tune it out — you don't tune it in." Lee Bargeron: "I
think that with cable TV expanding — it used to be that you had maybe
ten channels and now you have two hundred channels, satellite TV, pay per
view, Internet, everybody is sitting at their computer. I know I spend a lot
of time on the computer. I think that there are a lot more things vying for
people's attention, and I think the live music scene has probably suffered
from that." The devaluation of live music is especially hard on musicians.
Doug Lee: "It used to be that when you and I were in college and they
booked a band to come play, even if it was a band that you had never heard
of, if they booked a band into the gym or to play outdoors at the quad or
something, everybody was there, and everybody sat there and listened to
the band because we were not bombarded with live music all the time. Now
people have been around live music all their lives, and there is so much of it.
Every little bar has got a solo act or a duo or a band or something, and it is
a lot harder to get people's attention than it used to be. That is the biggest
change. People have gotten so used to live music that it is not a big deal to
them like it used to be."

Digital technology has also made it easy to get music for free. Preston
Lovinggood: "The economy affected the record labels and us — they were
going under and people were not buying albums... Not a lot of people
bought our album. The audience knew the songs but they had burned it
[the CD] themselves... People were not coming to the shows." People were
not coming out to live venues either. Bobby Horton: "One thing that really
hurt the Birmingham music scene was MADD [Mothers Against Drunk
Driving]. Another was cable television. Competition for the entertainment
dollar. People do not drink like they used to. Habits have changed." Musicians lament the demise of live entertainment in Birmingham. Michael
Goldsmith of Common Ground: "It's hard because it seems like there are a
lot of bands and not very many rooms to play. Southside and Otey's. Hell,
if it was not for Otey's, that is basically our best room by far and away. Not
because the crowd is so great — the crowd sucks for the most part, they
don't listen. They listen some, but you are always playing for a crowd, which
is better than the Nick, whereas the Nick is a cooler place, but if you are
playing for five people it is kind of lame, and making twelve dollars. Then

playing Otey's the next night and making seven hundred dollars with a packed house and people clap sometimes after a song!"

There are too many rock bands around and not enough places to play. Joe Burnes: "I haven't played Birmingham a lot. I have played outside Birmingham, there just ain't nowhere in Birmingham to play. Birmingham is not a nightlife city, really. They are not very supportive of shows." Michael Chandler: "I think that the terrible thing is that we have so many incredible musicians, and one by one you try and see them grow up in the music scene in Birmingham and mature on their instrument or their talents or their writing skills, but yet they have no venues. There is no place for them to showcase it. They wind up either giving up on music or else they leave town." Jamey Hollingsworth: "I know that in 1976 that could have been a kind of uplifting era and then the '60s, late '60s, early '70s ... when the people kind of bonded together in going out on the streets and having fun. That was a way of forgetting everything else ... I always hear people tell stories of what it was like back then when they used to play. Now it is just like every night is kind of the same ... [the clubs in Birmingham] getting all these good people playing and all of these people go down there to see them, but then they realize that they are not making any money off of it, so they start having a disco night, and then the place packs out! So then they do it two nights a week and they figure if they get disco night on Thursday and Friday and then get the Cheesebrokers in on Saturday then they are making a ton of money. Then they have lost their whole idea of what the place started for and that just seems indicative of what goes on." Doug Royale: "It would be cool if the city had more rooms for more than a duo or a single act ... You need more than just acoustic all the time. Louie's is gone, the Music Hall is disco and national acts. We [the Bluedads] did that thing at Zydeco on Thursday nights, but it was for $150! We just never tried because there were like ten people in there, 150 bucks and we got a truck and were unloading all this shit." Porter Landrum: "So we went and played the Gresham Junior High sock hop for 150 bucks, which is still the pay in Birmingham at some jobs. Twenty-four years later, the pay is still the same!"

Making it in the music business still has the same aura, and exerts the same attraction, as it did in the early days of rock 'n' roll, but changing technology and a different economic environment have taken the edge off becoming the Next Big Thing. Tony Lombardo: "There are two types of musicians in Birmingham. There are those of us who are waiting for a dream and there are those of us who are not. I am not. I think that the people who are waiting, a couple of them, have a good chance, and that might help the others such as me. The way Athens did in the early '80s or Austin in the late '80s: it became a scene. I think a lot of people want that for Birmingham. A lot of people will disagree with me, but I think there are. A lot of these people are my favorite musicians as well as friends."

Being a Musician in the Digital Age

Many players who started out in the 1980s and 1990s now work part-time. Doug Lee: "I have been playing part-time for twenty years now, and I have been real fortunate at putting together groups that would actually go out and not just play in the garage a couple of times a week. Go out and play jobs and build a reputation and make money and have a good time doing it . . . We were playing totally uncommercial music. We weren't playin' hits! . . . We worked cheap most of the time, because we had to pretty much take what we could get because of what we were choosing to do musically." Lee Bargeron: "For the last few years it seems to me that it has been a lot easier for solo acts to make a living than bands here in town. For a while you had a lot of clubs that have live bands, and it dwindled down. You started having smaller clubs, smaller bars that had solo acts."

Musicians have had to find alternatives to the bar or club. It is not only the declining club business but a greater awareness of the health issues playing all night in a bar. Ray Reach: "Bob [Cain] is another story of a guy who burned out on the smoky bar scene. Who wouldn't after doing it for years? You go in there and inhale everyone's secondhand smoke for a few years and it makes you crazy!" Many bands scaled back in the first decade of the twenty-first century, becoming duos or trios that played background music in smoke-free restaurants. Eric Essix: "There are other bands around here who will work for little or nothing or if you have a duo or trio you can make a decent living in Birmingham. There are a lot of places they can play." Don

Tinsley: "I am playing restaurants and bars so the people who come in are there to either hear me play or get drunk . . . With the crowds though, if they do not bother me I do not bother them. Sometimes with the audiences around here, it is like you have to play almost simple enough to just make sense to them . . . I know what it feels like to be onstage, and I know if it is sounding right, but it has nothing to do with how the crowd will react. People like it for whatever reason they like or dislike it. It is a weird thing." Alice Bargeron: "Another thing. Turn off the TV. By god, turn it off! Turn off sports. Why in the world does a club owner feel the need to throw money away on a group when nobody listens? People are sitting there looking over the person [playing] up at the TV watching a basketball game." Joe Burnes: "I play for parties that they are not interested in what we are doing. They are out there talkin', having fun. They didn't come to party. No clapping, nothing. They don't respond. So what we do on those jobs is we kind of cool out some, because we could turn cartwheels and it would not make much difference. Just cool out and take the money and run, because they did not come out to party and you ain't about to make them party. So we just go on about our business and leave and they say that they had a band . . . So they got everything when they got the band and the shrimp and the roast beef . . . As long as they are jumbo shrimp. That is it!" Randy Hunter: "Music in this town is you take out a two-top [table] and put a duo in there and you pay them seventy-five dollars and all they do is make the room louder. Like the Mill [a restaurant in Five Points] and all those places. I don't know why they even bother having music. There are more gigs in this town than there have ever been, but there are hardly any that are worth going to play . . . You cannot just put a duo in a noisy restaurant and expect them to draw a crowd. If anybody wants to listen to them, number 1, then they are not going in there to listen because they cannot hear a thing. The other side of the point is that most of the people already in there do not care a thing about listening to a musician."

Birmingham's musicians are returning to church. From the beginnings of rock 'n' roll, churches incubated musical talent. Foxxy Fatts: "I started off playing down the street from the house. It was a little sanctified church on the corner and I used to go down and listen to the band in the corner, and I just went in there one night and asked them if I could play there. So

I started playing on the snare drums and I liked it and went the whole two weeks . . . You would be surprised, we actually go play in churches now. The whole band plays now, horns and all . . . We are going to do some concerts at some churches during the spring and summer." Cleve Eaton: "I was born and raised in that church in Fairfield . . . So I am back home and back in my church and I like to do something for them too, to help them, period." Coming to music through attending church was as common in 2004 as it was in 1954. Preston Lovinggood: "We all grew up together . . . We grew up in church, hearing the music . . . Now there is pretty good pop music in the megachurches . . . Playing in front of people is an evangelical practice." Religion is big business in Alabama. Birmingham has fifteen megachurches (with weekly attendance of over two thousand people), and all of them are heavily invested in music. The Church of the Highlands has fifteen locations and is visited by nearly twenty-two thousand of the faithful each week. Its music, sound, and video equipment is valued at over $7 million. Even the smallest churches have music directors. Ray Reach: "I still do a church job. I am minister of music at St. Francis Episcopal on Highway 119. I do it all with electronic musical instruments. We have a little bitty church there, but I orchestrate all the hymns with a MIDI and play the keyboard part along with it." Joe Burnes: "Do you know what has happened to musicians now? They are playing in the churches. See, churches have started using bands. Church music has changed some from the old hymn thing to more of a gospel thing with a beat. So that is where the musicians are now, because there are a hundred churches that need you and I think that is paying some dividends to play for the Lord versus a nightclub. They would call that playing for the devil. I got so many musicians that I can't even reach. If they are in church, then they are getting a bonus. They are getting paid and a promise to go to heaven. With me they are underpaid and probably go to hell. That is a lot different. It is hard to get a cat out of the church, man! And they are paying them good. They are paying them better than I can pay them. I had one guy that I tried to get, he said that no he couldn't play for me on Sunday because he would be playing in church for the Lord. I said, 'Well, man, you are playing with me on Friday and Saturday. How much are they payin' you in the church?' He said, 'They are paying me $150 on Sunday, but if you give me $200 I will do it.'" Kevin Derryberry:

"You go downtown and see these people at the Mill playing and they have the band here and everybody is over there talking. The whole thing about it, playing music to me is a privilege. I do sometimes, when I get in front of people, I demand attention, but I earn it! Recently I have decided to go into more of a gospel Christian-type band. I have done all these albums and figured out that is all good stuff, I guess, but I have lost a lot of meaning. I want to write some songs that mean something . . . that go deep! Not 'I love her, she don't love me' . . . It is like starting all over! A sober audience — the most critical! I am excited though. It is like a brand-new beginning . . . I was totally confused at how my future was going to be and I was worried about it. That is changing my life. I know He has got something planned and that He has got it. As long as I keep myself in the center of [God's] will, I don't have to worry about it anymore." For musicians like Henry Lovoy, who remember when music really meant something to the audience, returning to church meant singing for people "who really care about the music. It means a lot to me."

Digital technology put the music and initiative back into the hands of musicians but also increased their responsibilities. Even weekend players had to become more professional as the business changed, and the old way of living the life of the carefree musician changed with it. Rob Thorworth: "Musicians are sleeping until noon and 1 o'clock. Man, you gotta get up and on the phone at 8 a.m., and a musician, that is against his nature . . . What musicians don't realize is that the business side is such a priority. You got to live to do it! Exactly. But it is all part of living from check to check, and it is a hard way to make a living . . . I went through a time and especially when I was in the Newboys, and of course I was twenty, twenty-one years old and I was chasing a bunch of skirt and drinkin' down everything I could lay my hands on! But you can't get anywhere doing that, man! I think bar owners respect that when you get paid out at the end of the night. They know that I am there opening my book and I am writing my log down, and it is like, 'Well, these guys are legit. They are out touring, they got their damn laptops. They are working on it.' What do I have to do to make this happen? Well, I am going to be a musician, I am going to structure this like a little business . . . so I busted my ass and I keep great numbers and everything and if we go through a toll booth and it costs fifty cents, I keep a damn receipt and I write it down . . . You have got to do that, but for years, hell! I bounced checks! I lived from check to check and spent it out . . . I think that a lot of musicians don't really have either the fire under their ass or they just don't have the know-how to do it."

Gone are the days when a garage band made up a business card and left it at Nuncie's. Also long gone is the art of making up flyers for gigs and posting them around the city. Jamie Thorn of Electric Circus: "We built up the band really by lots of legwork. We went to like every high school in the city and flyered every car in the parking lot." Judy Ranelli: "We used to get into trouble for putting flyers out on telephone poles and stuff . . . flyers, flyers everywhere. We would spend twenty dollars on flyers and make thirty dollars." Now a band's prowess is found on the Internet, where they have to maintain their web pages, mass-email their fans, and upload music and videos. Rusty Laquire said this of one Birmingham band: "Those guys did every bit of their CD themselves on their computer . . . They are graphics wizards and they have been really working at it . . . They are like on the street level and really beyond. They are marketing wizards. They are pumping their fans with information. They are hitting the streets, they are just infiltrating, pioneering the band on the home page . . . They just won a deal, they won one of the like top twenty-five web pages in the nation. They are really getting it out there." In the 1960s you had to convince radio deejays and record store owners to get behind your music. Now you have to place your songs on television, in movie soundtracks, in computer games, and in advertising.

Playing malls, restaurants, and record stores might have replaced the armories and clubs, yet the pressures remain the same. Doug Royale: "People were saying, 'You guys are great! And you guys blow me away.' Then you feel like you are on top of the world! The next night you feel like, being a musician is about that far from being a bum! Do you know what I mean? We are singing our nuts off and playing high-energy, just killing 'em, and we did that for like a year and a half, and we just went totally broke! You can play all these great gigs, and feel like you are really doing something that is great, and you are going broke every second. So what do we do? We go get a three-piece, play restaurants, pay our bills! You can do that, or you can flag it and get a day job. You don't want to do that! I don't want a day

gig! So you can do that or you can go play restaurants and play 'Mustang
Sally' and do weddings."

Entertaining people in restaurants and private parties requires special
skills. Doug Royale: "Playing restaurant shit you just have to have a whole
load of ammo. You don't have a written list, you call it as you go. So anything to make them happy." Porter Landrum: "Read the room. Read the
room like a road map! We played one wedding and we had these little old
ladies who were sitting there and they were tapping their feet. So we were
doing songs from way back! You kind of ride it like riding a wave if you
are a surfer. I sell industrial equipment during the week, and this musical thing is like having a child, or a pet, and you water it, and you plant a
flower. Every night is a little different, and you feed off it and it is magic! It
is spiritual. It really is!" Michael Goldsmith: "Then you have your private
parties, which, the money is great. There are always rich people that want
people to come to their house and play music and entertainment. I swore
that I would never play another private party one time because I hated it so
much, but of course I am playing four this month! . . . People usually come
up and tell you to play this and that, and 'Turn it down' and 'You are still
too loud' and 'Can you play something we can dance to?' 'Can I sing on
this song? It is my favorite one!' It sucks! . . . It is really true — if it were not
for this group of rich people in Mountain Brook, a lot of people would be
out of work!"

Musicians in Birmingham still depend on playing covers to make a live-
lihood and still dislike doing so. Ben Trexel: "I think the hard-core rock
'n' roll fans are mostly lower-middle-class people and don't have the money
to go out all the time to keep that kind of buzz going — the only gigs that
pay are cover gigs and sports bars. Unless you want to be the Cheesebrokers
and play the Music Hall and play '80s cover tunes, and they make a fortune,
but they are not trying to make any mark in the real music world." Matt
Kimbrell: "I have gotten to the point where a couple of years ago I had to
learn 'Sweet Home Alabama' . . . just so I could fucking play! That is like
committing suicide to me. I played 'Sweet Home' so much that I came
up with my own version in a minor key. That really drives people crazy."
Bryan Price: "You know what is funny? I have always wanted to do and
we have almost done it, but I always wanted to do a remake of Telluride's

'Birmingham Tonight.' I want to just rock the fuck out of it!" Playing covers is still lucrative. Rob Thorworth: "The Newboys are what I despise now.
Not despise: but I mean, hell, we were playing our own music, but we were
playing Beatles songs and Rolling Stone songs and we were pleasing the
public. If you play covers you are going to dig through deep money! — look
at the Cheesebrokers! But you are not going to get out of the state of
Alabama, and your career is limited, so to speak . . . We will go in and play,
seems like we are right behind them or the night before them, and those
guys . . . are going to be disappointed if they get eight grand at the door!
But I know where Gravy would go and we would be happy if we made two
grand . . . They are making ten grand, they all have day jobs, they are playing cheesy '80s music and they are playing badly even . . . God knows how
much money those guys are making a year . . . and I am making thirteen
thousand dollars or less a year . . . Hell, I just got health insurance. I am
thirty-three years old! Health insurance! People take that shit for granted,
but this is what I do and that is what I sacrifice by not playing cover songs
and trying to promote my own material."

The Great Recession of George W. Bush's presidency killed off a lot of
bands and venues and ended the careers of some of the generation of musicians who came of age in the 1980s and 1990s. Jamey Hollingsworth: "Playing with these veterans, their perspective on music has changed. They are
like, 'I am tired of this. I just can't do this anymore. I am still going to play
music for my own satisfaction.' It is in their blood and they are not going to
quit, but they are playing for themselves now . . . People are going out doing
what they really want, but they are not getting any success that they really
deserve for it. For me music is more of a hobby." Despite low pay, low expectations, and disinterested audiences, Birmingham musicians still want to
play. Alice Bargeron: "Sometimes I get real depressed about it and I am like,
'Why have I wasted all these years doing this,' but then I think how lucky
I am to get paid for what I love to do. There is nothing like having people
like what you do and actually hire you to do that . . . I am still doing what
I really like to do and making a damned good living doing it." Scott Boyer:
"I have been saying to myself for thirty years is that the business of music is
every bit as lousy as the business of playing music is wonderful. To me that
is the truth. I still enjoy, really enjoy writing, I really enjoy playing . . . so I

get up on stage and I am free. I am free from all my cares and woes. When I am onstage playing I am in nirvana." Marc Phillips: "If you don't truly have a love for it, a genuine love for it, then don't get involved in it. 'Cause there's too many, too much of a downside, and there's too little money in it. If you really have a love for it and it's really your heart, and you're really, truly talented, it's not just 'My cousin tells me I'm really good' or 'Mother thinks I sing well.' And you know, you've got the sense of it, that if you're really talented and it's something you really want to pursue — regardless of what happens — then fine." Judy Ranelli: "If it works out and you have a really great crowd, then it is the biggest rush you have ever had in your life."

Rock music in the twenty-first century does not exert the same influence over the audience it once had. Michael Chandler: "During the late '50s and early '60s were the most powerful time as far as rock 'n' roll in the world. It was defined as what it started out to be, and that was rebellion, vigorous and hard-driving sound for youth that is unlike today... That is what I thought music was." Topper Price remembered that musicians in the 1960s were driven by idealism: "Oh, you are going to change the world and make it a better place! My first motivation to get out there and do it was that I thought that I saw something that maybe someone else needed to see. I wanted to tell people that. I mean, that really and truly is what got me think that." Scott Boyer agreed: "If I didn't still think that I had some of that to give, I would get out of the business." Topper: "I think the vast majority of people who get into live music when they are teenagers do it for the same reason." Scott: "Yeah, I do too. They are convinced they can make the world a better place, that they have something they want to say that they feel other people want to hear." Rob Thorworth: "Topper Price inspired me! Not only from the blues standpoint. I mean, he made me cry at the Nick one time! I remember hearing him do a solo, man! I remember him, hearin' him do a solo, and it was just the most impassioned gut-felt blues that I had ever heard, and you know? It was good and he was fucking... couldn't talk, couldn't even walk on the stage, he was mumbling into the microphone in between songs, the band was completely in disarray and not knowing what he was doing, and you know — the usual Topper gig! This guy was such a bluesman and I was just getting into this blues thing and I was really studying... So my point is that I figure, well, if I am going to do it, man, I am going to find out what makes it authentic and I am going to study up on it . . . I don't make any bones about the fact that I didn't live on the railroad tracks or anything, but I mean, I just wanted to represent the art form somewhat authentically, and I feel like I have."

Being authentic, playing how you feel, remains a central part of a musician's identity. Topper reminisced about one gig: "They were a real hotshot band, they were from New York and they were real good. I made the mistake of going back to listen to their show after that and I was just so blown away I could not even get back on the stage. They just ate me alive. We went back to do the second show, and we were just awful. We said damn it, we play the blues, so damn it, let's play the blues, forget the fancy shit and let's play what we play. We did a lot better the next night: you have to be what you is." Jay Willoughby: "I remember being in the Newboys and after playing a gig one night looking back at my guitar on the guitar stand and talking to Rob. It just hit me then and I said, 'I think I am in trouble. I cannot imagine not making a living at this and without that Rickenbacker.' It just clicked. There is no turning back. This is what I do and this is what I am."

Musicians in Birmingham in the twenty-first century are no less critical of the music scene than they ever were, but they still love playing Birmingham. Mike Panepento: "When I am onstage it is better than any sex or drugs or whatever you can do. It is very euphoric! As long as I am making people happy and having a good time on stage, that's what it is all about. To sum it up, people play music here in Birmingham because they want to. There is work here, but they are not here because of the money. They are here for other reasons, because they love it or are climbing the ladder." Bryan Price: "My life ain't that bad . . . Always do what you want to do. Find somebody else that does. Don't think about what some other band is doing. Pulling in crowds at nightclubs in Canada and piss on that! Do what you want to do and do it because you have to satisfy yourself first . . . I don't care to be the most anything in this town. You can do it without catering to this town. Like I said, I hate cutting it down, but I mean, this is Birmingham. It is not a music industry [town], and I don't think it ever will be. I don't care if it ever is! If I wanted to I would move to Atlanta or Nashville. I don't want to. I grew up here. Houses are cheap. I am pretty happy here." Libba Walker: "You know there are so many people that think they are complimenting Glenn and myself by saying, 'You two should go to Austin or somewhere. You could do something.' I just say, 'Well, I like it here.' You can make a living here. I love Birmingham. Tell people that I like playing here in Birmingham, damn it, even when they do not show up."

Birmingham's Rock 'n' Roll Years

Despite all the changes to the making of music, digital technology has not displaced rock 'n' roll from the center of American popular music. Doug Lee: "We have kept it together now for going on fifteen years and gone through a lot of style changes. We haven't had that many personnel changes, but we have kind of changed what we have done. We started off as a real pop rock band, playing a lot of Police and Tom Petty. We used to do a lot of stuff by Marshall Crenshaw, even some Huey Lewis and the News! All that stuff that was popular in the early and mid-'80s. Then when Rick Byrd came on board with us we really went more in a country rock direction, and now we have kind of veered away from that. We are still playing some country rock, but we are playing more rock 'n' roll now than we were five years ago. We have gone back to playing a lot more rock 'n' roll . . . You know you cannot make a living in music if you are not playing rock 'n' roll."

In the sixty years rock 'n' roll has been played in Birmingham, there have not been that many changes to the sound. Lee Bargeron: "There is a lot of recycling of old stuff. I will hear groups come in, they play something and whether they know it or not because a lot of it was probably way before they were listening to music. You can hear something and say, 'That sounds just like so and so twenty year ago on this album or this song.' I think a lot of that has to do with the retro movement that has been coming about over the past few years. A lot of them are going back and listening to some of the old stuff and trying to get that feel. Of course the baby boomers will never grow out of the music of their youth, especially as the 1960s were *the* time to be young in America." Michael Chandler: "At age fifty you can tell that I am becoming an old fogy . . . I haunt old record stores looking for music from that era. A lot of kids today are missing out on that era because they are pretending to like country, alternative, and New Age stuff. They are missing that good emotional sound."

The eternal appeal of rock 'n' roll, and the nostalgia for the music of one's youth, are reasons why reunions of rock bands are so popular in the digital age. The great number of guitar bands now active in Birmingham owes something to the baby-boomer ideal of never growing old. In the twenty-first century many garage bands from Birmingham's 1960s are still playing live: Larry and the Loafers, the Distortions, the Ramblers ("they never really quit"), the Tikis, the Premiers, the Rockin' Rebellions, and the Bassmen. The reunion movement started in the early 1980s when '60s music became popular. Frank Ranelli: "I didn't play for ten years, and then in '83 WYDE radio had the Rock and Roll Reunion where they tried to get all these bands back together from the '50s and '60s — they had a thing at Boutwell Auditorium . . . I ran into all these people that I used to know or played with. So I kind of got the bug and called a few of them. We were just going to get together and mess around and stuff. One thing led to another and we ended up forming a band and started playing again. When we formed in '83, '60s music was just really coming back. I went down to Montgomery to do some kind of function . . . There were multiple banquet rooms and I don't know why but I went outside for something. I heard this music and there was this party for Auburn. It was for some fraternity or something and they had a band in there playing and it was all these young guys, but they were playing Jimi Hendrix stuff and Doors and these kids were just eating it up. I got to thinking, Man, look at this, they are playing stuff that I used to play and everyone is liking it so." Sammy Salvo: "The last time I got on stage was 1983. Larry and Dale Serrano had a rock 'n' roll reunion. They got a bunch of rock 'n' roll singers. My kids were grown enough to see me. We had a really good time. It meant a lot to me to have my kids and my nieces and nephews there. The place was just packed — it was great."

Digital technology has enabled collectors to access and distribute music from the 1950s and 1960s that had almost disappeared. Early examples of classic rockabilly, once highly prized and elusive 45 rpm discs, have been rediscovered and rereleased in digital format. Listeners born decades after Dinky Harris walked into Reed Studios in 1959 to cut "She Left Me Crying" are now enjoying his playing (on YouTube and MP3) and singing his praises. In the twenty-first century Dinky's recordings on the long-defunct Fad label have been given new life on the Internet and brought him invitations to play in faraway countries. The power of recordings have not only kept his music alive but also made him a star of rockabilly long after it passed into history. He is still surprised that his records have spread so far and opened so many doors for him. "I am amazed people know who I am," he says.

Now that recordings can be transformed into digital files and made available to anyone on the Internet, some of Alabama's outstanding musicians have earned recognition far away from Birmingham. It is fair to say that Eddie Hinton is pretty much unknown in his home state, yet he has a following in England, where he is revered as one of the great names of blue-eyed soul. Hinton grew up in Tuscaloosa and played in garage bands there and in Birmingham, and then he got the call to go to Muscle Shoals and join the legendary session men there. Hinton made several albums after his glory days at Muscle Shoals, but they did not get much attention in the United States and were soon out of print. Touring Europe had made Hinton many fans, and it was an Englishman, Peter Thompson, who began to compile and release Hinton's work after he died in Birmingham in 1995. Johnny Sandlin: "He knows more about Eddie than probably Eddie or Eddie's folks or anything, but he has put together a retrospective to a lot of the early stuff that he did that is just incredible." All of Hinton's albums are now available, as well as much of his session work, and his legacy grows with every album downloaded.

Ed Boutwell and Don Mosely have been active in recording Birmingham musicians for decades — so many, in fact that they only remember the really important ones. Yet years after the records were released, collectors and enthusiasts seek them out as they follow the trail of an unappreciated local artist on the Internet. Years after they cut the records, the Sound of Birmingham and Boutwell Studios receive inquiries about artists and songs that they have long forgotten. "I showed you a letter from England a while ago looking for records that we cut ten or fifteen years ago, wanting to try to get masters to release over there, and [asking about] certain groups that came through and artists that recorded here." Some investigators phone long distance from Europe, many write, and a few turn up at the studio, looking for the background story of their treasured discs. "How did they get them?" asks a perplexed Mosely.

Birmingham's record collectors have played a major part in bringing bands back together. The city has two active record clubs — the Birmingham Record Collectors and the Alabama Record Collectors Association — who seek out rare discs from the 1950s and 1960s and the musicians who played on them. Ben Saxon was one of the founders of the Birmingham Record Collectors: "About two years ago [1993] we got the Premiers back together. We have what we call a Duke's Reunion. We got all the people together from the old days. We got Sammy Salvo, Bo Reynolds, Dale Karrah, and all the guys together. We had a beach party! We were at the Homewood Armory on Lakeshore Drive. We had about five hundred people show up both times. The Premiers got back together. They got back together and wanted to play for us, honestly . . . They practiced three nights a week. They sounded terrible. They had not played together in thirty years. Eventually they ended up being better than they were. They were fantastic. Dale had a heart attack the night before the show. We thought that the show was over, because Dale was the lead guitarist and had written 50 percent of the songs. Bo Reynolds, the lead singer, had cancer. He could not come to any of the practices. I talked to Dale and he said for us to go on without him . . . During the night Bo Reynold walks in. The guys were up there performing. I said, 'Bo, do you feel okay?' He was going through chemotherapy. I said, 'They want you up there.' He said, 'Nah. Nah, I can't do it.' Eventually he got up there . . . Then they did 'Are You Alright?' It would not have been right without Bo's voice. It was their big song, and it was Bo's voice on there." The audience loved it, one of them concluded: "It puts you right back in there." In 1985 WVOK sponsored another garage band reunion. This one, "Reunion of the Sons and Daughters of the 60's," was held at Boutwell Auditorium. It featured seven bands, including the Hard Times, the Townsmen, and the Distortions. Michael Melton, now assistant city attorney: "I was just incredible that your kids got to see what you really played like. My seventeen-year-old son, who's pretty jaded, just thought it was awesome."

Each passing decade created nostalgia for popular music that was fed by radio programming and reunion shows. In addition to '50s and '60s oldies, there is always an audience for southern rock, although these days Lynyrd Skynyrd no longer have that enormous Confederate flag as a backdrop to their shows. Classic rock, "cheesy '80s music," and even folk and grunge all enjoy nostalgic status these days. Telluride and Brother Cane have both re-united for shows, and Three on a String have been playing more or less un-interrupted for forty-four years. Telluride came back to play in 2008, which marked eleven years of postbreakup reunions.[6] J. R. Taylor mischievously commented that many of the punk bands of the 1980s had played more reunion shows in the two decades after their breakup than they did when they were together. The Ho Ho Men reunited in the 1990s. Matt Kimbrell: "We did one gig at Otey's. We actually did two, but the first one, because these guys turned out, all the guys that we played for in the '80s, all the frat boys [now] lived in Crestline. The first time that we played, 150 of them came out, and it was the best gig we have done in years." The Shame Idols reunited in 2007 and played several shows. Don Tinsley: "Dogwood gets together every blue moon. We grew up in a college situation and we started at [the university of] Montevallo. We had a huge bunch of friends down there that were hippies and beer beaters and druggies and everything, and we still get together. We have people coming in from like Hawaii to Mon-tevallo. We play that every once in a while we will have a reunion or some-thing like that."

Sixty years on, rock 'n' roll is alive and well and still reminds the baby boom generation of their golden years. Rock music in all its forms still frames American popular music. Rick Kurtz: "When stuff really started breaking was about in the late '50s with the birth of rock 'n' roll. Everything progressed until about the mid-'70s, and after that it is like there was not anything that was brand-new that ever came out. It was like a derivation of everything that had been done. So it kind of runs in a cycle now. It is a lot like fashion. You can only invent the wheel one time. In this case rock 'n' roll is the wheel ... Everything is just multicultural, and there is just so many facets of what you call popular music right now. There are just so many choices now that it has kind of diluted the whole thing ... But there is still rock 'n' roll. Oh yeah. It will just keep on trying to reinvent the wheel. It is kind of hard to picture how the end of rock 'n' roll would be."

Notes

Introduction

1. C. S. Fuqua, *Alabama Musicians: Musical Heritage from the Heart of Dixie* (Charleston, SC: History Press, 2011). Organizations collecting information about Alabama musicians include the Alabama Blues Project, the Alabama Folklife Association, the Alabama Music Hall of Fame, and the Alabama Jazz Hall of Fame.

2. Michelle R. Scott, *Blues Empress in Black Chattanooga: Bessie Smith and the Emerging Urban South* (Urbana: University of Illinois Press, 2008), 5; Robin D. G. Kelley, *Race Rebels: Culture Politics and the Black Working Class* (New York: Free Press, 1999), 51.

3. Lawrence W. Levine, *Black Culture and Black Consciousness: Afro-American Folk Thought from Slavery to Freedom* (New York: Oxford University Press, 1977), 80; Grace Elizabeth Hale, *Making Whiteness: The Culture of Segregation in the South, 1890–1940* (New York: Pantheon, 1998), 16.

4. Zandria F. Robinson, *This Ain't Chicago: Race, Class, and Regional Identity in the Post-Soul South* (Chapel Hill: University of North Carolina Press, 2014), 17.

5. Karl Hagstrom Miller, *Segregating Sound: Inventing Folk and Pop Music in the Age of Jim Crow* (Durham, NC: Duke University Press, 2010), 4.

6. Robert C. Toll, *Blacking Up: The Minstrel Show in Nineteenth-Century America* (New York: Oxford University Press, 1974), 223; Lionel Hampton and James Haskins, *Hamp: An Autobiography* (New York: Warner Books, 1989), 25.

7. Miller, *Segregating Sound*, 8–9.

8. Robert Gordon, *It Came from Memphis* (New York: Pocket Books, 1995), 44, 47, 56.

9. Miller, *Segregating Sound*, 5, 6, 11.

10. Hale, *Making Whiteness*, 38. See also David Roediger, *The Wages of Whiteness: Race and the Making of the American Working Class* (New York: Verso, 1999); .

11. Hale, *Making Whiteness*, 38.

12. Martin Stokes, ed., *Ethnicity, Identity and Music: The Musical Construction of Race* (New York: Berg, 1997), 3–4.

13. Allen Tullos, Matt Miller, and Timothy J. Dowd, "Atlanta: City without a Sound?," *Footnotes* (American Sociological Association), 2003, http://www.asanet.org/footnotes/mayjun03/indexone.html.

14. Mike Butler, "'Luther King Was a Good Ole Boy': The Southern Rock Move-

ment and White Male Identity in the Post–Civil Rights South," *Popular Music and Society* 23, no. 2 (Summer 1999): 47.

15. Mark Kemp, "Coming Home to a New Strain of Southern Rock," *New York Times*, July 5, 1998, AR 27.

16. Robinson, *This Ain't Chicago*, 7, 11, 26.

17. Ibid., 43.

18. See Madhu Dubey, "Postmodern Geographies of the U.S. South," *Nepantla: Views from the South* 3, no. 2 (2002): 351–71.

19. Sara Cohen, *Rock Culture in Liverpool: Popular Music in the Making* (Oxford: Clarendon, 2001), 186.

20. Robinson, *This Ain't Chicago*, 149.

21. Michael Azerrad, *Our Band Could Be Your Life* (Boston: Little, Brown, 2001), 7–8.

22. Susan K. Cahn, *Sexual Reckonings: Southern Girls in a Troubled Age* (Cambridge, MA: Harvard University Press, 2007), 242–43, 264.

23. Ellen Willis, *Beginning to See the Light: Sex, Hope and Rock-and-Roll* (Hanover, NH: Wesleyan University Press, 1992), 57.

24. Patricia Kennealy-Morrison, "Rock around the Cock," in *Rock She Wrote*, ed. Evelyn McDonnell and Ann Powers (New York: Delta, 1995), 363. I do not mean to argue that all punk and New Wave bands were enlightened in this way. In Sara Cohen's study of punk bands in Liverpool, she points out that some bands excluded wives and girlfriends to rehearsals but played to an audience of women. Cohen, *Rock Culture in Liverpool*, 210.

1. Rock 'n' Roll Comes to Birmingham

1. John Ed Willoughby, round table on "The Golden Age of Radio," Vulcan Park, Birmingham, February 21, 2013.

2. Dick Stewart, "Up Close with Hardrock Gunter: I Claim to Have Named the Music [Rock 'n' Roll]," *Music Dish*, 2006, http://www.musicdish.com/mag/index.php3?id=11476.

2. Records and Rock 'n' Roll

1. Peter Guralnick, *Last Train to Memphis: The Rise of Elvis Presley* (Boston: Little, Brown, 1994), 5. Preston Lauterbach notes that the first African American recording studio in Memphis was that of Richard "Tuff" Green in South Memphis. See Lauterbach, *The Chitlin' Circuit: And the Road to Rock 'n' Roll* (New York: Norton, 2011), 188.

3. The Garage Bands

1. "The Ramrods," posted October 8, 2010, by Chris Bishop, accessed June 16, 2016, http://www.garagehangover.com/The_Ramrods.

4. On the Road

1. John Wyker of Rubber Band in J. D. Weeks, *Panama City Memories* (Birmingham: JD Weeks, 2011), 147–52.

2. Daniel D. Williams, "The Mystique of Muscle Shoals Music," *Birmingham Weekly*, December 2–9, 1999, 7.

3. Craig Werner, *Music, Race and the Soul of America* (New York: Plume, 1999), 75.

4. Distortions Reunion, Birmingham Record Collectors meeting, February 2010.

5. "Bad Betty" in Weeks, *Panama City Memories*, 117.

6. Sarah Bradford Wear, ibid., 43–44; "The Newspaper Boy," ibid., 216–17.

7. John Wyker of Rubber Band, ibid., 147–52.

5. Race and Music in Birmingham

1. Gary Sprayberry, "Interrupted Melody: The 1956 Attack on Nat 'King' Cole," *Alabama Heritage* 71 (Winter 2004): 16–22.

2. James Miller, *Flowers in the Dustbin: The Rise of Rock and Roll, 1947–1977* (New York: Simon and Schuster, 1999), 88–93; Craig Werner, *Music, Race and the Soul of America* (New York: Plume, 1999), 34.

3. Wayne W. Daniel, *Pickin' on Peachtree: A History of Country Music in Atlanta, Georgia* (Urbana: University of Illinois Press, 2001), 7.

4. Robert K. Oerman, liner notes to *Maddox Brothers and Rose*, boxed set, Bear Family Records (Germany), 1998, 11.

5. Brian Ward, *Just My Soul Responding: Rhythm and Blues, Black Consciousness and Race Relations* (Berkeley: University of California Press, 1998), 41–42.

6. Miller, *Flowers in the Dustbin*, 124.

6. Music in the Struggle for Civil Rights

1. Brian Ward, *Just My Soul Responding: Rhythm and Blues, Black Consciousness and Race Relations* (Berkeley: University of California Press, 1998), 104.

2. Ibid., 102.

3. Craig Werner, *Music, Race and the Soul of America* (New York: Plume, 1999), xi–xii.

4. Ward, *Just My Soul*, 130.

5. Werner, *Music, Race and the Soul of America*, 58.

6. "Six Held in Attack on Negro Singer: Police Study Charges," *Birmingham News*, April 11, 1956, 1.

7. Diane McWhorter, *Carry Me Home: Birmingham, Alabama, the Climatic Battle of the Civil Rights Revolution* (New York: Simon & Schuster, 2001), 172, 315.

8. Peter Guralnick, *Last Train to Memphis: The Rise of Elvis Presley* (Boston: Little, Brown, 1994), 5.

9. Peter Guralnick, *Sweet Soul Music: Rhythm and Blues and the Southern Dream of Freedom* (New York: Penguin, 1991), 193.

10. Robert Cantwell, *When We Were Good: The Folk Revival* (Cambridge, MA: Harvard University Press, 1996), 93.

11. David King Dunaway and Molley Beer, *Singing Out: An Oral History of America's Folk Music Revivals* (New York: Oxford University Press, 2002), 142.

12. John Lewis quoted in Howell Raines, *My Soul Is Rested: The Story of the Civil Rights Movement in the Deep South* (New York: Penguin, 1983), 98.

13. William Thornton, "Leeds High Band Drops 'Overcome' from Show," *Birmingham News*, September 3, 2005, 16A–17A.

14. Ed Gardener quoted in Raines, *My Soul Is Rested*, 141.

15. Dorothy Love Coates obituary, *New York Times*, April 12, 2004, http://www.nytimes.com/2002/04/12/arts/dorothy-love-coates-singer-of-gospel-music-dies-at-74.html; Werner, *Music, Race and the Soul of America*, 97.

16. Brian Ward, *Just My Soul Responding: Rhythm and Blues, Black Consciousness and Race Relations* (Berkeley: University of California Press, 1998), 189.

17. John Lee Hooker finally came to Birmingham many years later and was booked to play the Hollywood Country Club, but a fight broke out during the performance, and Hooker and his band stopped playing and left.

7. The Beatles Are Coming!

1. Andre Millard, *Beatlemania, Technology, Business and Teen Culture in Cold War America* (Baltimore: John Hopkins University Press, 2012), 39.

2. Steven D. Stark, *Meet the Beatles* (New York: Harper, 2005), 15, 32.

3. Dave Schwensen, *The Beatles in Cleveland* (Vermilion, OH: North Shore, 2007), 17; John Penuel interviewed by James K. Turnipseed, November 2009.

4. Tony Fletcher, *Moon: The Life and Death of a Rock Legend* (New York: Harper, 2000), 208.

5. Brian Ward, *Just My Soul Responding: Rhythm and Blues, Black Consciousness and Race Relations* (Berkeley: University of California Press, 1998), 333–34.

8. Birmingham and the Counterculture

1. David Hood (interview by David Gilchrist, August 7, 2003), *Birmingham Weekly*, July 31–August 7, 2003, 3.

2. Steve Jelbert, "Alabama Beat Goes On," *The Times*, T2 Magazine, April 1, 2005, 15.

3. Richard Younger, *Get a Shot of Rhythm and Blues: The Arthur Alexander Story* (Tuscaloosa: University of Alabama Press, 2000), 11.

4. Barbara Allen quoted in Garry Berman, *We're Going to See the Beatles! An Oral History of Beatlemania* (Santa Monica, CA: Santa Monica Press, 2008), 48.

9. The Muscle Shoals Sound

1. Peter Guralnick, *Sweet Soul Music: Rhythm and Blues and the Southern Dream of Freedom* (New York: Penguin, 1991), 179.

2. Daniel D. Williams, "The Mystique of Muscle Shoals Music," *Birmingham Weekly*, December 2–9, 1999, 7.

3. Richard Younger, *Get a Shot of Rhythm and Blues: The Arthur Alexander Story* (Tuscaloosa: University of Alabama Press, 2000), 57.

10. Southern Rock

1. Courtney Haden, "Rockola Is Here to Stay," *Southern Style*, December 15, 1977, 11.

2. Marley Grant, *Southern Rockers: The Roots and Legacy of Southern Rock* (New York: Billboard Books, 1999), 13.

3. Ibid., 17, quoting Jimmy Hall of Wet Willie.

4. Scott Freeman, *Midnight Riders: The Story of the Allman Brothers Band* (Boston: Little, Brown, 1995), 21.

5. Bo Emerson, "Allmans' Fans Gray but Groovin'," *Atlanta Constitution*, September 8, 2007, A8.

6. George Kimball, "At Fillmore East" (album review), *Rolling Stone*, August 19, 1971. You can read the review at http://www.superseventies.com/allmanbrothers.html.

7. Mark Kemp, "Coming Home to a New Strain of Southern Rock," *New York Times*, July 5, 1998, AR 27.

8. Patterson Hood quote: Drive-By Truckers, *Southern Rock Opera* (Lost Highway, 2002).

9. Van Zant quote: Lynyrd Skynyrd, *The Definitive Lynyrd Skynyrd* (MCA, 1991).

10. Alan Paul, "Southern by the Grace of God," *Maximum Guitar* 10, no. 4 (August 1998): 20.

11. Opportunity Knocks

1. *According to the Rolling Stones* (San Francisco: Chronicle Books, 2003), 156.

2. Phillip Jordan, "To the Top: Lasting Memories of Topper Price," *Birmingham Weekly*, May 24–31, 2007, 3.

3. Rick Carter, "Then and Now with Rick Carter and Telluride," *Leaf,* January 2015, 10.

4. Lee Ballinger, *Lynyrd Skynyrd: An Oral History* (New York: Avon, 1999), 90–91.

5. Marshall Hagler, "Roots: Jackson Highway," *Southern Style,* December 15, 1977, 11; Ballinger, *Lynyrd Skynyrd,* 2.

12. The Morris Avenue Boom

1. Chris Charlesworth, "Jimmy Carter: Rock 'n' Roll President?," *Guardian,* October 30, 2012, http://www.theguardian.com/music/2012/oct/30/jimmy-carter-president -interview.

2. Metropolitan Development Board, Birmingham, press release, August 8, 1974.

3. VIP Invitation, Oaks Street, November 25, 1974.

4. Dennis Washburn, "Night Capper," *Birmingham News,* April 2, 1976.

5. J. R. Taylor, "I Cover the War," *I Cover the War,* August 1987, 10.

13. Decline and Fall: The End of Southern Rock

1. Rick Carter, "Then and Now with Rick Carter and Telluride," *Leaf,* January 2015, 11.

2. Allen Barra, "New Wave Meets Southern Hospitality," *Trouser Press,* September 1981, 25.

3. J. R. Taylor, "I Cover the War," *I Cover the War,* July 1988, 29.

14. The New Wave

1. Allen Barra, "New Wave Meets Southern Hospitality," *Trouser Press,* September 1981, 25.

2. Ed Reynolds, "The Entertainer King," *Black & White,* November 11, 2010, 9.

3. J. R. Taylor, "Primitons Primeval," *Black & White,* March 8, 2012, 18.

15. The Next Big Thing

1. Jimmie Lewis Franklin, *Back to Birmingham: Richard Arrington, Jr. and His Times* (Tuscaloosa: University of Alabama Press, 1989), 62; see also the promotional pamphlet *Birmingham, a City Born Again: The Arrington Years* (Birmingham: Elements / Jesse J. Lewis and Associates, 1999).

2. Jere Chandler, "Is Alabama Home Sweet Home?," *Fun & Stuff,* February 1, 1999, 5.

3. Shawn Ryan, "Who Puts the Bop in Haley-Bopp?," *Birmingham Weekly,* April 9, 1998.

4. Jere Chandler, "Marchant and Deacon Ted of Virgo's Merlot," *Creative Loafing*, July 1999, 20.

5. Jere Chandler, "Record Reviews," *Creative Loafing*, July 1999, 21.

6. Darin Powell, "Brilliant and Insane: The Magic City's Own Verbena Hits It Big with Its Major Label Debut 'Into the Pink,'" *Birmingham Post Herald*, July 23, 1999, C1, C4.

7. Chuck Geiss, "Naked Birmingham," *Black & White*, June 10, 1999, 4.

16. Music and Community

1. Mark Kelly, "Fifty Years in the Making," *Weld*, June 18, 2013, 3.

2. Barbara Sloan, *Barefoot among the Thorns: The Story of Dance in Birmingham* (Birmingham: Arlington, 1998), 14, 18.

3. Fletcher Anderson, "Foundations of Musical Culture in Birmingham, Alabama, 1871–1900," in James L. Baggett, *The Journal of the Birmingham Historical Society: Anthology Honoring Marvin Yeomans Whiting* (Birmingham: Birmingham Public Library, 2000), 42; Martha Mitchell, *Birmingham: Biography of a City of the New South* (Chicago: University of Chicago, 1946), 186.

4. Don Ward Haarbauer, "A Critical History of the Non-Academic Theatre in Birmingham, Alabama" (Ann Arbor, MI: University Microfilms, 1973), 92.

5. *Birmingham Age-Herald*, September 11, 1922, quoted in Blaine A. Brownell, "Birmingham, Alabama: New South City in the 1920s," *Journal of Southern History* (1972), 47.

6. Lynn Abbott and Doug Seroff, *Ragged but Right: Black Travelling Shows* (Oxford: University of Mississippi Press, 2007), 141.

7. Mary Colurso, "Questions and Answers with City Stages Head George McMillan," *Birmingham News* online, Wednesday, May 13, 2009, http://blog.al.com /mcolurso/2009/05/questions_and_answers_with_cit.html.

8. Quoted in Dena McClurkin, "Success of City Stages Showed Others the Way," *Birmingham News*, June 13, 1999, 1–2.

9. David Pelfrey, "Hat in Hand: After 20 Years, City Stages Is Still Panhandling," *Black & White*, May 29, 2008, 16.

10. Sir Laurence, "Bring the Noise; Rap at City Stages? It's about Time," *Birmingham Weekly*, April 5, 2001.

11. "Drive to Save Music Club Series Begins," *Birmingham News*, September 26, 1963, 7.

12. Mark Kelly, "We're Okay, You're Okay: City Stages Sparks a Reflection on Birmingham's Numerous Paradoxes," *Black & White*, June 1997, 16–17.

13. Shawn Ryan, "Nuclear Polka Band Blasts onto Club Scene," *Birmingham News*, January 18, 1996, 8E.

14. Shawn Ryan, "Biggie for Bands: Five with State Ties at Music Convention," *Birmingham Post Herald*, March 15, 1997, 5A.

17. The Curse of Tommy Charles

1. Mark Kelly, "We're Okay, You're Okay: City Stages Sparks a Reflection on Birmingham's Numerous Paradoxes," *Black & White*, June 1997, 16–17.

2. Vox Populi, "1999 Reader's Poll," *Black & White*, April 1, 1999, 16.

3. David Pelfrey, "Character Is Destiny: A Chronicle of Birmingham's Decline," *Black & White*, May 28, 2009, http://www.bwcitypaper.com/Articles-i-2009-05-28-229404.113121_Character_Is_Destiny.html.

4. J. R. Taylor, "Set List," *Black & White*, December 10, 2009, 35.

5. J. R. Taylor, "Back in Black," *Black & White*, June 19, 2003, 30–33.

6. Andrew Weems, "Love Junkies Swimmin' in the Honey Jar," *Birmingham Weekly*, March 12, 1998, 20.

7. Darin Powell, "Get into the Groove: Local Nightclubs Find Harmony Together by Following Their Own Beats," *Birmingham Post Herald*, December 3, 1997, C3.

8. Janita Poe, "Bombingham," *Atlanta Journal Constitution*, May 11, 2002, 1.

9. Sam George, "Outsider Eyes," *Black & White*, July 8, 2010, 4.

10. John Seay, "They Are Mice: The Newfound Midwestern Sound of Azure Ray," *Birmingham Weekly*, November 20, 2003, 26; Jere Chandler, "Birmingham's Own Vallejo Signs Major Deal," *Creative Loafing*, December 1999, 31.

11. Daisy Winfrey, "Let There Be Rock: The Drive-By Truckers Celebrate Their Southern Roots," *Birmingham Weekly*, August 8, 2002, 23.

12. "Taylor Hicks Comes Home," *Excursions*, 2010, 29–31.

13. Mary Colurso, "Wild Sweet Orange Gets Its Juices Flowing," *Birmingham News*, July 25, 2008, 1; David Feltman, "A Taste of Wild Sweet Honey: A Birmingham Band Hits the Big Time," *Birmingham Weekly*, July 24, 2008, 9.

14. Jon Poor, "Mary, Mary Why Ya Buggin'?," *Black & White*, August 26, 2010, 16.

15. Amber Ritchie, "A Struggling Music Scene," *Weld*, October 4, 2012, 20.

16. Mary Williams Walsh, "When a County Runs off a Cliff, and into Bankruptcy," *New York Times*, February 19, 2012, 5.

17. Jere Chandler, "Is Alabama Home Sweet Home?," *Fun & Stuff*, February 1, 1999, 5.

18. Mark Kelly, "History Repeating," *Weld*, June 27, 2013, 3.

19. Kyle Whitmire, "Birmingham's Broken Promise," *Birmingham Weekly*, December 29, 2005, 5.

20. Marvin Whiting, quoted in Mark Kelly, "Write on Birmingham; Examining Ten Provocative Quotes about the Magic City," *Weld*, August 2, 2012, 14.

18. Birmingham Music in the Digital Age

1. Maura Johnston, "Brisk Timekeeping: Yelawolf's Gritty Performance on Bleecker Street," *Village Voice*, September 21, 2011, 52.

2. Daisy Winfrey, "Homegrown Stage: The Ackleys," *Birmingham Weekly*, June 13, 2006, 20.

3. Jon Caramanica, "Twin Rock Dreams Prevail," *New York Times*, September 2, 2012, 17.

4. Tom Lamont, "Alabama Shakes: From Small-Town Bar Band to Titans of Rock," *Guardian*, March 29, 2015, http://www.theguardian.com/music/2015/mar/29/alabama-shakes-interview-sound-color-festivals.

5. Comment on www.Lastfm/:wecanhavefun, accessed 2012. This now-defunct website was a forum for indie music lovers in Birmingham.

6. "Live Music," *Black & White*, May 29, 2008, 43; "Live Music Calendar," *Weld*, February 26, 2015, 18–19.

Index

Music:Interview

A SERIES FROM WESLEYAN UNIVERSITY PRESS

Edited by Daniel Cavicchi

The Music/Interview series features conversations with musicians, producers, and other significant figures in the world of music, past and present. The focus is on people who have not only made good music but have had insightful and profound things to say about creativity, politics, and culture. Each Music/Interview book presents an original approach to music-making, showing music as a vehicle for inspiration, identity, comment, and engagement. The interview format provides conversations between knowledgeable insiders. By foregrounding individual voices, the series gives readers the opportunity to better appreciate the sounds and music around us, through the voices of those who have experienced music most directly.

ANDRE MILLARD is a historian of popular culture and
professor of history at the University of Alabama in Birmingham.
He is the author of *Edison and the Business of Invention* (1990),
America on Record: A History of Recorded Sound (1995),
The Electric Guitar: A History of an American Icon (2004),
and *Beatlemania* (2012).

◆